MASTERPIECES
OF 20th CENTURY
PAINTING

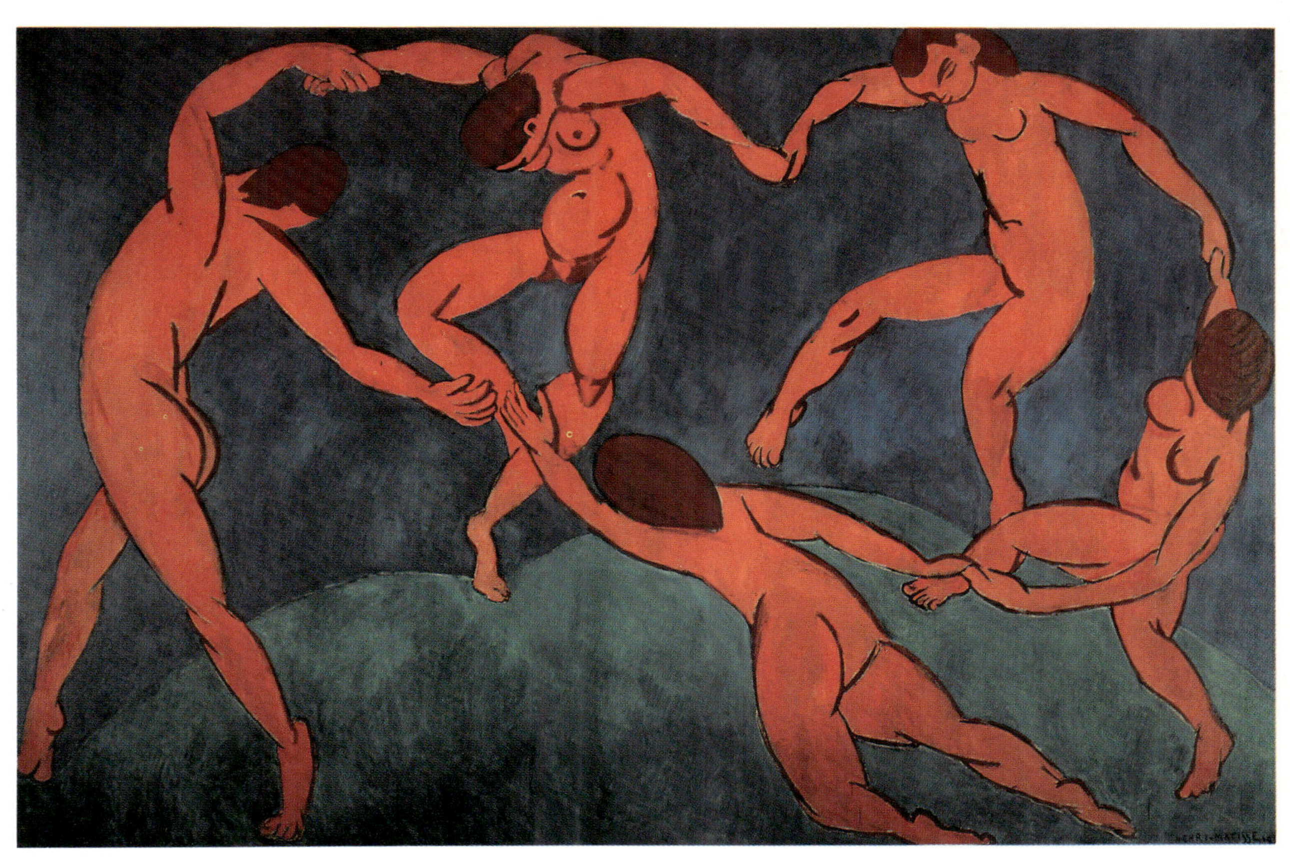

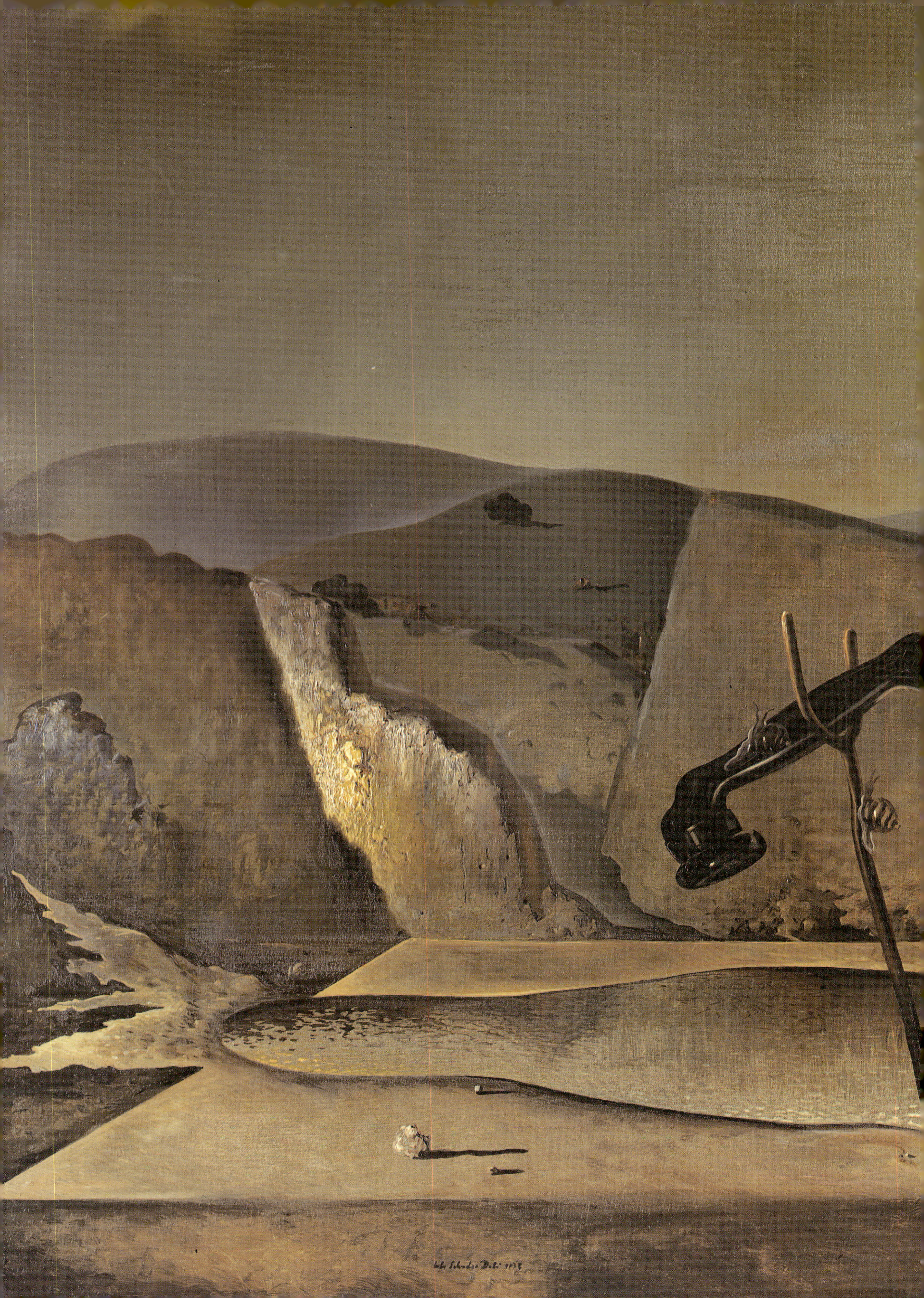
Gala Salvador Dali 1938

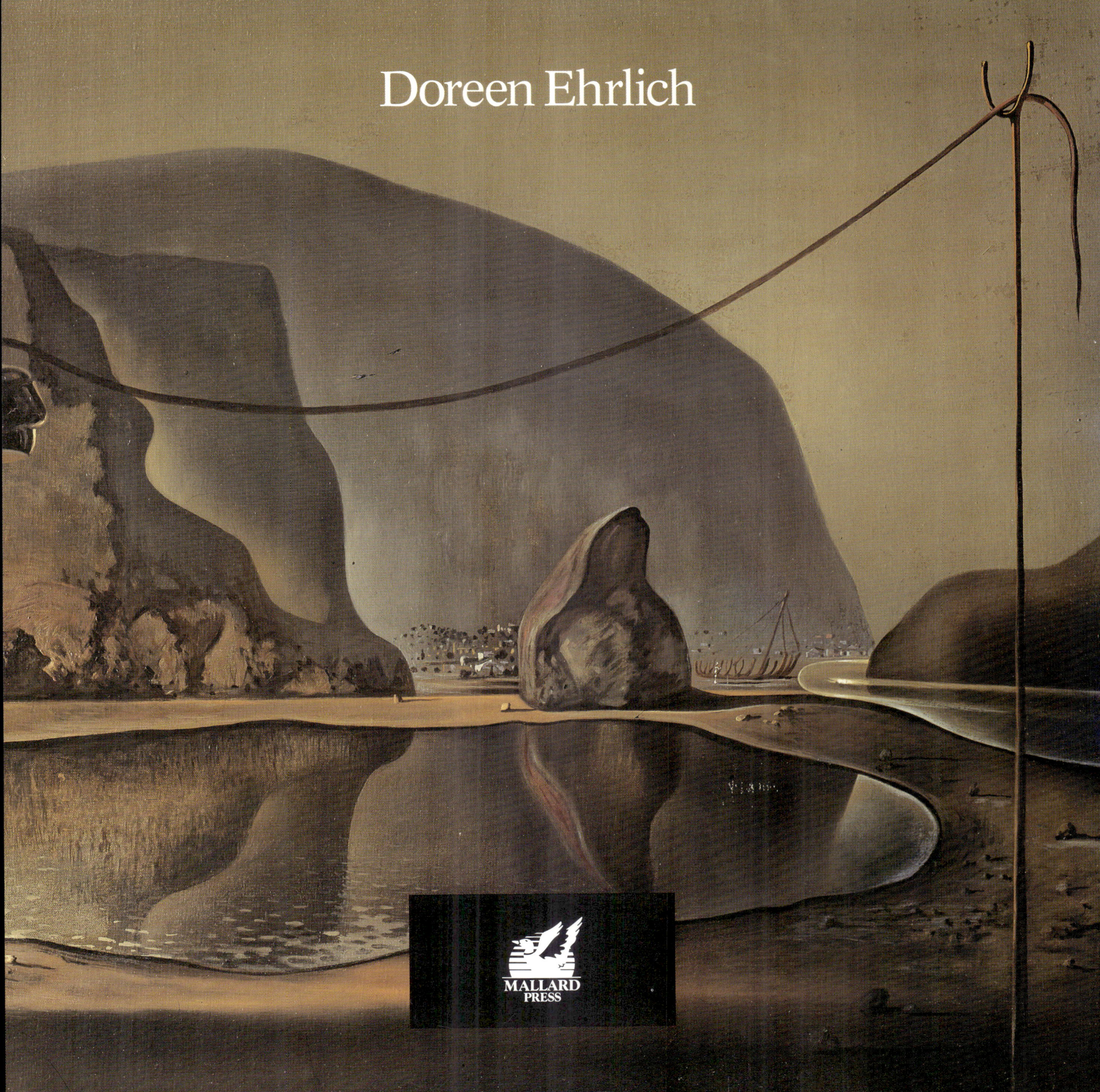

MASTERPIECES OF 20th CENTURY PAINTING

Doreen Ehrlich

MALLARD PRESS

ISBN 0-792-45198-8

Printed in Spain
by Graficas Estella, S.A. Navarra.

Page 1: *Dance* by Henri Matisse
Pages 2-3: *Mountain Lake* by Salvador Dali

Contents and List of Plates

Chronology

	World Events	Visual Arts	Culture
1900	Launching of first Zeppelin Boxer Rebellion in China	Cézanne: *Bathers* Munch: *The Dance Of Life*	Freud: *Interpretation of Dreams* Puccini: *Tosca* Picasso first visits Paris Death of Oscar Wilde Death of Nietzsche
1905	Revolution in Russia October Manifesto	Foundation of *Die Brücke* (The Bridge) in Dresden Matisse: *Portrait of André Derain* Vlaminck: *The Blue House*	R Strauss: *Salome* F Lehar: *The Merry Widow* Einstein: *Theory of Special Relativity*
1906	San Francisco earthquake	Picasso: *The Coiffure, The Brothers* Derain: *Pool of London*	Upton Sinclair: *The Jungle*
1907	Germany further isolated by Triple Entente (Russia, France, and Britain)	Picasso: *Les Demoiselles d'Avignon* Paula Modersohn-Becker: *Seated Nude Girl with Flowers*	Mahler Symphony No 8 Strindberg: *The Ghost Sonata*
1909	Blériot flies English Channel	Braque: *Violin and Palette*	Thomas Mann: *Royal Highness* Mahler: *The Song of the Earth* Strauss: *Elektra* Diaghilev founds Ballets Russes
1910	Edward VII dies Accession of George V	Matisse: *The Dance* Kandinsky: *Improvisation 13 No 10* Kirchner: *Self-Portrait with Model*	Marie Curie discovers radium
1912	First Balkan War Renewal of Triple Alliance between Italy, Germany, and Austria-Hungrary Sinking of *Titanic*	Picasso: *Still life with Chair Caning* Balla: *Dynamism of a Dog on a Leash* Severini: *The Blue Dancer* Duchamp: *Nude Descending a Staircase* Marc: *Rain* Macke: *Woman in a Green Jacket*	Jung: *Psychology of the Unconscious: A Study of Transformations and Symbolisms of the Libido*
1913	German arms production increases rapidly German Social Democratic Party (SPD) largest in Reichstag	Dissolution of *Die Brücke* Armory Show in New York Boccioni: *Dynamism of a Cyclist* Malevich: *The Knife Grinder* Delaunay: *Sun, Tower, Airplane* Braque: *Clarinet & Bottle of Rum on a Mantlepiece*	Frank Wedekind: *Lulu* Thomas Mann: *Death In Venice*
1914	Austria invades Serbia War declared	*Werkbund* exhibition in Cologne Gris: *The Sun Blind* De Chirico: *Premonitory Portrait of Guillaume Apollinaire*	Joyce: *Dubliners*
1916	Trench warfare. Battles of Somme and Verdun	First Dada proclamation in Zurich Rouault: *The Old King*	Kafka: *Metamorphosis* Joyce: *Portrait of the Artist as a Young Man* Holst: *The Planets*
1917	USA joins War against Germany Russian Revolutions	Chagall: *Double Portrait with Wine Glass*	First issue of magazine *Dada*
1918	Armistice on the Western Front World War I ends Tsar and family assassinated	Kokoschka: *The Power of Music*	Spengler: *The Decline of the West* Death of Debussy Prokofiev arrives in New York

The First of the Modern Movements

'Remember that a picture – before being a war-horse, a nude woman, or some sort of anecdote – is essentially a flat surface covered with patches of color arranged in a certain order.' The painter Maurice Denis, wrote this as a twenty-year old in 1890. His words were to be echoed and elaborated upon by many later artists: the idea that a painting is a two-dimensional artifact rather than a 'mirror' that reflects the way the world appears is a useful key to understanding much of the painting of our century.

It is, for instance, essential in understanding the work of Cézanne, whose group of large-scale late figure paintings, *The Bathers*, stands at the very beginning of the art of the twentieth century, and form a constant reference point for later painters from Matisse to early and late Picasso. *The Bathers* in the Philadelphia Museum of Art is one of this series, painted in the period 1898-1905. Here was a traditional subject, the female nude in a landscape, found in Greek and Roman painting and all subsequent periods of Western art, treated in a radical way and on a life-size scale that emphasized its importance. The figures are broken down into a series of facetted shapes in order to stress both their three-dimensional quality and the flatness of the canvas on which they are painted. The brilliant color is applied methodically to a pale ground in order to construct the complex interlocking planes of which the painting consists.

Cézanne's last years were spent as a virtual recluse in Aix-en-Provence, and it was not until after his death in 1906 that his work became widely known. The effect of the retrospective exhibition held in Paris in 1907 was immediate and lasting. His repeated advice to 'treat nature according to the cone, the cube and the cylinder' was taken up by a younger generation of artists, and can be most clearly seen as an influence on Cubism.

The young Matisse who, with Picasso, is generally acknowledged as the leading painter of the twentieth century, owned a small Cézanne, *Three Bathers*. He bought the painting in 1899 when he could ill afford it, refusing to sell it even at times of great financial need. It was evidently not the painting's geometrical aspects that most excited Matisse. He explained the work's importance in a letter accompanying the painting when he presented it to the Museum of the City of Paris in 1936: 'It has sustained me morally in critical moments of my venture as an artist; I have drawn from it my faith and my perseverance.' He particulary admired 'the sweep of its lines' and the richness 'in color and surface,' qualities evident in his own work and those of his fellow artists who shared his ideas and were termed 'Fauves' or 'Wild and dangerous beasts' at the beginning of the century. The Fauves were the first great movement of modern painting, although for most of the painters, including Matisse, Fauvism was a temporary phase, reaching its most intense form in 1905 and 1906, after which the artists went their separate ways, developing their individual styles.

The term 'Fauves' was first leveled by a hostile critic at a roomful of paintings by Matisse, Vlaminck, Rouault and others at the 1905 Salon d'Automne (Autumn Salon) in the Grand Palais of the Champs Elysées. The Salons d'Automne were the last of the notorious head-on confrontations in Paris between contemporary artists and their audience in a public gallery, confrontations of the type first made famous some forty years before with the showing of Manet's work and the early paintings of the Impressionists. After this, the radical work of the century was generally shown in dealers' galleries; one of the most radical of all twentieth-century works, Picasso's *Demoiselles d'Avignon* (1907), was not seen in public until thirty years after it was painted.

Criticism of the Fauves was violent; the paintings at the exhibition were described as having 'some formless confusion of colors; some splotches of pigment crudely juxtaposed; the barbaric and naive sport of a child who plays with a box of colors just given as a Christmas present.' The overwhelming characteristic of Fauvism was its use of intense, pure color. Matisse, who abandoned his law studies in 1892 to study art in Paris, acknowledged Cézanne 'who gave the definitive push when he showed us how to make volumes with pure color. . .we can trace the rehabilitation of color and the recovery of its power to work upon us directly.'

Portrait of André Derain, which has particular interest as a Fauve painting of a Fauve subject, was painted when the two artists were working in close association at Collioure in the south of France in the summer of 1905. Derain painted a portrait of Matisse in the same summer, and both portraits are now in the Tate Gallery, London. Matisse aimed to translate experience into a pictorial equivalent: 'I want to reach that state of condensation of sensations which constitutes a picture,' he declared. His portrait of Derain, which still has the power to shock, demonstrates the ideas of his Fauve years of what he termed 'construction by colored surfaces,' a technique derived from Cézanne that eliminates drawing. This can be seen in the methodical construction of his subject's face by the placing together of complementary colors (as in the scarlet of the hat against the green of the background). The boldly expressive application of the paint in what Derain termed 'deliberate disharmonies' is characteristic of Matisse's work at this period, and on this foundation was built his later use of color.

This emancipation of color can also be seen in Derain's painting of a year later, *The Pool of London* (1906), one of a series of London views painted on commission for the art-dealer Ambrose Vollard. Vollard was well known for his dealings with the Impressionists, and wished to repeat the success of Monet's views of the Thames exhibited in Paris in 1904. Derain's work is striking in its dynamic and deliberately unnaturalistic use of pure color, especially the clashing reds and blues. The 26-year-old painter's new concern with what he termed 'things which owe their expression to deliberate disharmonies' can also be seen in the distorted shape of the large foreground boat, seen from above (possibly from London Bridge) with the familiar shape of Tower Bridge in pale contrast in the background.

Derain, who had first met Matisse in 1899 and received a great deal of encouragement from the older painter, was also at this time very close to Maurice de Vlaminck, with whom he had shared a studio. Unlike Matisse and Derain, Vlaminck was virtually self-taught as a painter – among other things he had been a racing cyclist and violinist. The most extreme and violent of the Fauves, Vlaminck was the painter perhaps best deserving the term 'Wild Beast.' He was violently opposed to all academic institutions and proud of the fact that he had never set foot in the Louvre, although Van Gogh was a vital influence on his work, as can be seen in such a rawly expressive landscape as *The Blue House* (c. 1905). Vlaminck's technique at this time was to use pure primary colors squeezed straight from the tube on to the canvas. The deliberately unrepresentational use of color, the red tree trunks for example, are also characteristic of Vlaminck's dynamic style. According to Vlaminck, it was in Derain's studio that Matisse and Picasso first saw the African sculptures that were to be such a decisive influence on both young painters' work in the early years of the century. Matisse, Derain and Vlaminck all formed collections of such artifacts at this time: it is appropriate that the first response to the vigor and drama of such carvings should be from the 'wild beasts' in a period when it was relatively rare for artists to look outside the dominance of traditional European 'high art' for inspiration.

Matisse met Picasso as early as 1906, and his early work represents as much of a revolt in terms of color as Picasso's *Demoiselles d'Avignon* does in terms of form. Although the Fauves could never be considered a coherent group, Matisse was their acknowledged leader. The work of each of the painters developed in different directions after this period. Among the many artists associated with Matisse was Raoul Dufy, who evolved his colorful, witty style of the 1920s and 1930s under

Matisse's influence, as Dufy himself acknowledged: 'I grasped all the new reasons for painting; the realism of the Impressionists lost its charm for me as I contemplated the miracle of the imagination introduced into draftsmanship and color.'

Although excited by Negro sculpture, Matisse pursued a separate path from Cubism, preferring to explore the aesthetics of color. Matisse's early work reached its culmination in the large painting of *Dance*, painted in 1910. *Dance* and its companion painting, *Music*, were painted for the staircase of the Moscow mansion of Sergei Shchukin, a Russian collector. In terms referring to his sculpture, but which apply directly to the paintings of the same period, Matisse wrote that his work was intended 'to put order into my feelings.' *Dance*, for all its energy which might be seen to derive in part from Matisse's African collection, is the result of a long process of simplification, composition and adjustment, of drawings and preparatory oil sketches. Dance itself is an important factor in this work. Both Diaghilev's Ballets Russes and the work of the American dancer Isadora Duncan were to be seen on stage in Paris in 1909; each in their very different ways were revolutionary, mold-breaking forms. Matisse was later to design for Diaghilev and may well have seen Duncan dance. His life-size circle of dancing women is ecstatic and dynamic, as though the dancers were performing a timeless ritual. Such a painting illustrates Matisse's well-known definition of his dream as an artist to which he was to remain true until his death in 1954, a dream which was to separate his work from that of most of his contemporaries: 'What I dream of is an art of balance, of purity and serenity, devoid of troubling or depressing subject matter, an art which might be for every mental worker, be he businessman or writer, like an appeasing influence, like a mental soother, something like a good armchair in which to rest after physical fatigue.'

'To paint and nothing more. And to paint seeking a new expression, divested of useless realism, with a method linked only to my thought — without enslaving myself or associating myself with objective reality.' Picasso on Cubism

Picasso is the great chameleon of art. No painter of his stature has ever shown such variety and versatility. The three successive paintings reproduced here illustrate this, although it may be difficult, some would say impossible, to believe that they are by the same painter, still less that they were painted within a year of one other.

In 1906 Picasso painted *The Coiffure* and *The Two Brothers* two works of what was later to be termed his 'Rose period.' By this time, Picasso at 25 was already famous. An infant prodigy, he had trained at the School of Fine Arts in Barcelona at the age of 14 and the Madrid Academy two years later. In 1901, at the age of twenty, Picasso was given a one-man show in Paris by the well-known dealer Ambrose Vollard, and by 1904 he was living in Paris where he continued to work until the end of World War II, by that time the most celebrated artist of the century. *The Coiffure* and *The Two Brothers* are cooly classical, serene in the balancing of the figures against the neutral background. The subject matter of *The Coiffure*, of a woman contemplating herself in a mirror while having her hair dressed, is a traditional one. In French painting of the time, the most famous examples are the oil paintings and pastels by Degas with the same title. The nude figures of *The Two Brothers* are also classical in form, self-contained and with no eye contact with the spectator. There is nothing here to prepare for the shock of the watershed between the old and the new that he was to paint the following year, the celebrated *Demoiselles d'Avignon* (loosely translated as the 'young women of Avignon'). Picasso left the huge painting unfinished, rolled it up and did not exhibit it in public for another thirty years, at the Paris Exposition Universelle of 1937, where it caused a furore.

The painting is monumental in size and seemingly traditional in subject matter — the large-scale female nudes make obvious reference to Cézanne's *Bathers* series, as does the still life in the foreground. However Picasso's nudes are not timeless figures at one with nature but prostitutes in the interior of a brothel. The early studies make it clear that Picasso intended the figures on the right to be sailors, but this was altered in the process of painting, as was so much else about this extraordinary work. He repainted both figures to give their faces the force of both African sculpture and the force and vitality of the archaic stone sculpture of his native Spain. The rejection of conventional perspective and the restless overall treatment of the jagged, angular spaces between the figures are but aspects of this remarkable painting to prove so influential in the circle of painter and writer friends to whom Picasso showed the painting. Notable among these was the French painter, Georges Braque, who had been apprenticed as a painter and decorator, turning to the study of fine art in 1902. Through his friendship with Raoul Dufy, Braque was to paint in a Fauve manner from 1905.

From 1908 Braque and Picasso became equal partners in the evolution of the movement later to become known as Cubism, although neither painter used the term, considering it inappropriate. Braque, in a telling phrase, later described himself and Picasso as being 'like two mountaineers roped together,' and the sense of mutual endeavor this conveys is significant. In the next year Braque and Picasso took the major step of rejecting a perceptual pictorial idiom in favor of a conceptual one. That is to say that the idea of the imitation of the three-dimensional world on a two-dimensional surface which had been current in painting since the Renaissance was abandoned. As Braque wrote: 'Painting is a means of representation. It is wrong to imitate what one wants to create. One does not imitate appearances; appearances are results. In order to achieve pure imitation, painting must disregard appearances. Working from nature is improvisation.'

The still-life subject matter of Braque's and Picasso's paintings during the period 1908-11 was remarkably similar, sometimes the groupings of objects including a sitter. It appears that the two artists painted without reference to models, in strict contrast to Cézanne's concentration for long periods on his still-life models. He often used wax fruit as the painting process was such a lengthy one. Still life has been a category of subject matter or 'genre' in Western painting since the seventeenth century. The genre has a particularly rich history in French art, from the work of Chardin in the eighteenth century to Renoir and Cézanne at the end of the nineteenth. Braque and Picasso, who aimed to create a complete and 'realistic' pictorial representation of objects by evolving a new pictorial language to describe them, chose simple inanimate objects as their subjects, but also wished to evoke the viewer's knowledge of the still-life paintings of the past. Braque in particular, in his concentration on the genre in this and succeeding years, became the most innovative and important still-life painter of the twentieth century.

In Braque's *Violin and Palette* of 1909-10, the planes to the right of the violin recall the jagged edges of the curtains in *The Demoiselles*. The light appears to come not from one source, but to be flickering across the picture from different sources. Writing of this fragmentation of objects, Braque remarked that 'it was a means of getting closer to objects within the limits that painting would allow.' The nail which casts a shadow at the top of the painting points up the contrast between traditional perceptual methods of conveying 'truth' to appearance and the Cubist methods of simulating a three-dimensional quality and evoking reality. The special significance to Braque of musical instruments such as guitars and violins as constant subject matter in his work, he explains as 'it was possible to bring them to life by touching them.'

The period of artistic collaboration between Picasso and Braque in 'seeking a new expression' between 1909 and 1912 was later termed 'Analytical Cubism.' A prime example is Braque's *Clarinet and Bottle of Rum on a Mantlepiece*. This is a very much more complex and evolved still life than the earlier painting, although the pivotal element of the nail casting its shadow is retained from the earlier canvas. The subject here is altogether more difficult to define, although the clarinet and the sheet music are easily recognized and the stone curve of the mantlepiece can be seen at the bottom right. The limited range of colors used in this painting and the use of passages of stippled or mottled brushwork is characteristic of both Braque and Picasso's work at this period. The introduction of stenciled lettering – 'Valse' (waltz) on the sheet music here – is one of the many technical innovations introduced by Braque at this time. He explains their function as a recall to reality 'to get as close as possible to reality. . . They were forms which could not be distorted in any way, because being themselves flat, these letters were not in space, and thus, by contrast, their presence in the picture made it possible to distinguish between objects situated in space and those which were not.'

In the summer of 1912 the painterly association of Braque and Picasso underwent a radical change with the introduction of collage (from the French 'to stick or paste') into the work of both artists. The technique evolved from Picasso and Braque's use of lettering in their work, as seen in *Clarinet and Bottle of Rum on a Mantlepiece*. Both artists realized that the Analytical stage of Cubism had reached its logical conclusion. Although Braque is often credited with the innovation, *Still Life with Chair Caning* by Picasso is the first painting to use the new technique, that is to say it incorporates some elements of the 'real' world in its structure, in this case a piece of oilcloth printed to simulate chair caning. Here the oilcloth is amalgamated into the painting by being painted over in parts and the lettering 'Jou' is both part of a newspaper heading and an ingenious suggestion of the French word to play a game, 'jouer.' The painting is enclosed in a rope frame which at one and the same time suggests the edge of a café table and tells the viewer that this is indeed a painting, a 'two-dimensional surface covered with patches of color,' not an optical illusion of reality. Indeed the painting, like Braque's *Man with a Pipe* of the same year, which used wood-grained wallpaper for the 'paneling' plays complex tricks with appearances and our expectations of 'reality' reminding us that all 'representation' of 'reality' in its *trompe l'oeil* (eye-deceiving) sense, literally attempts to deceive the eye and is therefore a lie.

This second variety of Cubism is known as 'Synthetic Cubism,' which implies that the elements of the paintings were drawn from man-made sources rather than natural ones, as with the oil-cloth painted to simulate wickerwork. This deliberate introduction of discontinuous elements of everyday life directly into a picture quickly became a convention of modern art, not just in painting and sculpture but also in literature in, for example, the prose of James Joyce and the poetry of T S Eliot and in the work of composers as dissimilar as Mahler and Ives. Although the creators of Cubism rejected the use of the term, the label 'Cubists' was first applied to a group of artists exhibiting at the Paris Salon des Indépendants in 1911. The exhibition contained not a single painting by either Braque or Picasso, and the term generally is of limited use – it had first been applied derogatively to an exhibition of Braque's work as early as 1908, and thus like 'Impressionists' or 'Fauves' originated as an insulting term. Between 1911 and 1913 there were exhibitions of Cubist painting throughout Europe and the famous New York Armory Show of 1913 spread the influence of the style to America.

Cubism showed its incalculable influence in diverse forms. In the work of the Spanish painter Juan Gris, for example, it is possible to see a cool refinement which is distinctly separate from Braque and Picasso's work of the same period. Gris came to Paris in 1906 to live and work in the Bateau Lavoir (the Floating Laundry) in the same block as Picasso who introduced him to Braque and such literary associates as the poet and theorist Guillaume Apollinaire. Apollinaire contended that every work of art originates in the mind. Gris' paintings demonstrated that for him pictorial reality was of more significance than any object in the 'real' world. 'No glass maker' he wrote 'would be able to fashion any bottle or jug I have painted because they have not, nor could they have, any equivalent in the world of the mind.'

Gris' use of collage derives from Picasso and Braque but the incorporated fragments of the world outside the picture keep their original identity. In *The Sunblind*, for example, the collage newspaper *Le Socialiste* was in circulation at Collioure, where the picture was painted. The sunblind itself, in contrast to the collage newspaper, is meticulously painted, slat by slat. Gris did not consider himself a colorist and the overall effect is one of elegant austerity.

A radically different development of Cubism may be seen in the work of Robert Delaunay who broke away from what he saw as the limiting use of color in the work of Picasso and Braque of the time. His reaction on seeing their painting first was said to have been 'But they are painting with cobwebs, these people!' He also found the studio-based subject matter of their work limiting, and in his own work moved out of the studio into a blaze of color and celebratory references to contemporary technological achievement. In *Sun, Tower, Airplane* (1913), for example, Blériot's historic first flight across the English Channel is linked with another heroic French achievment, the Eiffel Tower, a recurring motif in Delaunay's and other artists' work at this period, used as a visual metaphor for all that was most dynamic and modern about Paris. Here too is the Ferris wheel that was once near the Eiffel Tower, symbolic of speed and excitement but also, like the biplane and Tower, a symbol of the conquering of gravity, and the new command of the element of the air.

The left side of the painting, a brilliantly colored series of disk-like shapes, shows Delaunay's growing concern with the primacy of color. 'Color is form and subject: it is the sole theme that develops, transforms itself, apart from all analysis, psychological or otherwise. Color is a function of itself.'

Delaunay's work was defined by Apollinaire as a new species of Cubism: 'Orphic Cubism' – that is a non-figurative, abstract Cubism without subject matter, akin to music. Delaunay's work became almost wholly abstract, with, as Delaunay expressed it, 'color' as 'the form and subject.' His work quickly became influential internationally. He exhibited with the *Blaue Reiter* group, and designed a series of color reliefs for the Universal Exhibition in Paris in 1937. His wife, Sonia Delaunay, worked with him on his researches into the possibilities of color Cubism and herself extended their use to textiles, ceramics and to theater design.

Cubism, from its genesis in the paintings of Braque and Picasso in the early years of the century, became the most influential movement in twentieth-century painting. Few artists were untouched by its influence. Of its co-founders, Picasso at this time had some sixty years of creative work ahead and continued to work with astonishing diversity and undiminished energy, often in several contradictory styles within the same year.

Braque was to continue to paint until his death in 1963, not making violent changes in his painting like Picasso, but consistently and subtly modulating his style in a series of brilliant innovations. The partnership with Picasso was brought to an abrupt end in 1914, when Braque was called up. He was seriously wounded in 1915 and only began painting again after a long convalescence in the summer of 1917. Braque continued to paint the humble objects of everyday life, returning again and again to the same subject matter in order to explore its possibilities.

Between 1928 and 1929 Braque was engaged on a series of large still-lifes exploring similar subject matter. Of this series, the 'Gueridon' (a gueridon is a small occasional table) paintings are perhaps the boldest, particularly in comparison with his earlier Cubist work. Here Braque paints a very elaborate still life in contrast to the simple arrangement in the earlier *Clarinet and Bottle of Rum on a Mantlepiece*. His objects in

The Gueridon are firmly anchored in space by the heavy and elaborate table. Braque is now stepping back from his objects and exploring their relationships not merely with one another but with the space of the room. To this end he employs a series of perspective devices: we are enabled to look up at the corner of the ceiling, view the still life itself from the front, but also to look down on to the floor and the top of the table. The objects themselves are flattened yet appear to exist firmly in space, and the rich color harmonies are in great contrast to Braque's earlier use of near monochrome. Braque, unlike his 'fellow mountaineer' Picasso, described art in the following terms. He is writing of art in general, but his words might well be applied to his own work: 'artistic progress does not consist in extension but in the knowledge of limits. In my own painting I return continually to the center. . . I always try to have a focal area of great intensity, I concentrate things.'

No movement of modern painting was more efficiently stage-managed to achieve maximum public awareness than Futurism. The movement was launched on a shocked Paris in 1909. The Italian poet and play-wright Marinetti, rejecting alternative titles such as 'Electricism' and 'Dynamism' for a movement that celebrated technological change, published the Futurist Manifesto on the front page of France's best known daily newspaper, *Le Figaro*, on 20 February 1909, simulta neously mailing hundreds of copies to influential people in Italy. This assault on public consciousness was followed up with public readings of the Manifesto of Futuristic Painters in Italy. The first of these in a Turin theater in March 1910 was greeted with catcalls, punches and the throwing of rotten fruit. Newspapers throughout the world from Chicago to Moscow published accounts of these events and of the ideas of the movement.

The Futurists mounted violent attacks on established values in both life and art. Marinetti, who stage-managed and financed the movement from the beginning of its brief life in 1909 until about 1915, defined its ideology in the following dramatic manner: 'We shall sing of the love of danger, the habit of energy and boldness. . . we shall extol aggressive movement, feverish insomnia, the double quick-step, the somersault, the box on the ear, the fisticuff. We declare that the world's splendor has been enriched by a new beauty: the beauty of speed. A racing car, its bonnet adorned with pipes like serpents with explosive breath, a racing car which seems to run on gunpowder is more beautiful than the *Winged Victory of Samothrace* (referring to the famous statue from ancient Greece in the Louvre). . . Italy has for too long been the great market of the second-hand dealers. We would free her from the numberless museums which cover her with as many cemeteries.'

Futurism was the most public and publicized of modern movements. The first Futurist exhibition opened in Paris in February 1912 and traveled to London, Berlin and Brussels that year, and the following year Futurist exhibitions accompanied by lecture programs reached Amsterdam, Munich and Chicago. In Italy itself, public presentations became a violent species of performance art, including Futurist music, political harangues and head-on collisions with the public. However, despite their high public profile the Futurists were not united in their aims and their work is varied in both form and content.

The most complex artist of the group, and its leading theorist was Umberto Boccioni, whose death in World War I at the age of 24 robbed Futurism of much of its impetus. Boccioni served on the Italian Front as a volunteer in 1915, and was killed during a cavalry exercise in 1916. Like other Futurists, Boccioni was well aware of new developments in French painting, particularly Cubism, although Cubism's essentially static nature is radically different from Futurism, and even the work of such artists as Delaunay and Léger, who also took modern urban life as their subject matter, differs essentially from Boccioni's work. The Futurist Manifesto's exaltation of speed is demonstrated in Boccioni's

Dynamism of a Cyclist (1913). This is one of a series of paintings exploring, in Boccioni's words, 'that new absolute *velocity* which the true modern temperament cannot disregard.' The year 1913 also saw the artist expressing the same idea in another medium, the sculpture of a dynamic striding figure *Unique Forms of Continuity in Space*, bronze casts of which are in the Museum of Modern Art, New York and the Tate Gallery, London. *Dynamism of a Cyclist* fuses man and machine in one dynamic form speeding through space in bursts of fluid color. The preliminary studies for the painting show Boccioni working from fairly representational drawings of rider and machine in an attempt to capture the near abstraction of the movement itself.

Movement of a totally different kind is seen in the best known work of another Futurist, Boccioni's former teacher, Giacomo Balla. *Dynamism of a Dog on a Leash* of 1912. Balla had put his signature to The Technical Manifesto of Futurist Painting in 1910, which had stated that 'movement and light destroy the materiality of bodies. . . a profile is never motionless before our eyes, but constantly disappears and re-appears,' an effect here wittily described in the swinging leash and the dachshund's legs and tail. Balla had long been interested in photography, particularly in photographic sequences of movement, and the analyses possible from photography into the nature of movement that are impossible to catch with the naked eye. 'Chronophotography,' the recording of successive movements by human beings or animals by means of a succession of photographs had been known since the late nineteenth century. The movement here, not only of the dog and the woman, but also of the dust on the city street is conveyed with wit and a remarkable degree of subtlety.

The delight taken by Balla in this light-hearted subject is also evident in the work of Gino Severini at this period. Severini had studied with Boccioni in Balla's studio, and from 1906 lived and worked in Paris, where he came to know Picasso and Braque during the years they were evolving Cubism. Severini signed the 'Manifesto of Futurist Painting' but had little active contact with the Futurist circle until 1911, and turned to a different style of painting in the 1920s. *The Blue Dancer* of 1912 is one of a series of night-club dancers, painted in a rich variety of fragmented tones to convey the motion of the dance. Severini was himself an enthusiastic dancer, and *The Blue Dancer* conveys some of his own pleasure in the dance, which is essentially of a sophisticated contemporary kind in strict contrast to Matisse's universally ecstatic and timeless *Dance* of the year before. The rich decorative effect of Severini's dancer is enhanced by the application of sequins to the canvas at strategic points, an example of the use of collage technique for an effect of movement undreamed of by the Cubists.

Futurism had a stimulating influence on artists throughout Europe in the years before World War I. In Russia, for example, Marinetti's Manifesto of 1909 was translated soon after its publication, and influenced many aspects of Russian culture in the years before the 1917 Revolution. However, the fusion of Cubist and Futurist ideas in Russian painting of the period differs significantly from French and Italian forms. Kasimir Malevich (who launched his abstract movement, Suprematism, with the poet Mayakovsky in 1915) painted *The Knifegrinder: Principle of Glittering* some two years before this. There is no idealization of the machine as in Italian Futurism in the Russian painting, the rhythm and power of the simple machine being dominated by the human figure. The simple knifegrinding machine is however supplanted in Malevich's later work. By 1914 Malevich had conceived the complex machine, the airplane as the ultimate symbol, as it had 'awakened the soul from its long sleep in the catacombs of reason.' In his famous *Suprematist Composition: White on White* first shown in 1919, all representation has disappeared, and the white square appears as a free-floating form in seemingly endless white space.

Futurism in its original form was shattered by World War I, along with the youthful idealism of its founder members. The excitement generated by the movement, however, was to have its effect on much of the art of the succeeding years.

Expressionism deliberately turned away from one of the traditionally most important aims of European art since the time of the Renaissance: the representation of Nature. For this was substituted the direct rendering of emotion and feelings. The immediate forerunner of Expressionism may be said to be Van Gogh, who, unlike the Impressionists, deliberately exaggerated nature's forms 'to express,' as he wrote, 'man's terrible passions.' In a letter to his brother Theo he wrote: 'instead of trying to render exactly what I have in front of my eyes, I use color arbitrarily in order to express myself more powerfully.'

The Expressionist painters took this still further, as the Dresden painter Max Pechstein had it: 'Van Gogh is the father of us all.'

Another immediate forerunner was Gauguin, who also broke with Impressionism in his anti-naturalistic, symbolic use of color to suggest mental pictures rather than a record of visual experience. Like Van Gogh, he believed in making 'the invisible, visible.' Gauguin, one of the first to find inspiration in the arts of ancient, non-European cultures, also believed in the symbolic power of line: 'there are noble lines, deceitful lines. . .color is even more indicative. . . there are noble tones, others that are commonplace, tranquil harmonies and others that excite you by their boldness.'

Developments in France were eagerly followed in Germany at the beginning of the century. Vienna, under the Secession founded by Gustav Klimt in 1897, was markedly cosmopolitan in its exhibition policy, introducing a whole generation of young artists into the vanguard of modern painting.

Although 'Expressionism' can be used in its widest sense to include visual art, literature and film over a lengthy period of time, here the term is used to describe the painting of Northern Europe, primarily Germany from the period from around 1905 to the end of World War I. The rapid growth of Germany at the beginning of this period to its position of world importance had a great influence on the art of the period. Whereas French art of the nineteenth and early twentieth century was focused wholly on Paris, German art was more disparate, and developments in painting in for example Dresden, Munich and Berlin were very different. The great majority of painters however reacted not only against their nineteenth-century German artistic heritage which has been described as at least a generation behind that of France but against the social and political life of their time, believing that art had no point unless it had a revolutionary effect on society. The ideas of the Expressionist generation were put forward in broadsheets with such titles as *The Cry, The Action*, and *The Storm*.

In 1902, 22 paintings by the Norwegian artist Edvard Munch were exhibited in Berlin, part of a sequence entitled 'The Frieze of Life, a poem of life, love and death,' which, influenced by Gauguin and Van Gogh, used line and color symbolically to convey (mostly fraught) emotional states, as in his painting and woodcut *The Dance of Life* (1900). The symbolic use of harsh, clashing color and the distortion of the figures and the space they inhabit conveys an extraordinary emotional tension and characteristically Nordic intensity which is deeply disturbing. These paintings had an impact on Munch's German audience similar to that of his contemporaries, the Scandinavian playwrights Ibsen and Strindberg.

In Dresden, where plays by Ibsen and Strindberg received their first performances, the first of the Expressionist movements *Die Brücke* (The Bridge) was formed, marking a watershed in German art. Like the Fauves, *Die Brücke* artists sought for 'expression' in their work, but, unlike Matisse and his associates who sought for 'balance, purity and repose,' their German contemporaries 'subordinated art to experience,' notably extreme and painful experience. The four young artists who formed the group were all architectural students, the leader and initiator being Ernst Ludwig Kirchner. In order to bring new life to contemporary German art, Kirchner sought to isolate specifically German qualities in the art of the past, in particular that of the late medieval and early Renaissance masters, especially Dürer and Lucas Cranach. Another major influence was that of the artifacts of ancient, non-European peoples. Kirchner studied Polynesian woodcarvings in the Ethnological Museum in Dresden declaring in later life that he perceived that 'they used exactly the same formal language as I did . . .and I began to believe that I was on the right track. . . my aim was always to express feeling and experience through large and simple forms.' Kirchner's *Self Portrait with Model* (which was one of several paintings he later redated to 1910) shows the artist nearly life size, pipe in mouth, directly confronting the viewer, wearing an extraordinary striped robe that seems almost tribal in its clashing colors. In the background, in contrast, is his model, in a state of contemporary undress. She appears wary and watchful like the great majority of urban female figures in Kirchner's work.

For the ten years or so of the group's existence the artists shared the same literary mentors who exerted a strong influence on their work. These included the playwright Strindberg, the German philosopher Nietzsche and the American poet Walt Whitman. They also exhibited together and had studios near each other first in Dresden and then in Berlin. This shared experience is reflected also in the shared subject matter of the group, which in the work of Kirchner, Erich Heckel, Karl Schmidt-Rottluff and Emil Nolde is restricted to a small number of themes, including the many aspects of the human situation, landscape and the life of the big city.

Emil Nolde was an influential member of the group although his background was radically different from that of his younger fellow artists. Nolde was proud of his peasant stock (in what was then south Denmark) and had a hatred of urban and intellectual life. His powerful religious paintings derived a great deal from early German art. Nolde traveled widely but always returned to the wild coastal landscape of his birth. Such a painting as *In the Lemon Garden* shows Nolde's ability to convey through startling clashes of color and looming, mask-like faces, not just strong emotion but scents – in this case of lemons and roses – with a force almost akin to folk legend.

In Munich, six years after the foundation of *Die Brücke* group, the second of the important Expressionist associations of artists with radical aims held their first exhibition. This was *Der Blaue Reiter* (The Blue Rider), which took its name from a painting by one of its number, the Russian Wassily Kandinsky. He and Paul Klee, Franz Marc and August Macke (the last of whom were to die prematurely in World War I), were never as unified in their work practices or shared ideas as the earlier group, and should really be considered as a loose association of artists. However the prospectus for the first exhibition contained the following statement of intent: 'We seek today, behind the veil of external appearances, the hidden things which seem to us more important than the discoveries of the Impressionists. . .we search out and elaborate this spiritual side of ourselves in nature.'

Marc's prime subject matter was the animal world. He used limpid, symbolic color in his oil paintings and watercolors, and sought for 'the thing as it really is, beneath the superficial appearance.' His search led him towards the symbolic rather than descriptive use of color as seen in his well-known, anti-naturalistic red and blue horses. In *Rain* (1912), Marc uses human and animal forms within diagonals of prismatic color to suggest the driving rain and what Marc himself termed 'the organic rhythm of all things. . . pantheistic empathy with the vibration and flow of the blood of nature – in the trees, in the animals, in the air.'

In the year before his death his painting was becoming more

abstract, more visionary – *The Fate of the Animals* in the Kunstsmuseum, Basel, is sometimes interpreted as an Apocalyptic vision of the War. Marc was killed at Verdun in 1916.

August Macke, who was killed in France two years before Marc's death, was Marc's close friend for the last four years of his life. Macke contributed to *Die Blaue Reiter* publications, traveled widely in Europe and made successive visits to Paris: the influence of the Fauves and Cubists show themselves in both his work and, through his influence, on Marc, with whom he visited Robert Delaunay in Paris in 1911. Like Kandinsky and Klee, Macke was interested in the correlation between music and painting: 'That which makes music so puzzlingly beautiful also works magically in painting. . . in color there is counterpoint, violin, ground bass, minor, major as in music.' Such a painting as *Woman in a Green Jacket* (1912) shows Macke's concern with urbanized nature in the form of parks and enclosed public places and of humankind's relationship with such everyday experiences. Here the two couples and the solitary woman by the river are painted in delicate facets of color, expressing Macke's own desire to celebrate contemporary life: 'for me work is a complete rejoicing in nature.' After a visit to North Africa in 1914, Macke returned to Germany for military service and within six weeks was killed in France at the age of 27.

However, the *Blaue Reiter* artist who had the most influence on his own, and indeed succeeding generations was Wassily Kandinsky. In 1910 Kandinsky produced a watercolor of a completely abstract subject, probably the first entirely non-representational painting ever painted. Kandinsky continued to explore abstract themes in his series of 'Improvisations,' 'Impressions,' and 'Compositions,' in the years 1909-14. Kandinsky's influence was extended by his theoretical writings, the most famous of which was *Concerning the Spiritual in Art* (1912). Kandinsky employed his considerable knowledge of psychology, philosophy, and science in the formulation of this complex work. His series of paintings of the period were differentiated both in their composition and intended effect on the viewer. The 'Improvisations,' for example, were intended as spontaneous abstract expressions of particular feelings, while the 'Compositions' were more calculated in their use of specific forms and colors. The musical analogies of the titles were deliberate, intended to convey the non-representational nature of the images. Kandinsky believed that painting can 'develop the same energies as music' and such a painting as *Improvisation 13 No 10* where the forms are visionary and dreamlike and the colors resonant is intended to have an effect on the beholder similar to that of music on the listener.

Kandinsky returned to Russia in 1914. He became Professor of Painting at the Academy of Fine Arts, Moscow in 1918 and founded the Russian Academy of Artistic Sciences in 1921. In 1922 he returned to Germany to teach at the Bauhaus, the enormously influential school of architecture and design, until 1933.

Oscar Kokoschka, who was of Czech and Austrian parentage, became a key figure in German art in Berlin before World War I, working as a writer and graphic artist on another Expressionist publication, *Der Stürm* ('The Storm'). Although his work was allied to that of *Die Brücke*, Kokoschka might be considered a constitutional outsider – as a young man he was called 'Chief Savage' at an exhibition in Vienna, his native city. He was seriously wounded in 1916 and spent most of the rest of his long life outside Germany, although his paintings are often considered to have retained their Expressionist character from his radical beginnings. Such a work as *The Power of Music* shows his characteristic use of bold color and heavy impasto, that is the application of the oil paint in thick, solid masses to convey the emotional and spiritual nature of the music.

The French artist Georges Rouault is sometimes associated with the Fauves because, with Matisse, who had been a fellow student at the Ecole des Beaux-Arts in Paris, he founded the Salon d'Automne and exhibited there. However, his work is nearer to that of the Expressionists in both style and subject matter: Rouault himself described it as 'a scream in the night, a stifled sob, a laugh that chokes on itself.' Rouault's subjects were often religious. *The Old King* has the look of a Biblical subject, and Rouault's early apprenticeship in stained glass making can be seen in the rich yet somber colors and the black enclosing lines, giving the effect of medieval stained glass.

Also associated with the Expressionists, and influenced as they were by the work of Edvard Munch, was Chaim Soutine, although his work showed a separate development from theirs. Born in Lithuania, Soutine lived and worked in Paris from 1913, becoming part of the colony of artists in Montmartre known as the Bateau-Lavoir that included Chagall and Modigliani at this time. *Woman in a Red Dress* shows his characteristic distortion and simplification of form for emotive effect. The woman's expression and direct eye contact with the viewer, expressive hands, and the searing red of her dress are all typical of Soutine's work at this period, a period of extreme poverty in which Soutine refused to exhibit his work, eventually attaining a measure of financial security by the purchase of many of his works in 1923 by the American collector, Alfred Barnes.

Paula Modersohn-Becker's early death in 1907 at the age of 31, soon after her only child's long-awaited birth, cut short a painting career of only ten years. Her work is set apart from that of her contemporaries by its distinctively female subject matter. She studied first in Berlin, at the Association of Berlin Women Artists, as women were not admitted to studies at the Academy, and then in Paris, where her interest in ancient art, particularly that of Fayum portraiture from Upper Egypt, was kindled. After her marriage to the painter Paul Modersohn-Becker in 1901, she divided her time between the artistic colony at Worpswede in Germany, and Paris. Much of her painting is concerned with the life of women at various stages from puberty to old age. *Seated Nude Girl* conveys the feeling of ritual solemnity and celebration so characteristic of the artist. The rite-of-passage is made poignant by the precise placing of the flowers, the girl's necklace and crown, and the positioning of her hands and feet.

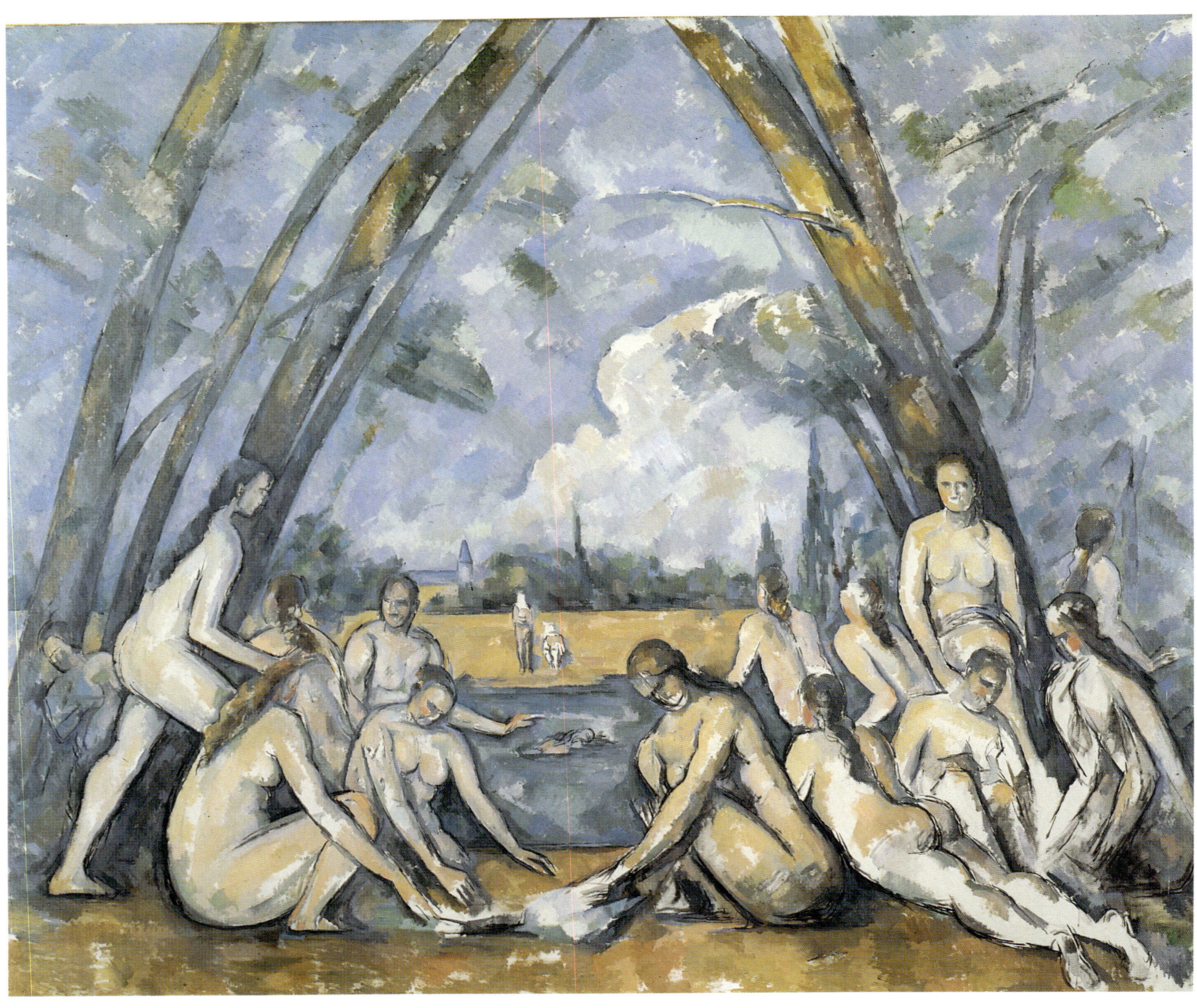

ABOVE:
Paul Cézanne
The Large Bathers 1906
Oil on canvas, 82×99in (208.3×251.5cm)
Philadelphia Museum of Art: Purchased
W P Wilstach Collection

RIGHT:
Henri Matisse
Portrait of Derain 1907
Oil on canvas, 15½×11⅜in (39.4×28.9cm)
Tate Gallery, London
© *Succession Henri Matisse/DACS, 1989*

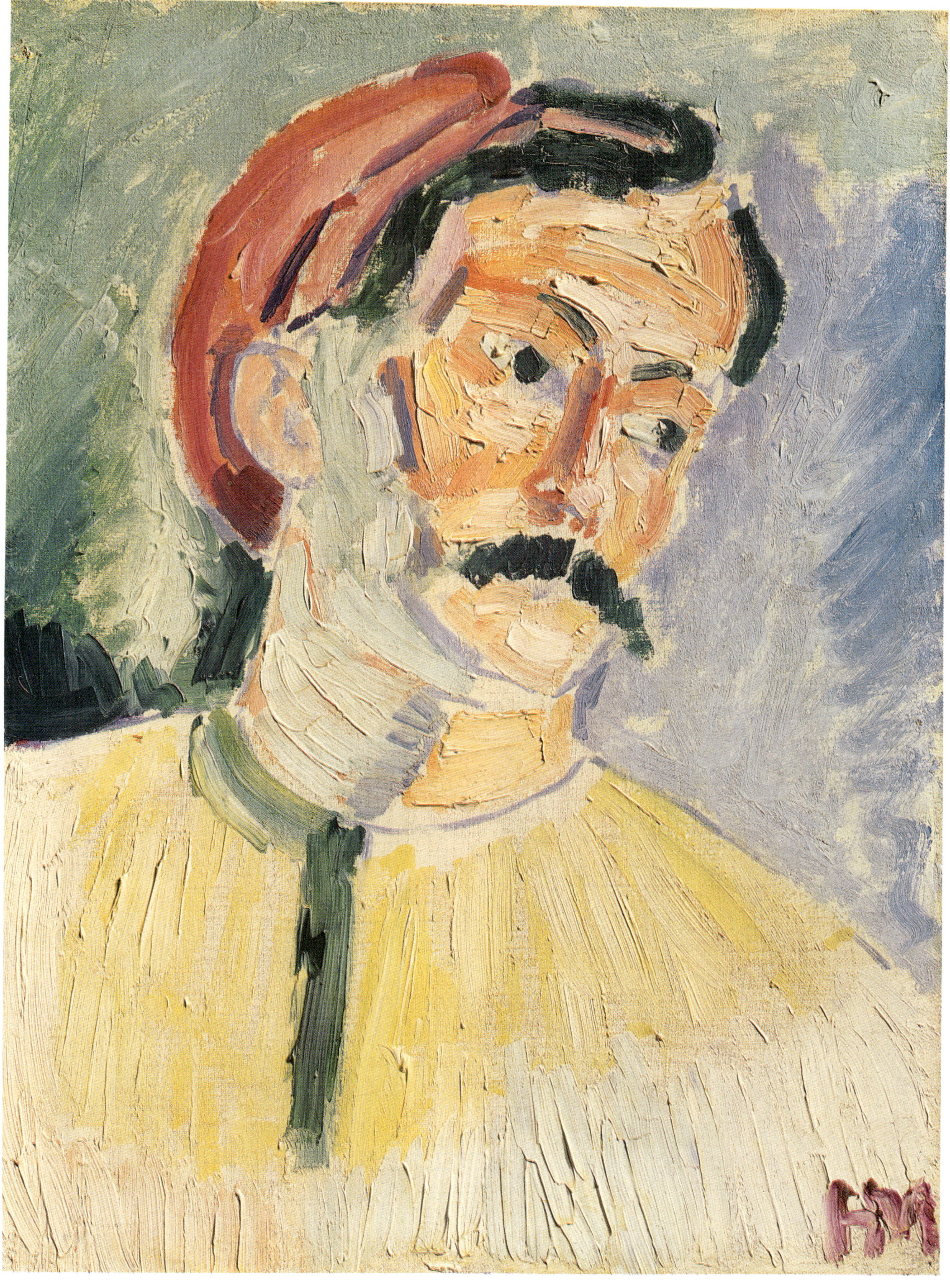

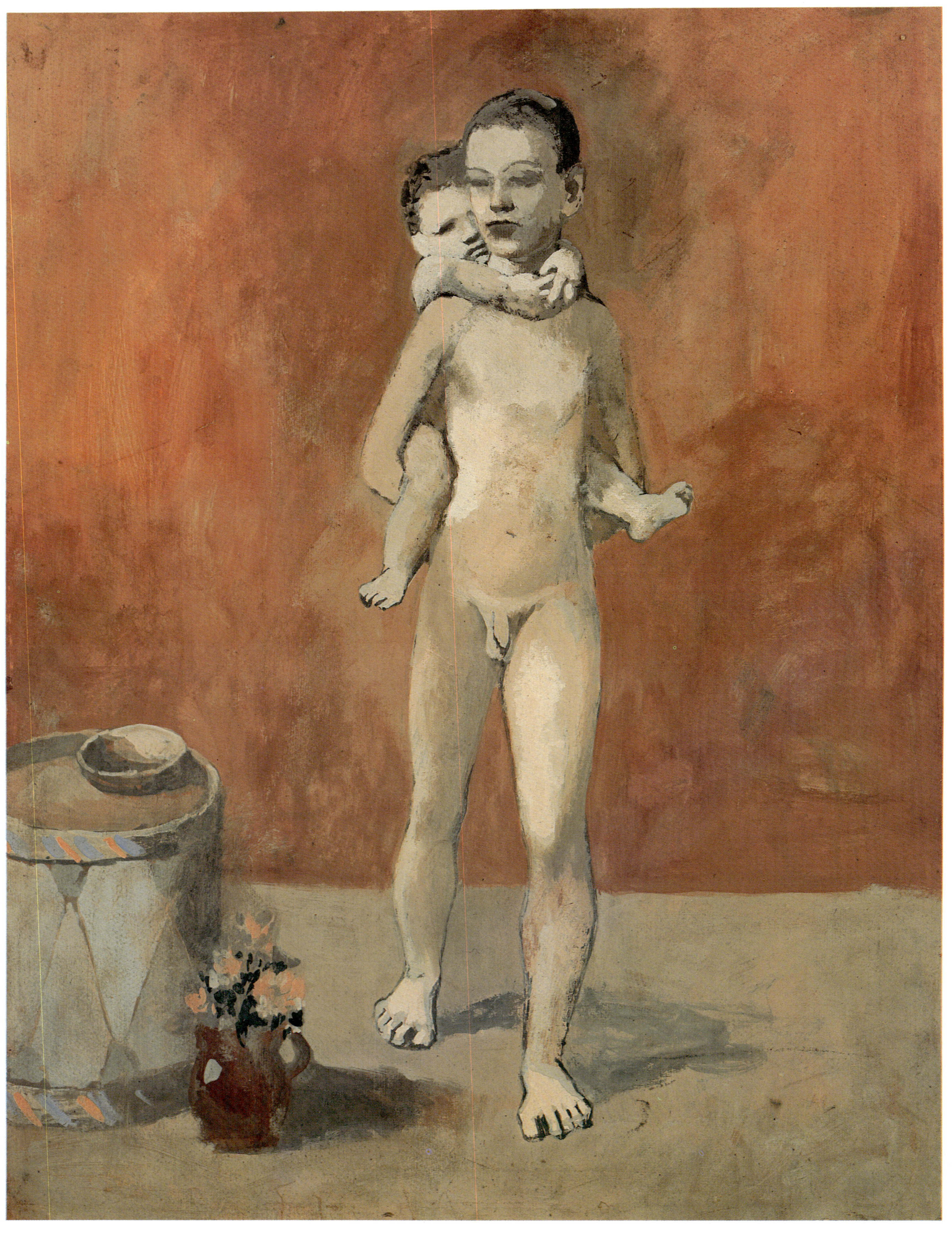

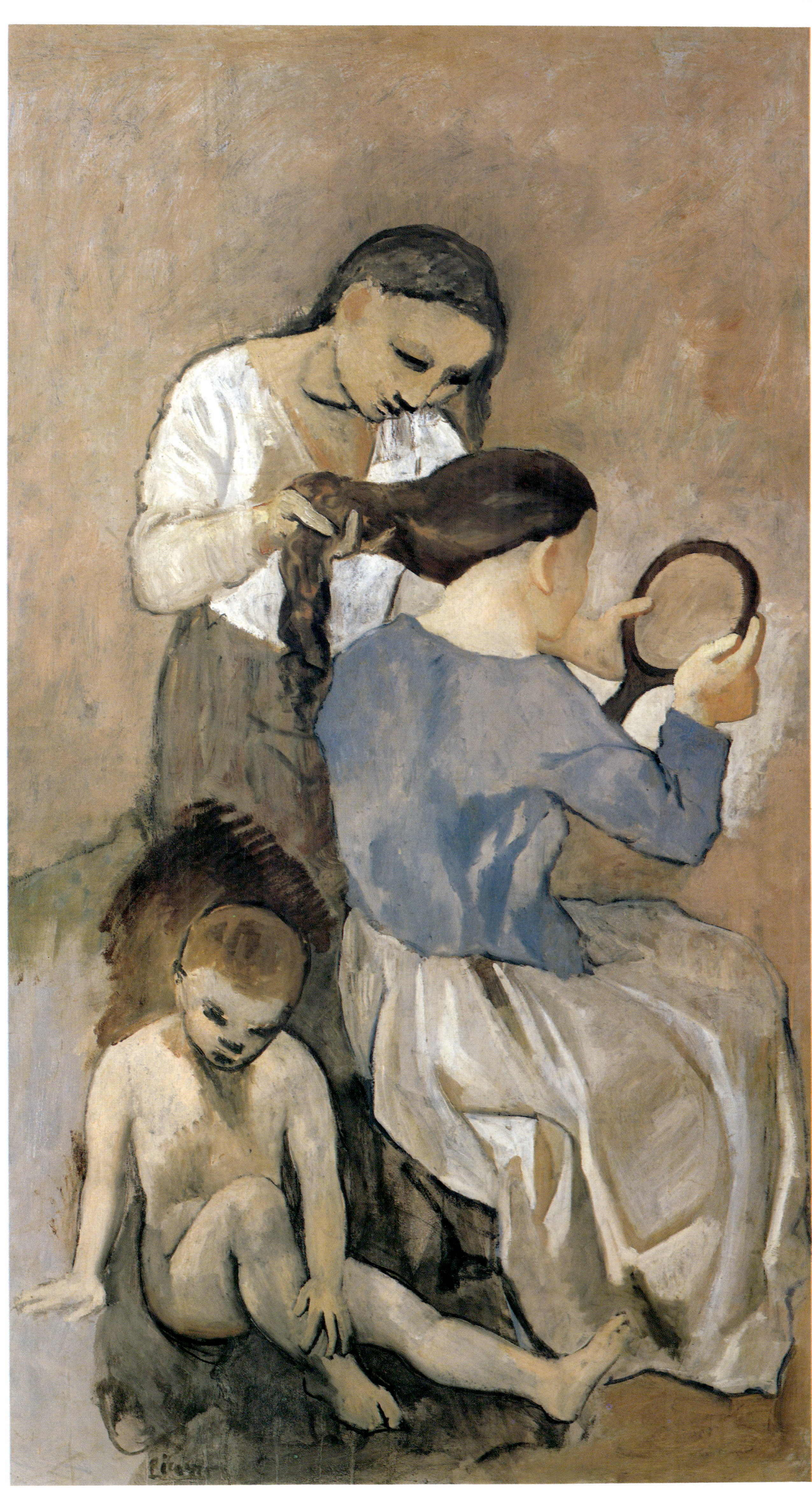

LEFT:
Pablo Picasso
The Two Brothers 1906
Gouache on cardboard, 31½×23¼in
(80×59cm)
Picasso Museum, Paris
© *DACS, 1988*

RIGHT:
Pablo Picasso
The Coiffure 1906
Oil on canvas, 68⅞×39¼in
(174.8×99.7cm)
*The Metropolitan Museum of Art,
New York
Wolfe Fund, 1951, from the Museum
of Modern Art,
anonymous gift*
© *DACS, 1988*

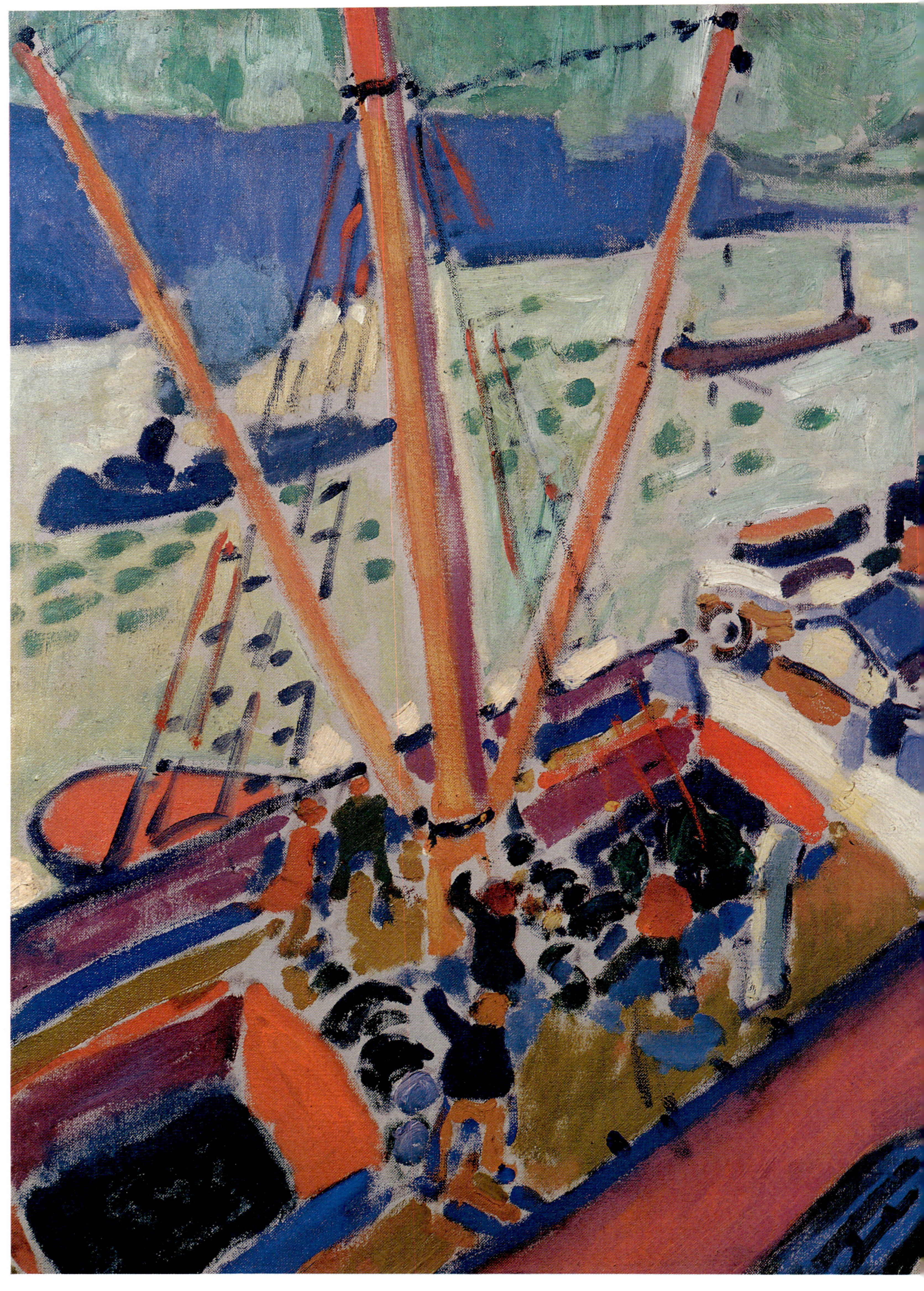

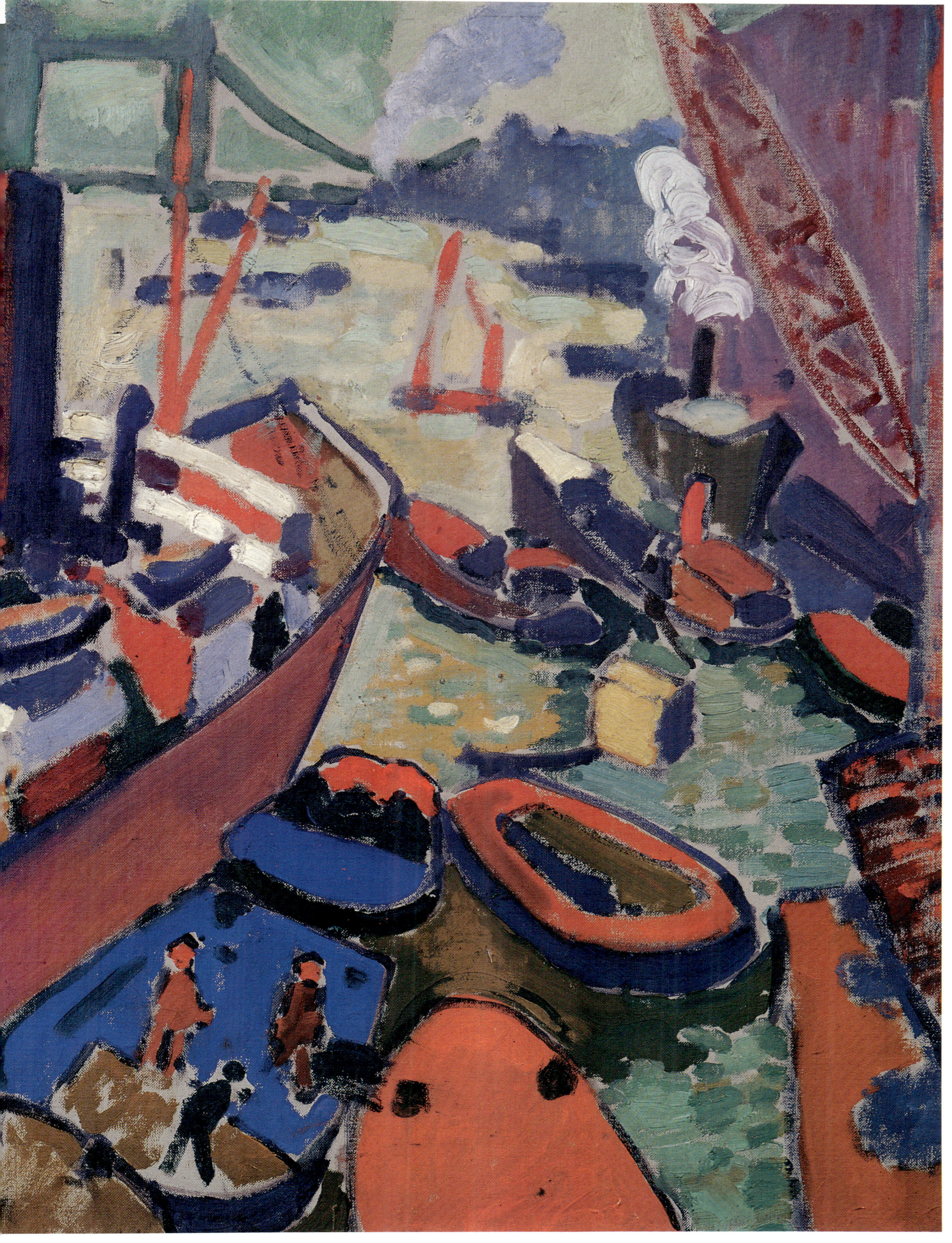

20

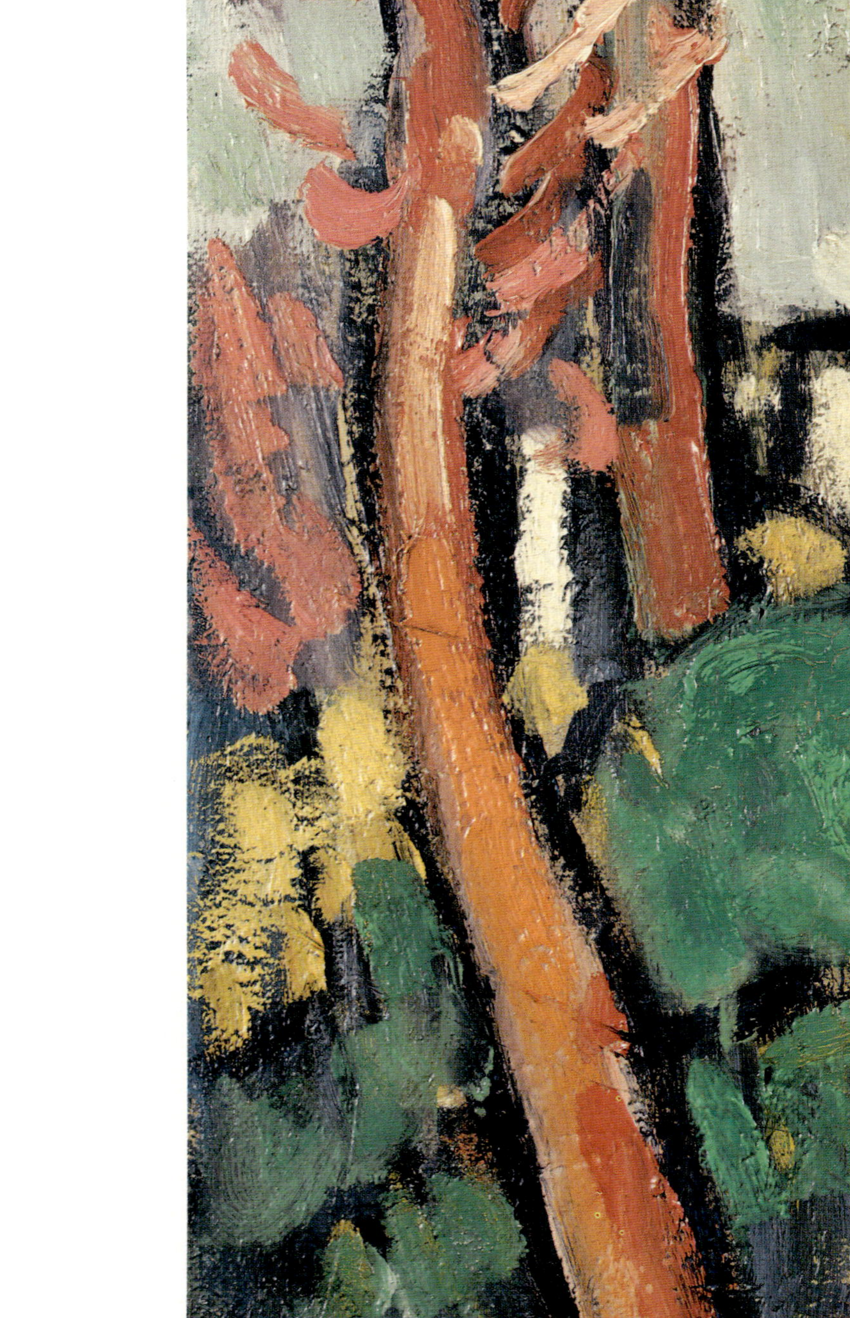

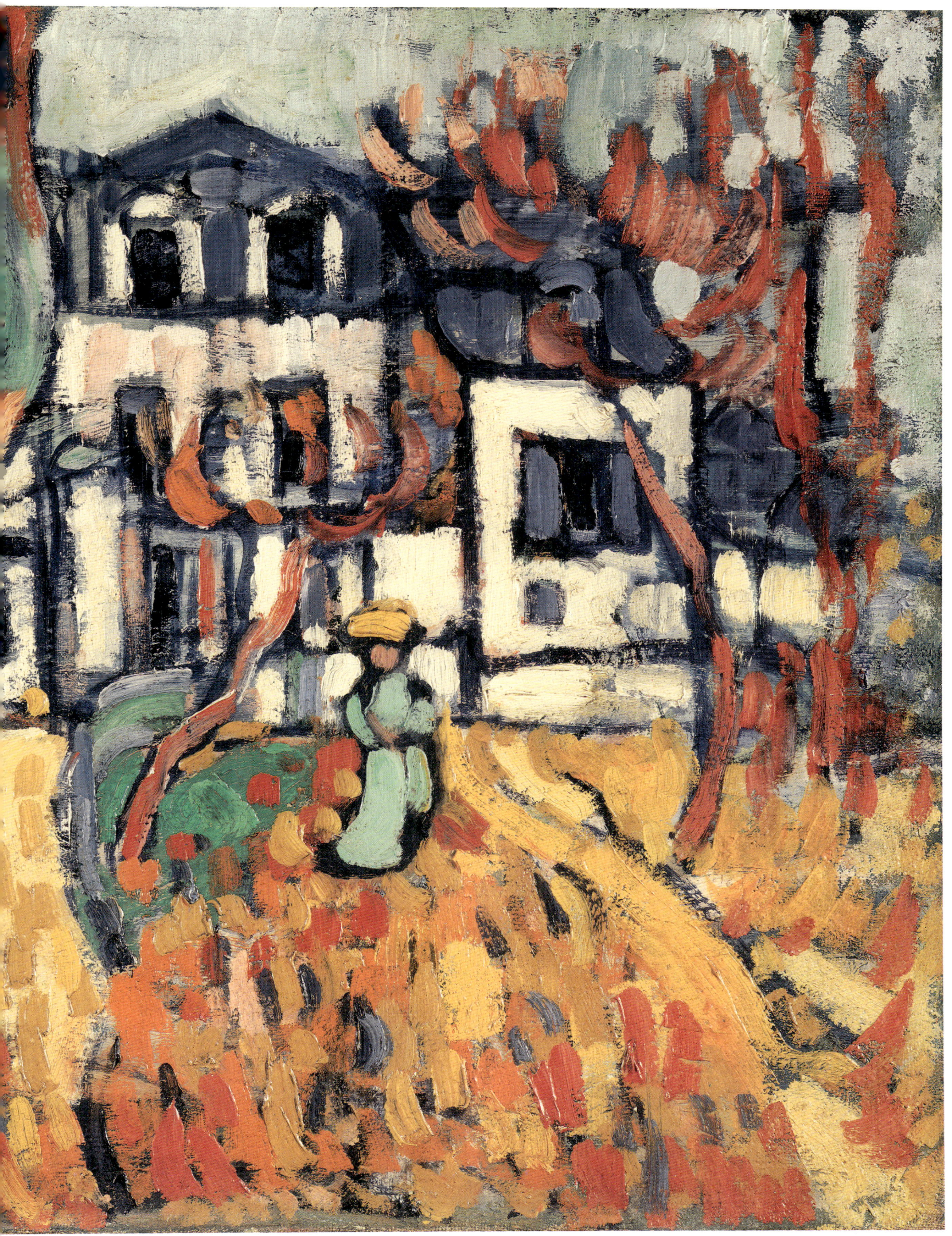

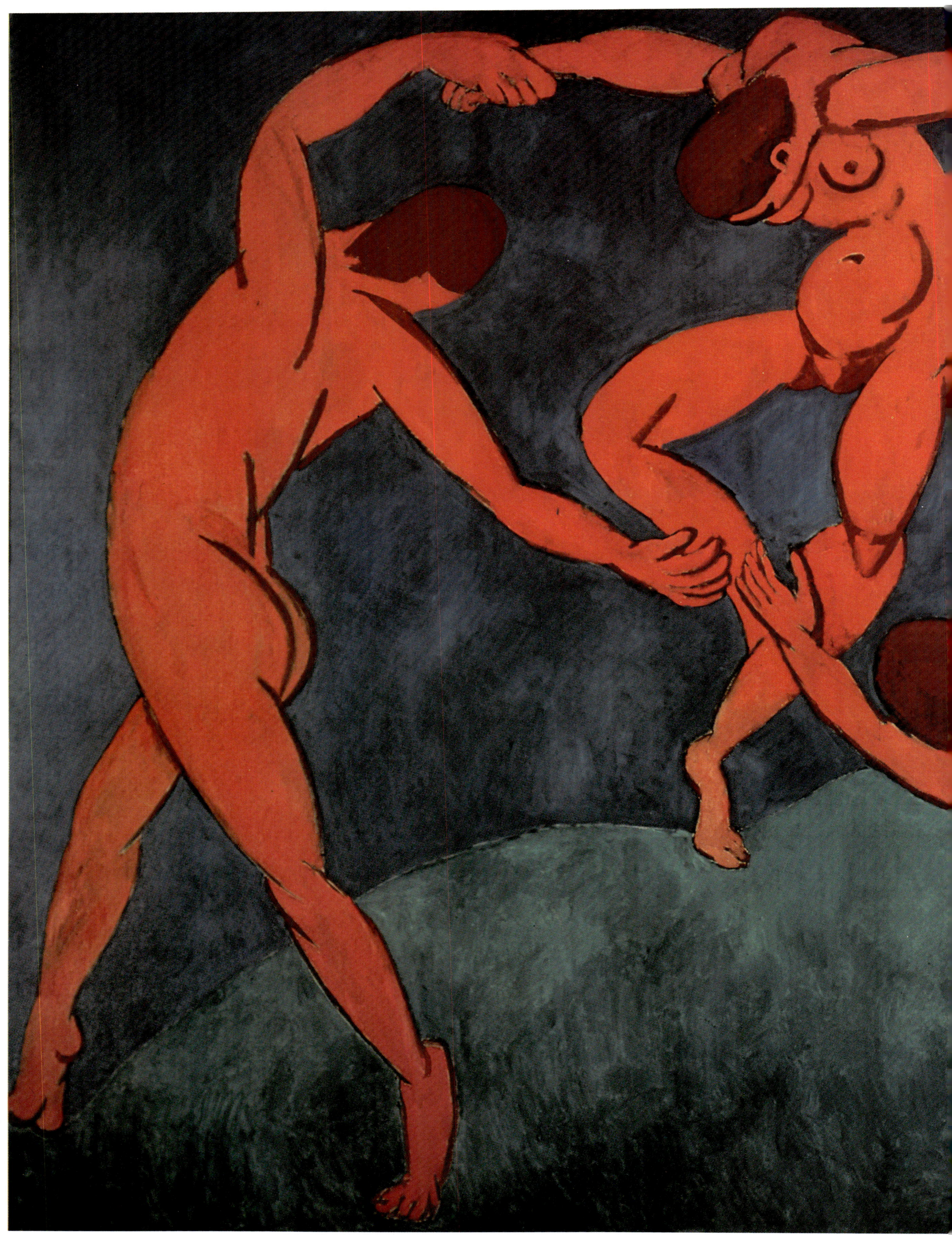

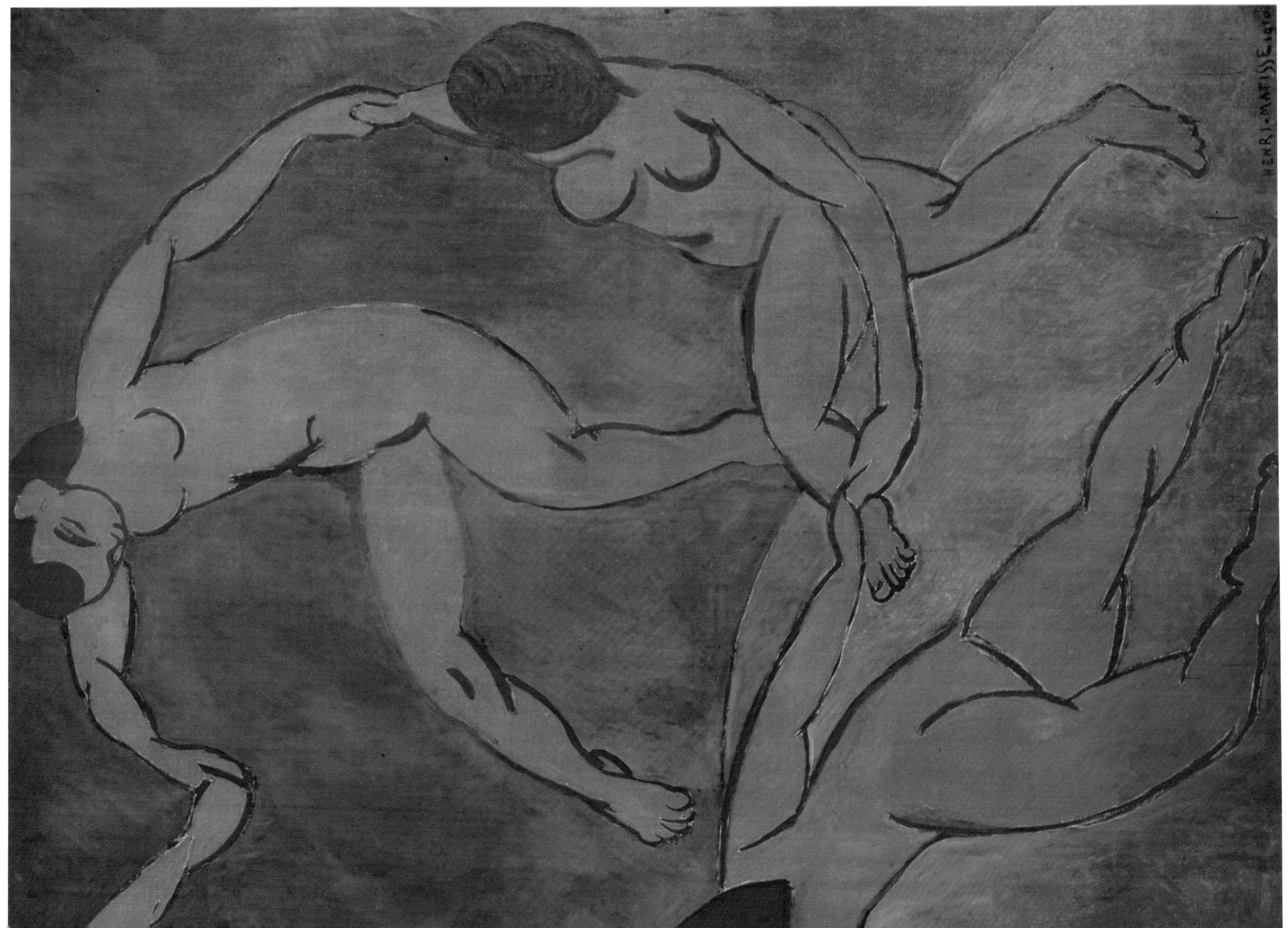

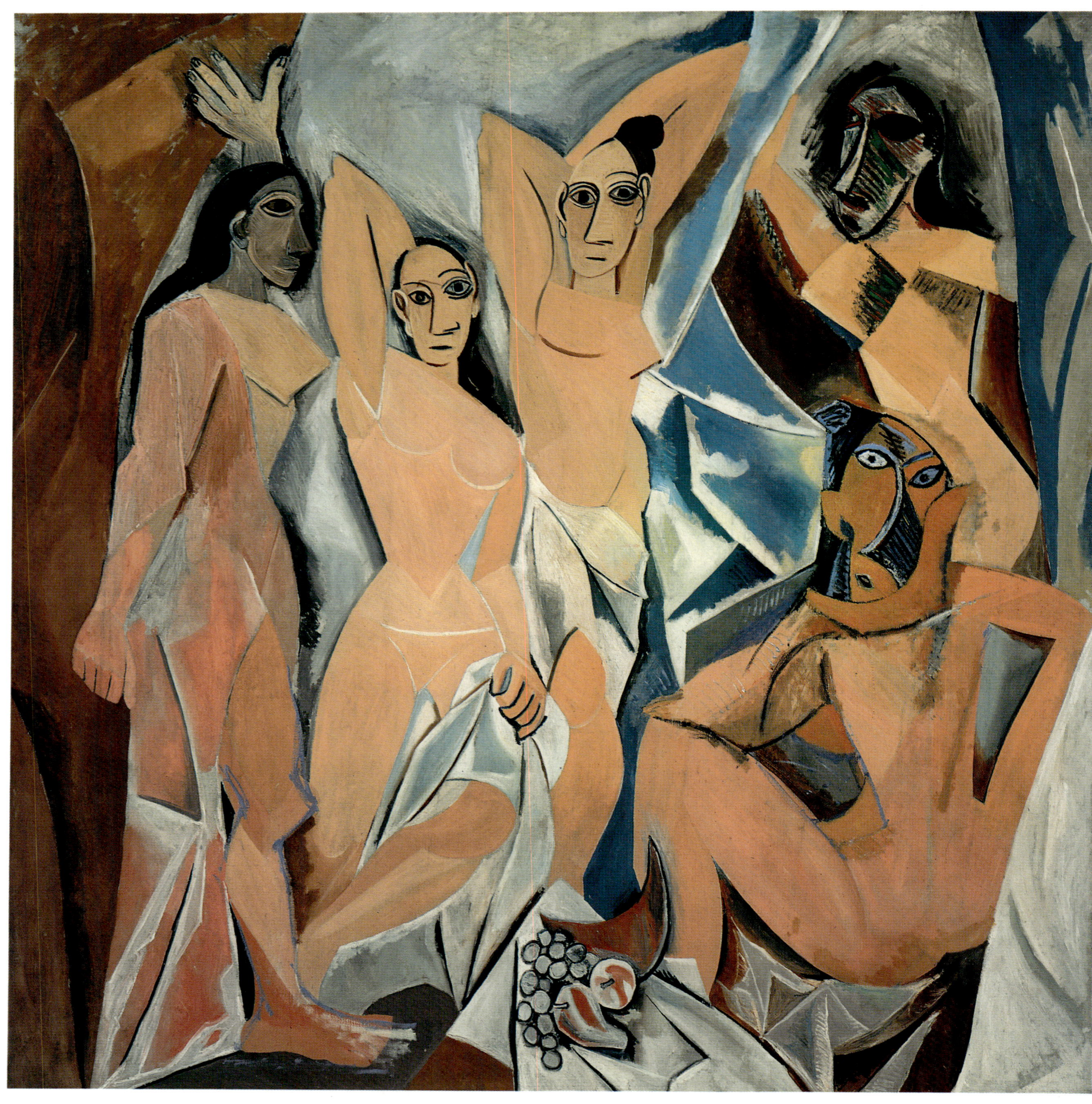

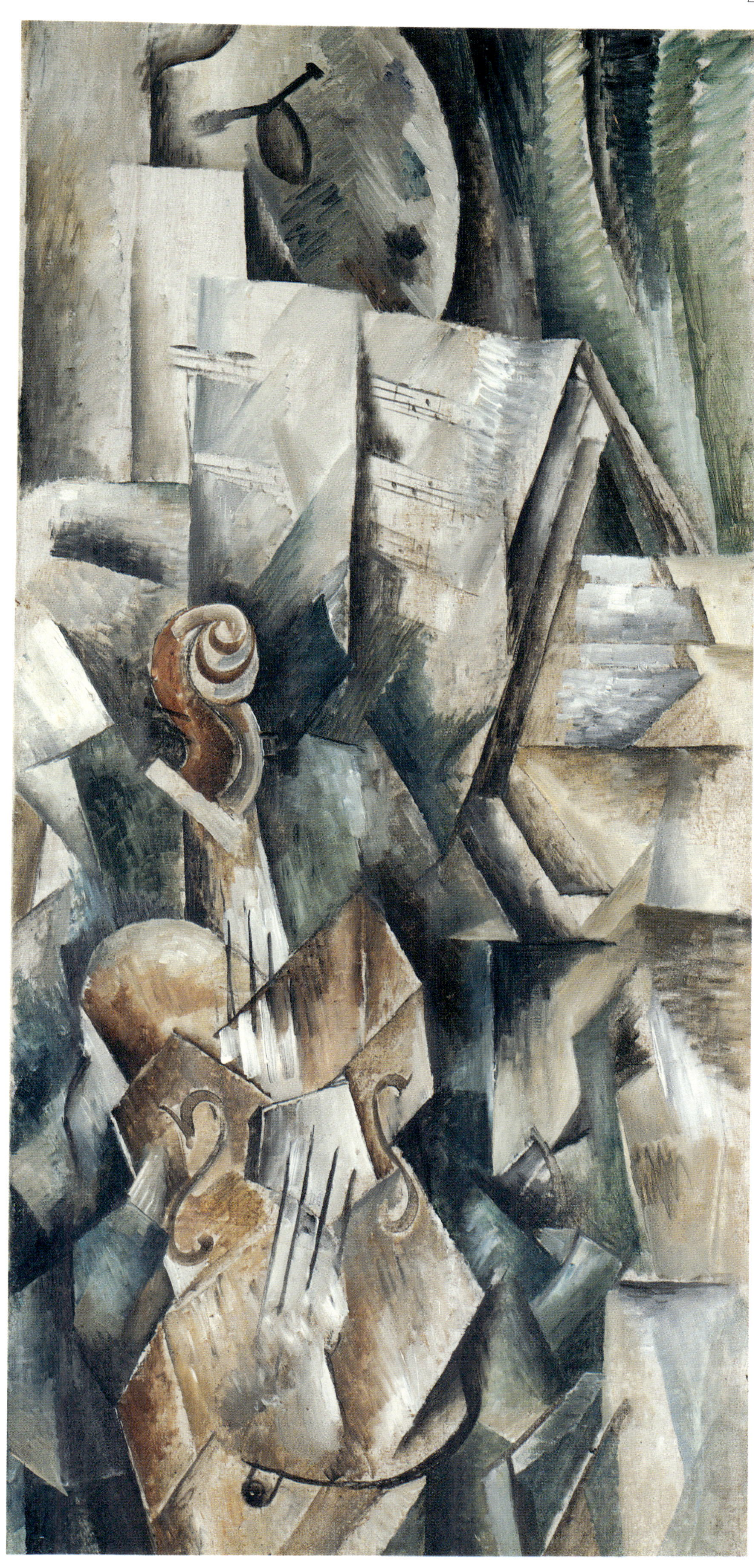

Georges Braque
Violin and Palette 1909/10
Oil on canvas, 36⅛×16⅞in (91.7×42.9cm)
Collection Solomon R Guggenheim Museum,
New York
© *ADAGP, Paris, DACS, London*

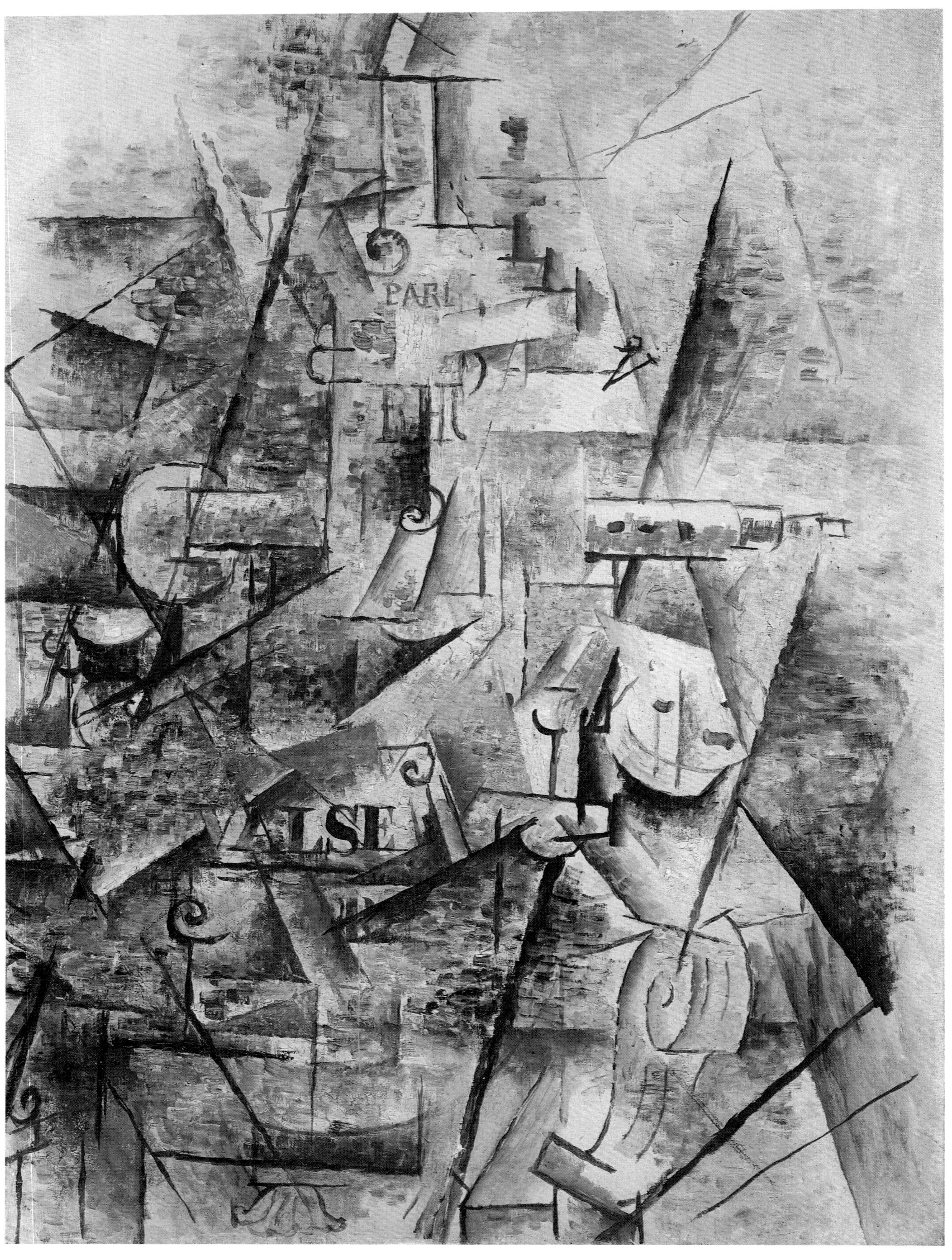

PARL
VALSE

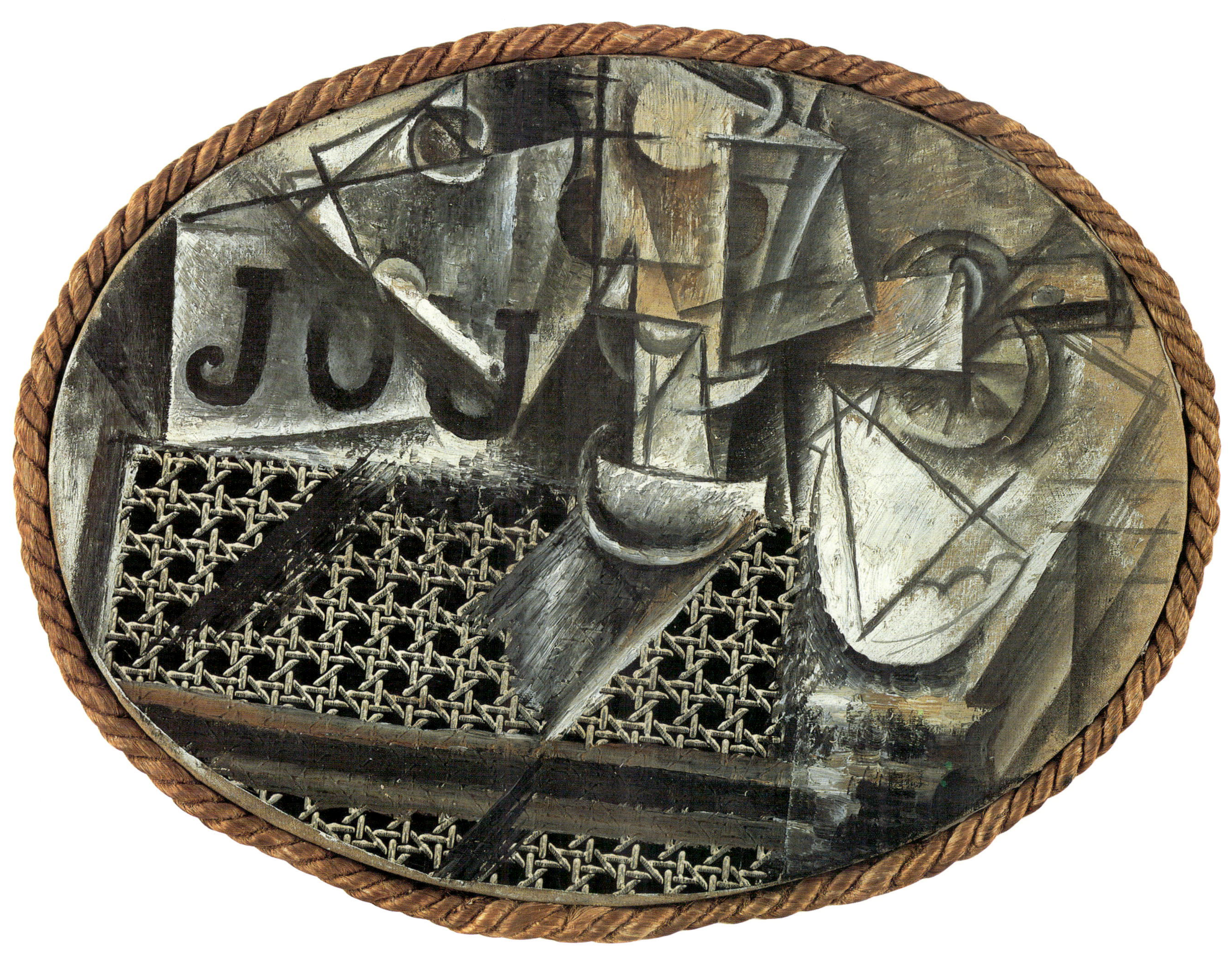

LEFT:
Georges Braque
Clarinet and Bottle of Rum on a Mantelpiece 1911
Oil on canvas, 31⅞×23⅝in (81×60cm)
Tate Gallery, London
© *ADAGP, Paris, DACS, London, 1989*

ABOVE:
Pablo Picasso
Still Life with Chair-caning 1912
Oil and oilcloth on canvas edged with rope, 29×37in (73.7×94cm)
Picasso Museum, Paris
© *DACS, 1988*

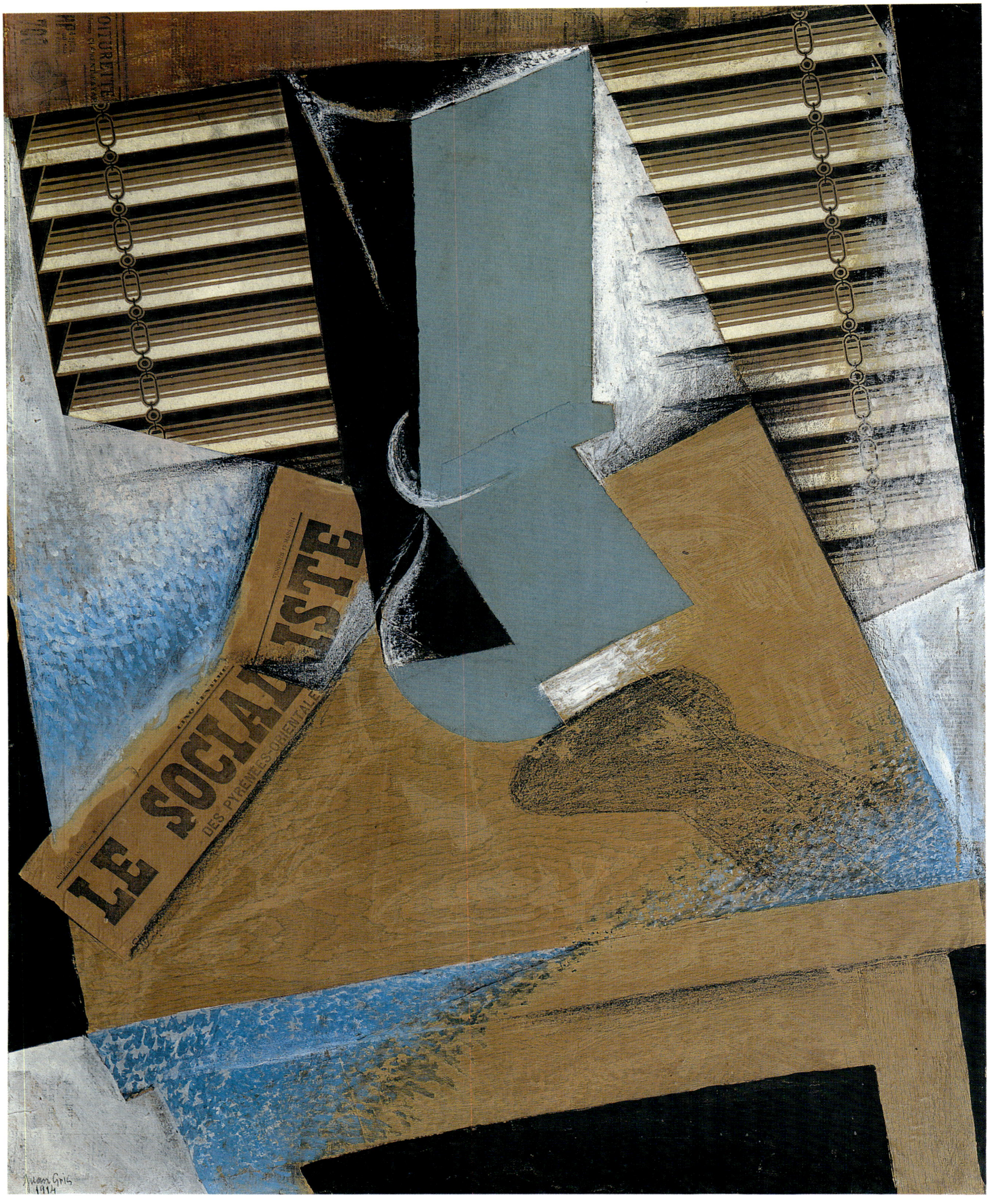

Juan Gris
The Sunblind 1914
Oil and collage on canvas, 36¼×28⅝in (92.1×72.7cm)
Tate Gallery, London
© *DACS, 1988*

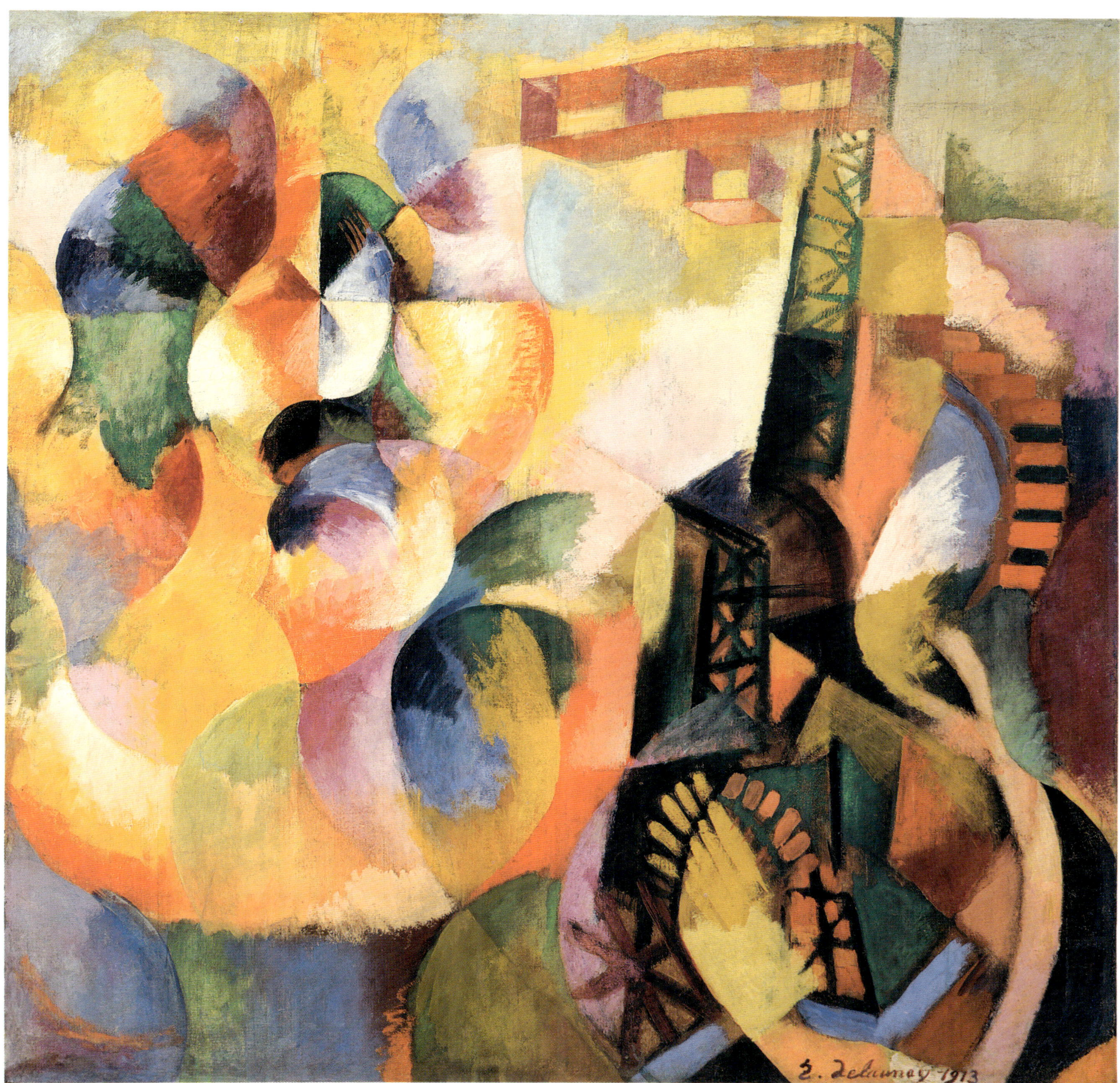

Robert Delaunay
Sun, Tower, Airplane 1913
Oil on canvas, 52×51⅝in (132×131cm)
Albright-Knox Art Gallery, New York
A Conger Goodyear Fund, 1964
© *ADAGP, Paris, DACS, London, 1989*

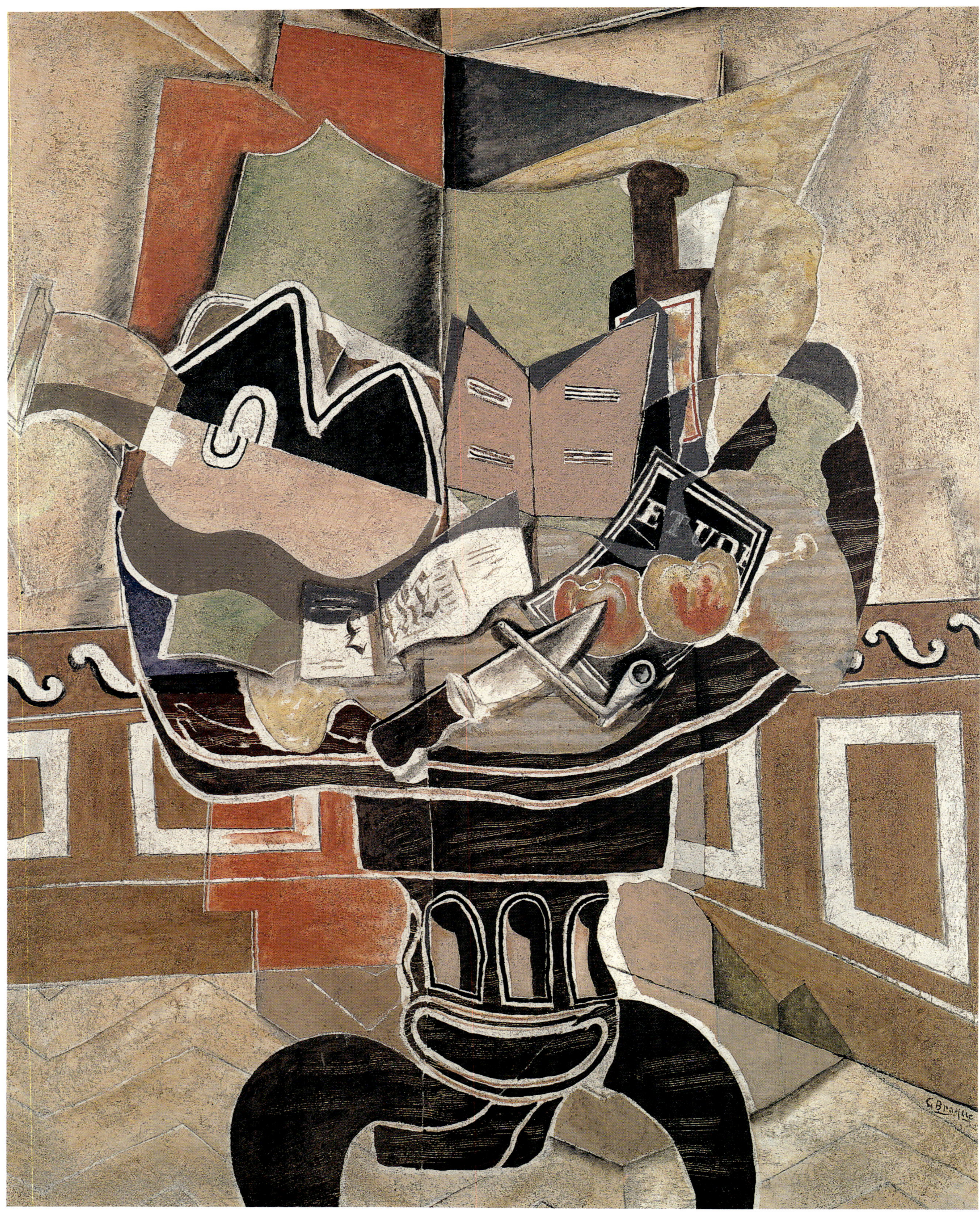

Georges Braque
The Round Table 1929
Oil on canvas, 57¼×44¾in (145.4×113.6cm)
The Phillips Collection, Washington, DC
© *ADAGP, Paris, DACS, London*

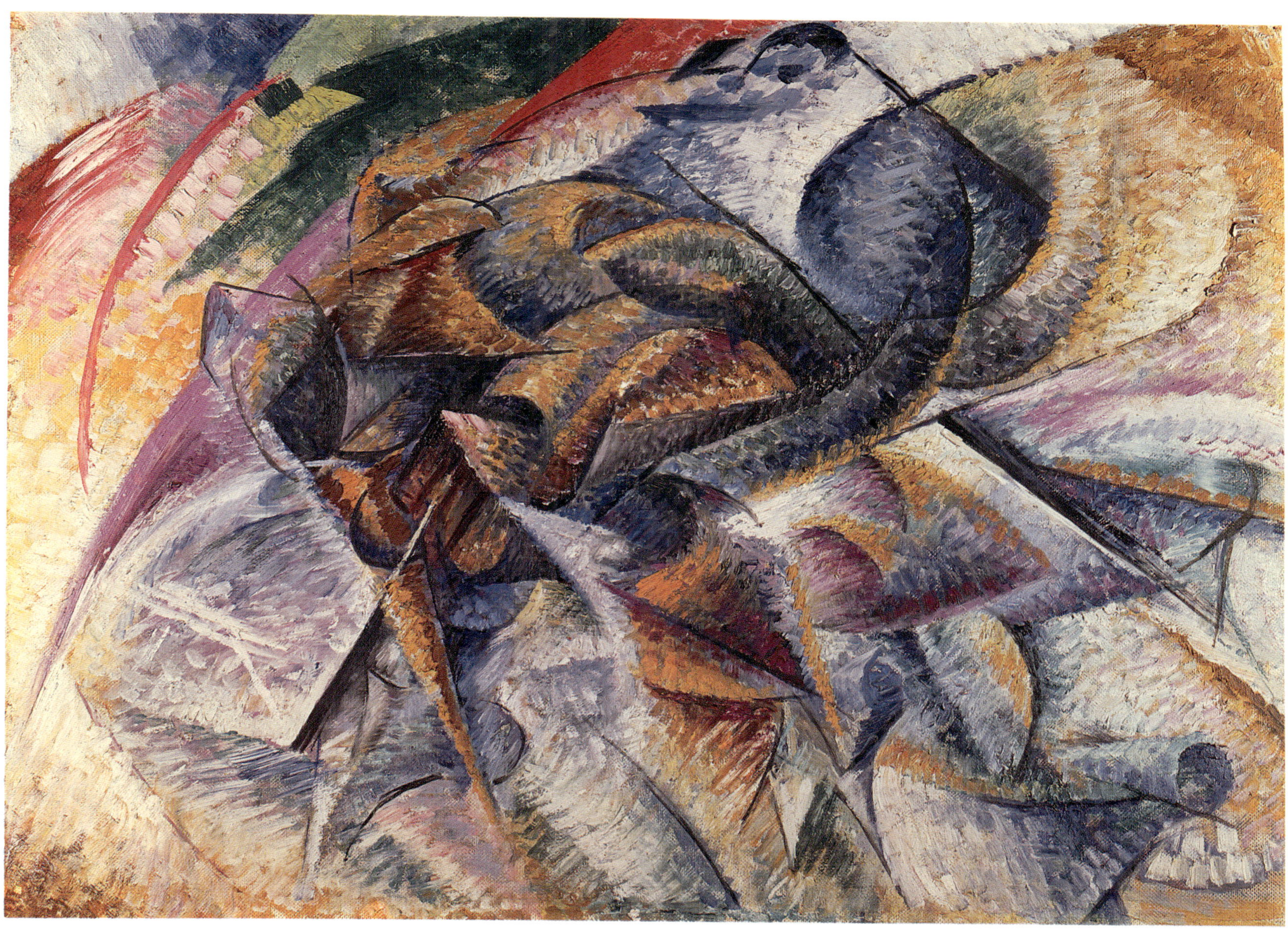

Umberto Boccioni
Dynamism of a Cyclist 1913
Oil on canvas, 27½×37⅜in (70×95cm)
Gianni Mattioli Collection, Milan
Photo: Scala

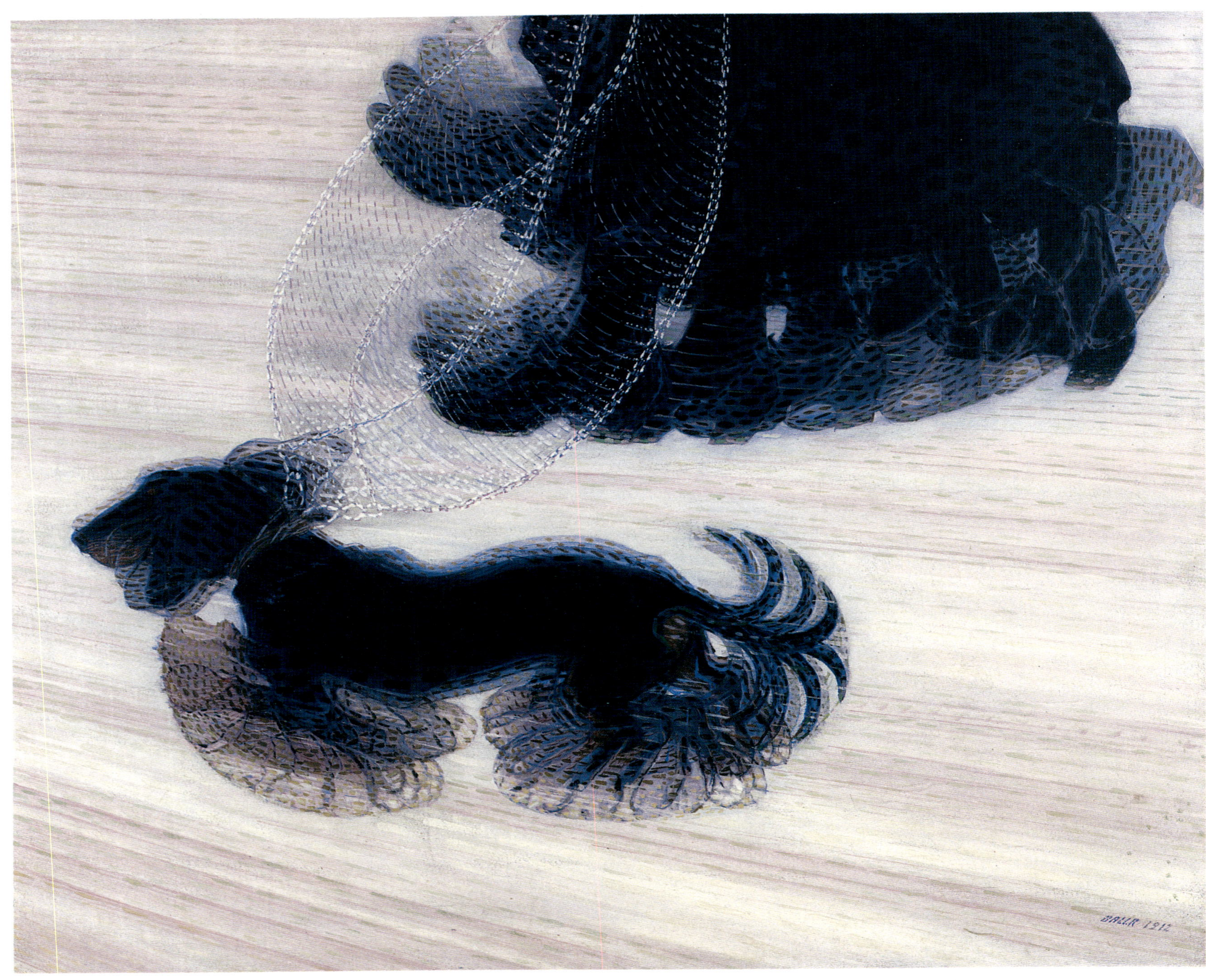

ABOVE:
Giacomo Balla
Dynamism of a Dog on a Leash 1912
Oil on canvas, 35⅜×43¼in (89.8×109.9cm)
Albright-Knox Art Gallery, New York
Bequest of A Conger Goodyear & Gift of George F Goodyear, 1964

RIGHT:
Gino Severini
The Blue Dancer 1912
Oll and sequins on canvas, 24×18⅛in (61×46cm)
Gianni Mattioli Collection, Milan
Photo: Scala
© *DACS, 1988*

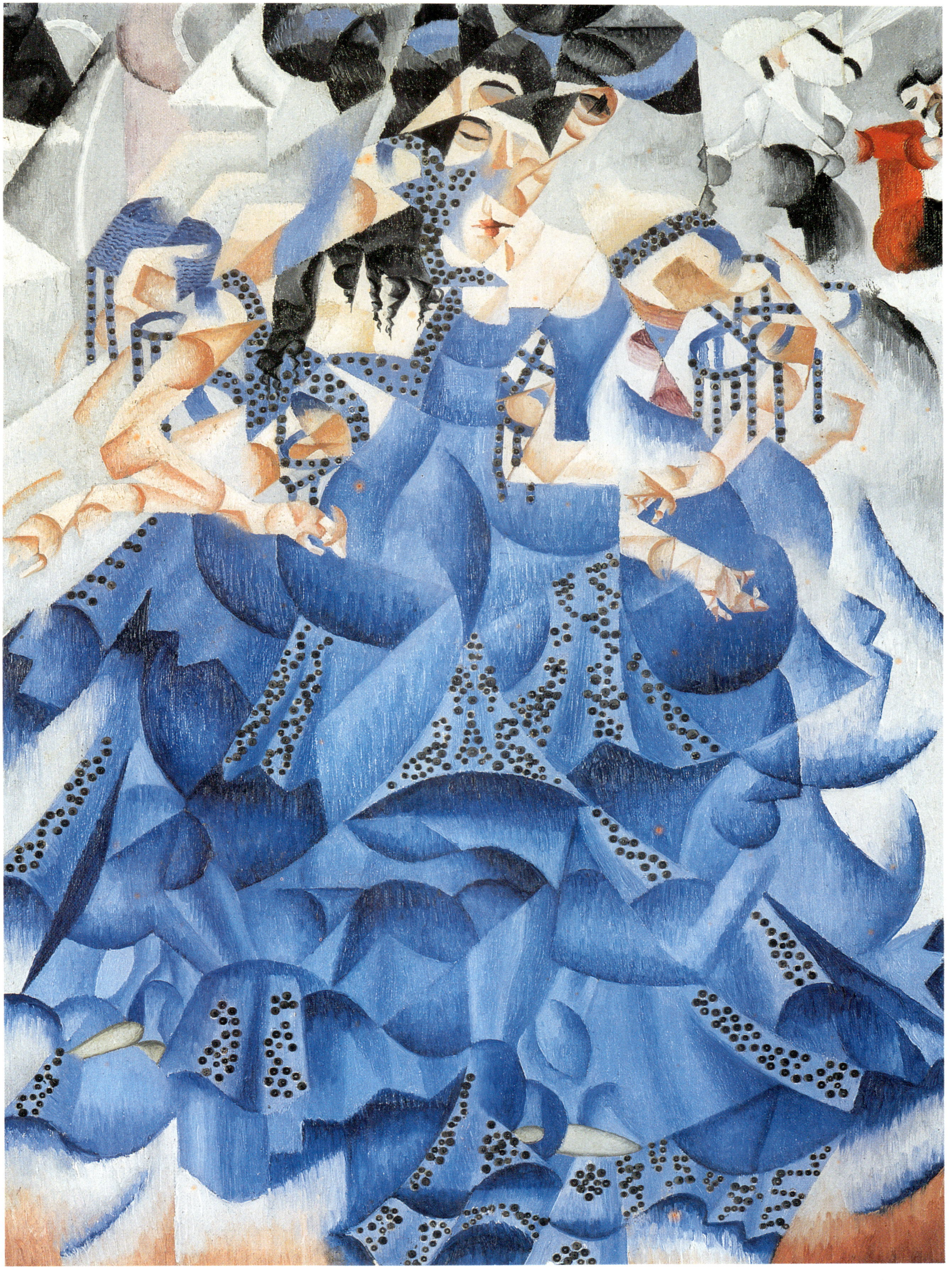

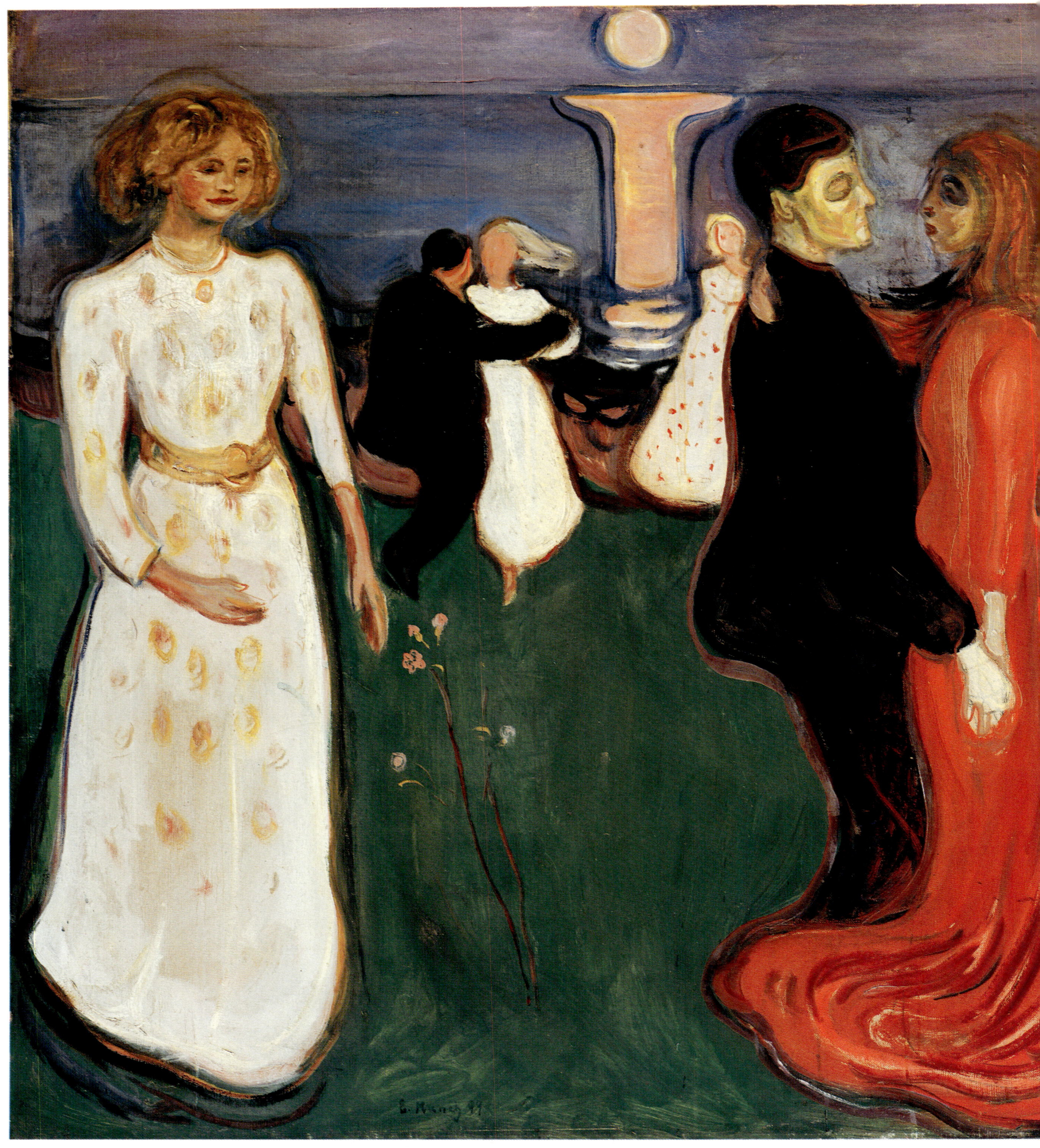

Edvard Munch
The Dance of Life 1899-1900
49½×75in (125.5×190.5cm)
Nasjonalgalleriet, Oslo
© *Munch-museum, Oslo*

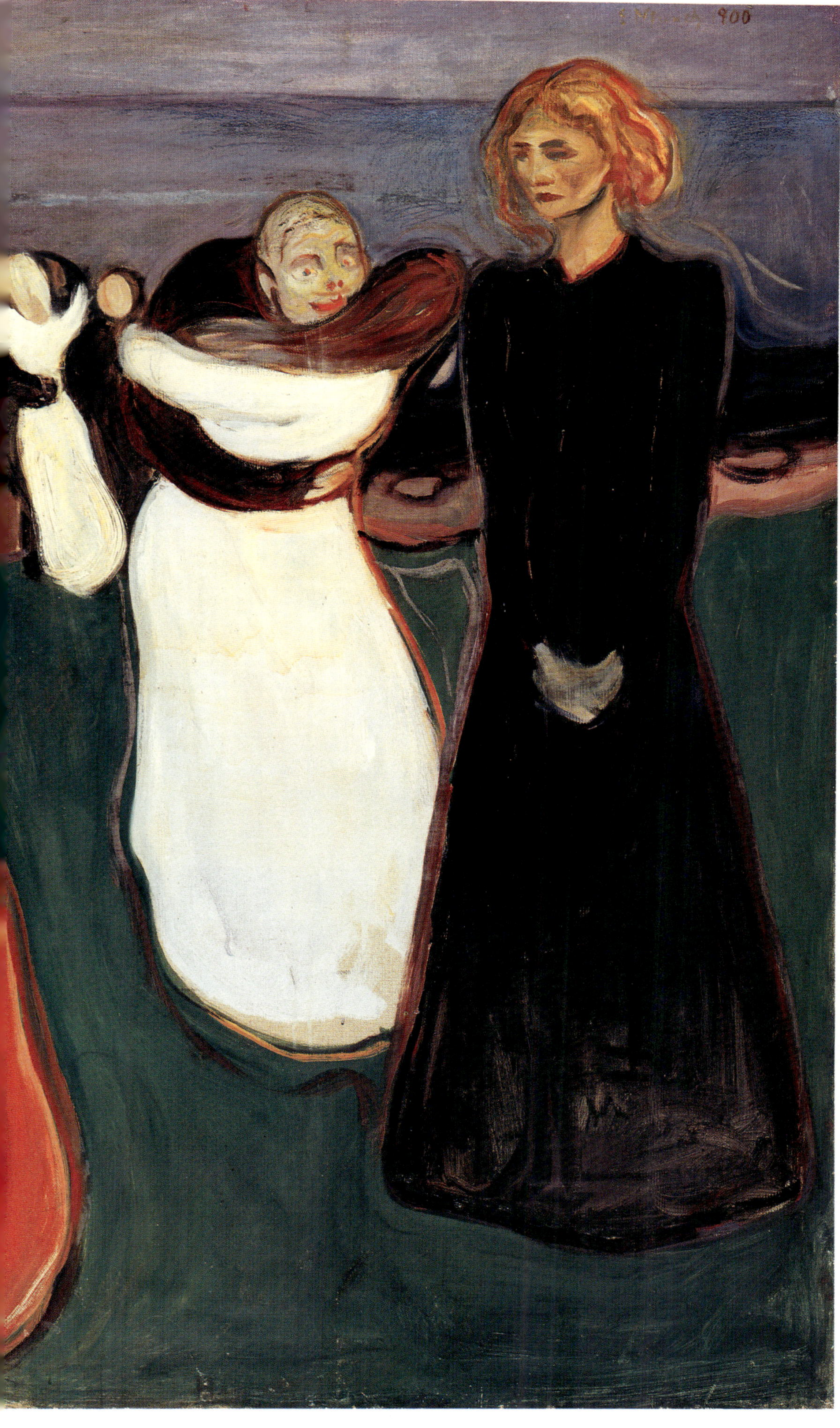

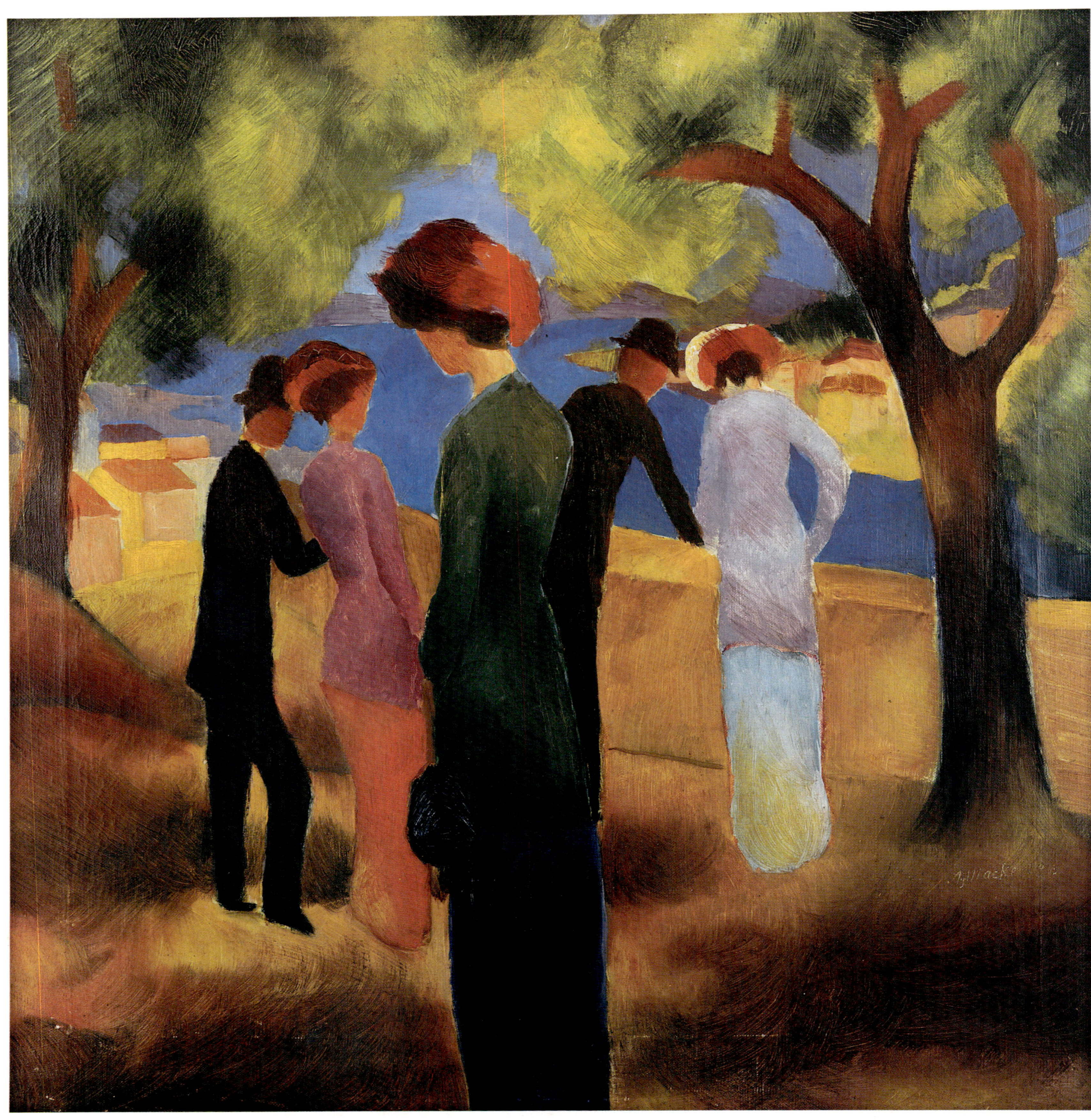

ABOVE:
August Macke
Woman in a Green Jacket 1912
Oil on canvas, 19⅓×16⅞in (49.2×42.9cm)
Museum Ludwig, Cologne

RIGHT:
Ernst Ludwig Kirchner
Self Portrait with Model c.1910
Oil on canvas, 59¼×39⅓in (150.4×100cm)
Hamburger Kunsthalle

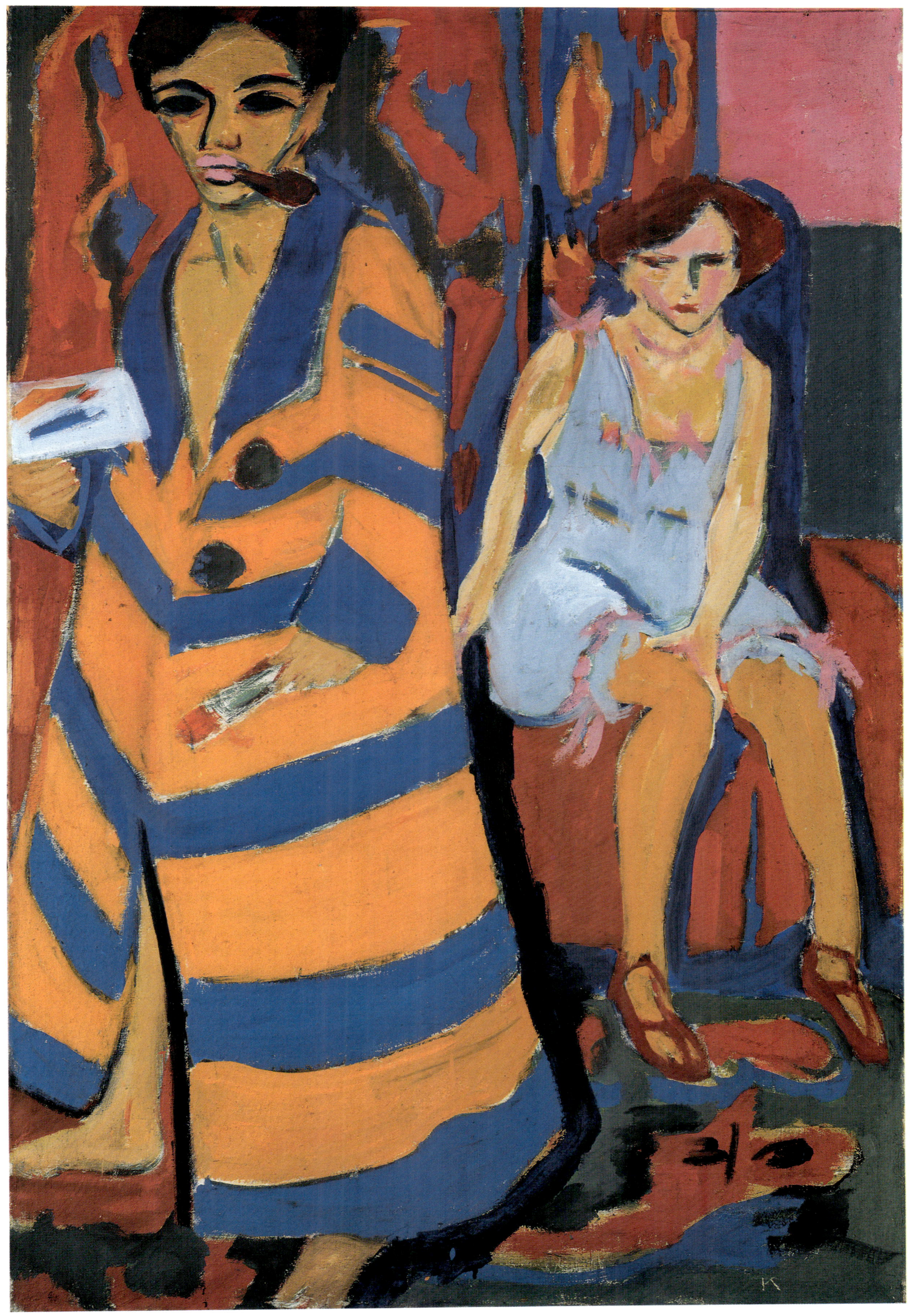

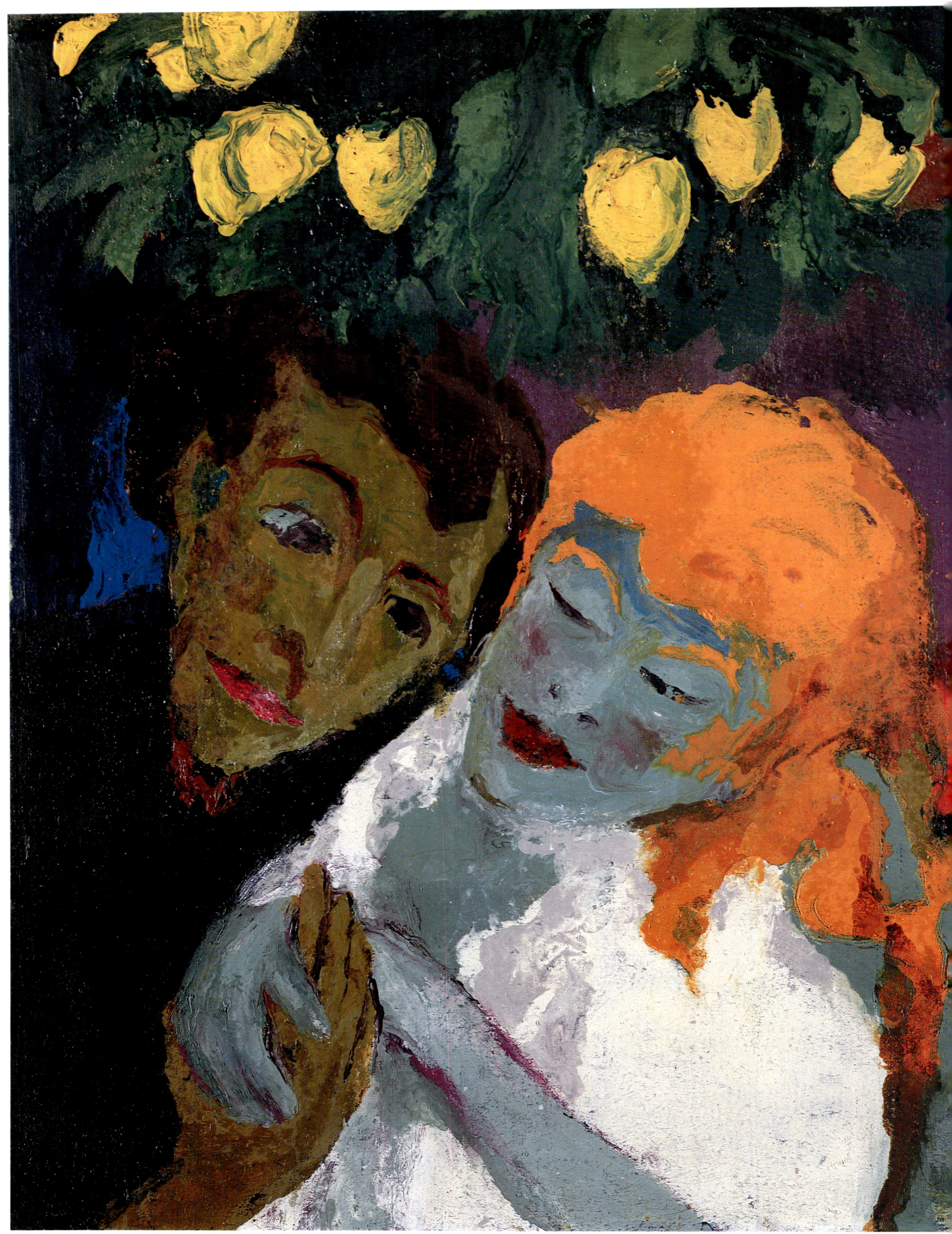

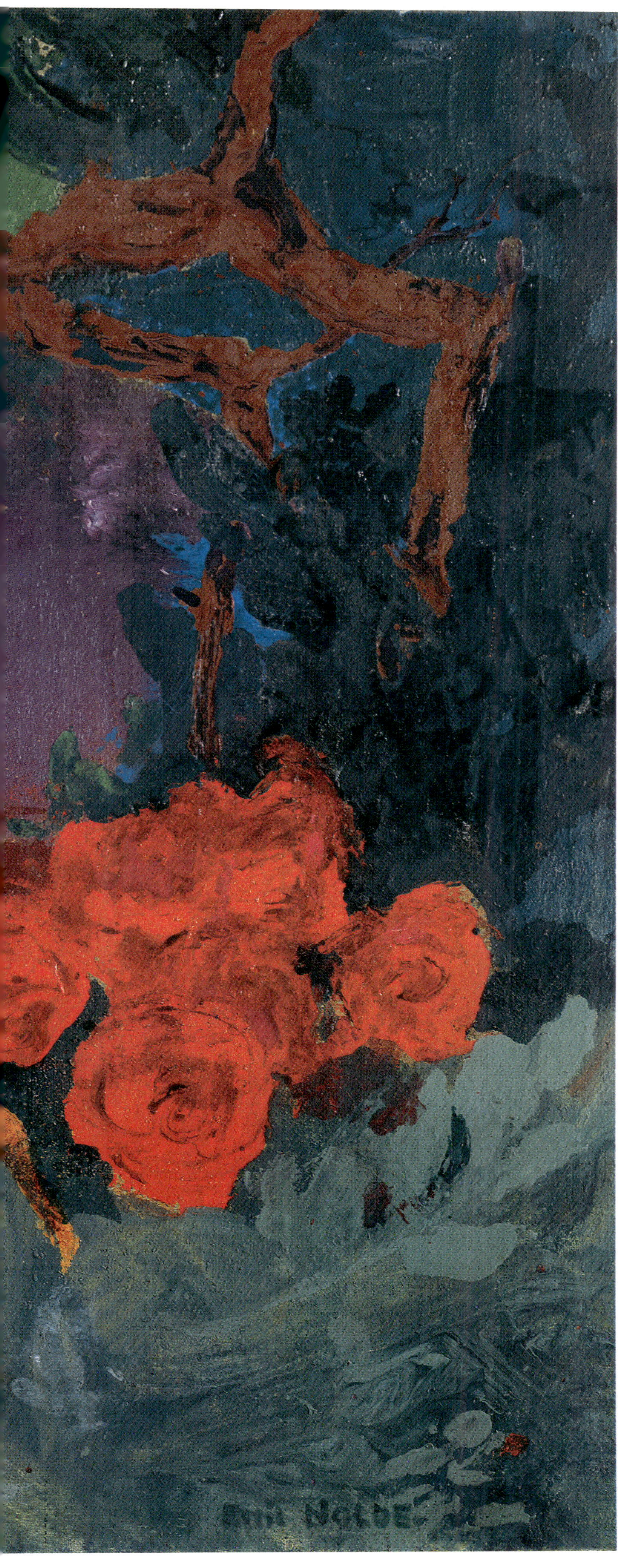

Emil Nolde
In the Lemon Garden 1920
Oil on canvas, 7¼×6in (18.3×15.3cm)
Staatsgalerie Stuttgart

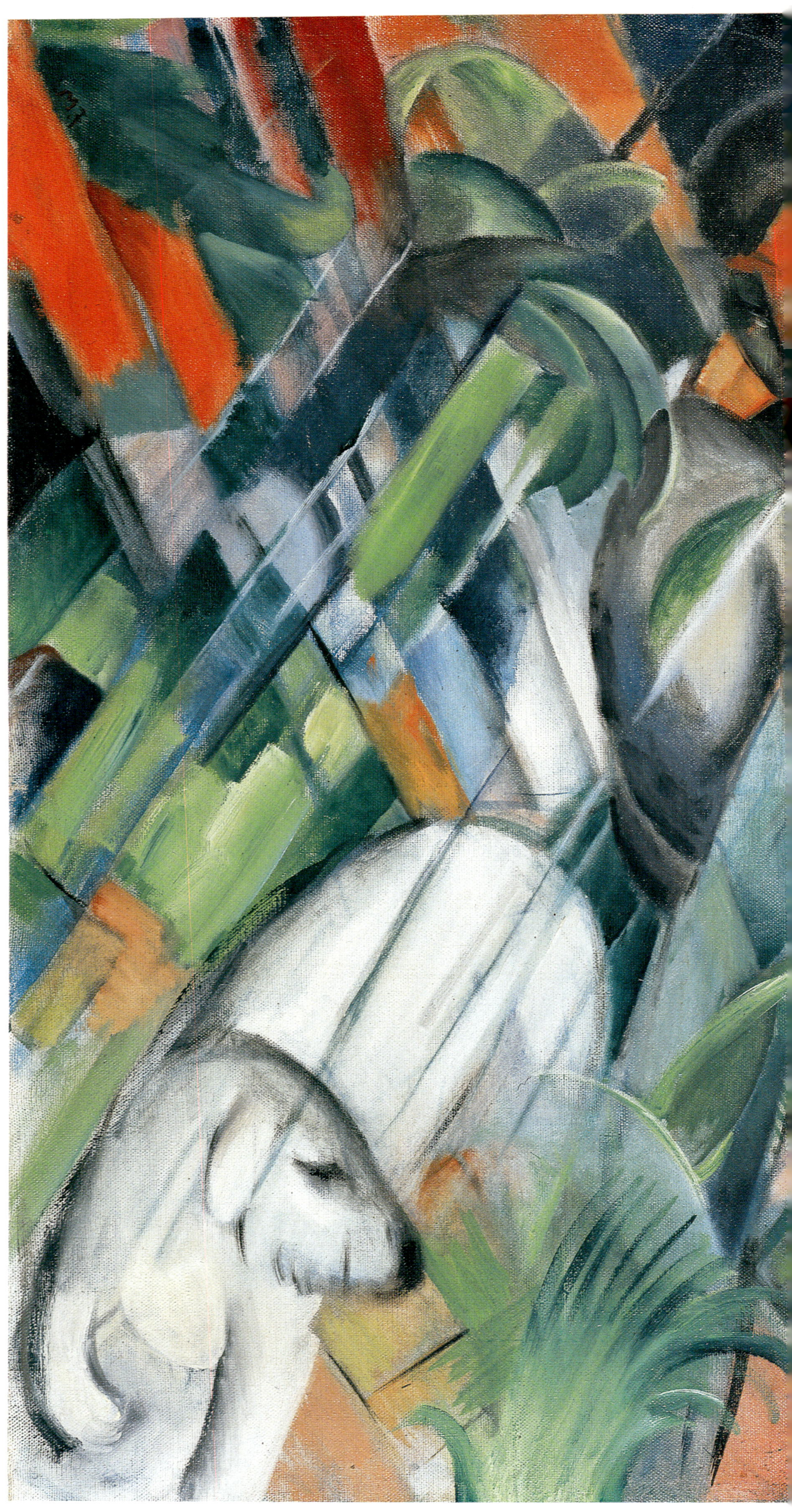

Franz Marc
Rain 1912
Oil on canvas, 31⅞×41⅓in (81×105cm)
Städtische Galerie im Lenbachaus, Munich

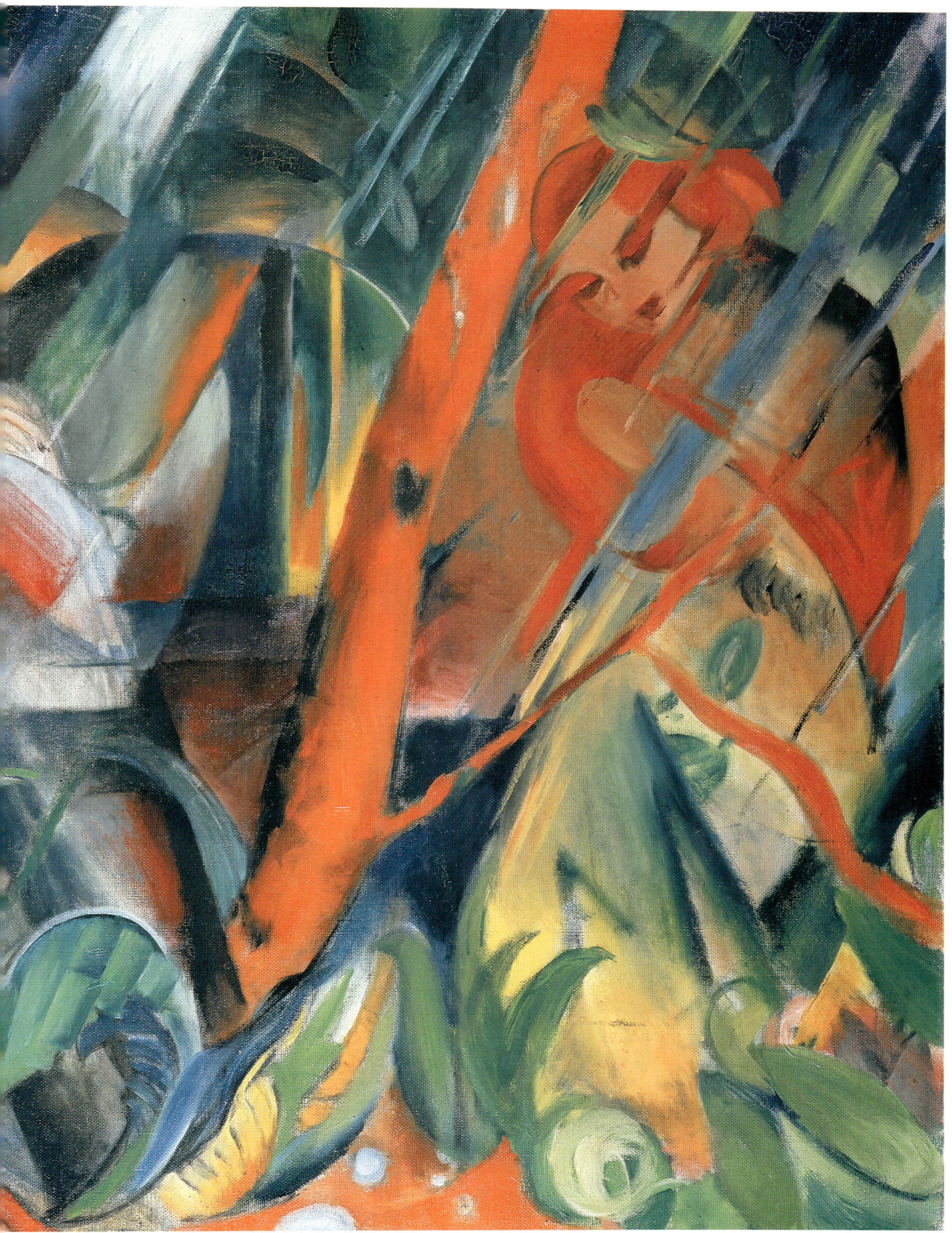

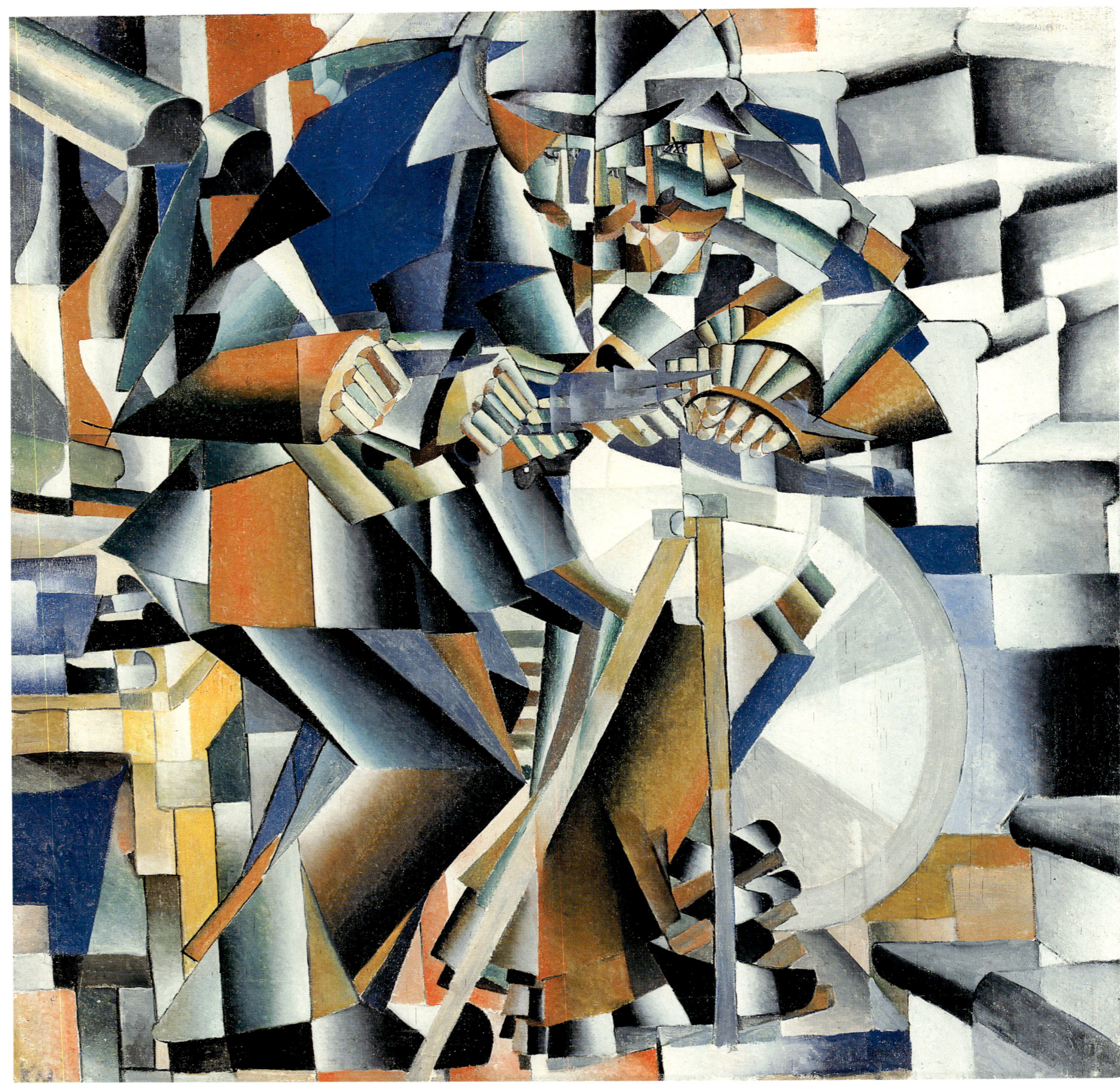

Kasimir Malevich
The Knife Grinder 1912
Oil on canvas, 31⅜×31⅜in (79.7×79.7cm)
Yale University Art Gallery, New Haven, Connecticut
Gift of Collection Société Anonyme

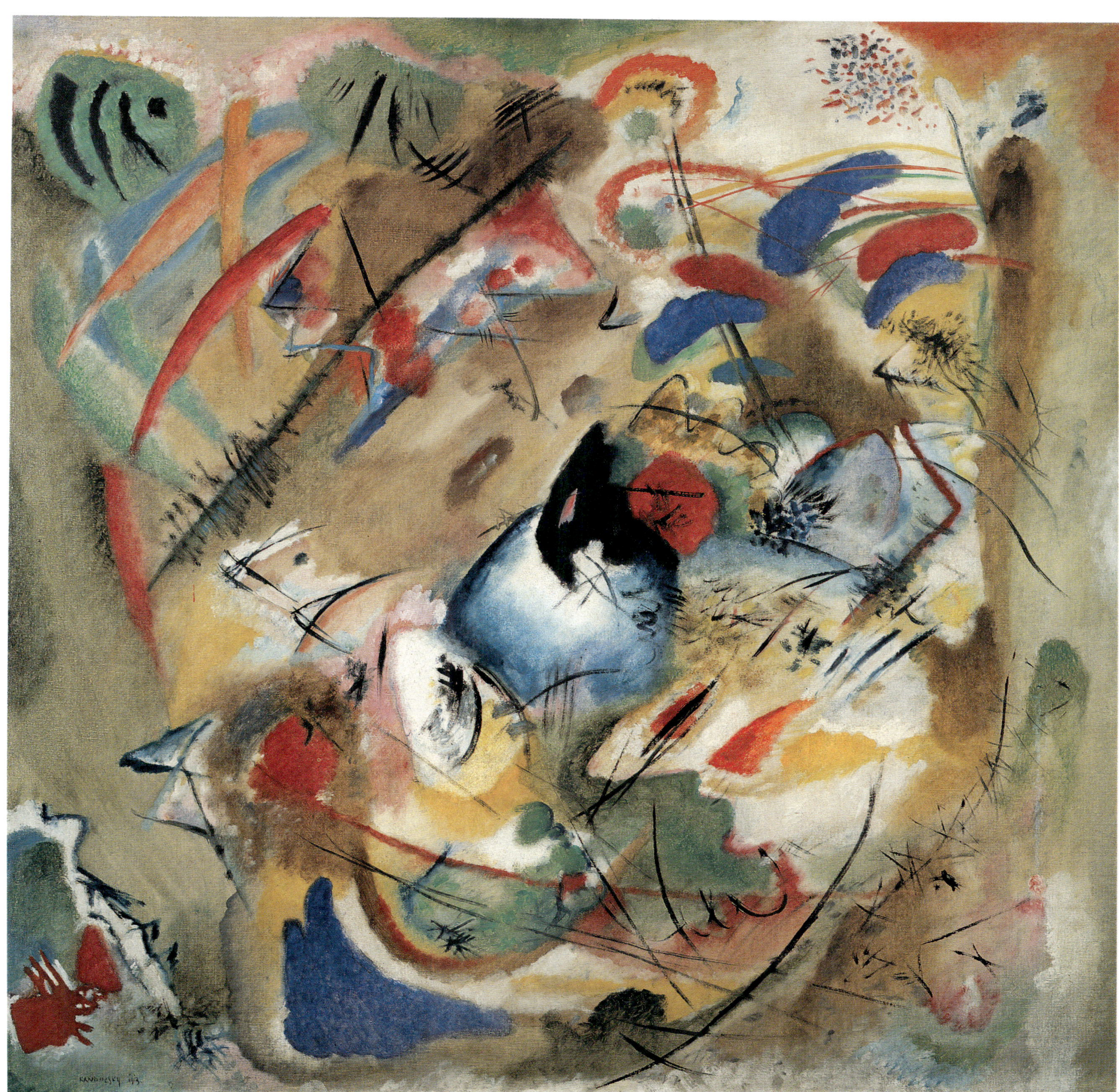

Wassily Kandinsky
Improvisation 1913
Oil on canvas, 51¼×51¼in (130×130cm)
Neue Pinakothek, Munich
Photo: ARTOTHEK
© *ADAGP, Paris, DACS, London, 1989*

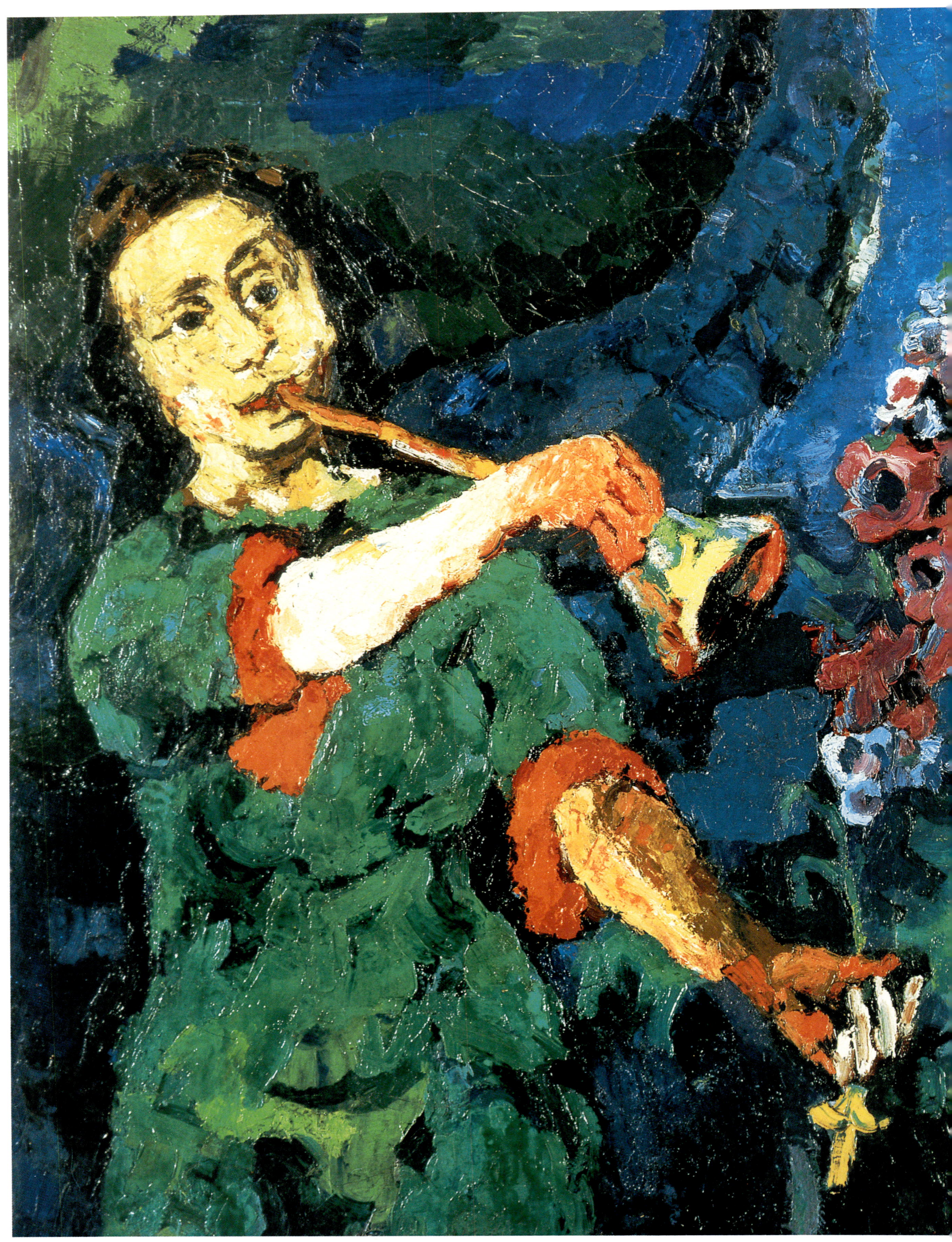

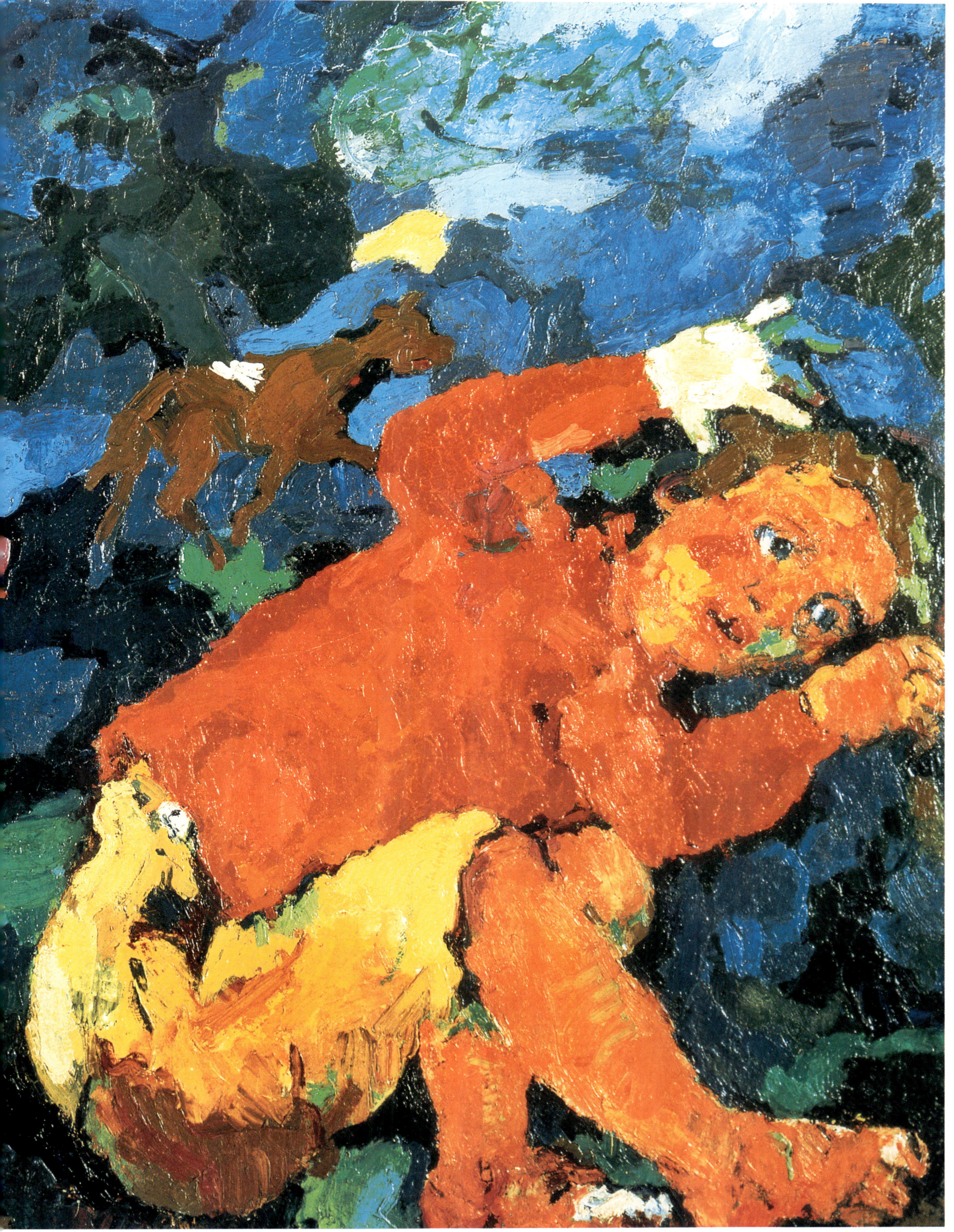

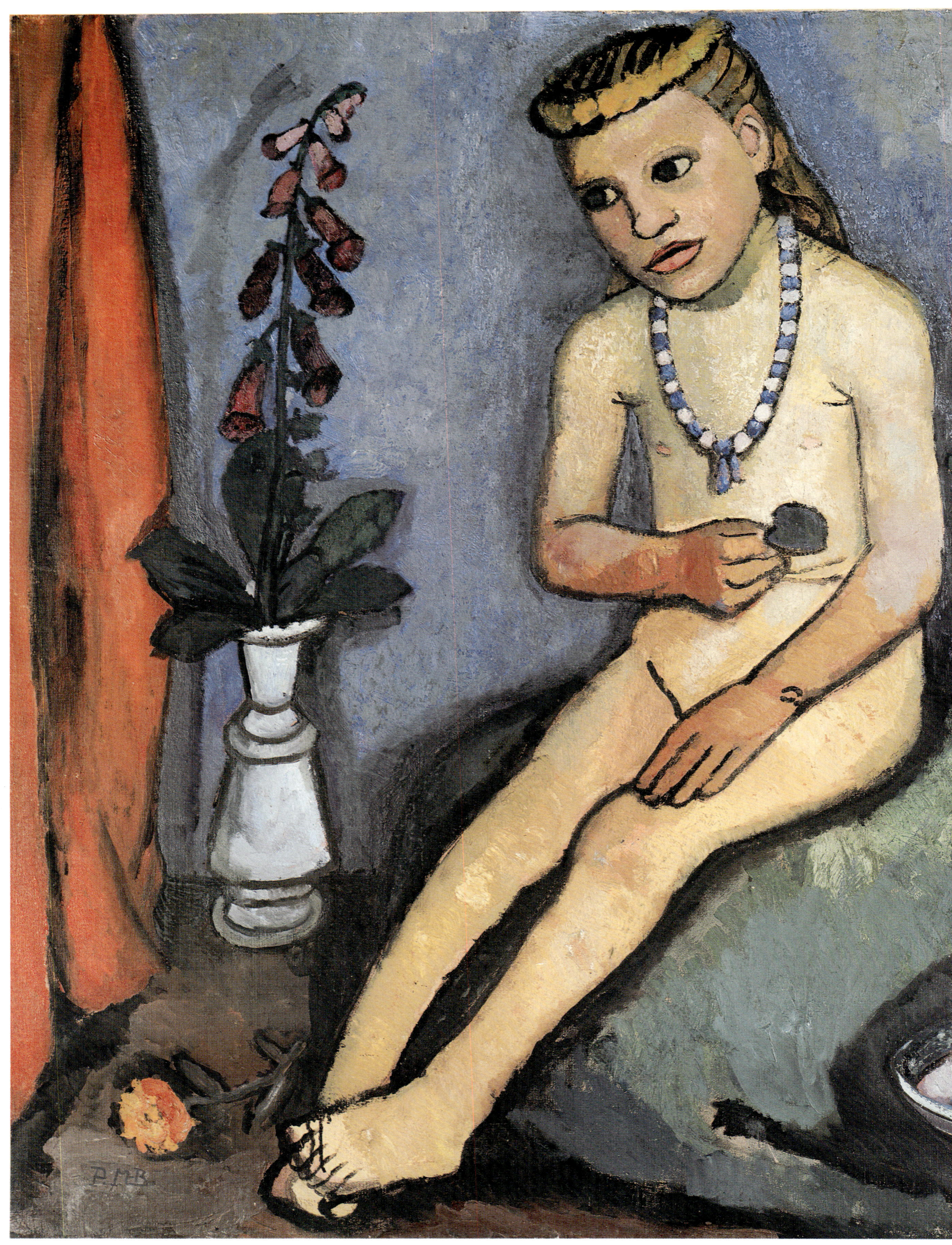

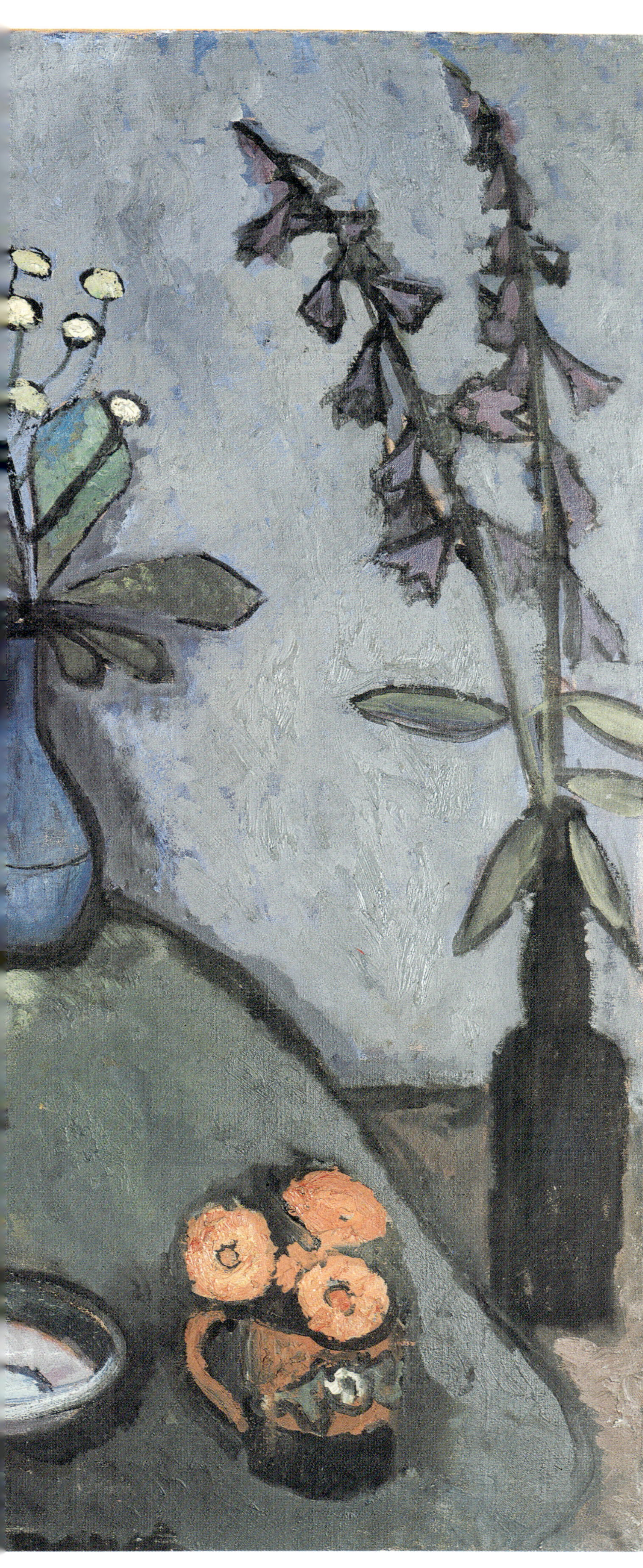

LEFT:
Paula Modersohn-Becker
Seated Nude Girl with Flowers 1907
Oil on canvas, 35×43in (89×109cm)
Museum Von der Heydt, Wuppertal

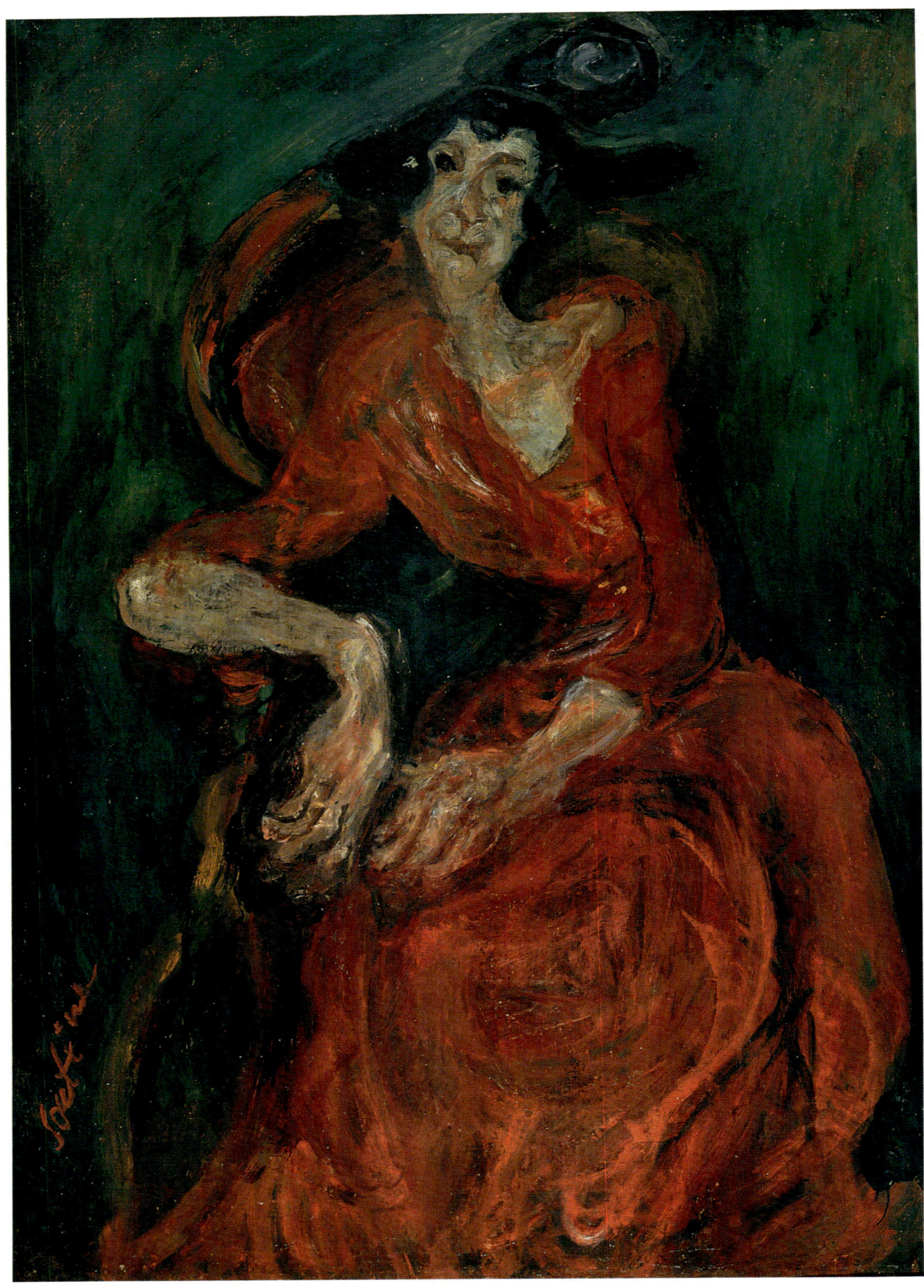

ABOVE:
Chaim Soutine
Woman in Red 1922
Oil on canvas
Musée du Petit Palais, Paris
Cliché Musées de la Ville de Paris
© *DACS, 1988*

RIGHT:
Georges Rouault
The Old King 1916
Oil on canvas, 30¼×21¼in (76.8×54cm)
The Carnegie Museum of Art, Pittsburgh
Patrons' Art Fund, 1940
© *DACS, 1988*

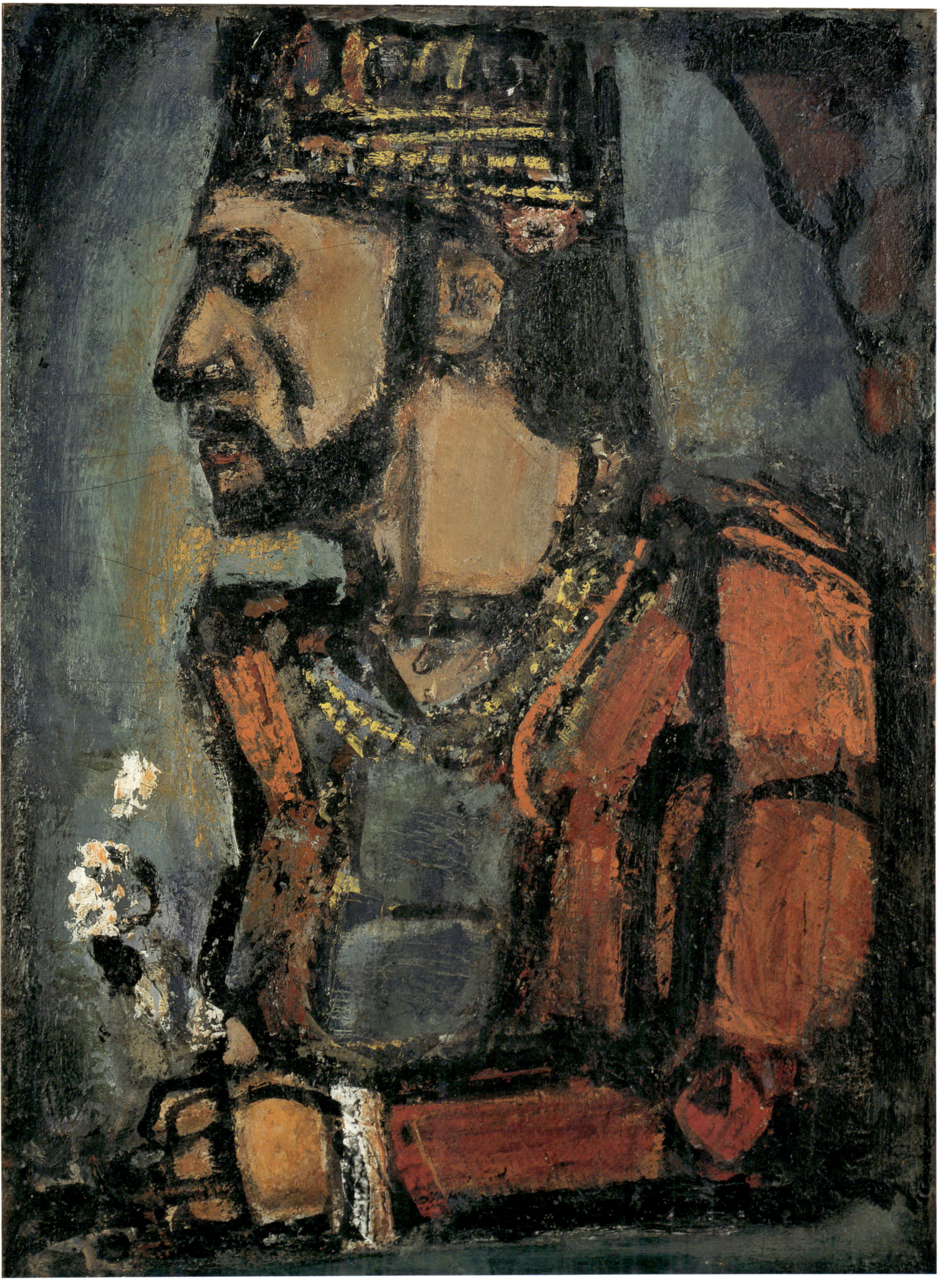

Chronology

	World Events	Visual Arts	Culture
1919	Treaty of Versailles Mussolini forms Fascist Party in Italy Alcock and Brown make first transatlantic flight	Léger: *La Ville*	Gropius founds the *Bauhaus* Kafka: *In the Penal Settlement*
1920	League of Nations founded Prohibition in USA	Nolde: *In the Lemon Garden* Mondrian: *Composition in Red, Yellow, and Blue* Bonnard: *The Bowl of Milk* Léger: *The Mechanic*	*The Cabinet of Dr Caligari*
1921	French occupation of Ruhr	Picasso *Three Musicians*	Prokofiev: *The Love of Three Oranges* Charles Chaplin: *The Kid*
1922	Mussolini marches on Rome and forms fascist government Stalin succeeds Lenin	Soutine: *Woman in Red*	T S Eliot: *The Waste Land* Joyce: *Ulysses* (published in Paris) Sinclair Lewis: *Babbitt*
1923	Fascist majority in Italy	Chagall: *The Green Violinist* (1923-24) Ernst: *Saint Cecilia-The Invisible Piano*	Eisenstein: *Battleship Potemkin* Le Courbusier: *Vers une architecture*
1924	Dawes Plan for German reparations Lenin dies	Kandinsky: *Shrill Peaceful Pink* Moholy-Nagy: *A II* Van Doesburg: *Countercomposition V* Miro: *Carnival of Harlequin* (1924-25)	Thomas Mann: *The Magic Mountain* Weimar Bauhaus closed André Breton: *Surrealist Manifesto* George Gershwin: *Rhapsody in Blue* Puccini: *Turandot*
1925	Locarno Treaty signed by Britain, Belgium, and France	Dix: *Portrait of the Dancer Anita Berber*	Kafka: *The Trial* Chaplin: *The Gold Rush*
1926	General strike in Britain	Grosz: *Pillars of Society*	Fritz Lang: *Metropolis*
1927	End of Allied control in Germany	Magritte: *The Reckless Sleeper*	Establishment of BBC First full-length sound movie, *The Jazz Singer*
1928	Start of first Five Year Plan in Russia Amelia Earhart first woman to fly Atlantic Fleming discovers penicillin	Schlemmer: *Fallen Figure with Column* Beckmann: *Aerial Acrobatics* Demuth: *I saw the Figure 5 in Gold*	Gershwin: *An American in Paris* Ravel *Bolero* Weil & Brecht: *The Threepenny Opera*
1929	Wall Street Crash World depression begins	Braque: *The Gueridon*	Foundation of Museum of Modern Art in New York
1930	4.4 million Germans unemployed Amy Johnson flies solo from Britain to Australia	Wood: *American Gothic*	Le Corbusier Villa Savoie – 'a machine for living'
1932	Roosevelt elected President in US Famine in Russia	Klee: *Ad Parnasum* Shahn: *The Passion of Sacco and Vanzetti* O'Keefe: *White Canadian Barn*	A Huxley: *Brave New World* D Runyon: *Guys and Dolls* E Hemingway: *Death in the Afternoon*
1935	Nuremberg Laws in Germany redefine the Jew	Dufy: *The Artist's Studio*	United States' New Deal programs for artists and architects begin
1936	Spanish Civil War begins Germany reoccupies Rhineland without Allied protest Constitutional crisis in Britain: abdication of Edward VIII – Accession of George VI	Dali: *Soft Construction with Boiled Beans*	Prokofiev: *Peter and the Wolf* Schönberg: Violin Concerto Chaplin: *Modern Times*
1937	Guernica bombed by German planes	Picasso: *Guernica* Nash: *Landscape from a Dream*	Steinbeck: *Of Mice and Men* Disney's first full-length cartoon: *Snow White and the Seven Dwarfs*
1938	German troops invade Austria. Crystal Night: large-scale program against Jews USA Roosevelt's New Deal	Dali: *Mountain Lake*	
1939	German invasion of Poland Britain and France declare war on Germany	Tanguy: *Indefinite Divisibility*	Steinbeck: *The Grapes of Wrath* Film of *Gone with the Wind*

Painting between the Wars

The optimism of the Futurists and their idealistic faith in modern technology was shattered by World War I, 'the war to end all wars.' Those of the generation of artists that survived the war turned to new means of expression. The diversity of styles is complex and confusing. It is difficult in this period to categorize artists into this or that 'movement' or 'ism,' particularly as many of the artists themselves resisted such categorization. In the most influential history of art of our time, E H Gombrich's *The Story of Art*, the author states 'There is really no such thing as Art. There are only artists.' It is only by examining the work of individual artists that it is possible to illuminate the painting of this otherwise puzzling period.

Kandinsky, for example, radically altered his style after the war. He returned to Moscow in 1914 and was given an important role in state education after the Russian Revolution of 1917, becoming Director of the Moscow Museum of Pictorial Culture in 1918 and founding the Russian Academy of Artistic Sciences in 1921. His theoretical work continued and his treatise *Point and Line to Plane*, an analysis of forms and colors was published in 1926. The painting style he evolved in these years, while not denying the importance of subjectivity, is more precise and clearer in form than the work of his *Blaue Reiter* years, as can be seen in *Shrill Peaceful Pink* of 1924 where geometric forms and a subtle interplay of rich colors is in striking contrast to his earlier work. The geometric form of such a painting was influenced by the work of the Dutch artist Piet Mondrian, although the austerity of Mondrian's work as well as its pure, primary color gives it an impersonality alien to Kandinsky's work of any period.

Mondrian's work is essentially Dutch, the flat planes and rectlinear forms reflecting the polders of his native country. He came to Paris for the first time in 1912 and his work, which mostly consisted of landscapes until that time, quickly absorbed the lessons of Analytical Cubism. After the war he moved back to Paris, living and working in isolation throughout the 1920s. Like Kandinsky, Mondrian's work reflects the influence of theosophy and music. In 1927 he wrote *Jazz and Neo-Plasticism*, exploring the relationship between music and his own art, which he saw as a lifetime's search for the abstract visual expression of a universal truth. Mondrian's Neo-plasticism is anti-expressionistic in its search for objectivity as can be seen in *Composition in Red, Yellow and Blue* of 1920. Like many of Mondrian's paintings, this was intended to be hung without a frame, flat against the wall, rather than tilted away from it in the traditional way, with the intention that the picture's space was also to be seen as extending to the space of the wall itself. Mondrian's elegant, austere abstractions and their use of pure, primary colors continue to have far-reaching influence on twentieth-century design in its widest sense, especially in architecture and advertising.

In Holland in 1917 Mondrian had collaborated with Theo van Doesburg in the foundation of the periodical *De Stijl* ('Style'). The name is also applied to the group of artists and architects associated with the journal and its ideas, although its most influential member, Mondrian broke with the group after 1924 and always preferred the term 'Neo-Plasticism' to describe his abstractions.

Van Doesburg's work is obviously influenced by Mondrian's, but the decisive difference (which led to Mondrian's resignation) is van Doesburg's use of diagonal grids, which cannot by their very nature extend to the space beyond the canvas but come into dynamic conflict with the picture's format, as can be seen in *Countercomposition V* of 1924. Van Doesburg was the driving force of *De Stijl*, taking its message of 'the new plastic art' and of 'collective effort' rather than 'individualism in quest of honors' to the newly established Bauhaus in Germany in 1921 where his influence had considerable impact, and his influence is perhaps best seen in architecture and the decorative arts, particularly on the work of his fellow *De Stijl* member, the architect and designer Gerrit Rietveld, famous for his 1917 red, blue, yellow and black-painted wooden chair which bears close comparison with both van Doesburg's and Mondrian's painting, as does Rietveld's best-known public building, the Van Gogh Museum, Amsterdam.

'The synthesis of all the plastic arts' was the ideal of *De Stijl* and also of the German school, and 'ideas laboratory,' the Bauhaus, founded by the architect Walter Gropius in 1919, for the ten years of its existence. Only the Bauhaus painters find a place in this book, although through the emigration of its members after 1933 when the school was dissolved by the Nazis, its ideas became influential throughout Europe and the United States.

Lyonel Feininger was American-born, although he lived in Germany from the age of sixteen, staying there throughout World War I and remaining active at the Bauhaus until the end, returning to America only in 1937, almost fifty years after he had left it. Feininger had worked as a caricaturist and came late to painting. His work was influenced by a stay in Paris where he met Robert Delaunay whose work, together with that of the Cubists, influenced his, although he evolved a personal style of transparent planes and glowing rectlinear forms which is seen at its most characteristic in his architectural and sea and river subjects. He was one of the first artists to be invited to teach at the Bauhaus, and taught painting there for some twenty years. Feininger's woodcuts illustrated Gropius's 1919 publication outlining the Bauhaus program, which stated that the 'structure of the future' would unite architecture, sculpture and painting and 'ascend to heaven conjoined as a crystalline allegory of a coming faith.' The crystalline structures of such a painting as Feininger's *The Red Tower in Halle II* (1930) seem almost to illustrate Gropius's vision of the future although the vision was to end when the Nazis came to power.

Oskar Schlemmer was the most versatile German artist of his period, working not only as a painter, sculptor and printmaker but also as set designer, ballet composer, muralist and inventor of a wide range of teaching programs at the Bauhaus. Schlemmer's first retrospective exhibition, due to be held in Stuttgart in 1933, was banned by the Nazis and many of his works were confiscated and exhibited at the notorious 'Degenerate Art' exhibition in Munich in 1937. This put an end to his freedom to work in Germany and in his later years he was also denied his freedom to teach, forced instead to paint camouflage installations.

Fallen Figure with Column (1928) demonstrates Schlemmer's wish to create a 'mystical objectivity.' The cool colors and the classical clarity of the composition reduced to a Doric column and a fallen nude figure are mysterious and almost dance-like in their disposition in the picture space. Schlemmer's versatile career of the 1920s included work as a theatrical set designer, and of particular relevance to this painting is the fact that in the early 1920s he also created the *Triadic Ballet* with music by Paul Hindemith, where the dancers' heads and limbs were encased in abstract forms to emphasize their movement in space.

The pioneering Hungarian artist, designer and educator, Laszlo Moholy-Nagy was working at the Bauhaus by 1923, editing with Gropius the 14 Bauhaus books and masterminding many of the industrial design activities at the Bauhaus, particularly the influential range of light-fittings which are among the best-known Bauhaus works. Moholy was fascinated by the properties of light and sought to overcome the traditional limitations of painting in order to create a universal vocabulary which would elevate the perceptions. 'Constructive art is processual, forever open in all directions. It is a builder of man's ability to perceive, to react emotionally and to reason logically,' he wrote.

A II of 1924 is one of a series in which Moholy attempted to transform the two-dimensional picture surface by means of intersecting planes, some transparent, some opaque into what he termed 'vision in motion.' His pioneering work in photography and film, which continued after he settled in the USA in 1937, can also be seen as an influence on his painting, as can his practice of painting on transparent plastic, which began in 1923. In explanation of his painting on canvas at this time, such as the *A II* series, he wrote: 'The fixed viewpoint, the isolated handling of problems as a norm is rejected and replaced by a flexible approach, by seeing matters in a constantly changing, moving field of mutual relationships.'

Josef Albers, onetime Bauhaus student and from 1923 to 1933 teacher there with Moholy, Kandinsky and Klee, settled in the United States in 1933 when the Bauhaus was closed. He was to have a decisive effect on the later history of American painting through his paintings, his teaching, and his treatise on color theory, published in 1963, *Interaction of Color*. His *Homage to the Square* series was begun in 1949, and developed at Yale, where he taught as Chairman of the Department of Design, until his death in 1976. Albers' lifetime study was the psychological impact of color, as he phrased it: 'The origin of art was the discrepancy between physical fact and psychic effect.' He evolved changing color combinations to explore this consistent format of squares, applying the pigment directly from the tube. Writing of the series in 1964, Albers analyzed his aims in the following manner: 'Choice of the colors used, as well as their order is aimed at an interaction – influencing and changing each other forth and back.' Of all the many remarkable artists assembled at the Bauhaus in this rich period, none was perhaps more remarkable than the Swiss Paul Klee. Indeed his ten years there from 1920 when Gropius invited him to join the Bauhaus marks a period when the Bauhaus was perhaps as much a center of experiment for painting as industrial design. Klee, although born in Berne, considered himself a German artist and fought in World War I. Before the war he had been associated with both Marc and Kandinsky, participating in the second Blaue Reiter exhibition and sharing his fellow artists' passion for folk painting, the art of primitive peoples and the drawings of children. As early as 1902 he was writing in the following manner: 'I want to be as though newborn, knowing absolutely nothing about Europe, ignoring facts and fashions, to be almost primitive.' The experience of both wars had a profound effect on his work. During World War I the two friends closest to him in their artistic vision, Marc and Macke, were both killed, as he wrote in 1915: 'The more horrifying this world becomes (as it is these days) the more art becomes abstract; while a world at peace produces realistic art.'

In 1914 he had taken a journey with Macke to Tunis, and the experience of 'the concentrated essence of the Arabian Nights' as Klee described it, caused him to define the importance of his experience in these terms: 'Color has taken hold of me: no longer do I have to chase after it. . . that is the significance of this blessed moment.' Such a work as *Ad Parnassum* ('To Parnassus') of 1932 (the culmination of a series of color constructions begun in 1923) shows Klee's delicate use of a mosaic of color forms.

Klee was immensely diverse in his technical application, using a wide variety of media throughout his life. Here, in his wish to 'reveal the reality that is behind things,' he refers to Mount Parnassus, where Apollo and the Muses lived. The golden disk of the sun also makes reference to Apollo and possibly to the Pyramids of Egypt which Klee visited in 1928. Klee believed that 'Pictorial art springs from movement, is itself fixed movement and is perceived through movement.' He believed 'Art to be a simile of Creation,' and that a painting 'should grow like a living organism.'

Klee's writings on art, which include the series of lectures he gave at the Bauhaus, is arguably one of the most influential bodies of theory conceived by a twentieth-century artist, yet he was denounced by the Nazis as a Cultural Bolshevist in 1933 and dismissed from his post as Professor at Düsseldorf Academy, returning to his native city of Berne where he had spent his childhood. The spirit of the times, as well as Klee's own struggle against the heart disease that was to prove fatal in 1940, can be seen in the isolated and imprisoned figures of the works

of his last months, such as *Captive* (1940), with its lattices of bars and single melancholy figure. It is an image apparently simple but of concentrated and complex power.

The horror experienced by Max Beckmann as a medical orderly in World War I profoundly influenced his art, which includes series of prints as well as canvases. His work was also included in the 'Degenerate Art' exhibition in Munich in 1937 and he left Germany for Amsterdam that year, and ten years later came to work for the last three years of his life in the United States, first in Washington and then at the Art School of the Brooklyn Museum of New York. Beckmann's work, which is often large-scale, has always been controversial. He has resisted definition as belonging to any group, although his work shows such diverse influences as the philosophy of Nietzsche and contemporary works by Picasso.

In the late 1920s Beckmann adopted the practice of spending some eight months of the year in Paris. Such a large-scale work as *Aerial Acrobatics* of 1928, reveals that he alone of his German contemporaries attempted to fuse the dynamism and psychological intensity particularly characteristic of German art of the time with the massive decorative forms being employed in Paris by Picasso and Léger in the 1920s. However *Aerial Acrobatics* is emphatically Beckmann in its distorted perspective and, despite its subject and size, curiously claustrophobic. In this painting, as in his major works of the 1920s, Beckmann explored the symbolism of carnival, cabaret and circus as an image of the artificiality of life's existence. The treatment of the picture space is always crucial. As he explained in *On My Painting* (1938), space is 'the infinite deity which surrounds us and in which we ourselves are contained.' Here the figures are suspended between sky and earth, the male figure in acrobat's costume encircled by the coils of his curious musical instrument, a 'serpent' as he hangs from the basket of the balloon. The faces are mask-like in their impassivity.

Otto Dix was one of the leading painters of the German style of the twenties known as *Die Neue Sachlichkeit* ('New Objectivity' or 'New Matter-of-Factness'). Dix evolved an extraordinarily exacting 'Old Master' technique. *Portrait of the Dancer Anita Berber* is executed in oil and tempera (an egg-based medium in use before the Renaissance) on panel. This gives his work an almost super-photographic effect, seen here in the minute handling of the woman's mask-like face and her meticulously painted hands. As he explained: 'Photography can never record more than a moment – and then from the outside. It can never create forms which are specific and personal, for this capacity depends on the artistic powers and intuition of the painter.' *Portrait of the Dancer Anita Berber* places its subject frontally, almost emblematically, recalling the work of such German fifteenth-century portrait painters as Lucas Cranach. The tension between Anita Berber's impassive face, with its mask-like stage make-up and her expressive dancer's body in the scarlet dress, symbolic of the vamp, makes this one of Dix's most dramatic paintings. Dix's sharp, often savage realism, has sometimes been termed 'magic realism,' to distinguish it from other 'New Objectivity' artists, who, like George Grosz, were more overtly political in their work.

Indeed Grosz made his reputation with his political caricatures for satirical journals before and during World War I, and is perhaps still best known for his work in this medium, which he continued to produce throughout his life, the last 26 years of which were spent in New York. Grosz was passionately anti-militaristic and anti-capitalist, views summed up in *The Pillars of Society* (1926). Here Grosz caricatures the Press, the Military, Politicians and the Church with a savagery reminiscent of both his own graphic work and the eighteenth-century English satirical tradition which began with Hogarth. The bloodstained sword brandished by the officer at the top of the picture is prescient, as is the burning house. The churchman, eyes closed, teeth bared, extends his hands in blessing to all, including the approaching conflagration.

Paris continued to act as a mecca to artists between the wars. The work produced in the city was hugely varied. The term 'School of Paris' is often used to describe the painting produced in the city in the first forty or so years of the century, roughly until the outbreak of World War II. Although the term has the most general application, as the artists can only be linked by virtue of the fact that they were working in the same city at the same time, it does serve to indicate the intense concentration of artistic activity in the city during this period of dealers and critics are well as artists.

Such an artist as Pierre Bonnard, two years older than Matisse and 51 at the end of World War I, developed and intensified his style in the period between the wars. Bonnard, along with his friend and fellow-painter Edouard Vuillard had developed a style known as 'Intimisme' by the turn of the century. The painters celebrated the intimacies of everyday middle-class life, shared meals and comfortable domestic interiors are affectionately observed. Bonnard, who had been one of the founder members of the Salon d'Automne along with Matisse, also designed stage decor and posters and undertook a radical revision of his painting in 1915. 'I returned to school,' he later explains, 'I turned against all that had previously excited me, the color which had attracted me. I had almost unconsciously sacrificed form to it but it is absolutely true that forms exist and that it is not possible either to arbitrarily reduce or transpose them. . . a picture which is satisfactorily composed is half made.' The asymmetrical composition of *Interior at Antibes* (1920) is characteristic of this later style: we do not immediately notice the figure of the girl as she stands against the warm Mediterranean light in the deeply shadowed room, and the cat, whose bowl of milk she holds, all but disappears in the shadow. Bonnard explained his aim in such a painting as wishing to show 'all that one sees upon entering a room hurriedly. . .what the eye takes in at the first glance.' The palette used here of rich, warm pinks, reds and blues is also typical of Bonnard's work at this period, drawing its tones in this case from the vase of anemones on the table.

Raoul Dufy developed his personal style under the influence of a painting by Matisse, that he saw first in 1905: 'When I saw this painting,' he later wrote, 'I understood at once the new *raison d'être* of painting.' Soon after this, his characteristically decorative style assured him his economic independence as a designer of fabrics for the famous Paris fashion designer, Paul Poiret. He also produced fabric designs for the silk manufacturer Bianchini-Ferrier, designed ceramics and, for the Paris International Exhibition of 1937, executed a huge and complex mural, *The Story of Electricity,* still to be seen in what is now the National Museum of Modern Art (the Palais de Tokyo) in Paris.

Dufy's art is characterized by its wit and bright color, his subjects often drawn from the glittering world of the promenades and casinos of the French Riviera, racing at Longchamps and yachting at Deauville. It seems probable that the calligraphic style he evolved for his applied art techniques, particularly the fabric designs and woodcut illustrations, helped form his mature painting style, here seen in *The Artist's Studio* (1935), an exploration of his own studio and paintings and the view to the world outside. Dufy's adaptation of his earlier use of Fauve color is seen here in the brilliant blocks of bright color (the blues are a particular Dufy characteristic) that overlay his linear structures, apart, that is, from the canvas still on the easel depicting a reclining nude, perhaps a witty reference to the artist's Muse. Dufy's later life was clouded by arthritis, for which he sought a cure in America.

Picasso continued to paint in a multiplicity of styles during this period. The two giant canvases *Three Musicians* (1921) may be seen as statements of a summing up of his work until that date. They are complex works, and the fact that he produced two such large-scale statements in the same year has its significance. The Philadelphia version reproduced here derives, as does the Museum of Modern Art canvas, from Picasso's years with Diaghilev's Russian Ballet. In 1919 Diaghilev invited Picasso to collaborate with the composer Stravinsky and the dancer/choreographer Léonid Massine in a ballet drawn from the traditional Italian street theater, the Commedia dell'Arte, to be called *Pulcinella*. Picasso had used the stock figures of Harlequin and Pierrot in his earlier work, but in a radically different form to suggest sadness and isolation, especially in the 'Blue Period' paintings. Here the figures are frontal in stance, and their masks give them an air which is at one and the same time genial and sinister, an effect heightened by the Cubist treatment of such elements as the musical instruments and the life-size scale of the figures.

The Italian artist Amedeo Modigliani came to Paris first in 1906 and worked as a sculptor, influenced by African tribal carvings and, especially, by the work of the Romanian sculptor Constantin Brancusi. As a child Modigliani contracted tuberculosis. His condition steadily worsened in the years of his poverty in Paris, where he lived and worked with such other expatriate Jewish artists as Chaim Soutine until both were helped by the dealer and collector Paul Guillaume. The stone dust produced by Modigliani's carving appears to have aggravated his condition and seems to have been the reason for his giving up sculpture in 1915 to concentrate on painting for the last five years of his life. *Woman with a Velvet Ribbon* is typical of his later style in its elegance and sharply linear quality, Modigliani's line in such works being reminiscent of Italian Renaissance masters such as Botticelli or of the earlier painters of Siena such as Duccio. The flatness of the composition, as well as the sinuous elegance of the forms used to describe the woman's body and her almond-shaped eyes, are all typical of Modigliani's fully evolved painting style.

Modigliani's figure subject is static and makes reference to tribal art and to the art of Italy's rich cultural past. Marcel Duchamp's mold-breaking *Nude Descending a Staircase No 2* of 1912 caused a sensation at the Armory Show in New York in 1913 by reason of its startlingly unconventional modernity. In this painting, Duchamp admitted his indebtedness to the photographic process known as chronophotography in which actions were recorded in motion, the dots on the subject's hands recall the points of light which highlighted the figure's movements in chronophotography. Duchamp appears to combine both Cubist and Futurist concepts in this complex representation of the nude, the most traditional of subjects, here shown as moving through both space and time on a two-dimensional surface. The year after this painting, Duchamp virtually gave up oil painting on canvas altogether in favor of 'machines,' ready-mades and experiments in three dimensions which were to have enormous influence on the history of twentieth-century art.

The idea of modernity so powerfully conveyed by *Nude Descending a Staircase* finds expression in an entirely different form in the work of Fernand Léger, who, although he trained originally as an architect, emerged in the years before World War I, together with Duchamp and Delaunay, as one of the most original and significant of the younger artists in the Cubist circle. Léger believed in what the great nineteenth-century French poet and critic Charles Baudelaire had described as 'the heroism of modern life,' particularly what he saw as the heroism of modern life in the city.

In his series of 'city' paintings produced when he was invalided out of the War in the years after 1917, Léger celebrated the modern city, particularly the modern metropolis in a personal reworking of both Futurist and Cubist elements into a form that is entirely his own. *La Ville* of 1919 shows the influence of synthetic cubism and indeed of Delaunay, applied to a new, and for the time extraordinary purpose, that of the celebration of the vitality of urban life in an age of machines. The bright colors and flat, formalized shapes of buildings, street signs, posters, street illuminations and the girders of building sites are presented here as a positive setting for the human figures whose creation they are.

In succeeding paintings, Léger abandoned his practice of fragmentation as an expression of the speed and vigor of urban life, concentrating rather on the human figure as a whole, calm and dignified in the achievment brought by their work in the City, worker-heroes and heroines, depicted often on a large scale, reminiscent of Egyptian and Assyrian art. *The Mechanic* (1920) exemplifies 'the heroism of modern life' in the form of a muscular mechanic, contemporary in his singlet, tattoo and handlebar moustache, who calmly surveys his work – the city in the background as he smokes his cigarette (echoed by the factory chimney) – at ease in this world of his own creation. The balance of the composition and the combination of frontal torso and profile head recalls both Egyptian art and the work of such French Neo-classical artists as Jacques-Louis David. In the year of *The Mechanic* Léger met the architect Le Corbusier. His first murals were designed five years later for the architect's influential pavilion at the International Exhibition of Decorative Arts, and Léger designed for theater, ballet and movies, taught at Yale and designed murals, tapestries, mosaics and stained glass for many buildings in Europe and America.

Marc Chagall first came to Paris in 1910 from the small Russian town of Vitebsk, 'with mud on my boots,' as he was to write later. Chagall's imagery is intensely personal, although he borrows stylistically from whatever suits his purpose, whether Cubism, in its various manifestations, or the stage designs of his fellow countryman Leon Bakst, under whom he studied in St Petersburg. Chagall was welcomed into the avant-garde circle of such artists as Léger and Delaunay on his arrival in Paris, and exhibited in Berlin before being made Commissar of Fine Art for Vitebsk in 1917. He returned to Paris in 1923, and maintained close links with the city throughout his long and productive life, which took his work as far afield as the United States, where he designed for the ballet and produced two murals for the Metropolitan Opera House, New York; and, in his seventies, the stained glass windows for the Synagogue at the Hadassah Medical Center, Jerusalem (1960).

The two paintings reproduced here belong to Chagall's earlier Parisian work, when he might truly be considered one of the most significant figures of the School of Paris. *Double Portrait with Wine Glass* of 1917 celebrates the anniversary of his marriage two years before. Chagall raises his glass in joyous celebration as he is carried on the shoulders of his wife, Bella above the town of Vitebsk. Bella, dressed in her wedding gown, appears to float in a golden glow, and the union seems to be blessed by the angel that surmounts the whole monumental canvas. Such blending of personal imagery and lyrical fantasy is unique to Chagall, although the belief, stated in *My Life* that 'Painting, like all poetry, participates in the Divine,' remained a constant feature of his work throughout his life.

Chagall's native country was seldom absent from his work, and in the monumental canvas *Green Violinist* completed in 1924, he returned to his early theme of the violinist as representative of all the arts in the remote Russian villages of his youth, who offers the people a means of transcending the harshness of their everyday lives through what Chagall conceived as the healing powers of music and the imagination. The snow-covered village square is symbolically dwarfed by the violinist and the device of the ladder, recalling Jacob's ladder that stretched from heaven to earth, is reinforced by the aspiring figure reaching towards the flying form at the very top of the canvas. When he died at the age of 97 in 1985 after a richly productive career, Chagall was the last survivor of the revolutionary years of early twentieth-century painting.

Of all the influential critics and theorists who helped make Paris such a power-house of aesthetic activity in the earlier part of the present century, the most important is undoubtedly Guillaume Apollinaire whose ideas helped shape many of the artistic movements originating from the capital. Chagall had completed his *Homage to Apollinaire* (Stedelijk Museum, Amsterdam) in 1912, and in 1914 the Italian painter Giorgio de Chirico painted *Premonitory Portrait of Guillaume Apollinaire*. De Chirico, who was born and studied in Athens originated 'Metaphysical Painting,' which he defined as 'standing completely outside human limitations: logic and common sense are detrimental to it. . .thus it approximates dream and infantile mentality.' De Chirico strove for 'metaphysical insights' into the reality of ordinary objects by deliberately juxtaposing them in incongruous and illogical relationships: here the curious cake-maker's molds are juxtaposed with the classical bust with sunglasses covering its eyes. The distinctive profile of the apparent subject of the painting is reduced to a silhouette in the background. The painting, which causes considerable unease in the spectator, is rendered more disturbing by the knowledge that de Chirico's target-like circle on Apollinaire's skull marks the spot where, two years later, Apollinaire was to be struck by the bullet that eventually killed him.

De Chirico's Metaphysical Painting had a brief influence on the work of the Bolognese artist Giorgio Morandi at the end of World War I. However, from the beginning of the 1920s Morandi (who lived all his life in his native city, and worked from 1930 to 1956 as Professor of Engraving at the Academy), in a consistent stylistic exploration painted still life almost exclusively. Morandi's exploration of inanimate objects, their existence in space and their relationship one to another is a subtle one, pure and restricted in its use of color, and seeking a clarity of form found in the early painters of the Renaissance, the contrasting shapes of long-necked flask and squat bowls here are characteristically blurred in outline, heavy in form and horizontal in composition.

André Breton, the French poet, critic, theorist and founder in 1924 of the first *Surrealist Manifesto*, defined the movement's purpose: 'to resolve the previously contradictory conditions of dream and reality into an absolute reality, a super-reality.' Within this general aim were a large number of conflicting ideas and a loosely grouped body of artists, writers and thinkers. The theories of Freud on the Unconscious were used extensively by the artists to support Breton's categorizing of Surrealism. In a definition that does much to explain the outrage felt by the Surrealists' contemporaries towards their works, as well as the continuing influence of the movement, Breton described Surrealism as 'purely psychic automatism through which we undertake to express. . . the actual functioning of thought, thoughts dictated apart from any control by reason and any aesthetic or moral consideration.'

This 'purely psychic automatism' may be seen in one of its forms in the work of the German-born painter Max Ernst. Ernst moved to Paris in 1921 after being at the forefront of such avant-garde movements as Dada, an extreme movement arising from profound disillusionment in the period after World War I, which placed emphasis on the irrational or absurd and declared itself against art in the conventional sense. Ernst had studied philosophy at the University of Cologne, and often twisted elements drawn from his culture's rich philosophic and artistic past, particularly from the medieval and nineteenth-century periods, into new and disturbing forms. In *Saint Cecilia, The Invisible Piano* (1923) Ernst depicted the blind Saint Cecilia, the patron saint of Music, walled up in a plaster mold used in the process of casting bronze monuments. The fragmented mold is covered with sightless 'eyes' and the saint reaches out towards the keys and pedal of an invisible piano. An organ and broken musical instruments are the means of recognizing the Saint in medieval and later representations. The mold imprisoning Saint Cecilia is linked with metal rods and may be about to break if the Saint can but release the energy of the music that appears to be within her.

Ernst is important not only for the complexity of the ideas he brought to Surrealism but for the variety of techniques he invented, thus extending both the conceptual and material boundaries of art. Together with the use of collage, which has a prominent place in his work, was the drawing technique which he later applied to painting and termed 'frottage.' Ernst explained his first use of it (in 1925) in the following way: 'To assist my contemplative and hallucinatory faculties, I took a series of drawings from the floorboards by covering them at random with sheets of paper which I rubbed with a soft pencil. . . I was surprised by the sudden intensification of my visionary powers and by the hallucinatory succession of contradictory images, superimposed, one upon the other.' The richness of the surface of such a key painting as *Europe after the Rain*, begun while Ernst was in hiding during the War, is similarly obtained in places by placing the canvas over a textured surface while the pigment is applied. Ernst also employs the technique of working up the chance effects of compressing half-dry paint. This 'automatic' technique sought to release the artist's imaginative faculty by removing the 'conscious' use of the brush. Such a complex work as *Europe After the Rain*, one of a series in which Ernst explored the condition of Europe in the war years (he was three times interned in France before escaping to the United States in 1941), demands a great deal of the spectator. Ernst was particularly interested in the chains of associations set up in the viewer's mind as the hallucinatory image of decay and rebirth is explored, and this major work is full of the irrational fears so often evoked by Ernst.

Yves Tanguy explored a different species of image drawn from the unconscious. A merchant seaman by family tradition, and uncertain of his future, he began to paint after seeing a painting by de Chirico and joined the Surrealists in 1925 soon after meeting André Breton. Tanguy explores Breton's notion of 'the future resolution of the states of dream and reality' by working on his canvas intuitively, without preparatory drawings, albeit with meticulous technique. He explained the importance of this practice in the following, typically direct fashion: 'I found that if I planned a picture beforehand, it never surprised me and surprises are my pleasure in painting.' Along with Magritte and Dali, Tanguy's Surrealism places his fantasy forms in an illusionistic, deep landscape setting, using precise techniques, apparently drawn from the masters of Renaissance painting. However, the forms in Tanguy's vast and lonely landscapes are intensely personal, as can be seen in *Indefinite Divisibility* (1942), where a vast, indescribable construction casts its giant shadow over a limitless space, that is lit in an eerie and inexplicable fashion from an undisclosed source.

Carnival of Harlequin is one of the Spanish painter and ceramicist Joan Miro's most inventive and light-hearted works. Miro lived part of the year in Paris from about 1920, where he moved in avant-garde circles until the invasion of France in 1940. Miro invented a Surrealist language of graphic forms in a restricted palette of symbolic colors. He particularly associated the clear blue used in this painting with the world of dreams. Here, for example, the familiar Commedia dell'Arte figure of Harlequin, employed consistently by Miro's fellow-Spaniard, Picasso, who Miro met in Paris in 1919, is seen as the woebegone moustachioed form to the left. Harlequin's sad masked face contrasts with all the carnival activity around him. In his work of the 1920s such as this, Miro's witty imagery enlarged Surrealism's vocabulary, leading André Breton in his history of the movement, *Surrealism and Painting*, to call him 'the most Surrealist of us all.'

However, the most notorious of Surrealism's adherents was another Spaniard, Salvador Dali who met both Miro and Picasso when he settled in Paris in 1929. Dali was the most public of artists for much of his long life and what he has described as 'the massive architecture of his egoism' has obscured much of his achievement. However, such a painting as *Mountain Lake* of 1938 demonstrates the style Dali developed from around 1929, which he termed 'critical paranoia' and put up in opposition to Breton's form of Surrealism. Dali's impeccable technique is seen here at the service of what has sometimes been termed 'magic realism' in order to convey the dream-like quality of the everyday telephone in extraordinary, indeed hallucinatory circumstances. It is huge in scale in a strange and ominous landscape. Dali exploits the viewer's expectations, the cord of the telephone is not connected, the lake is fish-shaped, and the snails are a disquieting presence, particularly when it is remembered that the Munich Conference, that sealed the fate of Europe, was arranged by telephone.

As Dali explained in one of his typically oblique pronouncements on his work in 1935: 'My whole ambition in the pictorial field is to materialize the images of concrete irrationality with the most imperialist fury of precision in order that the world of imagination and concrete irrationality may be as objectively evident, of the same consistency, of the same durability, of the same persuasive, cognoscitive and communicable thickness as that of the exterior world of phenomenal reality.'

Dali's efforts to 'materialize the images of concrete irrationality' are seen at their most powerful in the gruesome foreshadowing of the Spanish Civil War, *Soft Construction with Boiled Beans: Premonition of Civil War* of 1936. This diseased humanoid figure, cannibalistically destroying itself in what Dali himself termed 'a delirium of autostrangulation,' is the stuff of nightmare, rendered more terrible by our knowledge of the reality of the times. In such a powerful visual metaphor as this, it is possible to realize the validity of Dali's belief that he could 'systematize confusion and thus help to discredit the world of reality completely.'

The work of two Belgian Surrealist artists of this period, René Magritte and Paul Delvaux, is in the strictest possible contrast to that of Dali. It is proof, if proof were needed, of the continuing creativity and variety of Surrealism, the essence of which lay in what Breton termed 'interior perceptions.'

Magritte joined the Surrealists in 1925 but did not follow Breton's concept of 'purely psychic automatism,' choosing to concentrate on objects in the external world in relationships which are all the more disturbing by reason of their strangeness, and the matter-of-fact fashion in which they are painted. *The Reckless Sleeper* appears anything but reckless in his/her outward form, self-contained in bed, or perhaps it is a coffin. The figure's head is egg-like and vulnerable, and beneath is a brain-like form that may have reference to the sleep/death analogy of the painting as it also resembles a tombstone. Embedded within this form are various symbols common in both the analysis of dreams and art, the mirror, for example is used as a symbol of the transience of human life, and the bird is often a symbol of the human soul. However, too literal a reading of the symbols is to be avoided – the bowler hat for example is a common motif in Magritte's work, but its significance here is impossible to explain, especially as Magritte himself warned in the last number of *The Surrealist Revolution* of 1929, 'an object never fulfills the same function as its name or its image.'

Paul Delvaux was influenced by the work of both Magritte and Dali and by the classical architecture of Italy he saw on two visits in 1940. *Venus Asleep* was painted in 1944 during the bombing of Brussels. As Delvaux was later to write: 'The psychology of the moment was very exceptional, full of drama and anguish. . . I wanted to express this anguish in the picture, contrasted with the calm of Venus.' The disparate elements in the painting, the calm figure of the Goddess of Love watched over by the skeleton and black dressmaker's dummy restates and gives a new twist to the European legend of Death and the Maiden in the setting of a moonlit classical town of uncertain origin. Magritte said that 'perhaps unconsciously I have put into the subject of my picture a certain mysterious and intangible disquiet. . . I have tried in this picture for contrast and mystery.'

In England, source of much of the literature and ideas that had nourished Surrealism, Breton's manifesto found fertile ground in the work of Paul Nash, landscape painter and official war artist in World War I. His dream landscapes are both typically Surrealist in the manner in which they juxtapose incongruous objects and typically English in their lyrical treatment of the native landscape. *Landscape from a Dream* is set on the cliffs of Dorset where a stuffed hawk is reflected in a mirror set in the frame of a billboard-like structure. The symbolic sphere of the ball of grass and the 'real' and 'reflected' landscapes do not entirely correspond in various subtle ways, and the effect is one of disquiet, although Nash is characteristically reticent in his use of dream imagery and such a painting may be considered as a twentieth-century variant on the English landscape tradition.

In concluding this study of painting in the period to the end of World War II, it is fitting to look at the work of two of the 'Old Masters' of Modern Art, Picasso and Matisse. Picasso continued to work in a variety of styles and diverse media throughout the period. At the outbreak of war he was 58, with almost another thirty years of work ahead of him. For the Paris Exhibition of 1937 he was commissioned by the Spanish Republic to paint a large composition for the Spanish Pavilion, the subject to be of the artist's own choosing. The bombing of the Basque town of Guernica in April 1937 and the slaughter of some 2000 civilians decided Picasso's subject, often considered his major achievement. *Guernica* is a huge, near-monochrome canvas. The essentially private world of much of Picasso's work until this time is here turned into the powerful realization of a public nightmare. Picasso's nationality is nowhere more apparent than in this work which recalls paintings and etchings of the horrors of an earlier period by Goya. The woman with the dead child in her arms, the dying horse, impassive bull and the dead soldier are powerful images, so powerful indeed that the painting has always found a ready public response, despite its complexity.

In March 1948 the influential critic Clement Greenberg wrote that 'Matisse, with his magnificent but transitional style. . . is able to rest securely in his position as the greatest master of the twentieth century, a position Picasso is further than ever from threatening.' This was a startling concept at that time. Forty years into the future it seems prophetic, as the influence of Matisse's work in the period since his death in 1954 has been widespread in both Europe and America, particularly with regard to color.

From 1918 Matisse had made Nice his permanent home, painting murals and canvases, carving and designing stained glass and, after his illness in 1941, working in a new medium, gouache on cut-out pasted paper to produce influential works of monumental size and celebratory character, 'a flowering after fifty years of effort,' as Matisse himself described it. The extent of this flowering can be seen in such a late painting as *Interior with Egyptian Curtain* (1948), an exploration of exterior and interior worlds with the brilliant and joyful use of color that the artist had evolved over a period of fifty years. As Matisse explains with his characteristic lucidity: 'Seeing is of itself a creative operation, one that demands effort . . . the artist must see all things as if he was seeing them for the first time. All his life he must see as he did as a child.'

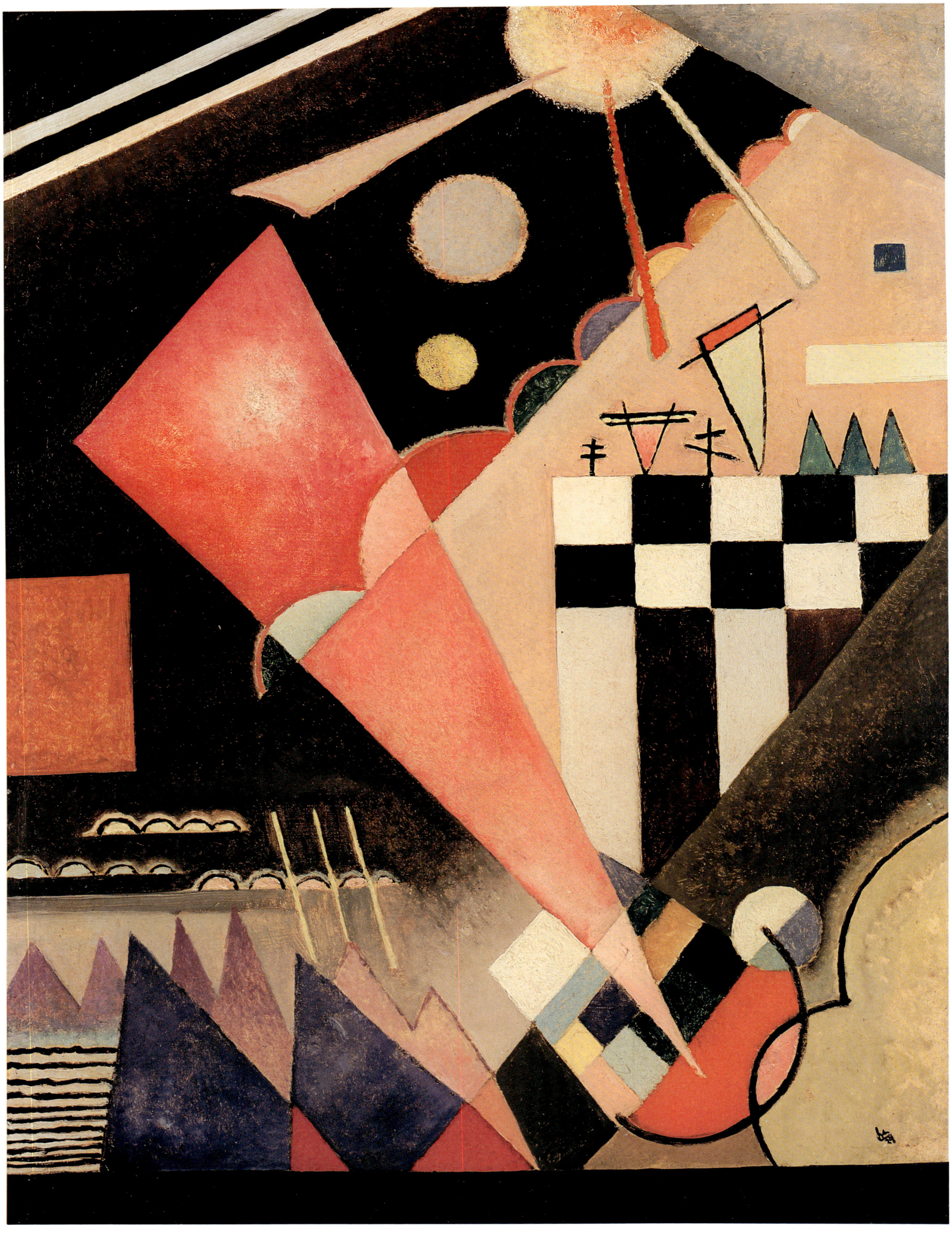

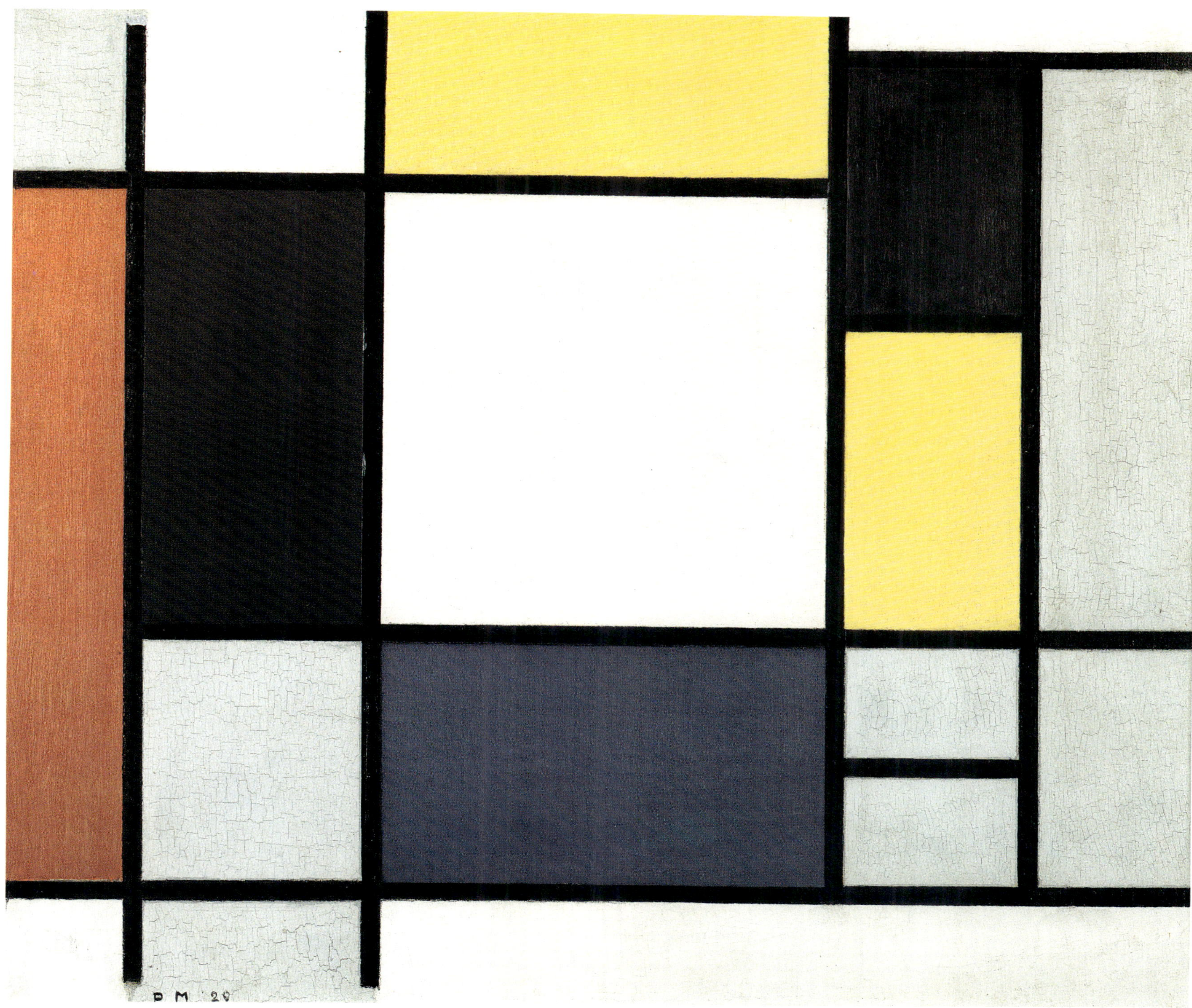

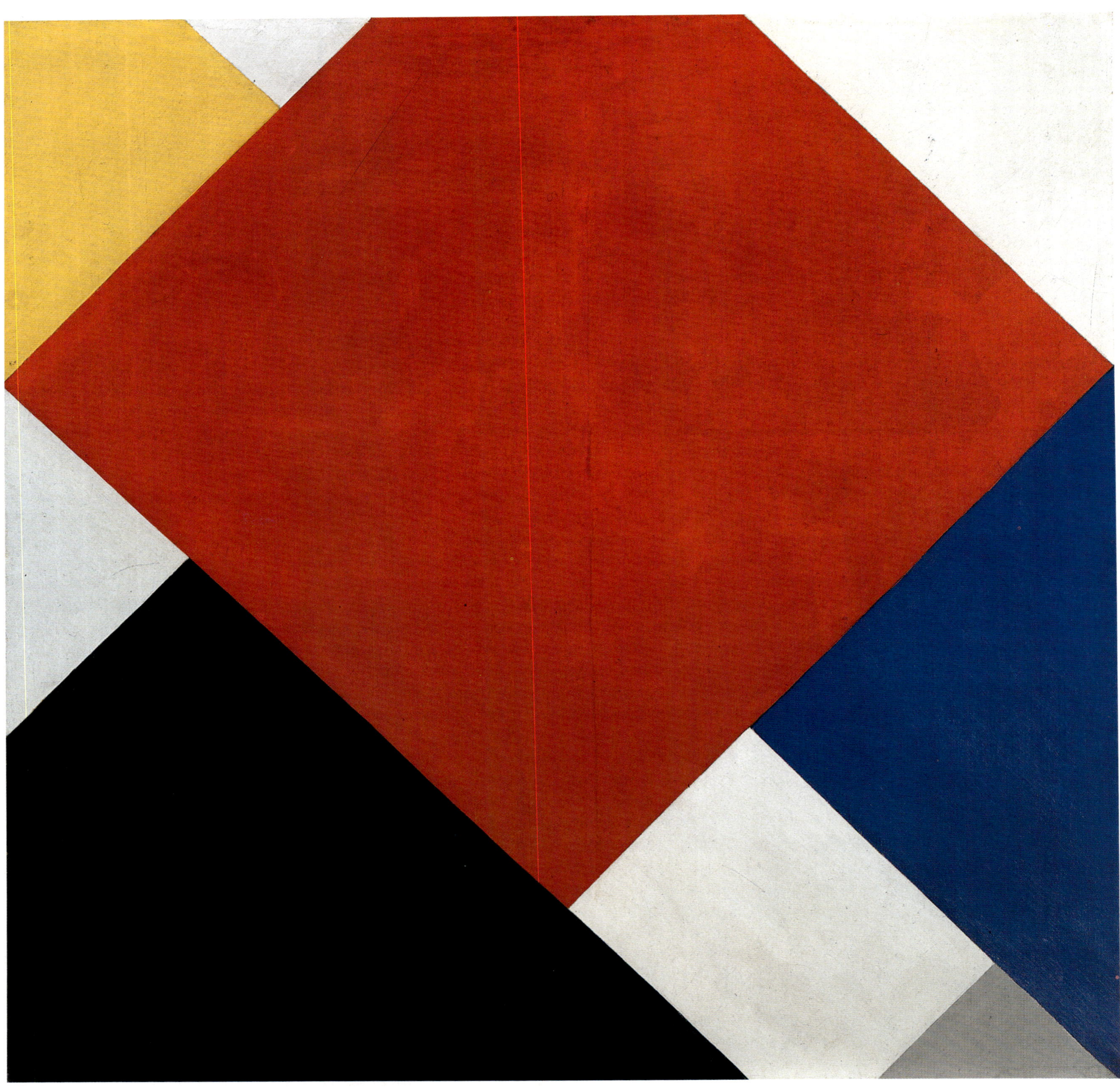

ABOVE:
Theo Van Doesburg
Countercomposition V 1924
Oil on canvas, 39⅜×39⅜in (100×100cm)
Stedelijk Museum, Amsterdam

RIGHT:
Oskar Schlemmer
Fallen Figure with Column 1928
Oil on canvas, 94×61in (239×155cm)
Staatsgalerie Stuttgart
© *1989 Oskar Schlemmer Family Estate,*
Baden Weiler, West Germany

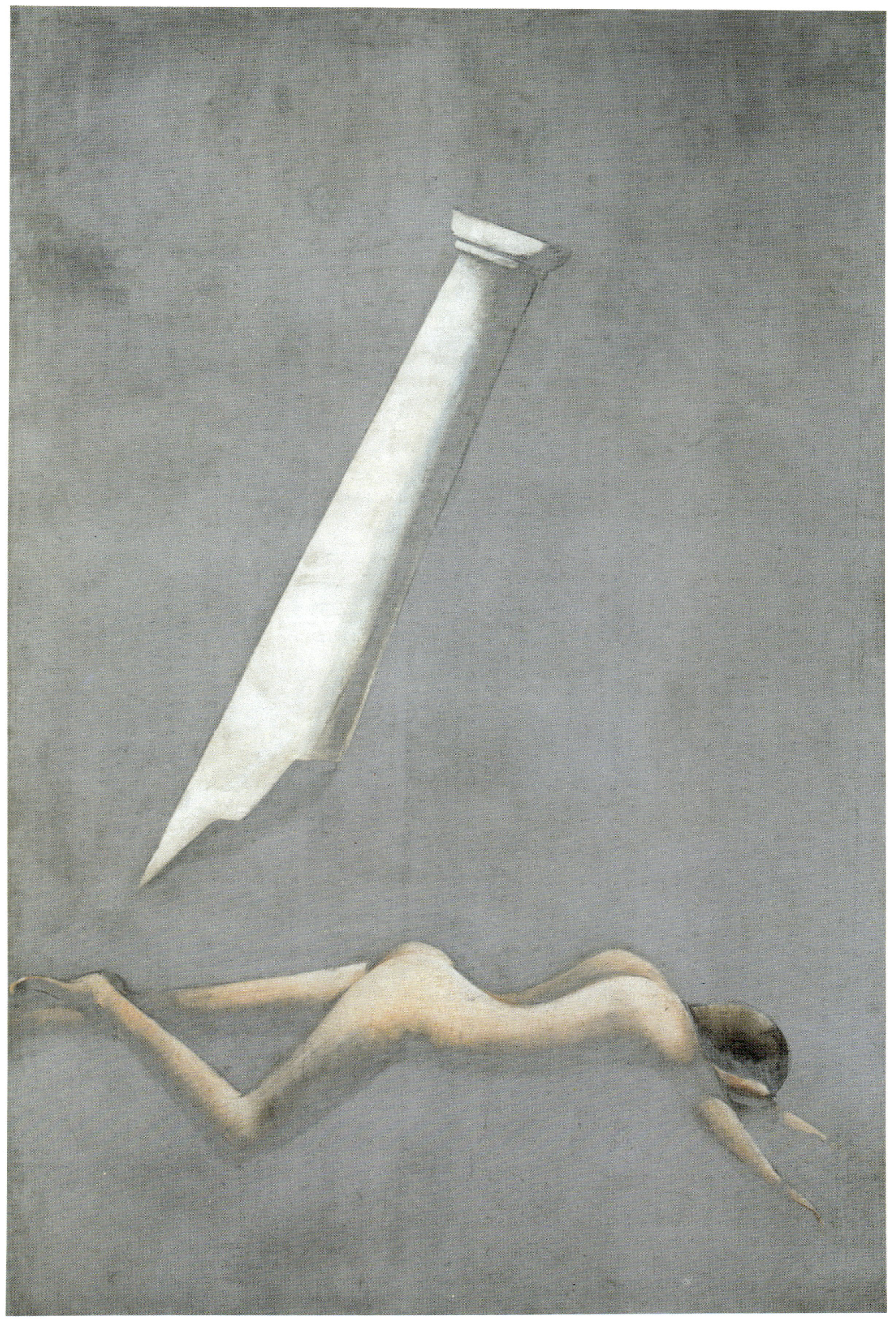

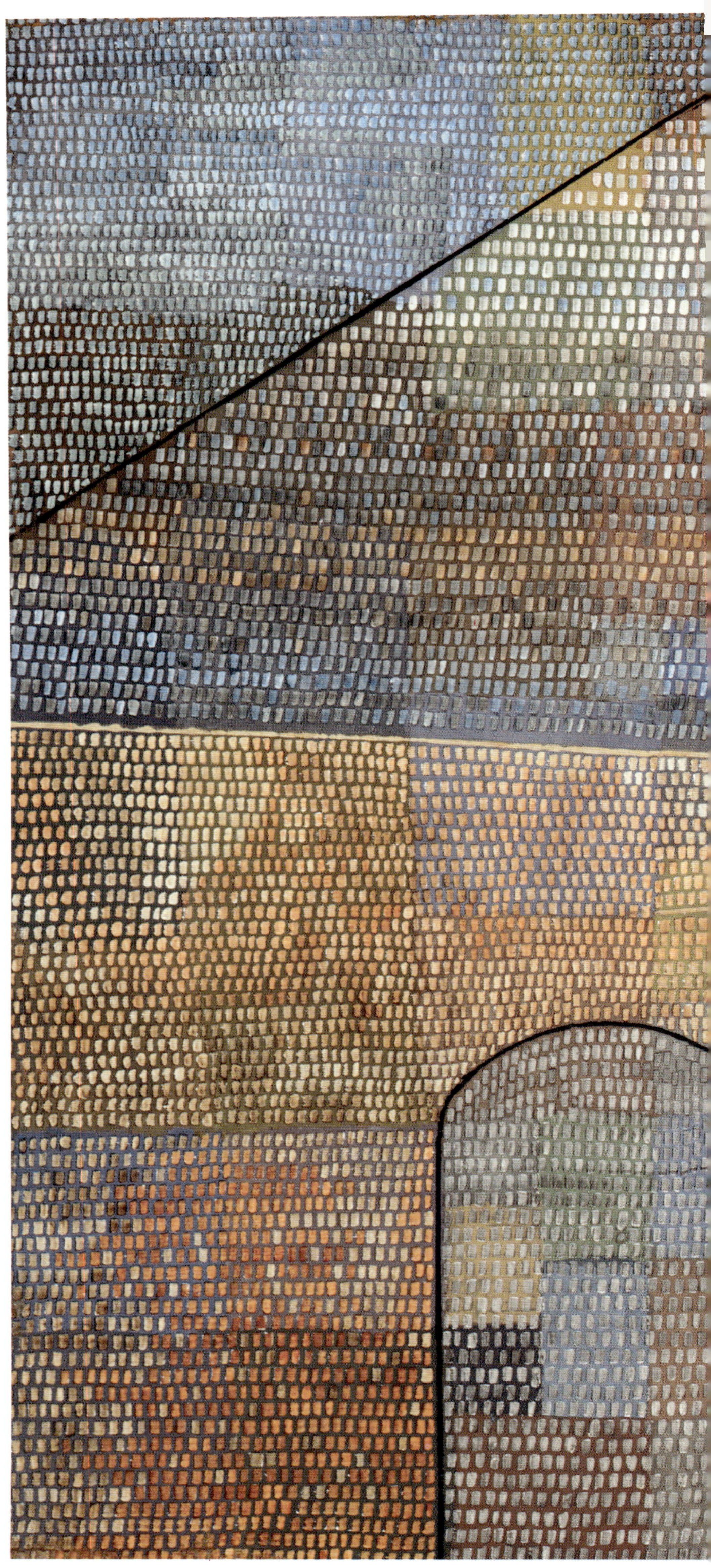

Paul Klee
Ad Parnassum 1932
Oil on canvas, 39⅜×49½in (100×126 cm)
Kunstmuseum, Bern
© *COSMOSPRESS, Geneva, DACS, London, 1989*

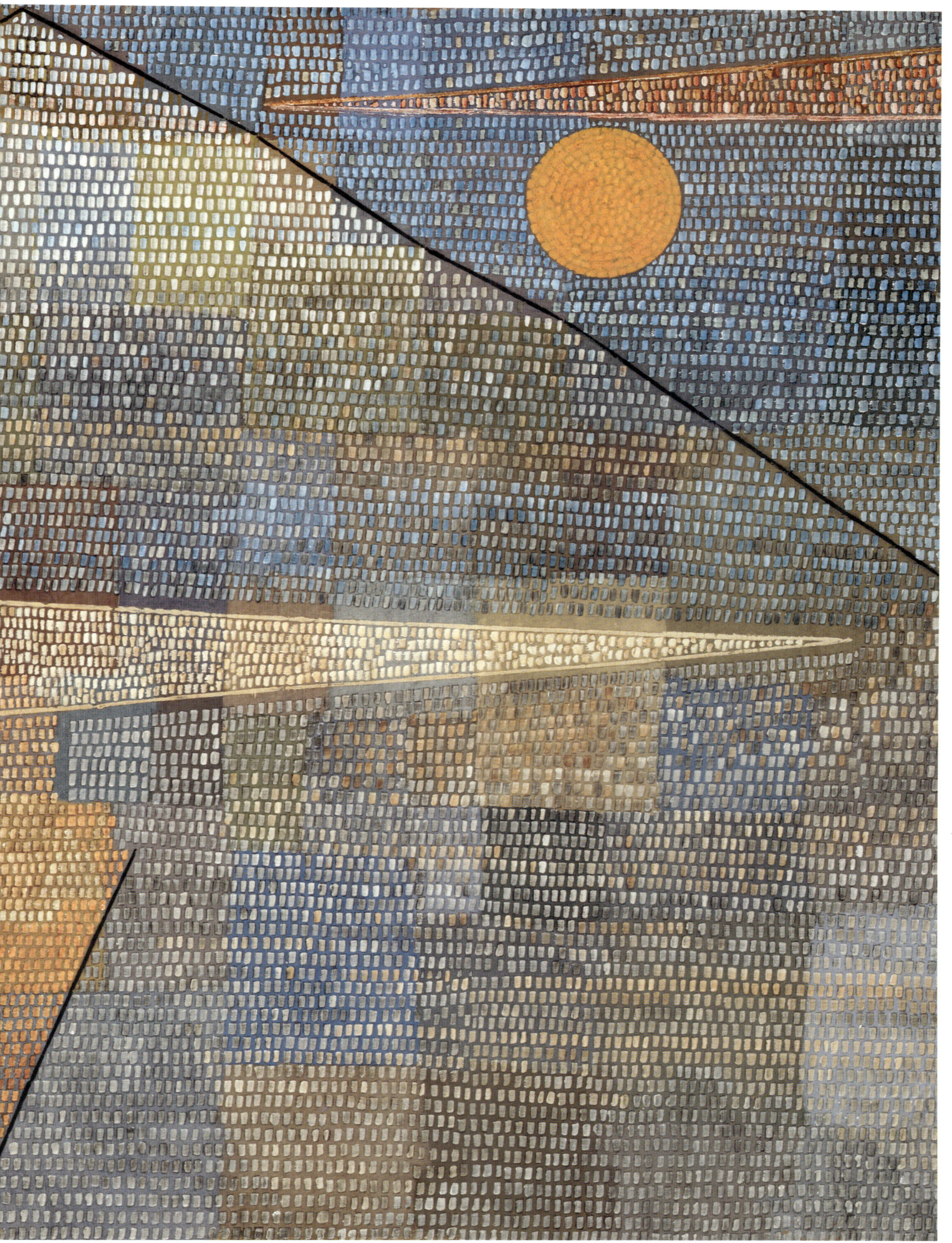

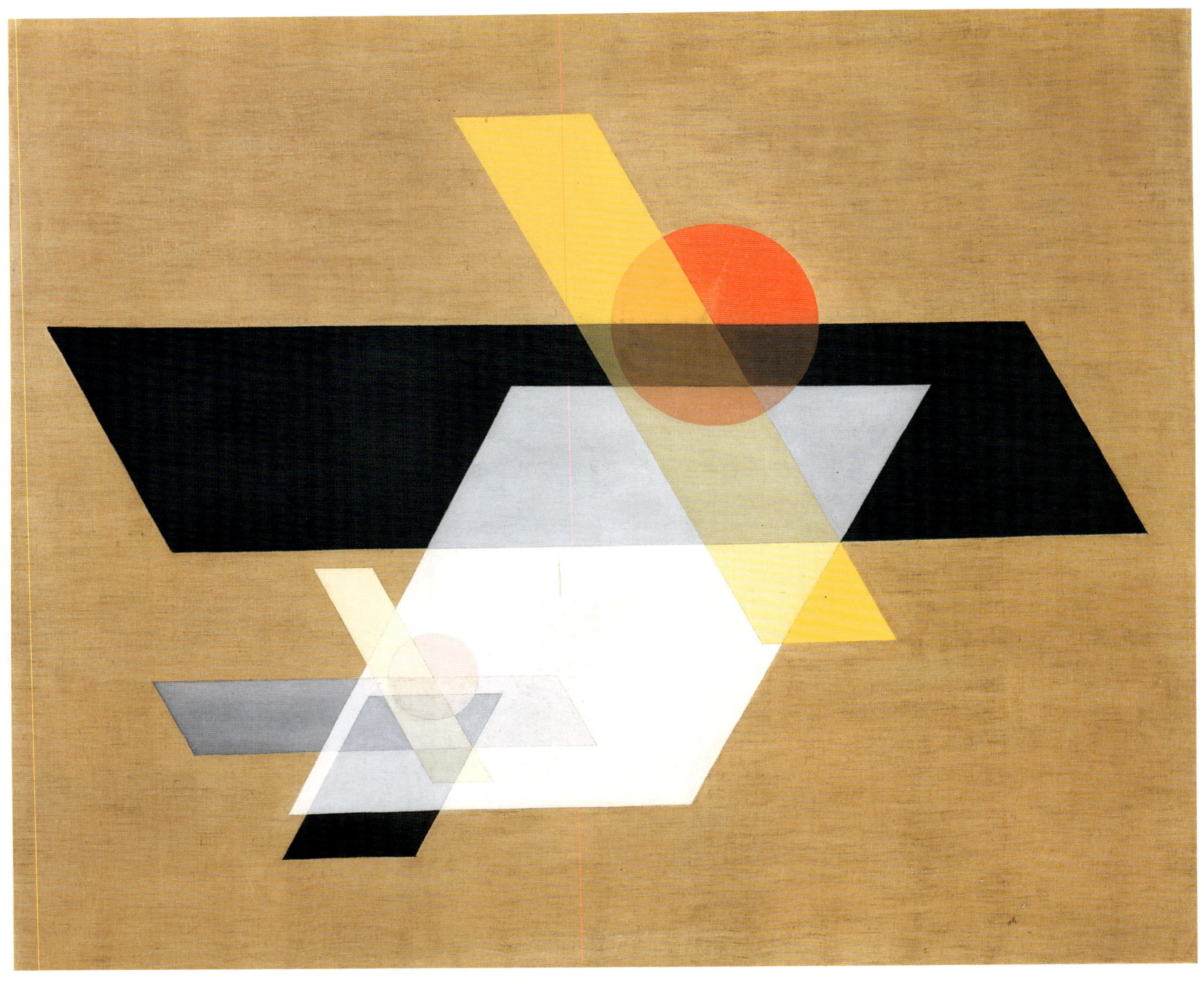

Laszlo Moholy-Nagy
A II 1924
Oil on canvas, 45⅝×53⅝in (115.9×136¼cm)
The Solomon R Guggenheim Museum, New York

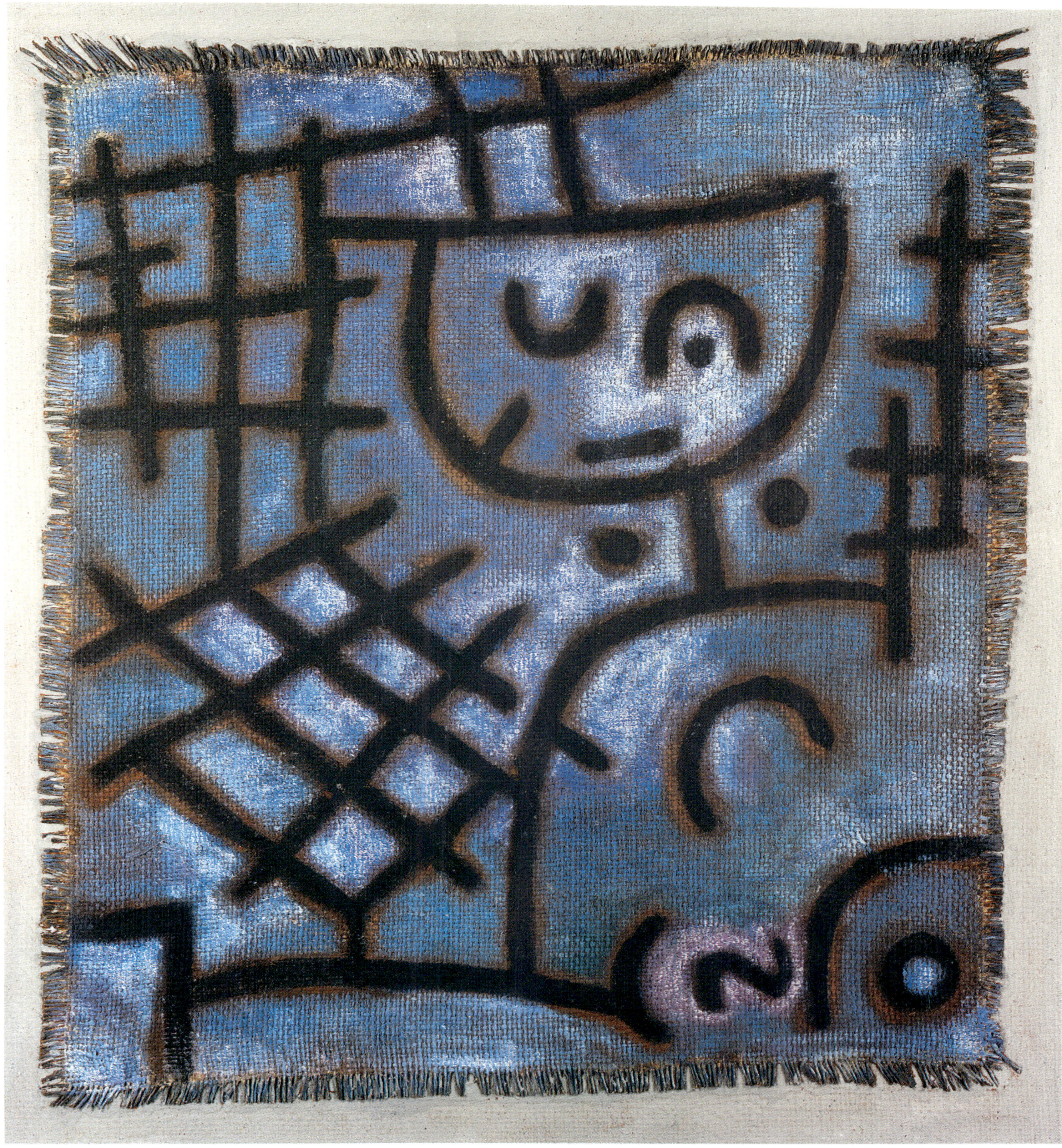

Paul Klee
Hither-beyond-Captive 1940
Oil on jute on canvas, 19⅝×19⅝in (50×50cm)
Galerie Beyeler, Basle
© *COSMOPRESS, Geneva, DACS, London, 1989*
(Estate LK 028 'Untitled')

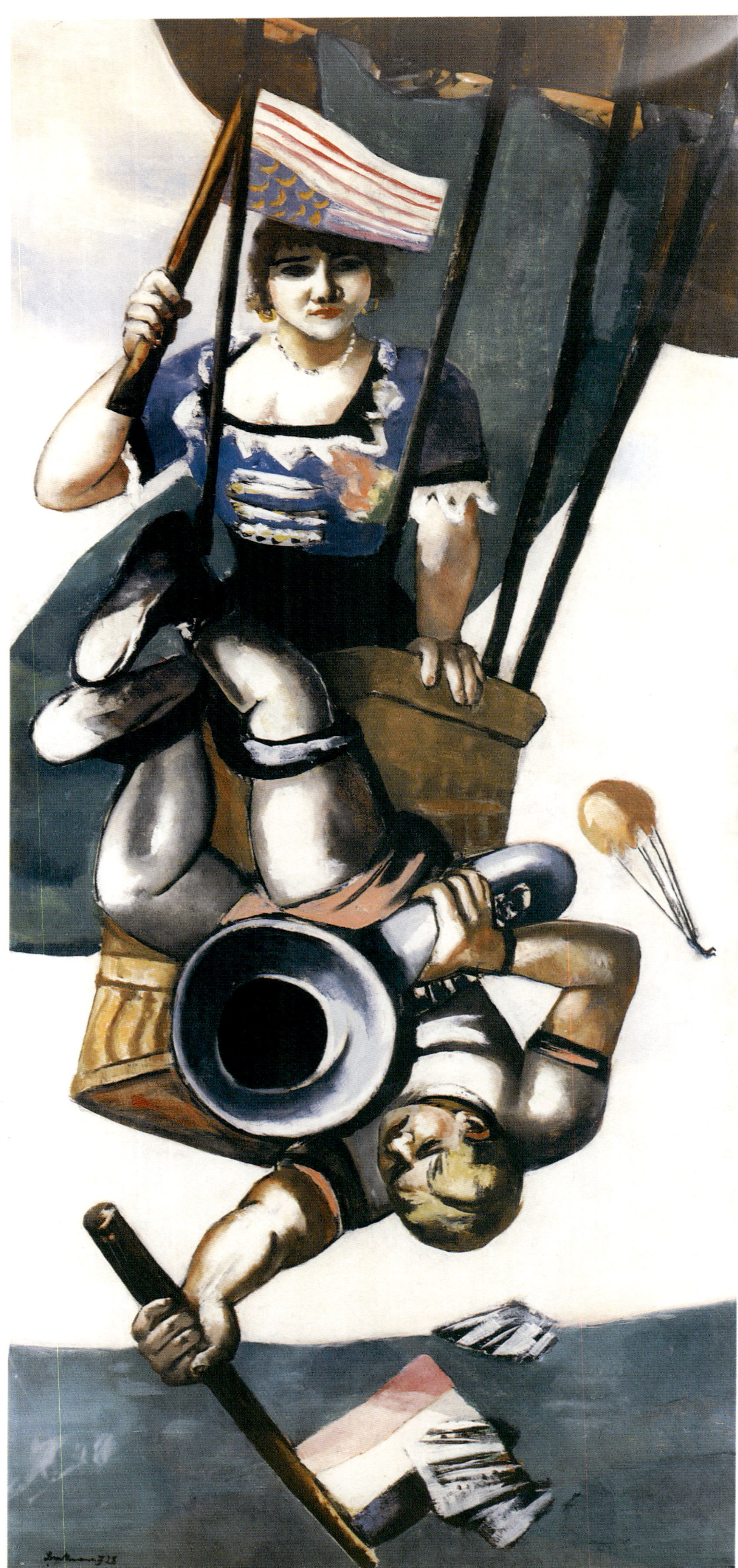

Max Beckmann
Aerial Acrobatics 1928
Oil on canvas, 84⅝×39⅜in (215×100cm)
Von der Heydt-Museum, Wuppertal
© DACS, 1988

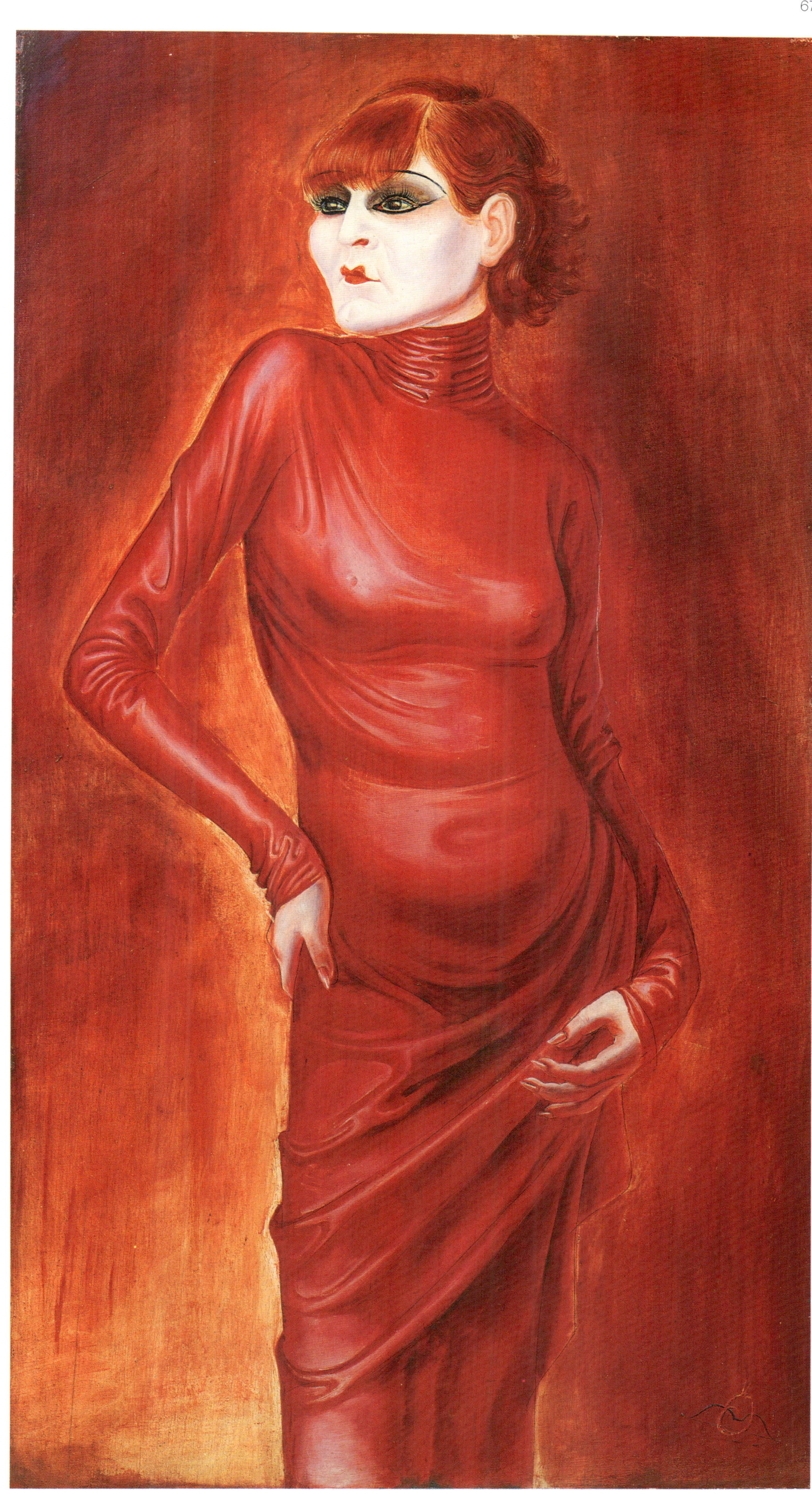

Otto Dix
The Dancer Anita Berber 1925
Tempera and oil on plywood
47½×25in (120×65cm)
Galerie der Stadt Stuttgart
Otto Dix Foundation, Vaduz, Liech-
tenstein

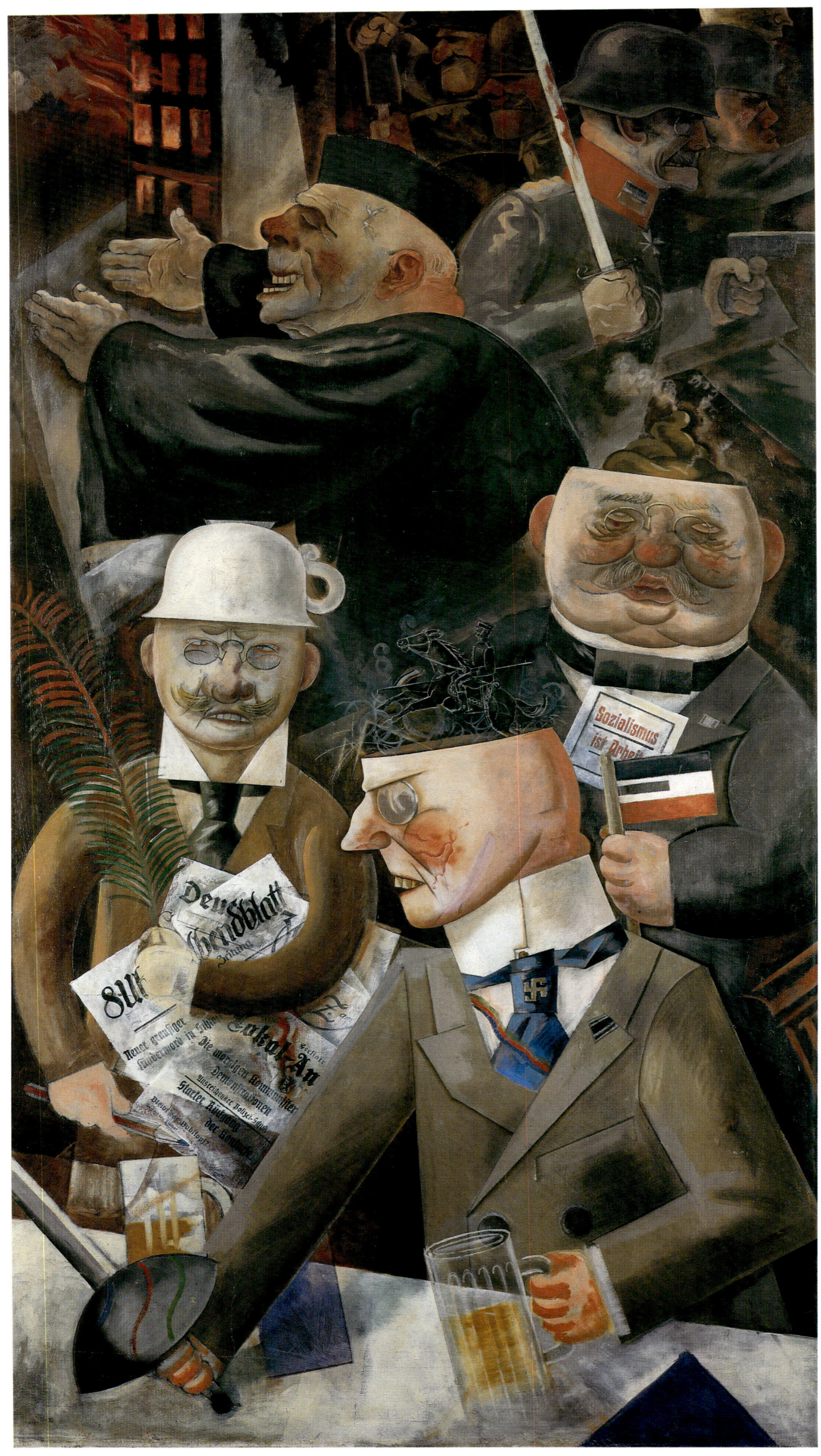

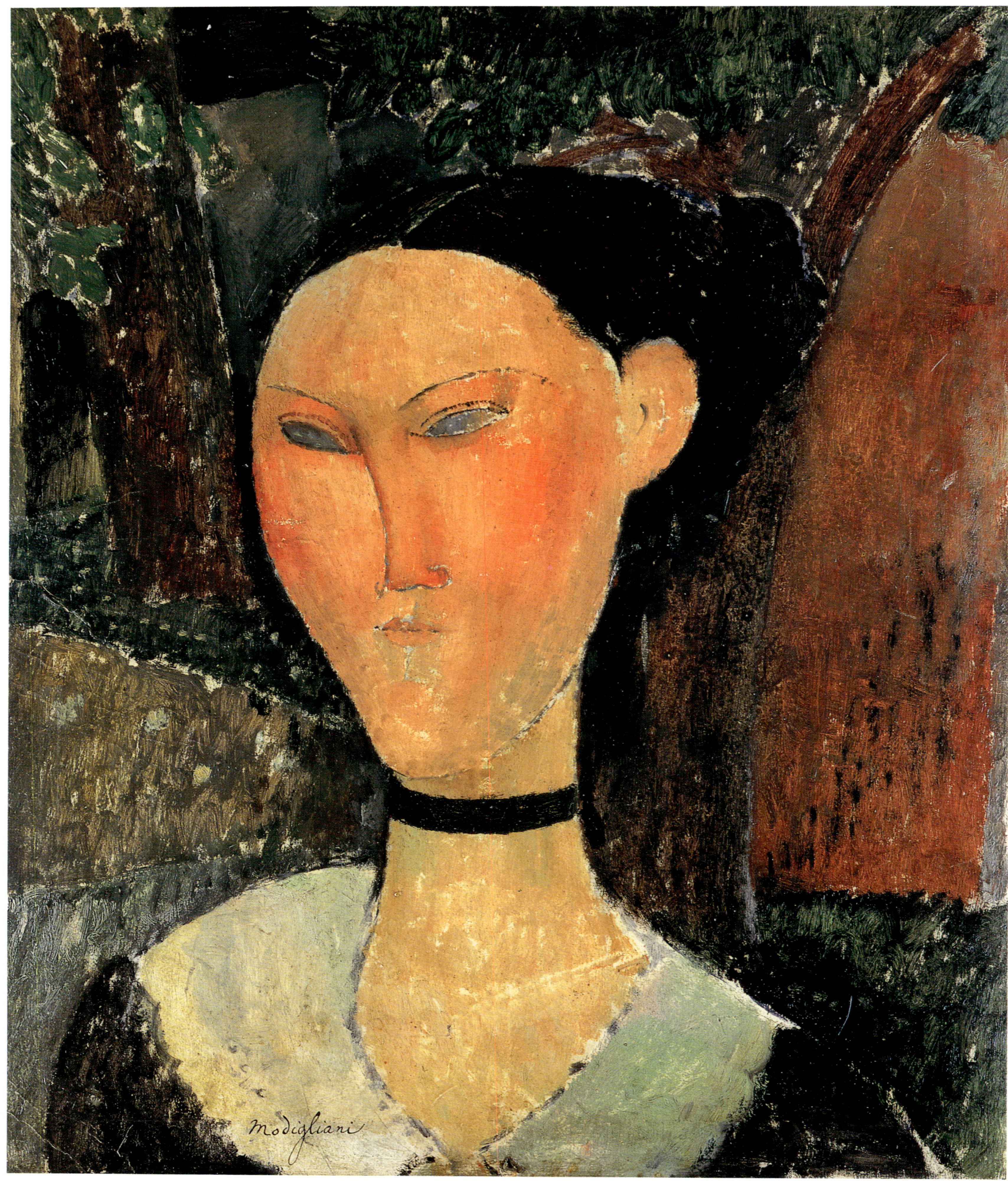

Amedeo Modigliani
Woman with a Velvet Ribbon c. 1915
Oil on canvas, 22×18½in (56×47cm)
Musée de l'Orangerie, Paris
Collection Jean Walter and P Guillaume

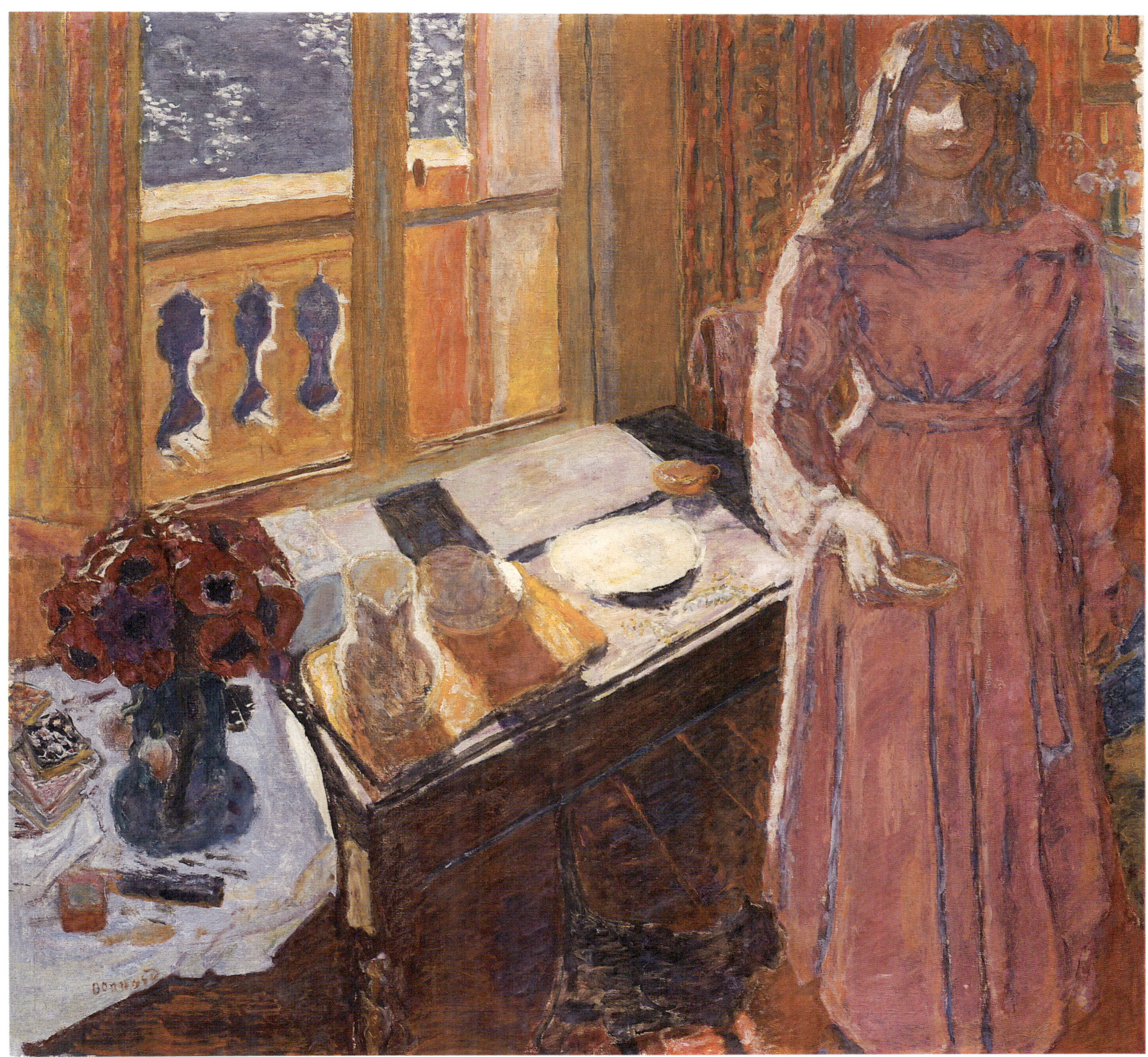

Pierre Bonnard
The Bowl of Milk 1919
Oil on canvas, 45¾×47⅝in (116.2×121.6cm)
Tate Gallery, London
© ADAGP, Paris, DACS, London, 1989

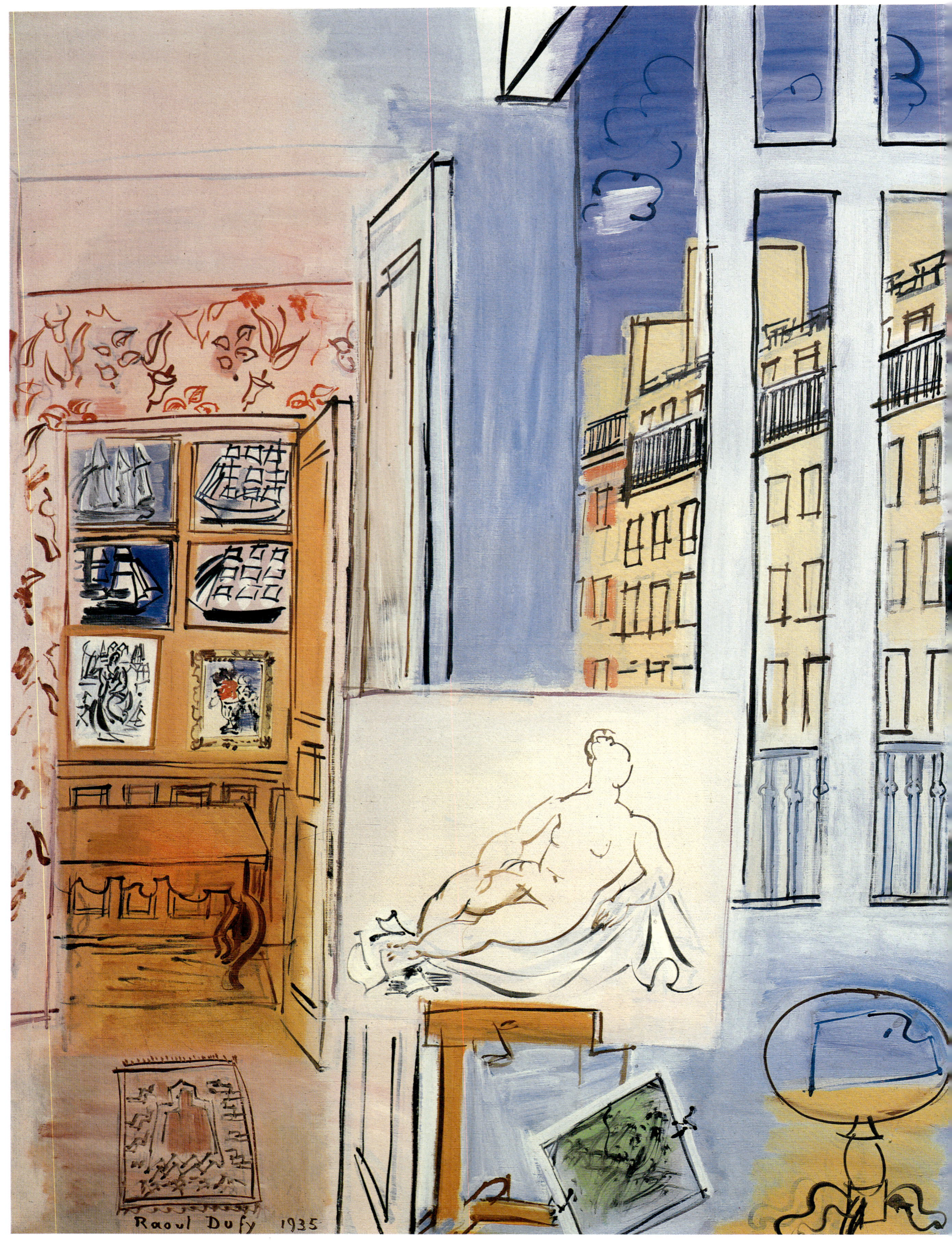
Raoul Dufy 1935

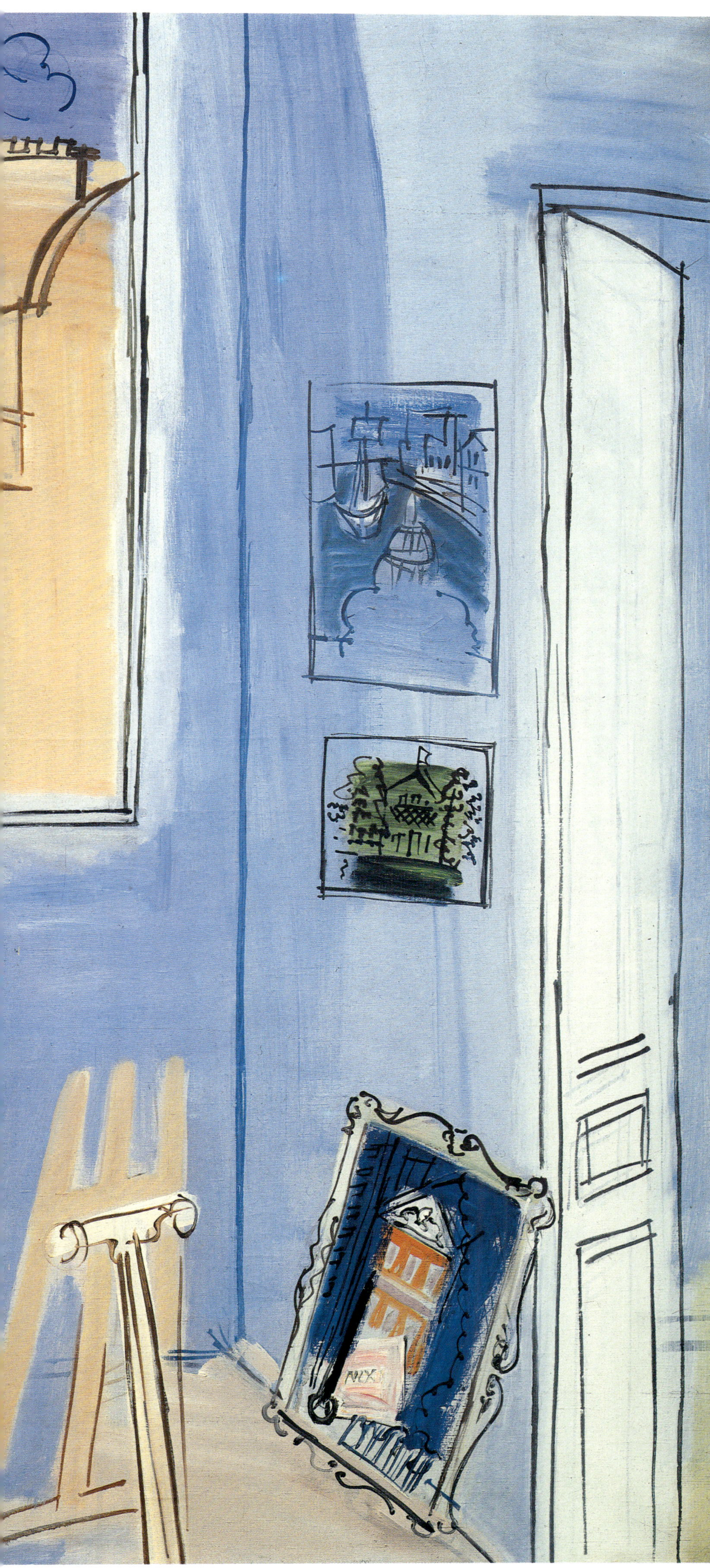

Raoul Dufy
The Artist's Studio 1935
Oil on canvas, 46⅞×58¼in (119×147.9cm)
The Phillips Collection, Washington, D.C.
© *DACS, 1988*

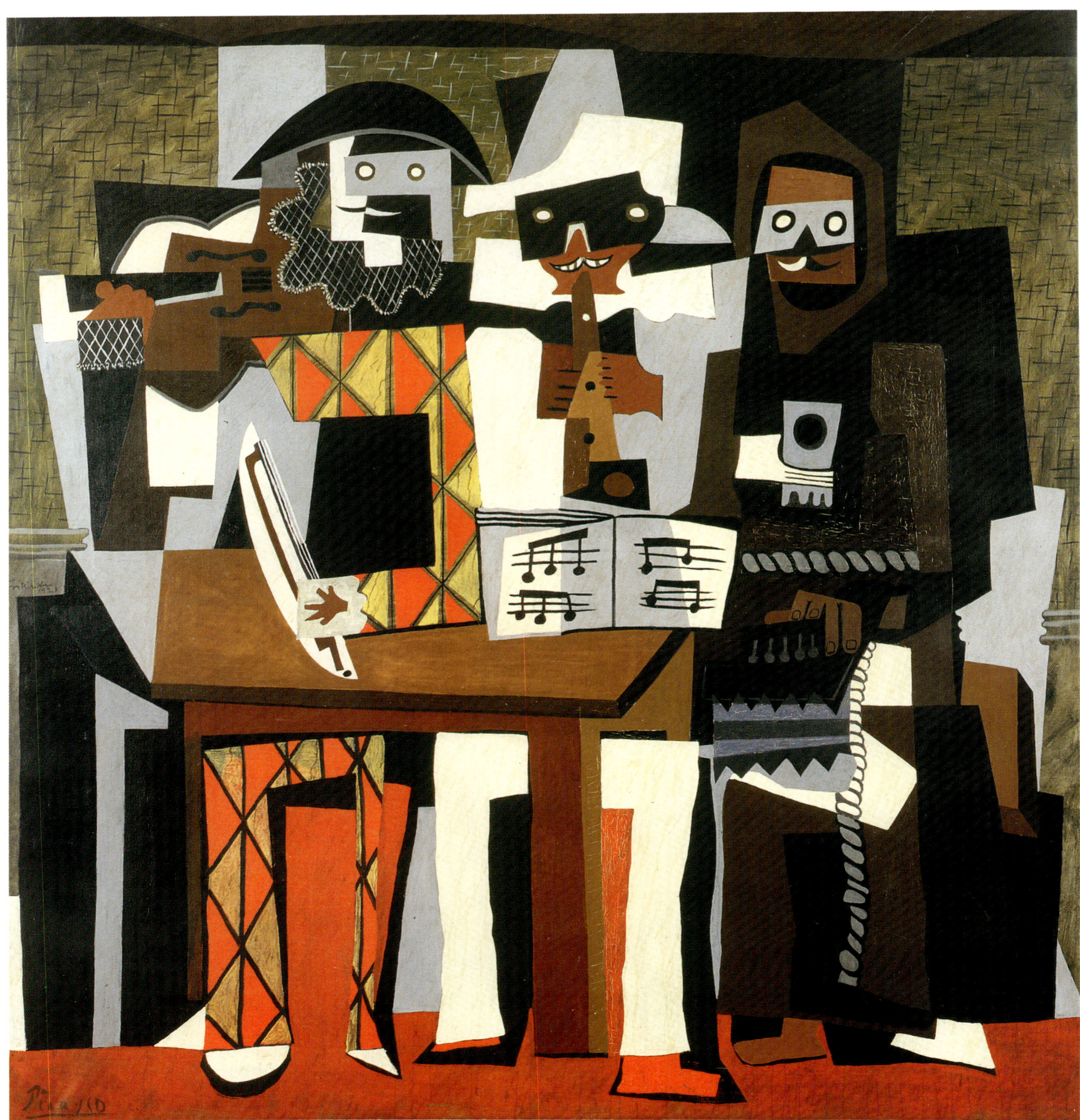

Pablo Picasso
Three Musicians 1921
Oil on canvas, 80×74in (203.2×188cm)
Philadephia Museum of Art
A E Gallatin Collection
© *DACS, 1988*

Marcel Duchamp
Nude Descending a Staircase No 2 1912
Oil on canvas, 58×35in (147.3×89cm)
Philadelphia Museum of Art
Louise and Walter Arensberg Collection
© *ADAGP, Paris, DACS, London, 1989*

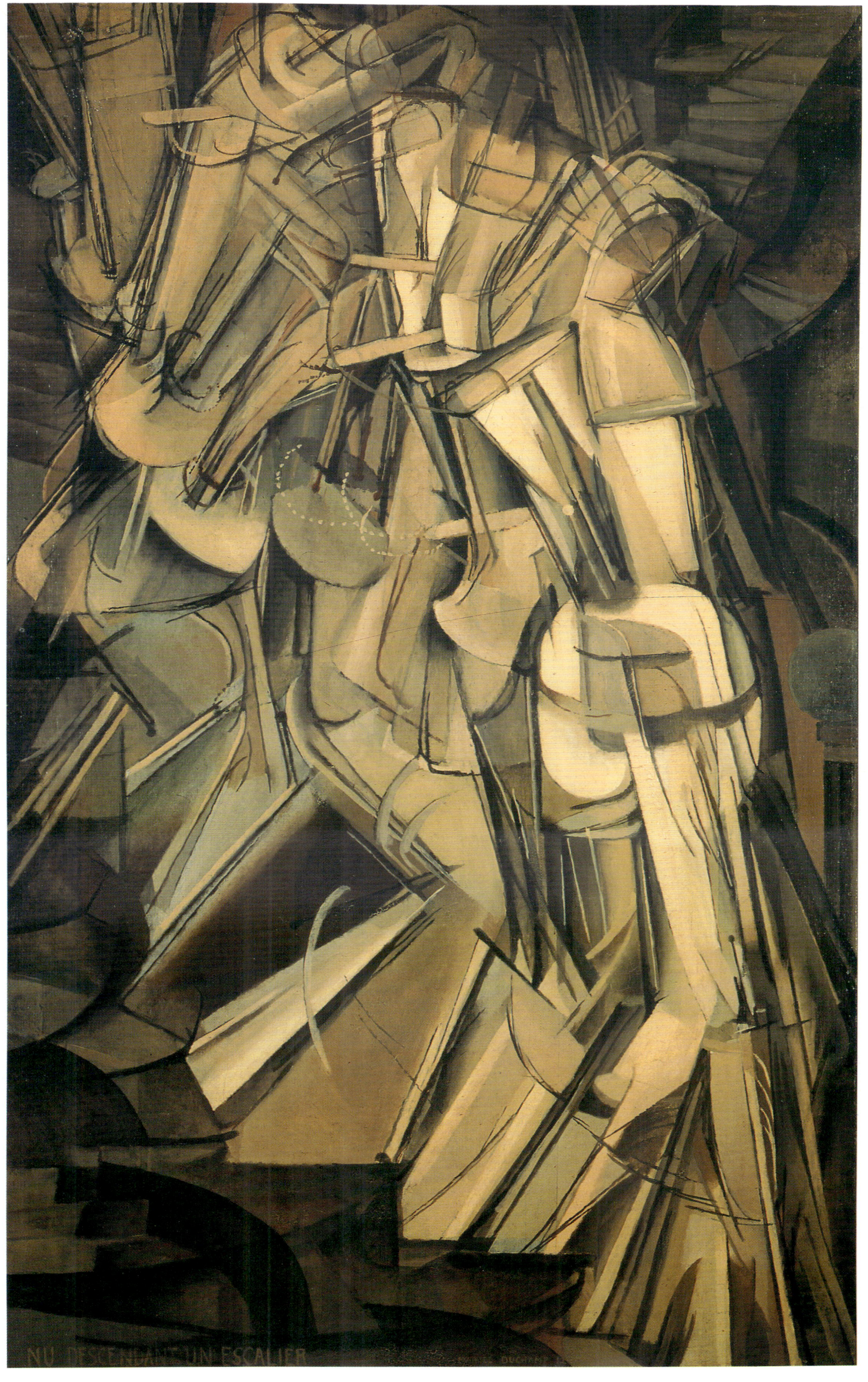

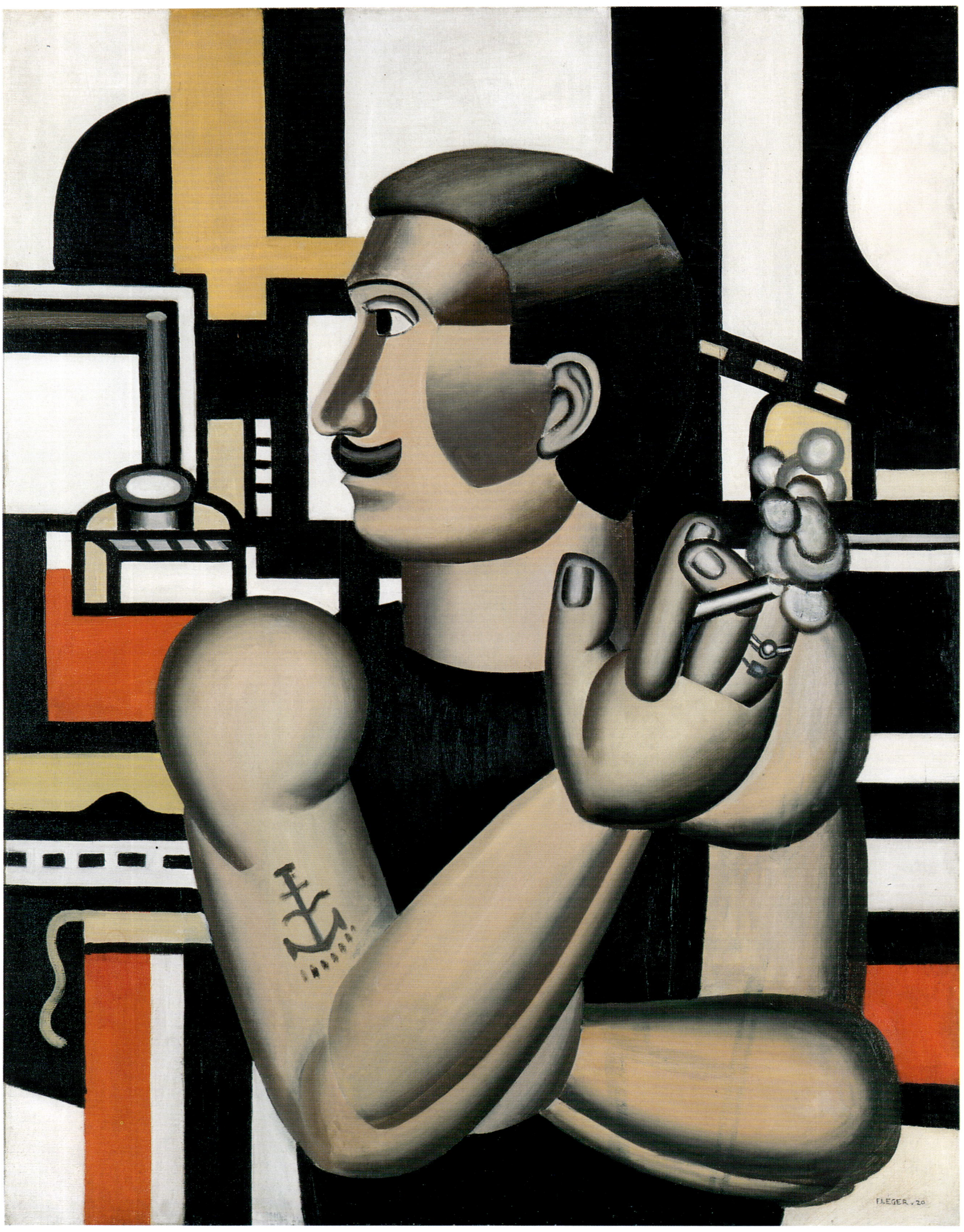

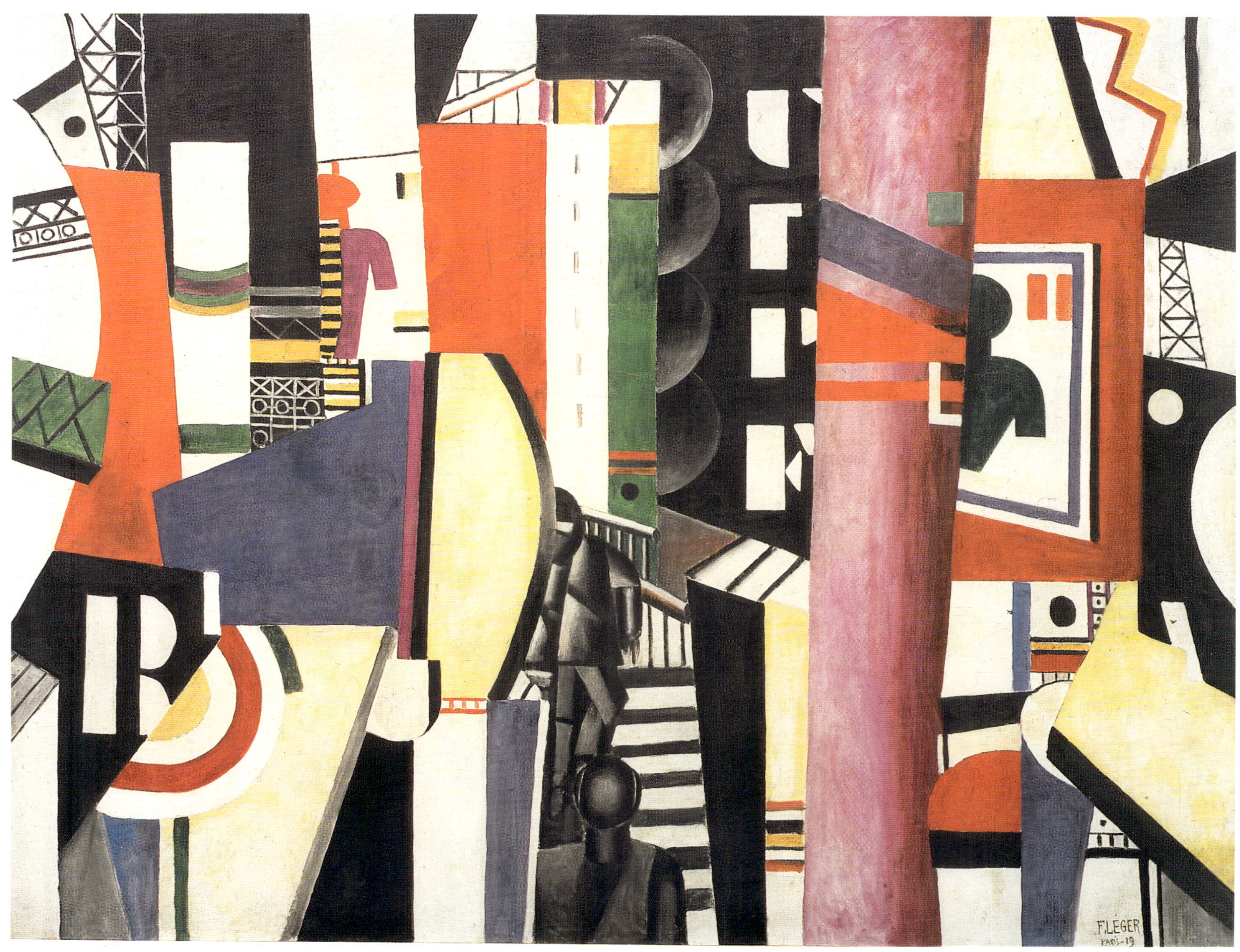

LEFT:
Fernand Léger
The Mechanic 1920
Oil on canvas, 45½×34¾in (115.5×88.3cm)
National Gallery of Canada, Ottawa
© *DACS, 1988*

ABOVE:
Fernand Léger
The City 1919
Oil on canvas, 90¾×117¼in (230.5×297.8cm)
Philadelphia Museum of Art
A E Gallatin Collection
© *DACS, 1988*

OVERLEAF LEFT:
Marc Chagall
Double Portrait with Glass of Wine 1917
Oil on canvas, 92½×54in (244×137.2cm)
Centre National d'Art et de Culture Georges Pompidou
Photo: Jacqueline Hyde
© *ADAGP, Paris, DACS, London, 1989*

OVERLEAF RIGHT:
Marc Chagall
Green Violinist 1923/4
Oil on canvas, 78×42¾in (198×108.6cm)
Guggenheim Museum, New York
Photo: David Heald
© *ADAGP, Paris, DACS, London, 1989*

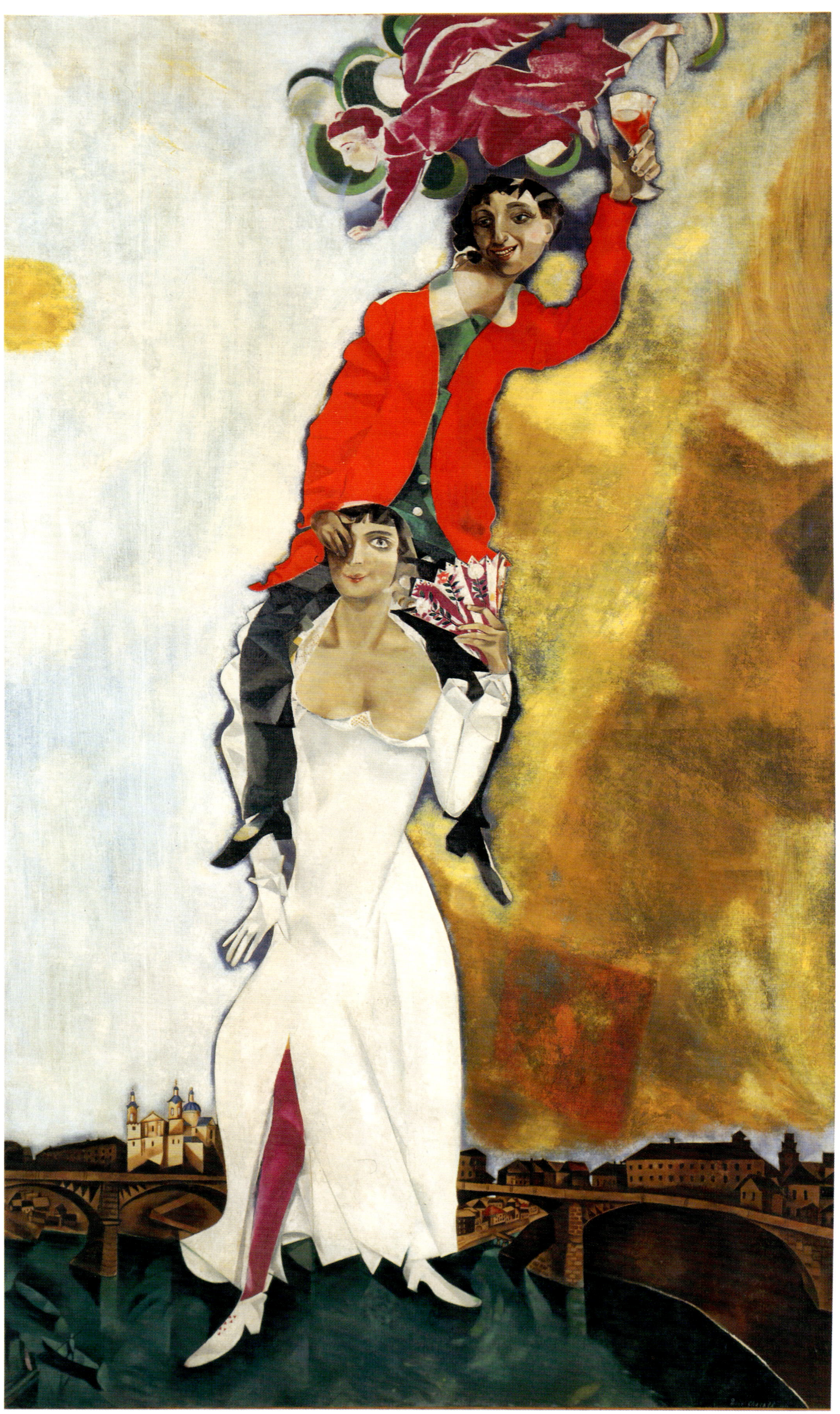

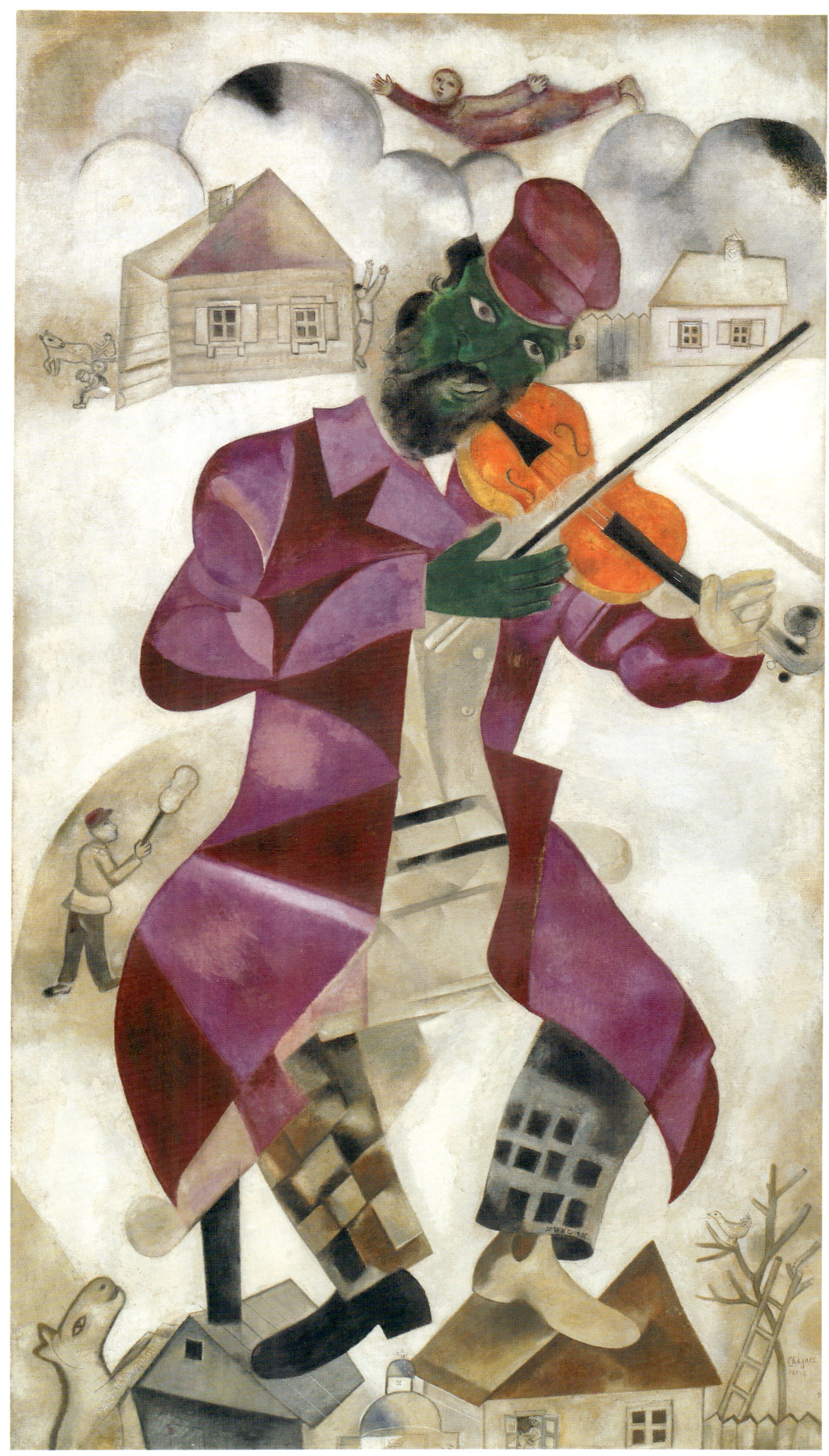

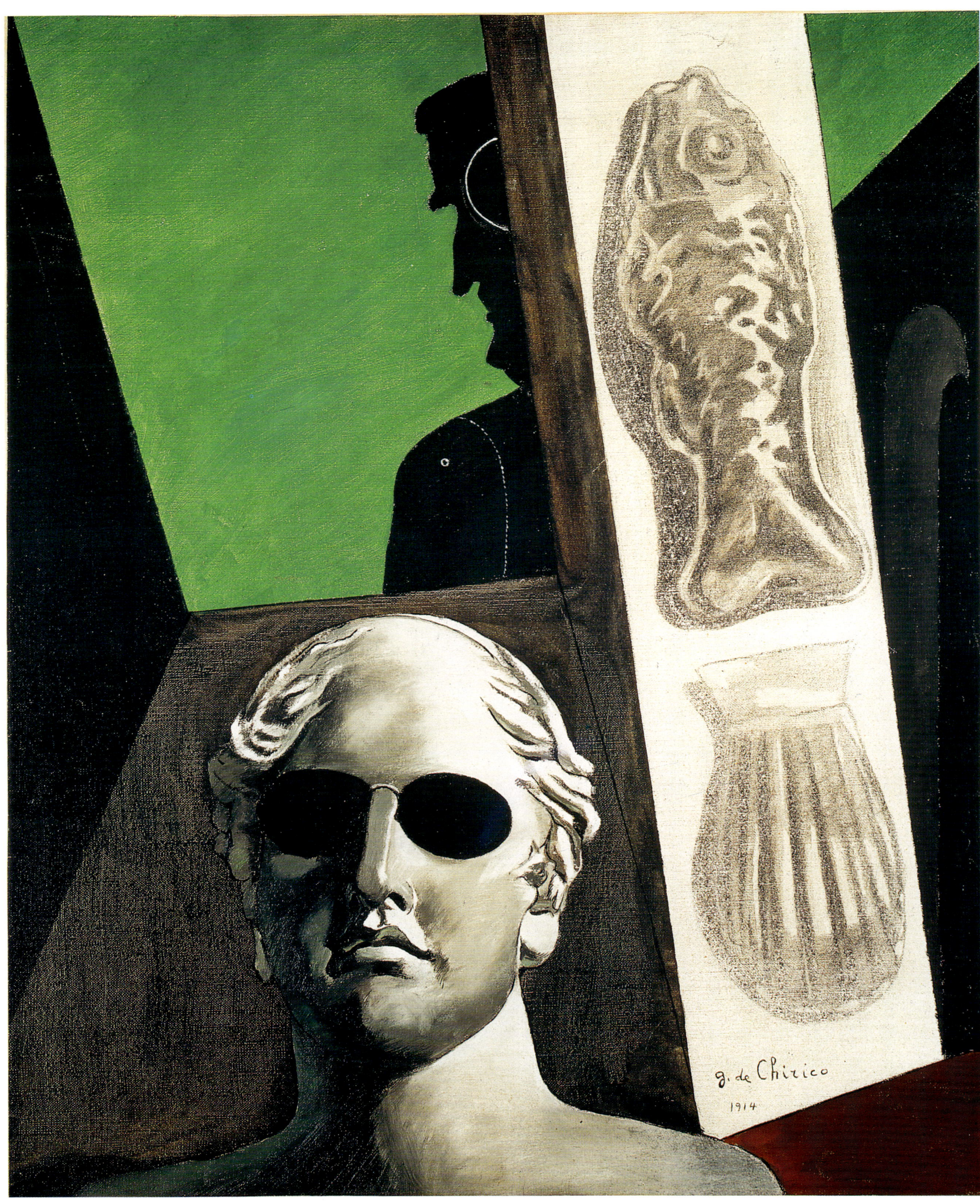

Giorgio de Chirico
Premonitory Portrait of Guillaume Apollinaire 1914
Oil on canvas, 32×25½in (81.3×64.8cm)
Centre National d'Art et de Culture Georges Pompidou
© *DACS, 1988*

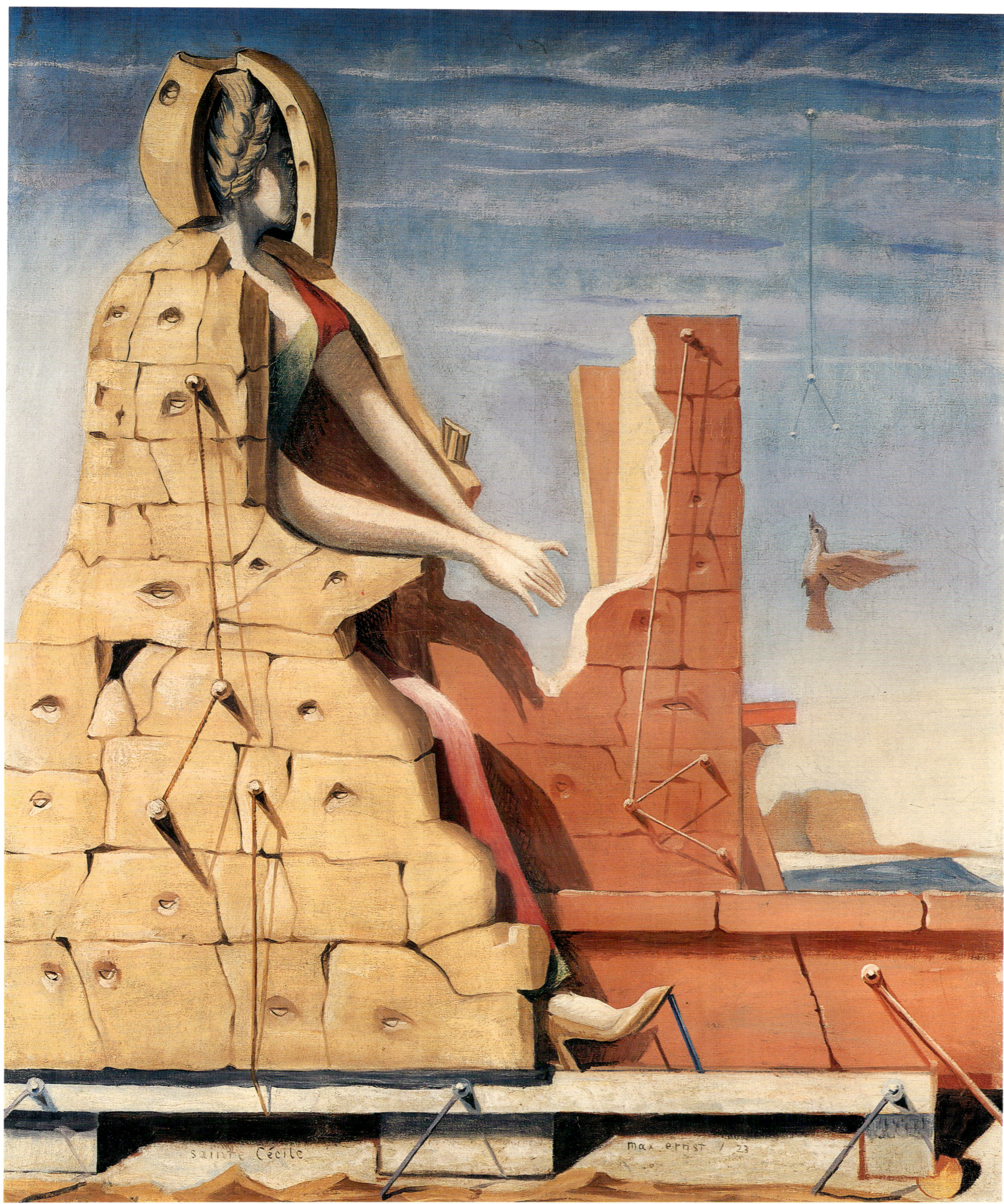

Max Ernst
Saint Cecilia – The Invisible Piano 1932
Oil on canvas, 40½×32¼in (103×82cm)
Staatsgalerie Stuttgart
© *DACS, 1988*

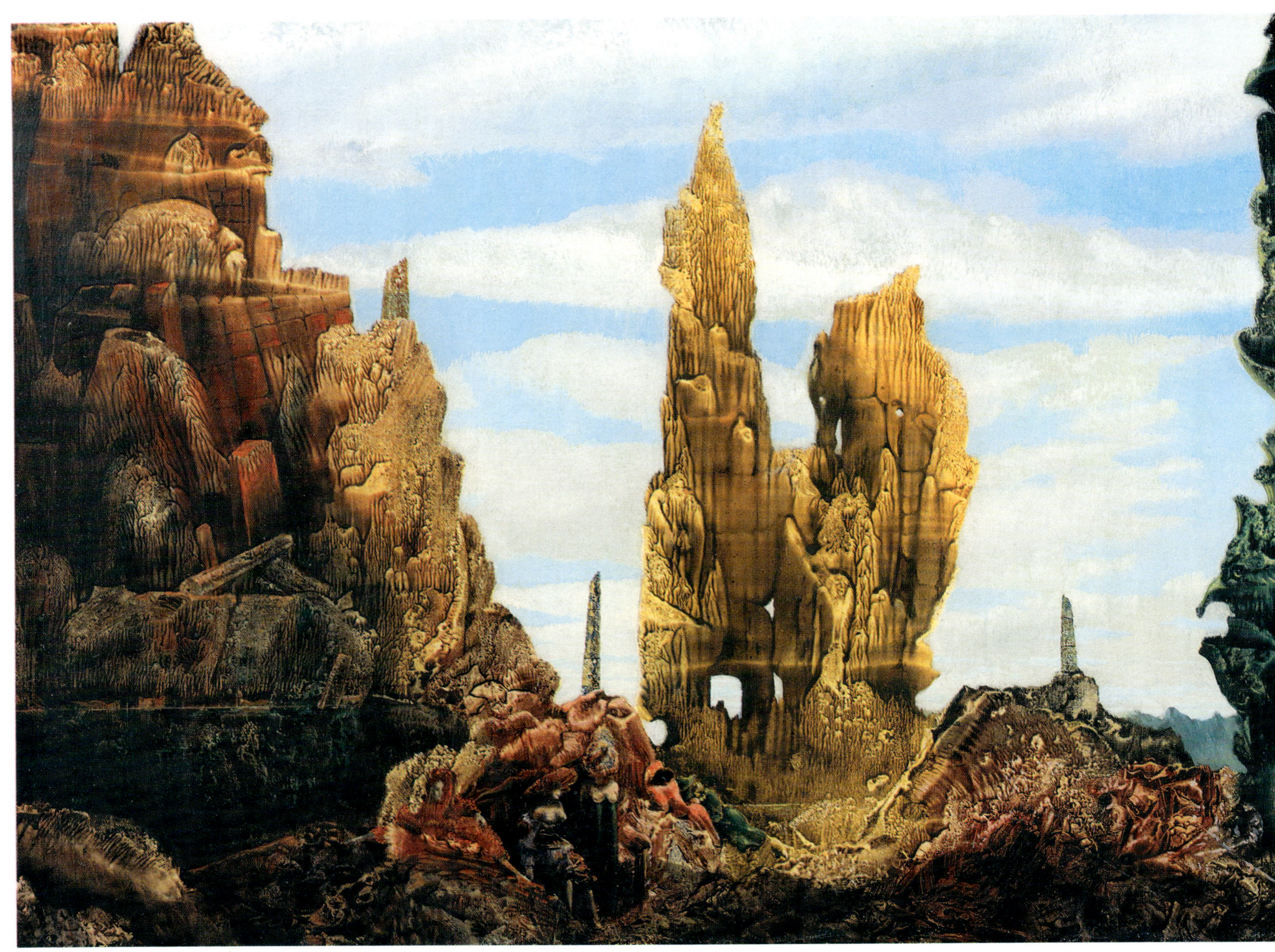

Max Ernst
Europe after the Rain 1940-42
Oil on canvas, 21×58in (53.3×147.3cm)
Wadsworth Atheneum, Hartford, Connecticut
Ella Gallup Sumner and Mary Catlin Sumner Collection
© *DACS, 1988*

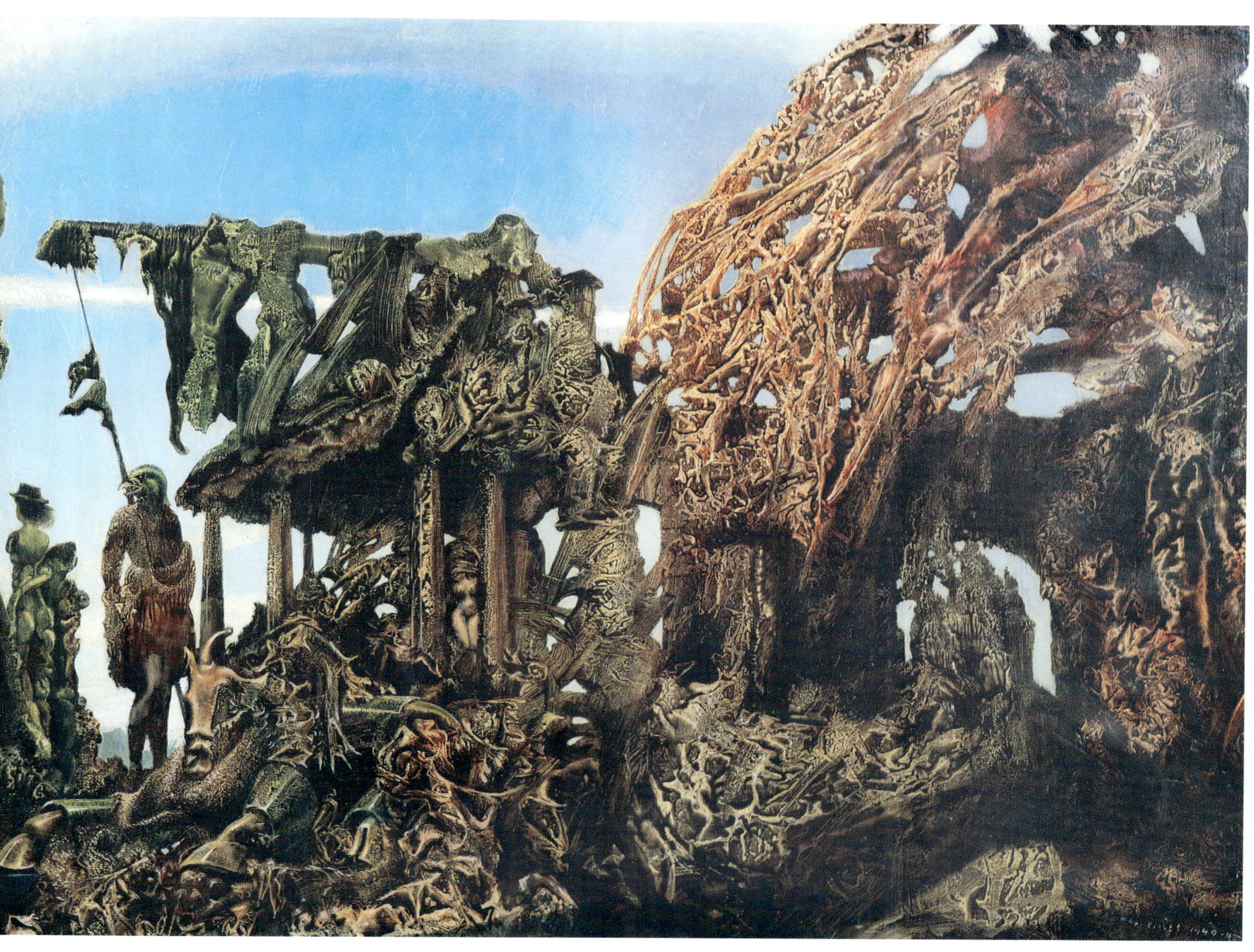

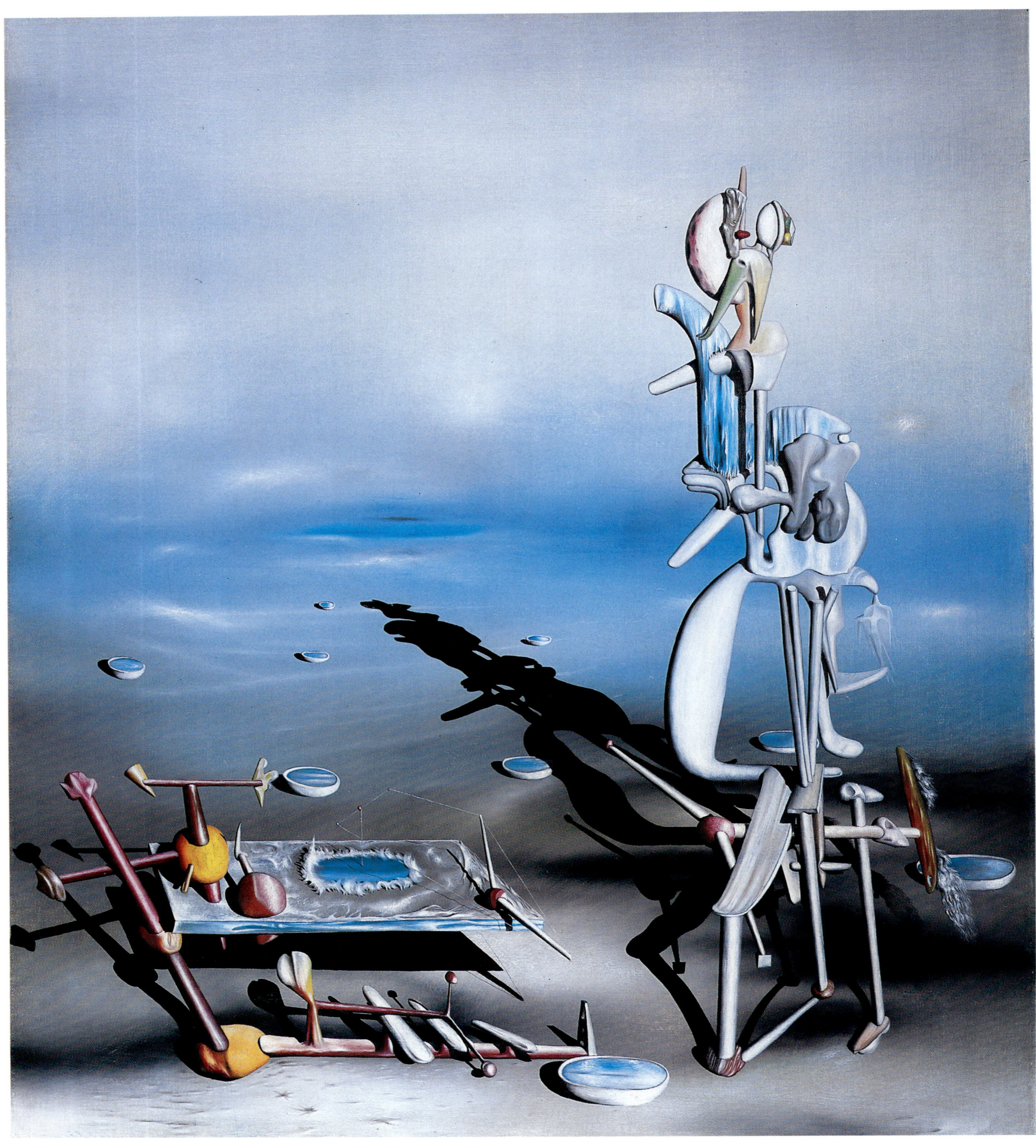

Yves Tanguy
Indefinite Divisibility 1942
Oil on canvas, 40×35in (101.6×88.9cm)
Albright-Knox Art Gallery, Buffalo
Room of Contemporary Art Fund, 1945
© *DACS, 1988*

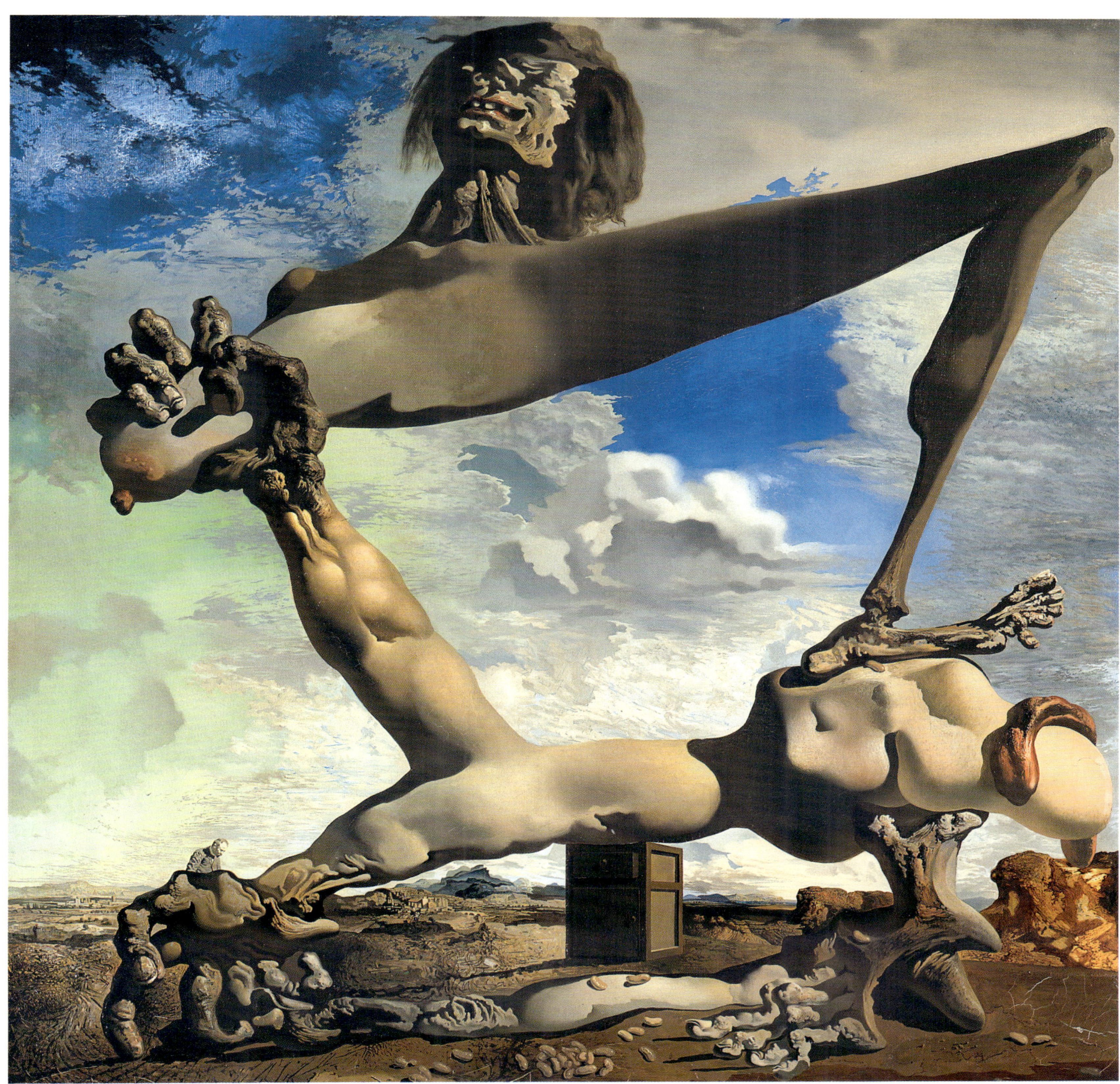

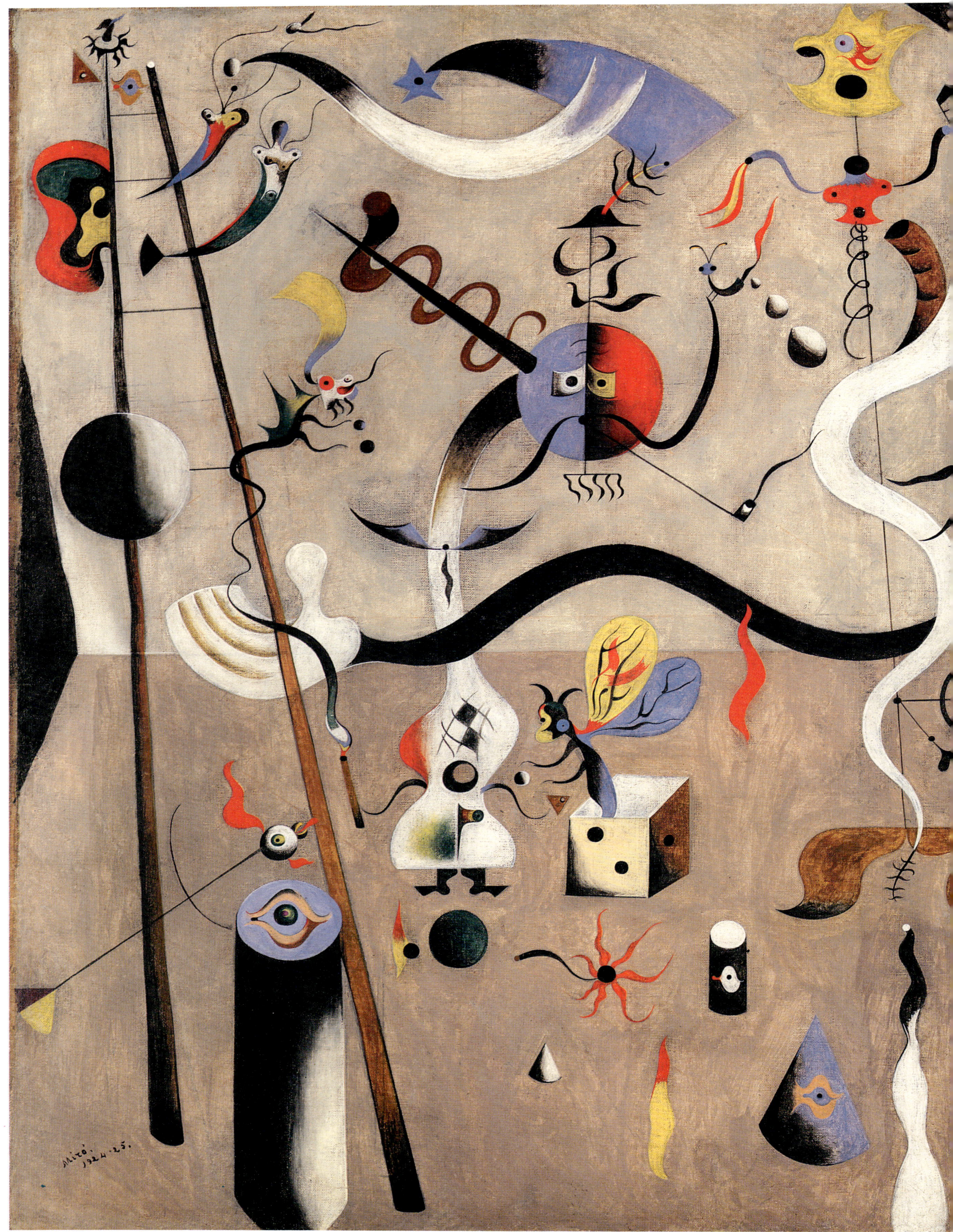

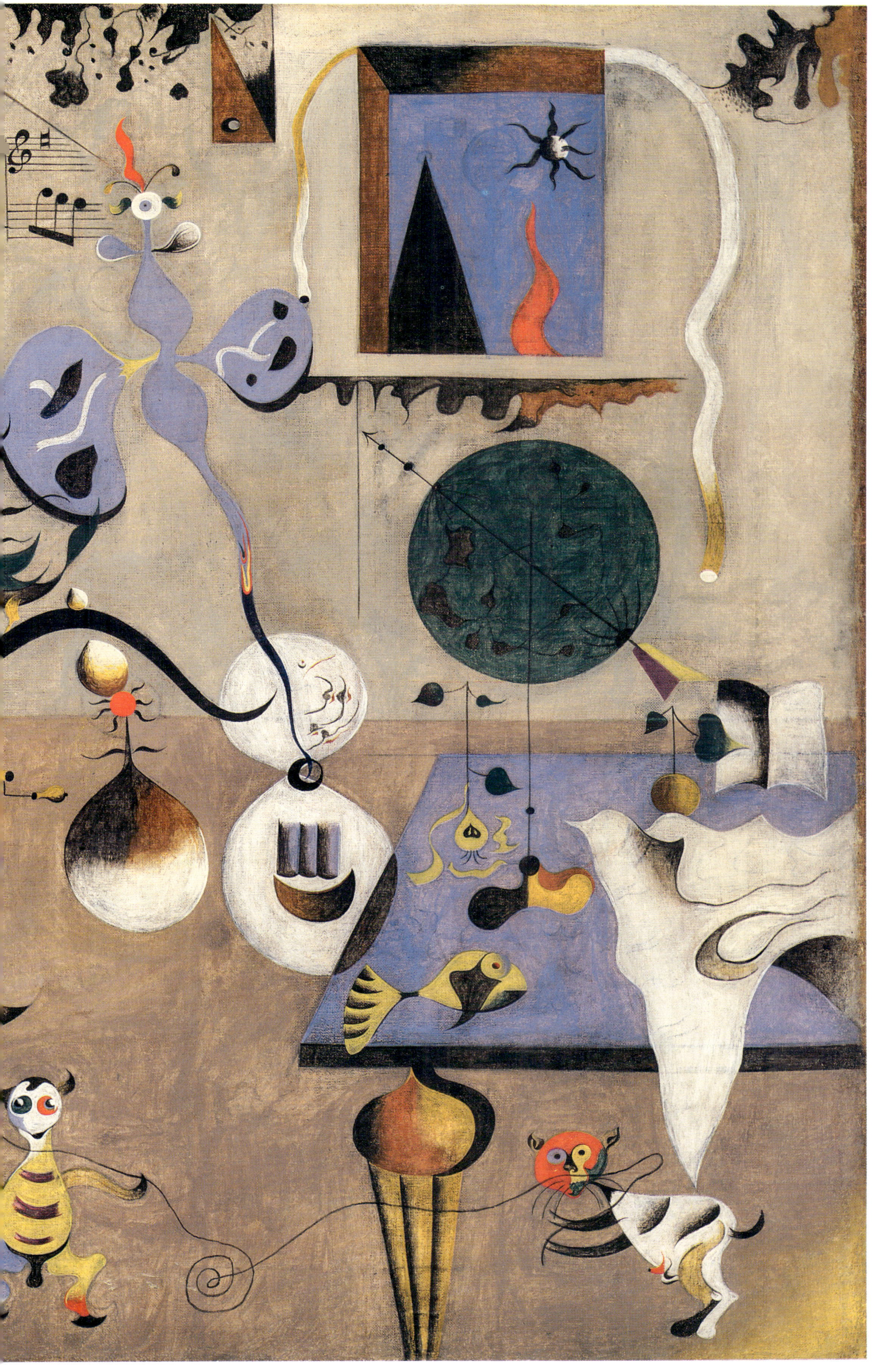

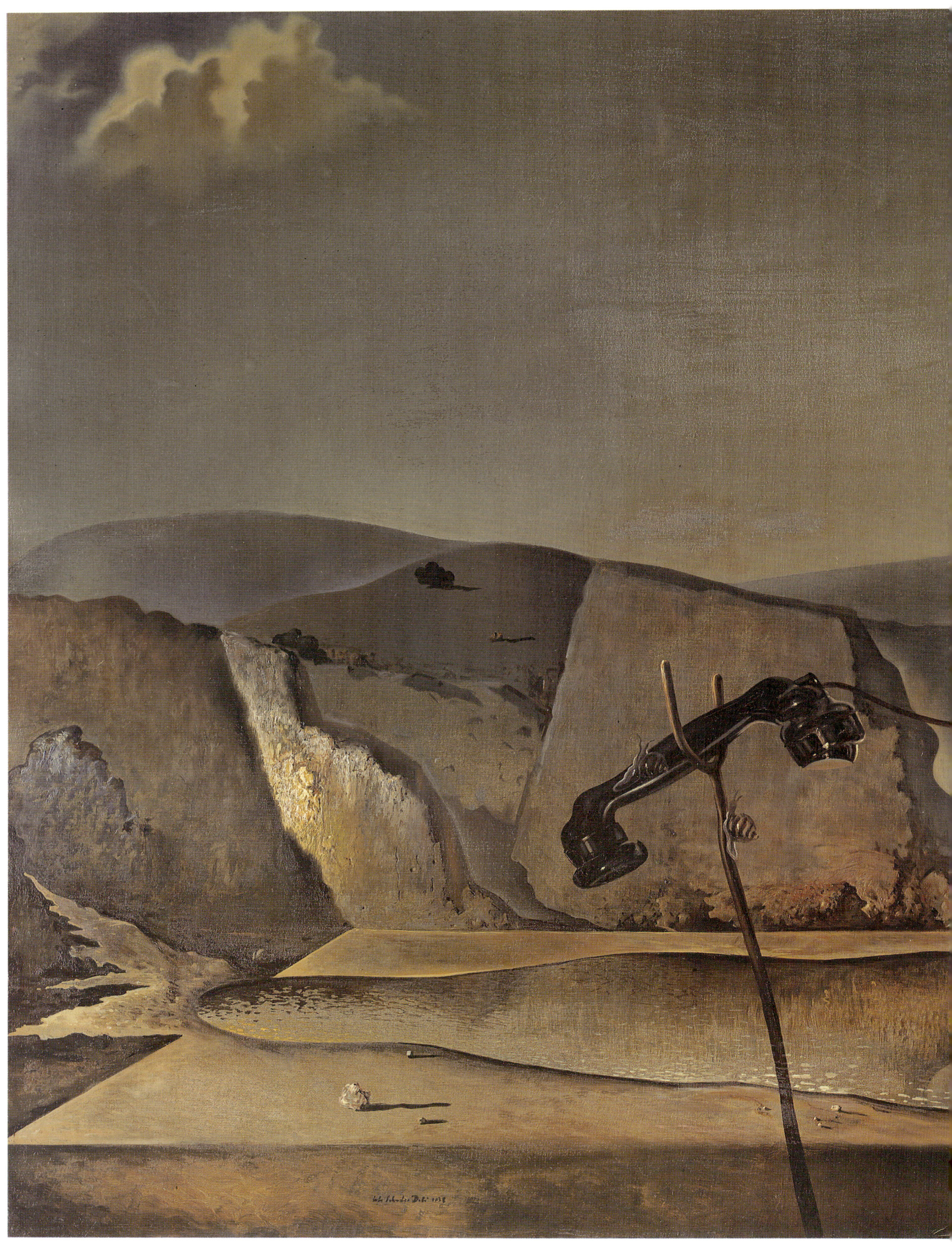

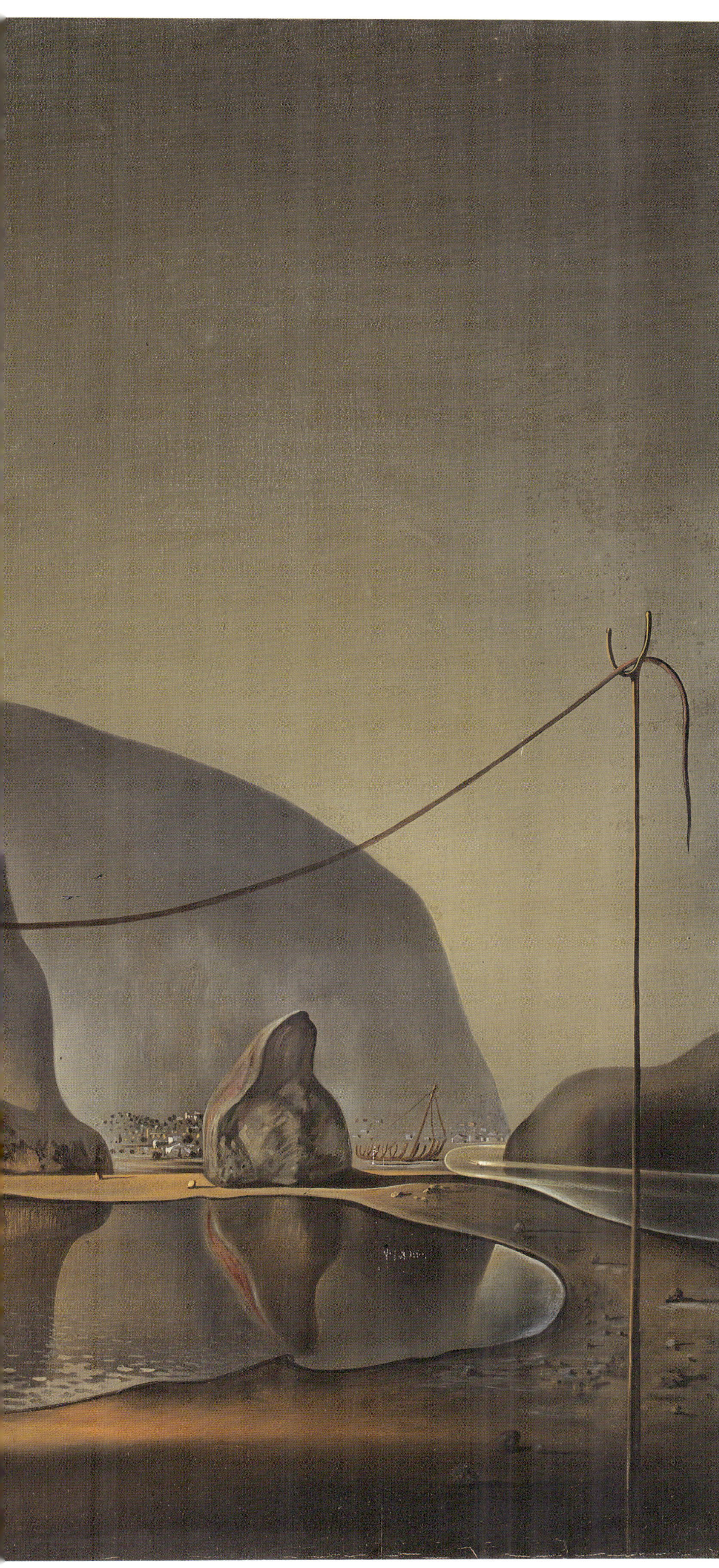

Salvador Dali
Mountain Lake 1938
Oil on canvas, 28¾×36¼in (73×92.1cm)
Tate Gallery, London
© *DEMART PRO ARTE BV/DACS 1989*

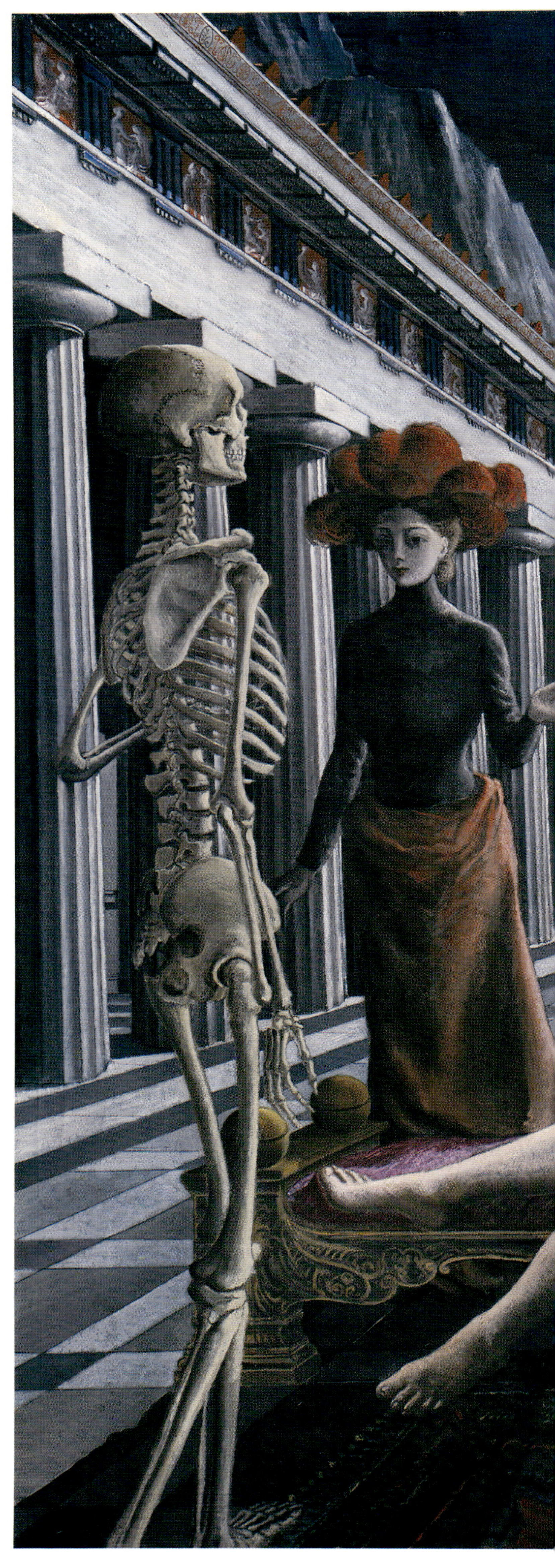

Paul Delvaux
Sleeping Venus 1944
Oil on canvas, 68×78⅜in (172.7×199.1cm)
Tate Gallery, London
© *Fondation P Delvaux, St Idesbald, Belgium*

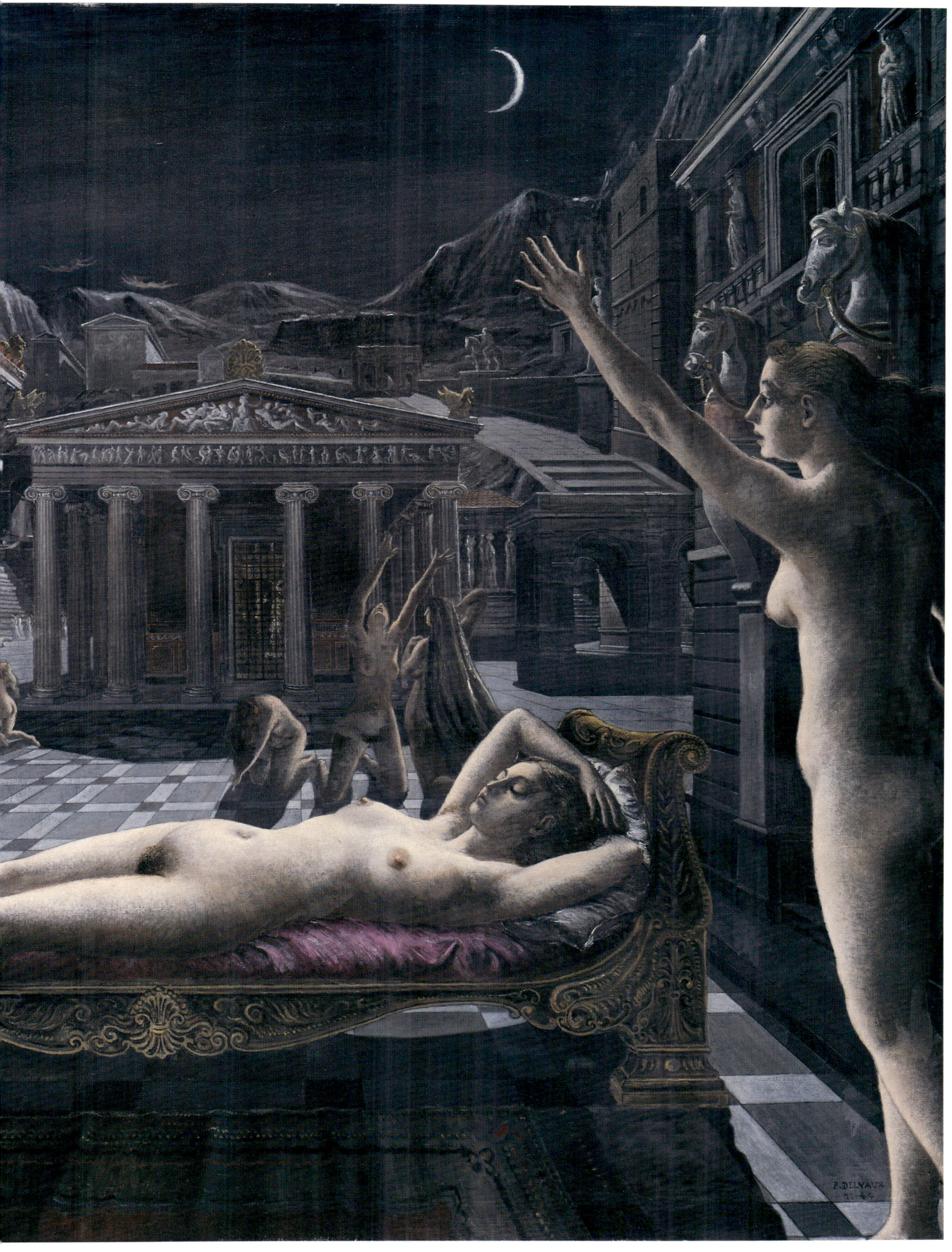

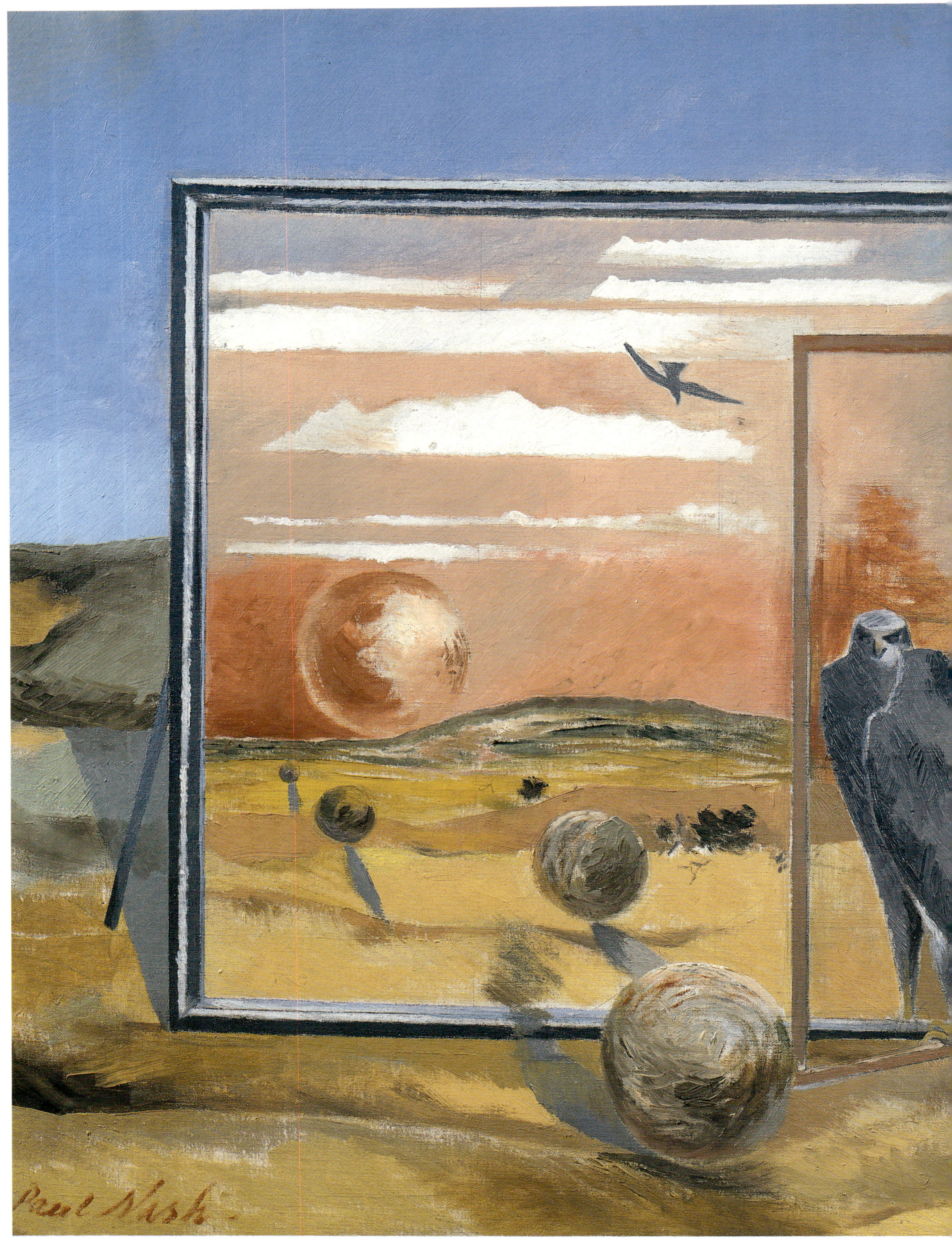

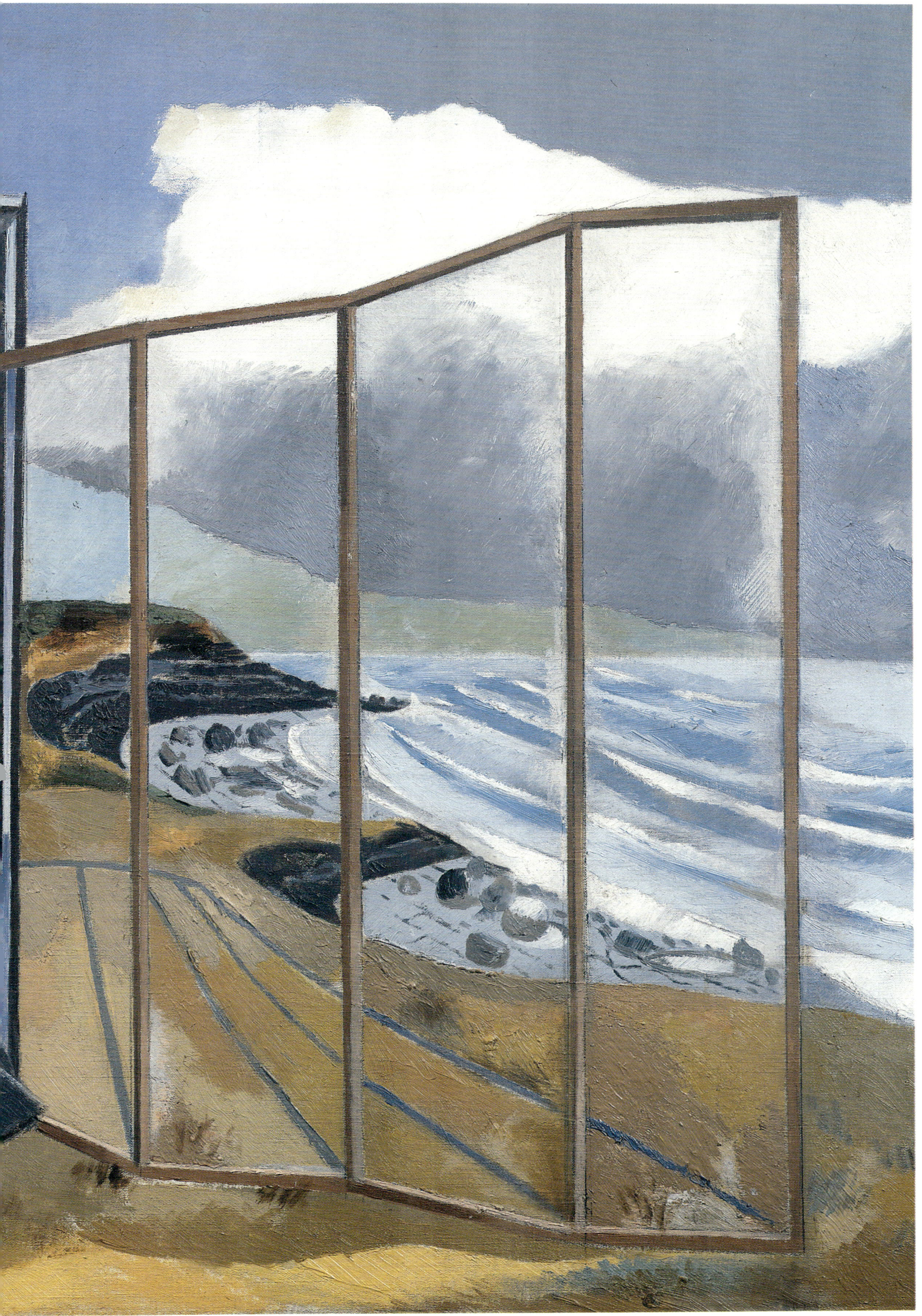

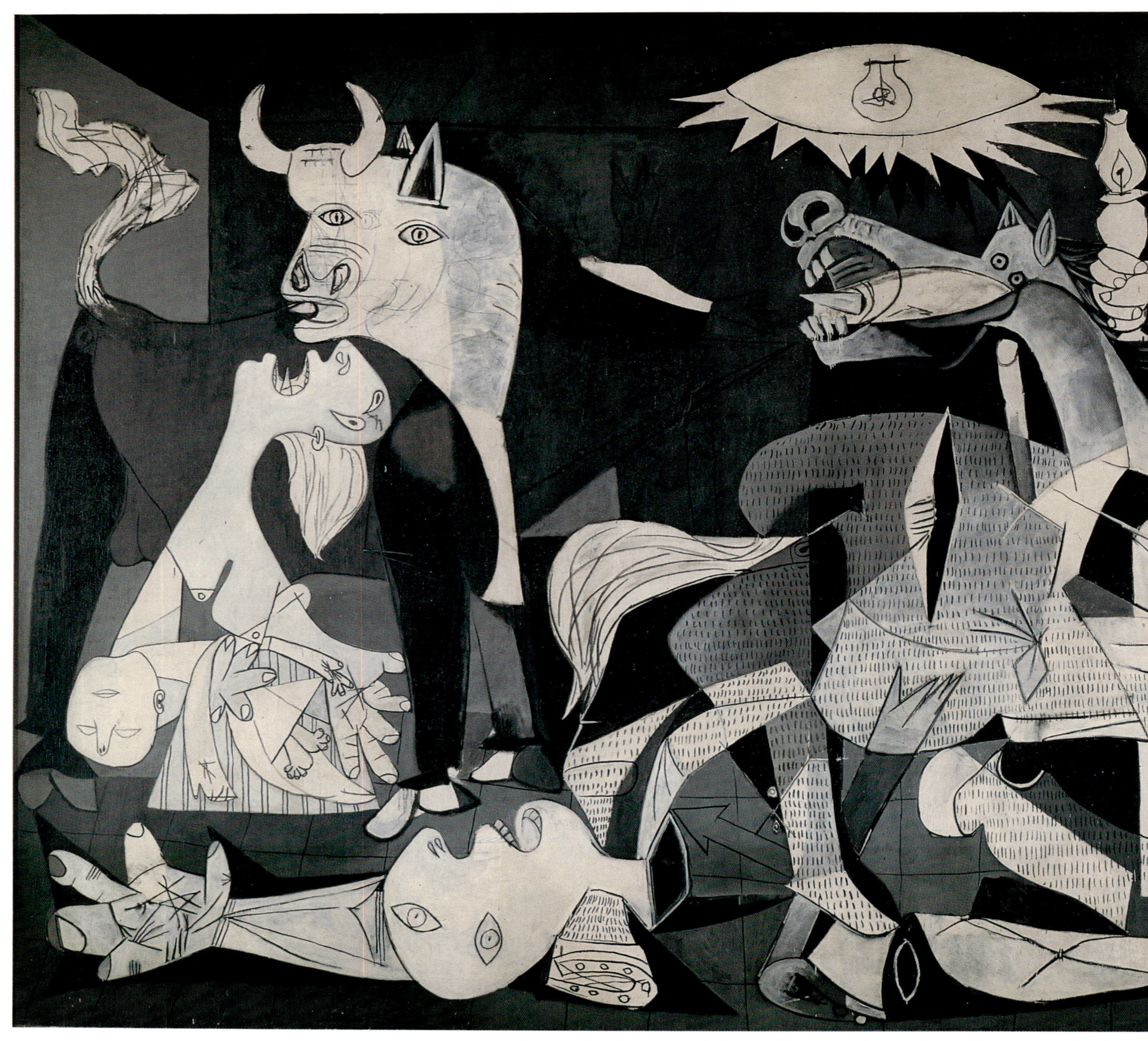

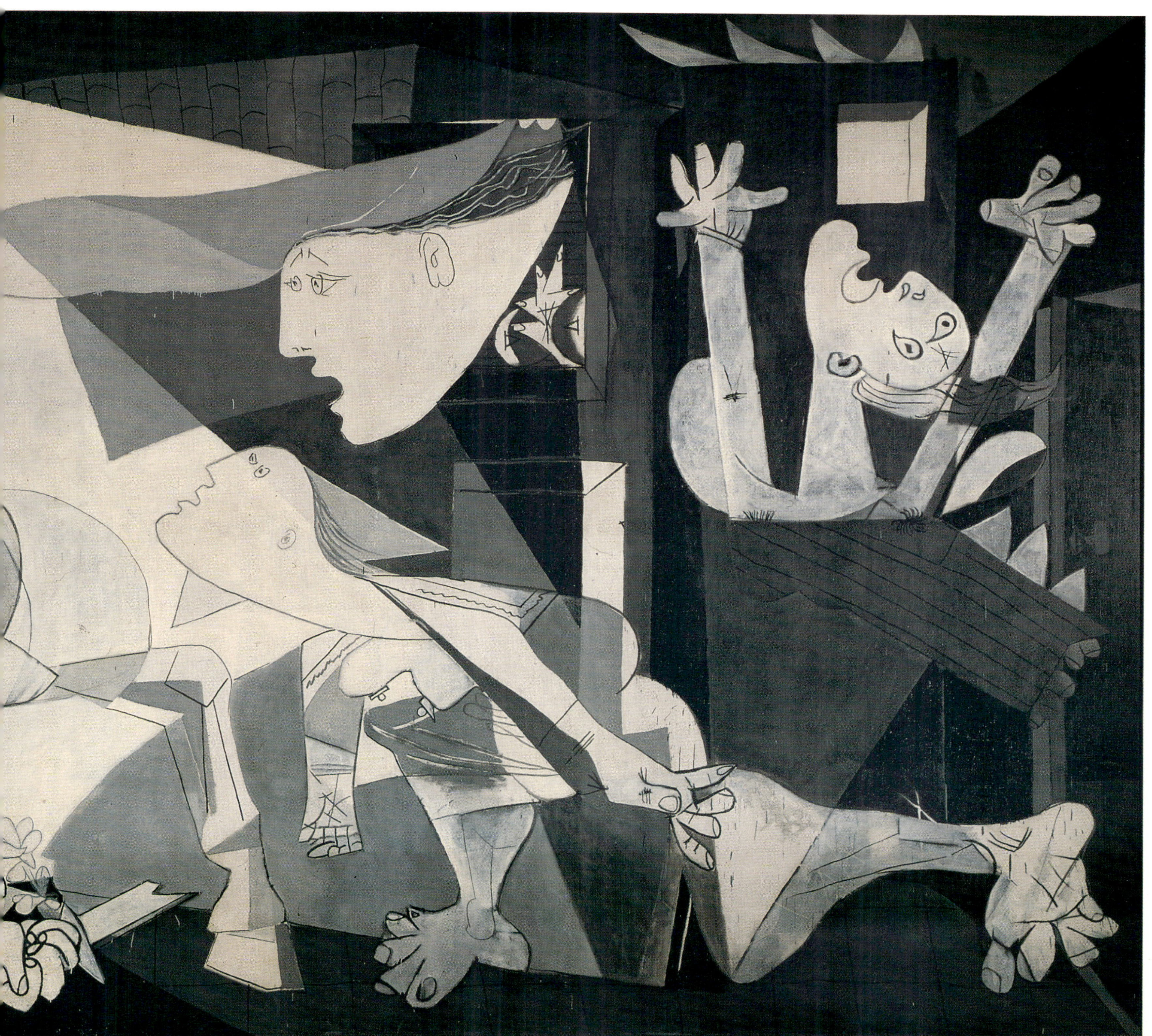

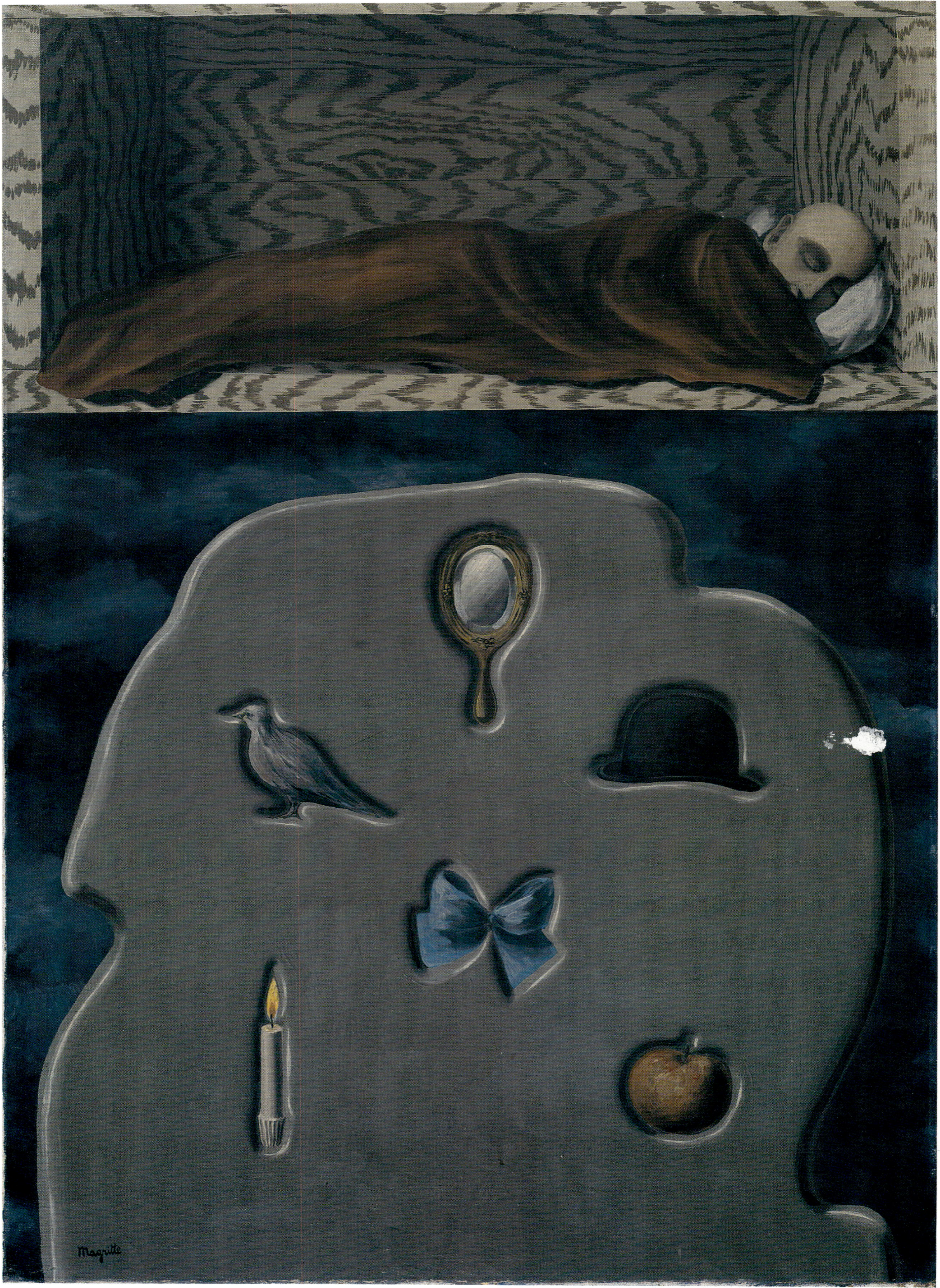

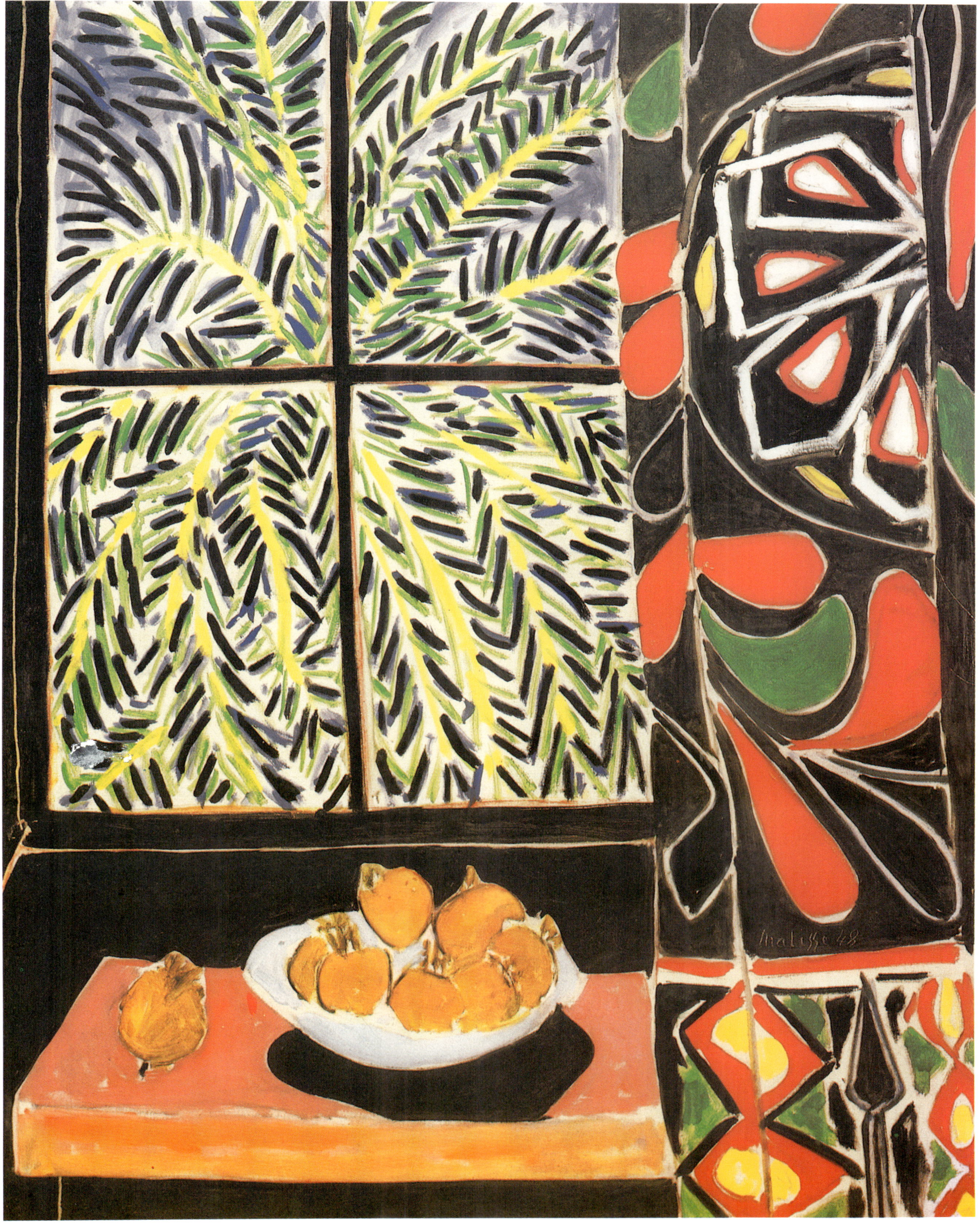

Chronology

	World Events	Visual Arts	Culture
1940	Fall of France Battle of Britain The Blitz	Klee: *Captive* Ernst: *Europe after the Rain* (1940-41) Davis: *Hot Still-scape for Six Colors*	Hemingway: *For Whom the Bell Tolls* O'Neill: *Long Day's Journey Into Night* Chandler: *Farewell my Lovely* Disney: *Fantasia*
1944	D-Day landings in Normandy Extensive air-raids in Europe	Delvaux: *Venus Asleep* Graves: *Brid Maddened by the Sound of Machinery in the Air* Gorky: *The Liver is the Cock's Comb*	J-P Sartre: *Huis Clos (Vicious Circle)* Copland: *Appalachian Spring* Bartók: *Sonata for Unaccompanied Violin*
1946	United Nations founded Cold War begins Nuremberg Trials	Hopper: *Approaching a City*	Prokofiev: *War and Peace* O'Neill: *The Iceman Cometh*
1948	Assassination of Ghandi	Matisse: *Interior with Egyptian Curtain*	A Huxley: *Ape and Essence*
1949	Federal Republic in West Germany	Newman: *Covenant*	Miller: *Death of a Salesman*
1952	US explodes first hydrogen bomb Accession of Elizabeth II	Pollock: *Convergence* De Staël: *Figure by the Sea* Levine: *Gangster Funeral*	Hemingway: *The Old Man and the Sea*
1953	Death of Stalin Korean armistice	Motherwell: *Elegy to the Spanish Republic #34* (1953-54) Rothko: *Green and Maroon on Blue*	Miller: *The Crucible* Britten: *Spring Symphony*
1956	Suez Crisis Hungarian revolution	Nolan: *Glenrowan* (1956-57)	Osborne: *Look Back in Anger* Bergman: *The Seventh Seal*
1957	Foundation of the EEC USSR launches Sputniks	Still: *1957-D No 1* Francis: *The Whiteness of the Whale*	Kerouac: *On the Road* Stockhausen: *Piano Piece XI*
1959	Cuban revolutions led by Castro	Vasarely: *Supernovae* (1959-61) Hofmann: *Pompeii* Johns: *Numbers in Color*	Grass: *The Tin Drum*
1960	Election of President Kennedy	Morris Louis: *Theta* Picasso: *Le Déjeuner sur l'Herbe*	Ionesco: *Rhinoceros* Pinter: *The Caretaker* Hitchcock: *Psycho* Fellini: *La Dolce Vita*
1961	Berlin Wall built Yuri Gagarin first man in space	Bacon: *Seated Man With Turkey Rug* Smith: *Panatella* Rivers: *Parts of the Face*	Williams: *Night of the Iguana* J Anouilh: *Becket*
1962	Algeria becomes independent Cuban missile crisis US astronauts in space	Warhol: *100 Cans* Stella: *Hyena Stomp*	Britten: *War Requiem* Coventry Cathedral consecrated
1965	US offensive in Vietnam Rhodesian unilateral declaration of independence War between India and Pakistan	Kelly: *Red Green Blue*	Schönberg: *Moses and Aaron*, first complete performance in London Bernstein: *Chichester Psalms*
1967	Six Day War between Israel and Arab States Che Guevara killed in Bolivia	Hockney: *A Bigger Splash* Riley: *Late Morning* Estes: *Food Shop*	Lowell: *Near the Water*
1968	Election of President Nixon Martin Luther King assassinated Senator Robert Kennedy assassinated Russian invasion of Czechoslovakia	Wesselmann: *Great American Nude* Hamilton: *Swingeing London* (1968-69)	Solzhenitsyn: *Cancer Ward* Kubrik: *2001: A Space Odyssey*
1972	Apollo 17, longest US lunar mission	Albers: *Homage to the Square* Close: *Nat*	Mishima: *Spring Snow*
1973	US troops withdraw from Vietnam Oil Crisis	Kiefer: *Father, Son, and Holy Ghost* Eddy: *New Shoes For H* (1973-74)	Solzhenitsyn: *Gulag Archipelago*
1975	Death of Franco, Spain President Ford on State visit to China	Penck: *Metaphysical Passage Through a Zebra* Caulfield: *After Lunch* Hodgkin: *Dinner at Smith Square* (1975-79)	
1977	Death of Mao Tse Tung Cambodia breaks relations with Vietnam	Dubuffet: *The Ups and Downs*	Grass: *The Flounder*
1982	Argentinian invasion of the Falklands First artificial heart transplant, Salt Lake City	Schnabel: *Winter*	Marquez: *Chronicle of a Death Foretold* Herzog: *Fitzcarraldo*
1983	US cruise missiles at British air bases	Baselitz: *Supper in Dresden* Kitaj: *Cecil Court WC2: The Refugees* (1983-84)	
1984	Indira Ghandhi, Prime Minister of India, is assassinated	Freud: *Portrait of the Artist's Mother*	Joffé: *The Killing Fields*
1985	Terrorist attacks at Rome and Vienna airports	John Walker: *Conversation*	
1987	Crisis on stock markets	·Rothenberg: *Vertical Spin* (1986-87)	New Clore Gallery at Tate Gallery opens

America
and after

World War II marked the end of Paris as the center of the art world and the impetus shifted to the United States. The German occupation of France meant that important European artists, many of whom were refugees in France, fled to the United States to work there, Ernst, Mondrian, Léger and Marcel Duchamp among them. America already contained magnificent collections of twentieth-century painting, and public attitudes to modern art had been given major impetus as long before as 1913 with that watershed of American cultural life, the Armory Show. This exhibition was visited in New York, Chicago and Boston by over a quarter of a million people.

The New York Armory Show (so-called because it was exhibited at the 69th Regiment Armory between February and March 1913) was formed by a radical group of native artists to exhibit both their own work and that of the most innovative foreign artists. The controversial International section of the show concentrated in the main on works produced in Paris at the time, including major paintings by Picasso and Braque, and, the focus of much critical attention, *Nude Descending a Staircase* by the 26-year-old Marcel Duchamp. The huge exhibition, containing some 1600 works, was a source of both controversy and acclaim. It is generally agreed that from the time of the Armory Show, twentieth-century painting became the live issue in American life that continues today. However, it is the work of the painters who largely resisted the influence of European modernism that must first be considered here.

Among the organizers of the Armory Show and one of the founders of both the Society of Independent Artists and the New Society of Painters was George Bellows. Bellows was at the forefront of much of radical American painting at the time, and an influential printmaker and teacher. His work reflects the influence of the American realist painters of the so-called Ashcan school in its realism. In his time Bellows, who died at the age of 42, was famous for depictions of such sporting scenes as the Dempsey-Firpo fight in 1923 which he both painted and lithographed, but his fame today tends to be concentrated on his portraiture. Bellows explained his own work in the following manner: 'I have no desire to destroy the past. I am deeply moved by the great works of former times, but I refuse to be limited by them.'

Distinctively American also is the work of Grandma Moses and the Iowan painter Grant Wood. Grandma Moses (whose real name was Anna Mary Robertson) did not begin painting until she was in her seventies, when arthritis in her fingers made embroidery difficult for her. *Hoosick Falls, Winter* shows the area of her home in upstate New York, and the charm which her naive vision and natural but untutored skill could produce. Although his work superficially resembles that of Grandma Moses, Grant Wood was altogether a different kind of painter. He began as a craftsman in metal at Cedar Rapids, Iowa and learned to paint at the Art Institute of Chicago and, briefly, at the Académie Julian, Paris. In 1942 he went to Munich to supervise the making of stained-glass windows to his design and discovered the works of the early German and Flemish masters that were to become the major formative influence on his work. Such a work as the celebrated *American Gothic* (1930), in its sharp detail, rigidly frontal postures and the hard, staring gaze of the figures recalls the work of such fifteenth-century masters as Hans Memlinc. Although Wood himself claimed that 'all the good ideas I ever had came to me while I was milking a cow,' his precise observation is combined with a knowing use of past forms. The social observation and sharply-lit, almost hallucinatory exactitude of his forms may be compared to the work of his German contemporary, Otto Dix who derived his style from similar sources.

The Lithuanian-born painter and graphic artist Ben Shahn came to the United States as a boy of eight. He worked as a lithographer until 1930, with a sharp eye for the social and political dilemmas of his time. His social awareness was heightened by two visits to Europe in the late 1920s in exploration of his European/Jewish roots, and much of his work is devoted to the isolation and alienation of dwellers in big cities. In the 1930s Shahn worked on a number of mural projects commissioned by government agencies, such as the Federal Security Building in Washington. His best-known murals are perhaps those at the Rockefeller Center on which he worked with the Mexican muralist, Diego Rivera.

Rivera's influence can be seen in *The Passion of Sacco and Vanzetti* (1931-32) commemorating the celebrated case and subject of a state investigation of 1920-27. Shahn devoted 23 paintings to the subject; here his precise technique and distorted, near-Surrealist use of space are devoted to the declared aim of his world: 'The making of a picture is an experience of intense and protracted awareness . . . communicating its pitch and intensity and arousing a responsive awareness within those persons who look at it.'

Social satire of a different form is seen in the work of Jack Levine. Levine's biting draughtsmanship is enhanced by his expressionistic use of paint. Although Levine declared 'considerations of modernity fill me with horror,' such a characteristic subject as *Gangster Funeral* of 1952 shows Levine's indebtedness to Expressionism, particularly to the work of Soutine and Rouault, in its expressive brushwork and distortion of space. The enlargement of the heads of his subjects is also characteristic of Levine, as is the flickering light in the painting and the inclusion of the spectator's viewpoint into the picture's space. This last pictorial device of drawing the spectator into the picture, here contrived by the grouping of the figures and the extraordinary foreshortening of the coffin derives from seventeenth-century Baroque art: the composition is reminiscent of Rembrandt's *Anatomy Lesson of Dr Tulp.*

Edward Hopper is the best known of the artists of the American scene. Hopper worked in what has been called the interpretative realist mode, decisively American in both style and subject matter. His three early European visits seem to have had little influence on his style. Indeed in 1950 Hopper declared that 'the nation's art is greatest when it most reflects the character of its people. . . The domination of France in the plastic arts has been almost complete for the past thirty years or more in this country. If an apprenticeship to a master has been necessary, I think we have served it.' Although Hopper exhibited his first painting at the Armory Show in 1913, he was fifty before he found his distinctive style and lived in voluntary isolation in New York City, the better to observe his subject matter, the human loneliness of big city life. In his sparsely populated cityscapes, Hopper paints his human subjects in public places, cafés, offices, hotels, cinemas, railroad stations: the figures are observed from unexpected angles, either from very high or very low viewpoints or glimpsed through windows. However, many of his most remarkable paintings are unpeopled. *Approaching a City* (1946) shows Hopper's mastery of the fabric of the city – the blank windows, the masses of the architecture and the railroad track convey an air of disquiet as the track plunges into the darkness of the tunnel. Hopper uses this metaphor of the transitory nature of modern life, so potent in the literature, music and film of the time, to telling effect. The idea of displacement and transience is central to his work. Such paintings have an accessibility and universality that is rare in the art of the period.

While the influence of European modernism was resisted by some American artists, by others it was embraced with enthusiasm. For Stuart Davis, a precocious realist painter of 19, the Armory Show was 'the greatest shock to me – the greatest single influence I have experienced.' He absorbed Cubist influence into his work along with the strong colors and urban and domestic subjects of Léger yet remained essentially American, as Arshile Gorky expressed it in 1931: 'this man, this American, this pioneer, this modest painter who never disarranges his age. . . who renders new forms and new objects.' A year in Paris in 1928 strengthened and clarified Davis's style of large, simplified forms and specifically American subject matter such as *Lucky Strike* (1921). Typically, Davis's compositions often incorporate the lettering, signs and other everyday details of American life that were to be an important influence on Pop Art of the 1960s. The subject matter of *Hot Still-Scape for Six Colors – 7th Avenue Style* (1940) is explained by Davis as 'well within the everyday experience of any modern city dweller. Fruit and flowers; kitchen utensils; Fall skies; horizons; taxi-cabs; . . .fast travel; electric signs; dynamics of city sights and sounds; these and a thousand more are common experience and they are the basic subject matter which my picture celebrates.' He added that it is '7th Avenue Style because I have had my studio on Seventh Avenue for 15 Years.' Like Léger, Davis conveys his own pleasure in the everyday sights and sounds of the metropolis in bright, hot color, conveying a cheerful busyness that is recognizably American.

Davis was not alone in his use of specifically American machine and urban imagery. Charles Demuth's *I Saw the Figure 5 in Gold* of 1928 uses signwriting devices and magazine layout techniques to convey William Carlos Williams's poem 'The Great Figure': 'I saw the figure 5/in gold on a red/firetruck/moving/tense/unheeded/to gong/clangs/siren howls/and wheels rumbling/through the dark city.' Such a specifically American everyday experience is depicted with reference to Cubist and Futurist techniques to convey the dynamism of the vehicle as it moves and the '5' appears to approach and recede again. Demuth ingeniously includes his own initials, as well as Williams's Christian and middle names into the composition.

The elegant Demuth, who was also a doctor, had studied in Paris until the outbreak of World War I, and later became a close friend of Marcel Duchamp. He invented what he termed 'poster portraits' such as this oil painting of his friends in artistic and literary circles, including symbolic 'portraits' of the playwright Eugene O'Neill and the painter Georgia O'Keeffe. Demuth's work owes not a little to avant-garde movements in Europe and yet retains an elegance and distinction that is specifically his own.

Joseph Stella was born in Italy and emigrated to America at the age of 19. He met Boccioni and the Italian Futurists and from 1913 began to paint American themes in a style heavily influenced by theirs. The most famous of these themes is that of the Brooklyn Bridge, a structure that had fascinated him since his arrival in America. In his *Autobiographical Notes*, he explained his excitement at finding 'America so rich with so many new motives to be translated into a new art. . . A new architecture was created, a new perspective.' He interpreted the towers and cables of the bridge in a series of huge canvases, *New York Interpreted* (1920-22), that attempted to convey the dynamism of New York. *Bridge* of 1936 is a later reworking of the same theme, refined and monumental in its rendering of the obsession Stella termed 'the shrine containing all the efforts of the new civilisation of America,' and moving him as if 'in the presence of a new DIVINITY.' Indeed the painting has the aspect of an altarpiece with its soaring lines and paired pointed arches. The effect of a religious panel is heightened by the inclusion of the lighted circles at the base of the composition which are reminiscent of the subsidiary 'predella' panels of fifteenth-century altarpieces. Stella's colors here are simplified to the colors of the metropolis at night, black, gray, whites and blues that seem to scintillate in their brightness.

American painting of the period is not confined to depictions of the urban scene. The much traveled Marsden Hartley was familiar with European trends from the first decade of the century and traveled to Europe for the first time between 1912 and 1914, exhibiting with *Die Blaue Reiter* in 1913 and painting a richly colored and powerfully symbolic abstraction *Portrait of a German Officer* in 1914. Hartley traveled from Mexico to Switzerland treating his landscapes in an expressionistic manner, apparently searching for a sense of permanence in life and landscape, settling finally in his native Maine for the last ten years of his life for what is generally agreed to be his finest period. Hartley wrote of his own work in the following terms: 'I would rather be sure that I had placed two colors in true relationship to each other than to have exposed a wealth of emotionalism gone wrong in the name of richness of personal expression.'

From Hartley's generation come several painters who, like him, form a link between the artistic avant-garde of the Armory Show years and such mid-century painters as Mark Rothko. Arthur Dove, who gave up his career as a successful illustrator and cartoonist in 1912 for a life of considerable hardship as a painter, reached a turning point in his life on an extended visit to Paris in 1907 to 1908 in the first years of the Fauve and Cubist movements. In evolving his abstract style in the 1920s Dove declared 'I don't like titles for these pictures, because they should tell their own story.' The sea was an important part of Dove's life and work. He lived and painted for a period on a houseboat he sailed around Long Island Sound and in the years of his final illness lived in an old converted post office on the edge of Long Island. *Motor Boat* (1938) with its rich, glowing colors, shows Dove's use of simplified forms to depict the boat's prow as it cuts through the water and the landscape beyond, all 'simplified' as Dove has it 'in most cases, to color and force lines and substances, just as music has done with sound.'

Milton Avery, although younger than Dove, was also influenced by his rural background: he lived in Connecticut and exhibited first in New York at the age of 42, working in an Impressionistic style. After this first group show he was introduced to the work of Picasso's early Rose period which influenced his work and to the work of Matisse, the strongest influence on his style. This can be seen in the flat blocks of color employed in *Clear Cut Landscape* (1951). Color is of essential importance in Avery's work. As Avery himself described his working methods: 'The two-dimensional design is important, but not so important as the design in depth. I do not use linear perspective, but achieve depth by color – the function of one color with another.' When Avery died in 1965, Mark Rothko paid tribute to the older painter, whose work was seen as a crucial influence by the Abstract Expressionists: 'his is the poetry of sheer loveliness, of sheer beauty. Thanks to him this kind of poetry has been able to survive in our time.'

From a similar background in the mid-West came Georgia O'Keeffe. From 1916 she was one of the group of young artists promoted by the photographer Alfred Stieglitz at his gallery of avant-garde European and American art familiarly known as 291. O'Keeffe is famous for her austere landscapes, simplified architectural forms and giant-size flowers seen in close-up, paintings that are part-abstract, part-representational. *White Canadian Barn No 2* is characteristic of her use of isolated forms that fill the picture space with a clean-cut monumentality, a characteristic seen from the 1930s in her work when she and Stieglitz, whom she had married in 1924, spent their summers in New Mexico. *White Canadian Barn* shows her immaculate line and precision of form in a characteristically unpeopled landscape. On Stieglitz's death in 1946, O'Keeffe moved permanently to New Mexico, whose vastness and color she often celebrated in her landscapes. O'Keeffe survived into her hundredth year.

A contemporary of O'Keeffe whose work was of major importance for the succeeding generation of American artists was Hans Hofmann, born in Germany. Hofmann spent his formative years in Munich where he later worked, and in Paris from 1904 until 1914, crucial years for the development of European art. Hofmann shared a studio with Matisse who became a major influence on his work, and met Picasso and Delaunay and other avant-garde artists of this exciting period. Hofmann is of crucial importance as a teacher, first in Munich from 1915 and then in the United States after 1930. As he expressed it: 'I opened my school. . .to clarify the then entirely new pictorial approach.' Hofmann's 'new approach' shaped a generation of American painting and critical theory through his work at the Hans Hofmann School for Fine Arts in New York from 1932 until he retired from teaching in 1958. Hofmann's own painting had a late flowering when at the age of 78 he was able to close his school and devote himself to painting.

His influential essays such as *Search for the Real* published in 1948, emphasized the importance of the picture plane: 'the creative element of all the plastic arts, painting, sculpture, architecture and related arts. Colors, commonly color-bearing planes, are creative elements in painting.' Hofmann's stressing of the picture surface can be seen in *Pompeii*, and the brilliant color complementary pairings of yellow and blue, red and green can be read as Cubist-derived natural forms. The images in the picture appear to change to the view — Hofmann demands that the spectator work hard at the painting. He used his own works in his teaching practice, teaching that color is a 'means of creating intervals,' and that depth could be created not by the use of traditional perspective but 'by the creation of forces in the sense of *push and pull*' shown in *Pompeii* by the parallel fields of opposing colors, that give a sense of shifting balance.

These theories, particularly the 'push and pull' theory and Hofmann's own painting practice which involved radical forms of expressive paint application that stressed the two-dimensionality of the picture surface made a huge impact on two generations of Abstract Expressionism in America. Arshile Gorky was of a later generation of painters who emigrated to America, and his work was recognized posthumously as belonging to Abstract Expressionism, although the sources of his work are many and various and his painting practice differs in many respects. He is perhaps more appropriately regarded both as a transitional figure in American painting and as an artist of considerable interest in his own right. Gorky was born in Turkish Armenia and emigrated to the United States at the age of 15 in 1920, changing his name to Gorky ('the bitter one' in Russian) after the Russian writer Maxim Gorky. Gorky's was a tragic life, with but a few stable years after his marriage in 1941, before a series of disastrous happenings in 1946 that included the burning down of his studio and his own operation for cancer. After a severe automobile accident two years later he committed suicide. Gorky drew on both the culture of his native country and his personal experience in much of his work. This was blended with a precise knowledge of many of the most radical movements of the twentieth century, derived from his study of contemporary painting in New York. American collections both public and private were particularly rich in the work of modern masters at this time. In 1942, for example, Peggy Guggenheim's Art of This Century Gallery in New York was opened which exhibited the famous Guggenheim collection of Cubist, Futurist and Surrealist works together with works by such radical contemporary American painters as Jackson Pollock.

Gorky was particularly influenced by Kandinsky and Miro, although his passionate study of contemporary and past masters resulted in a highly personal style of what might be termed Abstract Surrealism, a more accurate term in describing such works as *The Liver is the Cock's Comb* (1944). The significance of this work was recognized by the father-figure of Surrealism, André Breton. Breton wrote that *'The Liver is the Cock's Comb* should be considered the great open door to the analogy world. Easy-going amateurs will come here for their meager rewards in spite of all warnings to the contrary, they will insist on seeing in these compositions a still life, a landscape, or a figure instead of daring to face the hybrid forms in which all human emotion is precipitated. . . Here is an art entirely new.'

The melancholy that is so marked a feature of Gorky's mature style can be seen in the work despite the brilliant colors and the seemingly spontaneous working of the picture surface. In fact Gorky's working methods indicate the careful planning and draftsmanship that underpin the apparently improvisatory nature of such a large-scale work as this.

The strange, dream-like shapes are dominated by Breton's 'hybrid forms' of liver and cock's comb which are seen on the right. Gorky makes reference to the Greek belief that the liver was the seat of the soul in an expressive and personal image of considerable power.

The terms 'Abstract Expressionism' or 'Action Painting' although not synonymous and of limited usefulness are often applied to the work of a number of painters born between 1903 and 1915, most of whom worked in New York, and were in consequence termed 'New York School Painters.' The painters were influenced both by the new emphasis on Surrealist and psychoanalytic techniques brought to America during the war years by such leading figures as Max Ernst, Duchamp, Salvador Dali, Tanguy and André Breton. The presence of such important figures of the Modern Movement in New York after the Fall of France in 1940 served as a powerful influence on such painters as Pollock and de Kooning, who were working in considerable isolation and to whom success was slow in coming.

Abstract Expressionism had its genesis in both Cubism and Expressionism, but it was Surrealism that gave it birth, and Breton's definition of Surrealism is helpful in approaching an understanding of Abstract Expressionism: 'purely psychic automatism through which we undertake to express. . .the actual functioning of thought, thoughts dictated apart from any control by reason and any aesthetic or moral consideration. Surrealism rests upon belief in the higher reality of specific forms of associations, previously neglected, in the omnipotence of dreams and in the disinterested play of thinking.'

The painters who first came to public notice during the War and may inexactly be described as Abstract Expressionists were diverse in their expression and technique, although both the dynamism of their work and their predominantly existential attitude were hugely influential in both America and Europe. Indeed Abstract Expression was so influential in its domination of American painting at one time that it is often described as the new orthodoxy of the postwar period.

The most celebrated figure of American painting in the postwar period was undoubtedly Jackson Pollock. Pollock was born in Wyoming, moved to Arizona when young and grew up in Southern California. His work is permeated with the consciousness of the power of his native landscape and his awareness was enhanced by a geological study of the Grand Canyon in which he participated on leaving school. He studied at the Art Students' League, and admired the work of Diego Rivera and other Mexican muralists. The mythical qualities of such ephemeral art as Pueblo Indian techniques of forming ritual images with trickles of sand (so-called sandpainting) and the ritual art of Indian masks were also highly influential on his work. He was to describe his later influential method of working from all sides of the canvas as it lay on the floor with poured paint (Pollock's celebrated 'action painting' or 'gestural painting' technique) as 'akin to the methods of the Indian sand painters of the West.'

Guardians of the Secret (1943) was first shown at Peggy Guggenheim's Art of This Century Gallery, that famous center for Surrealist art. Indeed the Surrealist advocation of automatism is central to the work, as are the psychoanalytic theories of Freud and Jung (Pollock underwent intermittent Jungian analysis from 1943). The flanking, totem-like figures, the guardians of the title are fused on the picture plane with the cryptic symbols of the central 'secret.' The representational nature of Pollock's art at this period is nowhere better conveyed than by the third guardian, a large dog, an accessible image in powerful contrast to the personal and abstract nature of the richly worked mythic forms of the 'secret.' The rough, expressive brushstrokes of the central panel of the painting which seem to have a life and nervous energy of their own were to be developed over the next few years in such works as *Convergence* so that the process of painting itself became of paramount importance. Pollock described his work in the following statement, which is central to the understanding of Abstract Expressionism: 'When I am *in* my painting, I'm not aware of what I'm doing. It is only after a sort of 'get acquainted' period that I see what I have been about. I have no fears about making changes, destroying the image, etc., because the painting has a life of its own. I try to let it come through. It is only when I lose contact with the painting that the result is a mess. Otherwise there is pure harmony, an easy give and take, and the painting comes out well.'

The energy and gestural nature of Pollock's work – the 'action-painting' aspect of Abstract Expressionism that first engaged the public's attention – is also found in the work of the Dutch-born Willem de Kooning, although the results are radically different. Indeed, forty years on de Kooning is often considered to be the key figure rather than Pollock, who lived more in the public eye and died in an automobile accident in 1956.

De Kooning, schooled in the European tradition, left his native Rotterdam at the age of 22 and shared a close working relationship with Gorky, both painters' early work being influenced by Miro and Kandinsky. De Kooning's first exhibition consisted of black and white abstract paintings, using enamel housepaints for their immediacy and ease of execution. In 1950 he began painting the first of his series of *Woman* paintings, only to abandon it after some 18 months' work. The art historian Meyer Schapiro persuaded him to continue with this figurative and violent work, which was developed into a series of six controversial paintings whose seeming spontaneity is deceptive. The fracturing and distortion of the female figure, reminiscent in some respects of Picasso's *Demoiselles d'Avignon* was taken, forty years later, to extremes in *Excavation* (1950).

This monumental canvas has the underlying structure of a Cubist painting. De Kooning described Cubism as 'a poetic frame where something could be possible, where the artist could practice his intuition.' The forms that appear and disappear within this structure are abstract yet, as Kooning has said 'even abstract shapes must have a likeness,' and the 'likeness' here is to dislocated parts of the female anatomy, including disturbing eye forms that seem to engage the eyes of the spectator.

Mark Tobey's work, although still considered part of the gestural or 'action painting' current of Abstract Expressionism, is markedly different from that of Pollock and de Kooning, who were both of a younger generation. Tobey was raised in the Mid-west and traveled widely to Europe and the Orient, becoming an early convert to the Baha'i World Faith, which had a profound effect on his life and work. He traveled to China with the express intention of studying Chinese brush painting, explaining, 'pressure and release. Each movement like tracks in the snow is recorded and often loved for itself.' Influenced by this ancient technique he developed his famous 'white writing,' described by the artist Lyonel Feininger as 'the handwriting of a painter who has created a new convention of his own, one not yet included in the history of painting.' *Shadow Spirits of the Forest*, as in much of Tobey's work, makes reference in its 'white writing' to the 'electric night' of the contemporary city and at one and the same time to the artist's own rural past in a complex web of associations. The closely worked surface of such a painting reveals Tobey's debt to Zen in the fusion of such subjective realities as the busy metropolis and the Indian mounds near Tobey's childhood home in Wisconsin, described by the artist as 'rounded forms full of fantastic objects never found.' Tobey's work may be seen to be gentler in spirit than Pollock's, although like Pollock's it ranges across the entire canvas 'field.' Significantly Tobey centered his work not on New York but Seattle and spent his final years across the Atlantic in Switzerland.

Robert Motherwell, with a background in philosophy and art history, was perhaps the most intellectual of the Abstract Expressionists, taking up painting fulltime only in his forties while pursuing his diverse careers as teacher, writer and advocate of avant-garde art: he is generally regarded as the spokesman of Abstract Expressionism.

His own work is monumental in scale and often uses the organic black and white forms that dominate such a series as *Elegy to the Spanish Republic* painted from 1948 onward, and numbering over a hundred canvases. The funereal forms of *Elegy to the Spanish Republic #34* (1953-54) represent a nostalgic memory of Motherwell's youth as its subject, a subject commemorated in a very different way in Picasso's *Guernica* of 1937. This canvas of the series has more color than most, and as Motherwell relates: '*#34* is certainly one of the half-dozen most realized of the series. . . it could have had a more "finished" aspect, but I chose to stop at the moment that I thought the expression of feeling was complete, and I do not regret it.'

Although Clyfford's Still's works are generally classified as belonging to the 'color field' range of Abstract Expressionism, Still himself disclaimed any influence whether past or contemporary on his work, rejecting all European art as 'the sterile conclusion of Western European decadence.' He exhibited first in New York in 1945/46, returning to the city in 1950 after a period spent teaching at the Californian School of Fine Arts. Distrustful of the politics of the New York art world for much of his working life, Still lived and worked in Maryland for the last twenty years of his life.

Still desired to eliminate all pictorial representation from his paintings: 'space and figure in my canvases had been resolved into a total psychic entity, freeing me from the limitations of each, yet fusing into an instrument bounded only by the limits of my energy and intuition.' Claiming to paint only for himself and concerned to control the presentation and setting of his work, Still explained that 'each painting is an episode in a personal history, an entry in a journal.' *197-D No 1*, a typically huge canvas, is conceived as part of an organic whole. The canvas has a strong vertical emphasis and the dark, dramatic shapes seem shot through with bright color. Still, in denying any descriptive character to his work, stated: 'Imagination, no longer fettered by the laws of fear, became as one with Vision. And the Art, intrinsic and absolute, was its meaning and the bearer of its passion.'

In 1943 Still had assisted the painters Mark Rothko and Adolf Gottlieb in the writing of a letter to the *New York Times* which made the following assertions about Abstract Expressionism, and might be used still to explain the 'color field' wing of the movement: 'To us art is an adventure into an unknown world, which can be explored only by those willing to take the risks. . .We favor the simple expression of the complex thought. We are for the large shape because it has the impact of the unequivocal. We wish to reassert the picture plane. We are for flat forms because they destroy illusion and reveal truth. . . we profess spiritual kinship with primitive and archaic art.'

The emphasis on color and Rothko's 'large shape' is seen as distinct from Pollock and de Kooning's emphasis on gesture surface, the so-called 'action painting' current of Abstract Expressionism. Rothko's own work and the art of Barnett Newman are generally seen as the final stage of the movement, surviving into the 1960s as 'color field' painting or 'chromatic abstraction' when action painting was only being practiced by de Kooning.

Newman's work is generally termed non-relational, as he paints his single image in relation not to other images on his picture space but to the edges of the canvas, taking the color evenly through the picture in contrast to Pollock and de Kooning's concentration on the center of the canvas.

Newman declared his intention to create 'an art that would suggest the mysterious sublime rather than the beautiful,' a key phrase that does something to explain such a work as *Covenant* of 1949. The Sublime was a term that came into general use in Europe in the eighteenth century to describe a new aesthetic concept of the awe and wonder felt by the spectator in the face of certain of the grander aspects of nature, and, by extension, of art. Newman wrote of mankind's 'poetic outcry . . . of awe and anger at his tragic state, at his own self-awareness and at his own helplessness before the void.' The often monumental size of Newman's work is an essential part of this concept of the Sublime, as are the vast red spaces of such a work as *Covenant.* The thin vertical lines that break through this color field like lightning, serve to emphasize its affinities with the Sublime.

Mark Rothko was born in Dvinsk, Russia and came first to New York as a child of ten. He was to spend all his life there after 1924, participating in artists' movements in the 1930s, and during the Depression in the Works Progress Administration scheme which gave many artists of his generation the opportunity to work on a wide range of projects with Government funding. Rothko's work was influenced by the theories of Jung and Nietzsche, and from the 1940s his work explored Christian and mythical themes in a form that is sometimes described as Abstract Sublime. Rothko praised the limited use of simple shapes: 'the simple expression of the complex thought . . .they have no direct association with any particular visible experience, but in them one recognizes the principle and passion of organisms.' In Rothko's monumental *Green and Maroon on Blue* of 1953, the luminous horizontal planes seem to suggest sky, land and water and trigger the emotions of the viewer by acting as what Rothko himself termed 'measures' of feeling. However, Rothko's works are difficult to interpret, particularly in reproduction, as they need to be experienced in the original: Rothko himself refused to explain his work after 1949.

Like Barnett Newman and Clyfford Still, Rothko considered the presentation of his work of great importance to its understanding, which for him was equated with religious or mystic experience. As he explained in 1947: 'Pictures must be miraculous: the instant one is complete, the intimacy between the creation and the creator is ended. He is an outsider. The picture must be for him, as for anyone experiencing it later, a revelation, an unexpected and unprecedented resolution of an eternally familiar need.' The 'chapel paintings' for the Chapel of the Institute for Religion and Human Development in Houston, Texas were painted in conditions approximating to the unique site in which they would eventually hang. An earlier commission to paint a series of canvases for a specific hall in the Seagram Building in New York now hang in the Tate Gallery, London as Rothko withdrew the paintings when he discovered that the room was to be used as a restaurant – an inappropriate setting for his work.

Allied to Abstract Expressionism, although of a younger generation, is the work of Sam Francis, who spent extensive periods in hospital as a young man being treated for spinal tuberculosis. As he explained: 'In the hospital I was in love with things. I was a prisoner in love with the products of my imagination. So they appeared to me as things embedded in space. The space also was a thing.' Francis took up watercolor painting while immobilized in hospital during World War II and later studied at the California School of Fine Arts where he came under the influence of Rothko who taught there. The floating luminosity and rich color characteristic of Rothko's work was to become a marked feature of Francis's mature style.

Francis went to Paris in 1950 where he lived for the next seven years before journeying to Japan: Japanese art and culture has had an important effect on his work and his reputation both there and in Europe is perhaps higher than in his native America.

The Whiteness of the Whale (1957) is characteristic of Francis's richly colored forms on a white field. His structures, which are often primary colored, appear to resemble cell forms seen under a microscope recalling Francis's medical and psychological studies at the University of California. However the title of the painting is a quotation taken from Herman Melville's *Moby Dick* which consists of a discourse on the subject of 'the elusive something in the innermost idea of this hue (white) which strokes more panic to the soul than the redness which affrights the blood.' The use of a mass of color to enliven a white field echoes Francis's interest in both the sky and oriental art.

The experience of World War II and Oriental art was also influential on the figurative work of a very different artist, Morris Graves. Graves lived and worked in the Pacific Northwest for much of his career, although he first traveled to the Orient as a boy of 17. In 1938 he met Mark Tobey and incorporated Tobey's pictorial language of 'white writing' into his own painting vocabulary, although with different intent, as can be seen in *Bird Maddened by the Sound of Machinery in the Air* (1944) which relates to Graves's experience of the War when, in spite of registering as a conscientious objector, he had to spend a year in military service. Released to his retreat on remote Fidalgo Island in Pughet Sound, he painted a series of works which took as their subject the horrors of war, using the symbolism of birds to express what he termed 'the disheartening discrepancy between the vision and the painting – the transferring with paint – the difficult and limited and often impossible medium of paint.' Graves uses an adapted form of 'white writing' to convey both the ghostly, exposed form of the bird and the space it inhabits as it contemplates the approach of the ominous mechanistic form at the top of the painting. The intrusion into the space occupied by the bird and the attempt to depict a sensation of sound is graphically conveyed with a striking economy of means.

Abstract Expressionism was such a powerful movement by the 1950s that it was described as the 'new orthodoxy.' It placed emphasis both on the expression of the artist's subjectivity and on the high seriousness of artistic activity. As Mark Rothko expressed it: 'Subject matter is crucial, and only that subject matter is crucial which is tragic and timeless.' Pop art, a style developed mainly in the United States and Great Britain in the decade from about 1955 to 1966 may be seen as a reaction against such subjectivity and high seriousness. The American Pop artist Roy Lichtenstein has defined Pop art's radical difference from Abstract Expressionism. Writing in the 1950s he stated that '. . . art has become extremely romantic and unrealistic. . . it has less and less to do with the world, it looks inward,' and on a later occasion: 'Outside is the world, it's there. Pop art looks out into the world.'

The world it looks out into and depicts in such a literal manner is typically that of the contemporary city, a world rich as never before in objects to be consumed in the affluence of the later 1950s and 1960s. American Pop takes as its starting point aspects of everyday urban culture which appeared inappropriate to its first audiences as the subject matter of art. The everyday objects included various popular mass-media forms drawn from comics, packaging and advertisements, Hollywood movies and pop music and entertainment generally; vehicles of various kinds, consumer durables in the home and fast food – from tinned soup to ice cream.

This striking subject matter was treated in a prosaic manner, often on a monumental scale that demanded attention, and in a technique that sometimes incorporated objects from the real world into the structure of the work. This was a technique first used in Cubist collages at the beginning of the century, and developed into one of the central innovations of the Dada and Surrealist movements as the so-called 'ready-made.' The first ready-made was the 1913 *Bicycle Wheel*, a bicycle wheel mounted on a stool, a characteristically 'anti-art' Dadaist object by the French artist Marcel Duchamp. In this respect, American Pop art in particular derived direct impetus from Duchamp, whose *Nude Descending a Staircase* had caused such a sensation at the New York Armory Show of 1913.

Duchamp first came to New York to work in 1915 and had been

based there ever since. Pop artists' (who were first termed 'Neo-Dadaists') use of real objects in their work may be seen to derive from his use of assembled objects in such a complex work as *The Bride Stripped Bare by her Bachelors, Even* (1915-23) which incorporates lead wire and dust from Duchamp's studio between the two glass panels of its supporting structure.

Robert Rauschenberg and Jasper Johns are considered the leading figures of American Pop in the later 1950s. The two were friends, working in neighboring studios and having such avant-garde friends as the composer John Cage and the dancer Merce Cunningham (with whose dance company Rauschenberg has often collaborated as designer). Rauschenberg grew up in Port Arthur, Texas and studied in the late 1940s at the Académie Julian, Paris, then with Josef Albers at the Black Mountain College, North Carolina and finally at the Art Students' League, New York. Rauschenberg started his career as a painter with a series of entirely monochrome paintings, first all-white, then all-black, and finally all-red. After these minimalist experiments, Rauschenberg began his so-called 'combine paintings' of which *Charlene* of 1954 is one of the most famous. He presents his own experience of New York 'a city where you have on one lot a forty-story building and right next to it, you have a little shack.' The unexpectedness of changes of scale in the ten-foot space of the picture area is one of the most striking aspects of the work, as is the combination of collaged postcards, richly worked surface texture (which recalls the gestural mode of the Abstract Expressionists), and the opened umbrella at the top right. Rauschenberg's work asks the spectator to participate in the images he evokes, projecting his or her own ideas and emotions on to the work. It is an activity which has analogies to listening to John Cage's music which the composer describes in *Silence* (1961) as 'New music; new listening. . .an attention to the activity of sounds.'

Rauschenberg's use of past art is a literal one – there are printed reproductions of works by Goya, Degas, two Van Goghs, Vermeer, Renoir and Pieter de Hooch and other painters affixed to the surface of *Charlene* with a postcard of the Statue of Liberty at sunset set apart from the rest at the bottom edge of the picture. The reuse of such 'waste' as the postcards and the torn and painted newspapers and comics elsewhere in the picture, is explained by Rauschenberg as a concern with the transformation of material objects: 'the fact that the material is re-used is, in truth, the paradox. It ceases to be waste. . .Painting relates to both art and life. . . I try to act in that gap between the two.'

Jasper Johns, five years Rauschenberg's junior, arrived in New York in 1952, joining Rauschenberg's circle. He became well known in the 1950s for his series of field paintings, including the American flag sequence and the target series, which became a sensation. The deadpan manner in which Johns presented his familiar images was found shocking by a public grown familiar with the intensely subjective nature of Abstract Expressionism.

Numbers in Color of 1959 is typically commonplace in its apparent subject matter and uses a technique of melted wax mixed with pigment called 'encaustic painting' known from Roman times – this gives the painting a resonant color and richness of surface texture unobtainable by other techniques. Johns sought common images as vehicles for ideas, explaining that his choice of the American flag, for example 'took care of a great deal for me because I didn't have to design it. So I went on to similar things. . . things the mind already knows. That gave me room to work on other levels.' Of his use of numbers in the *Numbers* series paintings, Johns explains: 'I'm certainly not putting the numbers to any use, numbers are used all the time, and what's being done is making something to be looked at.'

The other levels in *Numbers in Color* are complex, as the familiar numbers appear to have no logical sequence and, on such a large scale and removed from any recognizable context seem to appear and disappear as elements in a design, giving the spectator the choice of constructing their meaning. As Johns explains: 'meaning is determined by the use of the thing, the way an audience uses a painting once it is put in public.' Johns's stress on the importance of the spectator's share in the work of art derives from Duchamp and his view of the artist's intention is in strict contrast to Abstract Expressionist theories that a work of art should either reveal the state of mind of the artist or communicate a transcendental experience to the viewer. Johns's words are characteristically matter-of-fact: 'Publicly a work becomes not just intention, but the way it is used. If an artist makes something – or if you make chewing gum and everybody ends up using it as glue, whoever made it is given the responsibility of making glue, even if what he really intends is chewing gum.'

The work of Larry Rivers, who studied with Hans Hofmann from 1947 to 1948, is generally considered to combine Pop art with the painterly qualities of gestural Abstract Expressionist technique, as can be seen in *Parts of the Face* of 1961. The source of the painting (whose subject is the artist's wife) is a language-school diagram, and it is one of a series, where models differ as does the language of the vocabulary labeling, varying from Polish to Persian. As in the work of Stuart Davis earlier in the century, the words become visual objects in themselves as well as denoting verbal information, and there are some parallels with Johns's work. However Rivers's information is given in the stenciled lettering of a language-school diagram or an advertisement, a use of mass media references wholly characteristic of Pop art. The presentation, despite the lively gestural passages of brushwork, particularly about the apparently uncompleted areas of the face, is generally deadpan, in a typical Pop style.

The most famous American Pop artist, famous for his life-style as well as for his work, was Andy Warhol. Born in Pittsburgh, Warhol studied at the Carnegie Institute of Technology and worked in New York throughout the 1950s as a highly successful graphic artist, the only American Pop artist to achieve such a reputation by working directly in the mass media before turning to painting. Warhol exploited the repetitive nature of advertising in the imagery of his paintings, which took as their subjects well-known American icons. Whether it was the most famous painting in the world, the Mona Lisa, a dollar bill, Marilyn Monroe, Elvis Presley or a bottle of Coke these were all instantly recognizable images – part of a common Western culture. They were presented without apparently undergoing any transformation into 'art' as in *100 Cans* (1962), one of Warhol's last direct paintings on canvas, before he developed the practice of silkscreening the images. The hundred cans, meticulously painted, are arranged like a print run or a limitless pile, filling the canvas. The bottom line disappears below the picture plane to suggest an infinite number of cans, which are almost twice life-size. The cans are presented in Warhol's characteristic deadpan manner. He explained his choice of subject by his liking for the particular brand of soup. His prosaic utterances include the famous statement, made in 1968: 'The reason I'm painting this way is because I want to be a machine. . .In the future everybody will be world famous for fifteen minutes. . . if you want to know about Andy Warhol, just look at the surface of my paintings and films and me, and there I am. There's nothing behind it.'

Warhol had started his career as a painter in 1960-61 by using enlarged subjects from comic strips, a device he soon abandoned. Independently, but more or less at the same time, Roy Lichtenstein, the most technically consistent of American Pop artists, began working with such popular imagery because, as he explained: 'Signs and comic strips are interesting as subject matter. There are certain things that are useable, forceful, and vital about commercial art.' Lichtenstein studied at the Art Students' League and at Ohio State University and his early works, drawn from advertising were misunderstood as simply enlarged versions of his commonplace sources. Lichtenstein explained that 'My work is actually different from comic strips in that every mark is really in a different place, however slight the difference seems to some.'

In the face of the actual canvases the differences are clear enough. Lichtenstein does not simply mimic the mechanical processes used in comics: the dots in his paintings for example form abstract patterns, of interest in themselves and of course the paintings are of monumental size. The two canvases forming *Whaam!* (1963), for example, measure some nine feet in width. In the 1960s Lichtenstein's work derived from comic strip subject matter is divided into three distinct groupings: science fiction, war and love and romance. All three groupings combine the conventional word and image comic strip form, although often, as in *Whaam!*, the subject is of Lichtenstein's invention. Preparatory drawings show that the painting was originally devised for only one canvas, the work was developed into two panels of the same size showing both the fighter plane and the plane it is shooting down, with the added dimension of, as Lichtenstein himself expressed it: 'one painting shooting another.' *Whaam!* emphasizes the explosion in close-up – another favorite device of comic-strip. The two canvases give the effect of a giant comic book and the strong diagonals of the compositon form a strong linking device between the two. The violence of the subject is in the strictest contrast to the dead-pan fastidiousness of the technique, giving the whole work an ironic sophistication typical of the artist.

Tom Wesselmann is best known for the series of works entitled *Great American Nude* which date from the early 1960s. Wesselmann trained at the Cincinnati Art Academy and the Cooper Union Art School in New York, experimenting from 1960 with mixed media including collage. Some of the *Great American Nude* series have collaged still-life elements that are incorporated into the painting in an illusionistic manner that emphasizes the flatness of his faceless female nudes. Wesselmann's *Great American Nude No 57* uses the tradition of the reclining female nude common in Western painting from the Roman period to Titian's Renaissance nudes and Manet's *Olympia* of 1865. This type of nude presupposes a male viewer and was taken over as a photographic form in mass-circulation magazines such as *Playboy*. In his satirical comment on the values of contemporary society, Wesselmann makes his nude as much an object of consumption as the flowers or fruit in the background, emphasizing the depersonalized eroticism of the image by its isolation and facelessness. Wesselmann acknowledges a debt to Matisse's series of reclining 'Odalisques,' or nudes with an Eastern setting, and sometimes includes versions of these paintings in his pictures. The glossiness of the polymer paint used by the artist emphasizes the slickness of the image and its large scale underlines its affinities with advertising billboards.

Although not a Pop artist in the same sense, Richard Lindner also makes shrewd comment on the popular imagery of the period in his works. In the case of *Rock-Rock* (1966-67), he comments on the importance of the pop idol in contemporary Western culture. Lindner was brought up in Nuremberg and fled to America at the age of 23. *Rock-Rock* shows his interest in performance art as well as his use of a rigid frontality and bright color that gives his work an almost heraldic appearance. The androgynous rock idol who overwhelms the picture-space by filling it so completely, appears bisected by the guitar, that at one and the same time seems part of his/her body. The disturbing effect of such an image is enhanced by the harsh synthetic color and large size of the painting as well as by such details as the mirror lenses and mask-like face of the figure.

Pop art in Britain was a simultaneous yet separate development. In 1953, at the Institute of Contemporary Arts in London, a group of young artists, writers and architects calling themselves the Independents'

Group staged an exhibition called 'Parallel of Art and Life,' following it a year later with an exhibition on the theme of popular culture. As Lawrence Alloway, the critic and chronicler of the movement, who coined the term Pop art explained: 'We felt none of the dislike of commercial culture standard among most intellectuals, but accepted it as a fact, discussed it in detail, and consumed it enthusiastically.'

Richard Hamilton, a founder member of the group, produced a small collage for the 1956 exhibition 'This is Tomorrow,' incorporating elements of mass-market consumer culture entitled *Just What is it that Makes Today's Homes so Different, so Appealing?*, a work that is seen as a landmark in the development of British Pop, incorporating as it does an anthology of key Pop subject matter as Hamilton defined it in answer to the question raised by the title of his painting. The list reads as follows 'Man Woman Food History Newspapers Cinema Domestic appliances Cars Space Comics TV Telephone Information.'

Hamilton received a traditional British art school training at the Royal Academy Schools and the Slade School of Art yet commented that 'the return to nature came at second hand through the use of magazines rather than as a response to real landscape or still life objects or painting a person from life.' In his works of the 1950s and 1960s, Hamilton explored the categories on his definitive list, using complex mixed-media techniques, often incorporating elements of collage into his works, as in the acrylic, collage and aluminium relief on silkscreen of acrylic on canvas *Swingeing London*. This takes as its subject a newspaper photograph of the arrest of the Rock artist Mick Jagger and Hamilton's dealer, Robert Fraser on drugs' possession charges in July 1967. The title makes ironic reference to the contrast between the currently fashionable term 'Swinging City' to describe London's 'permissive society' and the imposition of 'swingeing' sentences on the two men. Hamilton's use of a newspaper photograph is dramatic, the shining aluminium of the handcuffs being particularly striking. The work is one of a series of the same title that comments on the manipulative techniques of the mass media. His sophisticated use of popular imagery and exploration of innovative techniques makes him an influential figure.

Peter Blake, who studied at the Royal College of Art, is ten years younger than Hamilton and a very different artist. As he has explained: 'For me Pop art is often rooted in nostalgia: the nostalgia of old popular things.' *On the Balcony*, painted between 1955 and 1957, explores 27 variations of the theme of the title, a subject set for the Royal College of Art diploma in his first year as a student there. The apparently collaged elements, including Manet's version of the subject, and the photographically realistic magazine covers are all in fact painted: 'when you might think I might collage it, I paint it – it's a kind of aesthetic game. . .A picture like *On the Balcony* was purely a photo-realist, magic-realist picture where one was trying a *trompe l'oeil* technique.' The space is ambiguous as is the relationship between the figures: the figure at the top of the canvas, who appears to be adult is cut off above the waist, and another dressed in American clothing has *Life* magazine (featuring 'London's Lavish Season') in front of his face. The four younger figures sitting on the park bench face the viewer prosaically amidst the welter of imagery, three of them (the boy on the right is in school uniform) wear an Anglo-American mix of badges, including the Union Jack and 'I Love Elvis.' Nostalgia for Blake's childhood is evident in such elements as the girl's candy cigarette, and the artist himself is painted as a reflection in the spectacles of the figure on the left.

The patriotism of the postwar period in Britain is evident not merely in the Union Jack badges but in the three representations of the Royal Family. Blake has said that he does not see it as his task 'to make social comment in a critical way. It's purely to record.' The record is often a personal one, the packaging elements of the composition are particularly striking in this respect and there is an interesting contrast between these commercial elements and Blake's rendering of three fellow students' supposed paintings of the 'On the balcony' subject brief that are propped up on the bench in the center of the painting.

As Andy Warhol was the best-known American Pop artist, so David Hockney is the most famous of the British Pop artists to emerge in the period. Like Warhol he is an international celebrity, famous for his life-style as well as his art. Hockney studied first at Bradford College of Art and subsequently at the Royal College of Art from 1959 to 1962. Hockney became well known for both his painting and graphic work while still a student and had his first one-person show a year after leaving the Royal College. He has since traveled extensively from his home-base in California, winning additional fame as a designer for opera and as a photographer using complex, multiple images.

In evolving his highly personal painting style which mixes figurative and abstract elements, Hockney has, from the early 1960s, used acrylic – a medium that retains its intensity of color longer than oil and allows greater flexibility of handling and color contrast. In 1961 he visited America, where he now lives, for the first time. 'Somehow I instinctively knew I was going to like it,' he relates. *A Bigger Splash* of 1967 is the last of a series of three paintings of increasing scale of similar subjects, painted in California. The contrast of abstract and figurative elements is particularly stylish. Hockney acknowledges the tension between the two: '. . .if you take away the chair, for instance, and the reflection in the glass it becomes much more abstract.' The splash itself, 'found in a book about how to build swimming pools. . .,' implies the presence of an unseen diver beneath the surface of the pool. Hockney conveys his pleasure in the rendering of it in the following manner: 'And I loved the idea of painting this thing that lasts for two seconds, it takes me two weeks to paint this event that lasts for two seconds.'

Hockney's paintings are usually autobiographical in content, when he paints portraits, they are normally of friends. His best-known London portrait is *Mr and Mrs Clark and Percy* (1970). The life-size figures are the designers Ossie Clark and Celia Birtwell, close friends of the painter, who, the painter recalls, posed for a long time for the portrait. Use was also made of a series of drawings and photographs. The heads of the figures are painted with extraordinary fidelity and depth of focus, the treatment of Celia Birtwell's hair is particularly striking in this respect, whereas certain passages, notably the balustrade and Percy the cat are painted in a near abstract manner. Hockney makes reference to the tradition of eighteenth-century British portraiture in his title, echoing that of Gainsborough's *Mr and Mrs Andrews* (in which, as is characteristic of such portraits, Mrs Andrews is seated, while Mr Andrews stands), and in the depiction of the material objects that surround the couple. Such details as Celia Birtwell's dress and stance, the currently fashionable design-classic Bauhaus chair and the Hockney print on the wall all serve to substantiate the details of the couple's lifestyle – that of so-called 'Swinging London' of the period in which Hockney himself was such a famous figure there.

Patrick Caulfield is one of a number of British artists whose work is sometimes associated with Pop art, by reason of his use of popular imagery. Caulfield is another Royal College of Art student, although of a rather younger generation, graduating in 1963. Such a work as *After Lunch* demonstrates his typical use of popular mass-produced photographic reproductions, here in the form of a 'photo-mural' of the Château of Chillon in a Swiss-style restaurant with fondue still in a pot on the table. Caulfield explores the tension between the meticulously depicted 'photographic' image and the near-abstract structure and unmodulated color of the restaurant, making the viewer question the relationship between popular representation and the 'real world.' The ironic impassivity of the image and the use of different forms of representation within a highly formalized picture structure are perhaps more reminiscent of American Pop than British developments.

The Australian artist Sidney Nolan might be regarded as a precursor of Pop, as the first of the series of paintings that made his name on the theme of the Australian outlaw, Ned Kelly were produced in the 1940s. Nolan is one of a group of Melbourne painters who exhibited with the Australian Contemporary Art Society from 1939 and was associated with the journal *Angry Penguins* from 1941 to 1946. Nolan is known for his exploration of specifically Australian imagery and in particular the myth of Ned Kelly represented in *Glenrowan* (1956-57). Ned Kelly was the last and most famous of the nineteenth-century Australian bushrangers and an Australian folk-hero. Nolan represents him in his extraordinary home-made armor at Glenrowan township, site of Kelly's last stand against authority, where Kelly and his men were wounded and captured in June 1880. Nolan uses thin washes of color on a prepared board surface which are then scraped and worked to give a richness of color and texture appropriate to such a mythic subject. Indeed Nolan's work has interesting parallels with American and British Pop art in its use of imagery that represents the uniqueness of its country of origin.

In both Europe and America during the 1950s and 1960s, abstract painting movements ran concurrently with Pop art. In America the leading trend is known as Post-Painterly Abstraction, in which color and a craftsmanlike, impersonal technique are of prime importance.

Morris Louis and Kenneth Noland were close friends and painting associates from 1952 when both were teaching at the Washington Workshop Center. In April 1953 Louis' work (which until then had been a form of gestural Abstract Expressionism) was transformed after a visit to the studio of Helen Frankenthaler in the company of Noland and the critic Clement Greenberg. Frankenthaler was working with the then newly developed acrylic paint poured and rubbed directly into the weave of the canvas, a process Louis took up and developed in a series of large-scale canvasses called *Veils, Florals, Unfurleds*, and *Stripes* in the last eight years of his life before his death from lung cancer at the age of fifty.

Louis acknowledged his debt to both Pollock's drip technique and Frankenthaler's *Mountain and Sea*: 'she was the bridge between Pollock and what was possible.' *Theta* (1960), painted two years before Louis' death, displays two lines of color poured in diagonal sequence across the corners of the painting field, which is some nine feet in width. The rivulets of acrylic paint saturate the unprimed canvas, becoming an integral part of it in a process that of its essence deliberately denies the artist's individual 'handwriting' and has a resulting coolness and detached elegance characteristic of Louis' finest work.

Noland had studied at Black Mountain College, North Carolina and for a period with the Russian sculptor Zadkine in Paris, before taking a teaching post at the Institute of Contemporary Art in Washington and the Washington Workshop Center. He worked very closely with Louis in the early 1950s and at one time they even painted on the same canvas. The visit to Helen Frankenthaler's studio was also a turning point in his career and he and Louis spent a considerable period working out new techniques of staining acrylic into unsized canvas. Like Louis, Noland tends to paint in series, exploring a single motif, and working in acrylic to stain rather than paint the canvas. Noland's work develops after Louis's death in 1962 into a series of 'shaped' canvases using bands of color in chevron shapes in 1962-64, the period of *Bend Sinister*, and subsequently in diamonds (1964-67, horizontal bands 1967-70, etc.). *Bend Sinister* is a canvas of monumental size, measuring 7 feet 8 inches by 13 feet 5 inches: the very size of the canvas renders the color of prime dynamic importance as the giant asymmetrical chevron appears to hang in space. The handling of the paint is deliberately impersonal, and the eye is forced across the sharply differentiated bands of contrasted colors.

Frank Stella explored the Abstract Expressionist style while still a student at Princeton, experimenting also in new materials such as acrylic paint. His major concern is not with color, however, as with Louis and Noland, with whom he is often classified, but with the painting as an object in its own right without reference to anything outside itself. Indeed, in 1958 after a series of works showing the influence of Jasper Johns's target and flag paintings, Stella produced a series of 'black' paintings which concentrated on structure by eliminating color completely. *Hyena Stomp* of 1962 is one of a series of paintings in which Stella explored the possibilities of a square form of 77 × 77 inches. The composition can be 'read' in a variety of ways, the form here can be seen as that of an angular 'spiral' shape which begins in the top right hand corner of the canvas and is broken by the diagonals which seem to interrupt its brightly colored symmetry. It can, alternatively, be read anti-clockwise.

Stella aimed 'to see the whole idea without any confusion,' the title reflects Stella's interest in jazz and syncopation: its title is that of a composition by Jelly Roll Morton and the painting itself explores the tension between brilliant color and a cool and highly organized structural form. Nothing could be further from the subjective nature of much postwar painting, particularly gestural Abstract Expressionism. Stella's blunt statements are also in sharp contrast to those of the Abstract Expressionists: 'One could stand in front of any Abstract Expressionist work for a long time, and walk back and forth, and inspect the depths of the pigment and the inflection and all the painterly brushwork for hours. But I wouldn't ask anyone to do that in front of my paintings. To go further, I would like to prohibit them from doing that in front of my paintings. That's why I make the paintings the way they are.'

The very lack of subjectivity in such a work is a reminder of the fact that such key figures in the development of geometric abstraction as Mondrian and Moholy-Nagy had worked in the United States for many years of their productive lives and that Josef Albers, whose *Homage to the Square* series was begun in 1949, was an influential teacher, not least in the post he took up on leaving the Bauhaus at Black Mountain College, where Noland was a student.

Ellsworth Kelly, painter, lithographer and sculptor, studied first in Boston and then at the Ecole des Beaux-Arts in Paris, living in Paris from 1948 to 1954. His art is thus more European than that of his American contemporaries, owing much to the sculptured reliefs of Hans Arp and other abstract artists whose work he saw while living in Paris. Kelly aims to 'erase all "Meaning" of the things seen' in his abstractions. Yet his observation of everyday things such as shadows and plant forms is the starting point for his abstractions, which can take the form of painting, collage or sculptured relief. The curved and straight forms in the large canvas *Red Green Blue* are austere in themselves yet in sequence they set up a powerful series of evocations and connotations for the viewer to construe.

The work of the English artist Richard Smith has certain affinities with British and American Pop Art, although it has more in common with the work of Stella and other Post-Painterly Abstraction painters. Smith was a student at the Royal College of Art with Hockney and Peter Blake and at one time shared a studio with the latter. In the early 1960s, however, he worked in America and is an important link between the development of painting in both countries. His work is always distinguished by its color, which he has described as 'sweet and tender,' aiming to give a 'general sense of blossoming, ripening and shimmering,' as in *Panatella* (1961). *Panatella* also shows Smith's characteristic use of packaging forms in his work, a device of Pop Art, here turned to different ends – the title refers to the cigar-band from which the image derived. As Smith explains: 'My interest is not in the message so much as in the method. . . . You don't buy cigarettes – only cartons. The box is your image of the product.' *Panatella* is a large-scale work painted in an orthodox oil on canvas technique. Subsequent paintings have been acrylic on shaped wood supports.

The British artist Bridget Riley is one of the foremost exponents of the movement of the 1960s known as 'Op Art' (abbreviation for 'optical'). The term described a style of abstract art which appears to give the illusion of movement across the canvas and induces sensations in the viewer by the use of optical effects. Riley studied at Goldsmiths' College of Art, London and from 1952 to 1955 at the Royal College of Art. She exhibited regularly in England and America from 1962, and six years later won the International Prize for Painting at the 34th Venice Biennale which ensured her fame internationally. *Late Morning* of 1967 aims to set up physiological and psychological reactions in the viewer and to capture the experience of what she terms her 'visual life' and communicate it to others. As she explains: 'Vision can be arrested, tripped up or pulled back in order to float free again.'

Riley's exclusively black and white paintings of the 1960s attempted to reproduce natural effects such as she describes in the following, writing of her childhood in Cornwall: 'all was bespattered with the flitter of bright sunlight and its pinpoints of black shadow. It was as though one were swimming throught a diamond.' From 1966 she experimented with the use of color, often brilliant intense colors as used in *Late Morning*. Like much of her work of this period, this canvas is monumental in size and appears to surround the viewer with dazzling effect. As the artist herself describes the sensation of looking at such a work: 'There will be nothing to look at one moment and the next second the canvas seems to refill, to be crowded with visual events.'

Optical phenomena of a different kind can be seen in the work of the Hungarian artist of an older generation, Victor Vasarely. Vasarely studied medicine in Budapest before undertaking both conventional art-school training and a year at the Hungarian version of the Bauhaus, where he learned what he has called 'the functional character of plasticity'. He first worked as a graphic artist in Paris in 1930, and his first work as a painter, which was not until 1943, was in a Surrealist style. From 1947 he concentrated on constructive-geometric abstraction. He was a pioneer of the Op art style in the later 1950s, his work includes paintings in oil on canvas, screen-prints and designs for tapestries. *Supernovae* of 1959-61 grew mainly out of a series of 'kinetic' experiments (images which appear to move or change as the viewer looks at them) inspired by current scientific and psychological theory. The brilliant contrasts in the patterns of *Supernovae* produce a fluctuating effect on the retina – Supernovae are stars which have the property both of shedding proportions of their mass and of shining more brightly under certain conditions. Vasarely uses simple abstract forms to make the work accessible by avoiding reference to representation. He wished such a work to reach a wide public by means of current technology, or as he had intended in the case of *Supernovae* as part of a scheme that would integrate his work on a monumental scale in a setting of public architecture.

Abstract painting of a very different kind is seen in the work of the Russian aristocrat Nicolas de Staël, who was exiled to Europe in 1919 as a child of five. De Staël settled in Paris in 1943 and his work became well known internationally in the early 1950s. An exhibition of mosaics from Ravenna in Paris in 1951 was an important influence on his work as can be seen in *Figure by the Sea* (1952). Here the rich, glowing color is applied partly with a spatula to build up a pattern of forms reminiscent of mosaic. In a later work such as this it is evident that de Staël is attempting a synthesis between figurative and abstract painting, the broad patches of color here suggesting the landscape of the south of France and a human presence. Through the thickly applied blocks of brilliant color can be seen the colors of the surface below. At the time of his suicide in 1955, de Staël was one of the most admired painters in Europe. He is widely regarded as the last major figure of the School of Paris.

Jean Dubuffet, who declared himself against conventional forms of art and particularly antipathetic towards the School of Paris, had his first one-person show in Paris in 1944; his second, two years later, caused a public scandal. His work and theoretical writing have had an influence on artists as various as Willem de Kooning and David Hockney. 'My art' wrote Dubuffet, 'is an attempt to bring all disparaged values into the limelight.'

Dubuffet spent six months at the Académie Julian in Paris in 1918, and was largely self-taught, studying literature and ethnology extensively. By 1924 he had given up painting for the wine trade, and it was not until 1942, when he was 41, that he concentrated on painting. At about this time he started collecting what he termed 'Art Brut' (raw art), children's drawings and paintings, graffiti, unselfconscious art of a variety of kinds including the work of the mentally ill. From such sources Dubuffet evolved his own distinctive painting and sculpture style, one that shocked the public in its time by its rawness and totem-like qualities but became a style that was to prove highly influential on a younger generation of artists. Dubuffet's work of the fifties combines materials such as ashes, sand, and coal dust on the surface of his oil paint, troweling these substances in with a palette knife until the surface of the canvas appears to be modeled. He explained his methods in the following manner: 'art should be born from the materials and, spiritually, should borrow its language from it. Each material has its own language so there is no need to make it serve a language.' The forms produced in such an unorthodox way are richly suggestive, organic forms reminiscent perhaps of the earth's surface, given an almost totemic power. Dubuffet has written: 'Look at what lies at your feet! A crack in the ground, sparkling gravel, a tuft of grass, some crushed debris offer equally worthy subjects for your applause and admiration.'

Throughout the 1950s and 1960s, indeed until the year before his death at the age of 92 in 1973, Picasso, the most celebrated artist of the twentieth century, continued working in a wide variety of media, ranging from sculpture to ceramics. His oil paintings of this period are on a scale that is larger than life and often rework some of the themes of his earlier paintings, seemingly with undiminished vigor. The last twenty years of Picasso's life are characterized by his series of variations on themes suggested by paintings of the past: the most famous work of his seventeenth-century compatriot, Velasquez, *Las Meninas* ('The Maids of Honor'), and Delacroix's *Women of Algiers* are other examples. The theme of the female nude in a landscape setting is a traditional subject in oil painting from sixteenth-century Venice onward. At the age of 78 he began to work on a series of paintings based on Manet's *Déjeuner sur l'Herbe*. The forms are reduced to their essence and the distortions of the figure and the space it occupies has, it is suggested, some affinities with the key of work of Picasso's career, the *Demoiselles d'Avignon* of 52 years earlier. Images of the female nude punctuate Picasso's long and fruitful career, and are the subject of his very last paintings. One of the many ironies attending the last years of Picasso was the fact that this acknowledged 'Old Master' of twentieth-century art, famous for the radical nature and diversity of his art and its media, should have continued to the last to paint so traditional a subject in such a conventional medium on so monumental a scale.

In Britain the postwar figurative tradition continues until the present day. The best known internationally of the artists of what has recently been termed the School of London are Francis Bacon and Lucien Freud. The so-called School of London artists are radically different from each other but share certain ideas in common. In a period when such abstract movements as Abstract Expressionism held sway, these artists took as the central subject of their work the human figure and its surroundings, using it as a vehicle for the expression of emotional involvement and laying particular importance on the handling of the paint.

Bacon was born in Dublin of English parentage and worked first as an interior decorator and designer of furniture and rugs when he came to London at the age of 16 in 1925. Bacon had no formal training as a painter and indeed the public response to his painting was such that he all but gave up painting for seven or eight years during the war period. Bacon did not achieve public notice until 1945 when *Three Figures at the Base of a Crucifixion* had an enormous and shocking impact on the postwar public, achieving Bacon's stated 'desire for ordering and for returning fact onto the nervous system in a more violent way.' Since that time Bacon's work has been exhibited frequently in Europe and America and in September 1988 in Moscow, the first living British artist to be the subject of a Russian one-person show. *Seated Man with Turkey Rug* (1961) shows a typical Bacon subject, modern urban man with a disturbingly distorted face and body seated in isolation in a richly furnished room with his loneliness emphasized by the white lines drawn around him. These seem to suggest that he is enclosed in a glass box – a motif that is also seen in Bacon's series of paintings of Popes, which derive from his study of the seventeenth-century Spanish painter Velasquez' portrait of Pope Innocent X. In a tribute to the British painter Matthew Smith published eight years before this painting, Bacon is revealing about his own work: 'real painting is a mysterious and continuous struggle with chance – mysterious because the very substance of the paint . . . can make such a direct assault on the nervous system, continuous because the medium is so fluid and subtle that every change that is made loses what is already there in the hope of making a fresh gain. I think that painting today is pure intuition and luck and taking advantage of what happens when you splash the bits down . . .' *Seated Man with Turkey Rug* is not as horrifying as many of Bacon's canvases but is disturbing nonetheless. Bacon has gone on record as saying that his pictures were not intended to have any one precise meaning: 'They are just an attempt to make a certain type of feeling visual.' As ever in his work the feeling here is a disquieting one.

Bacon's friend and younger contemporary Lucian Freud, a grandson of Sigmund Freud, was born in Berlin and came to England at the age of ten in 1932, becoming naturalized seven years later. He began to paint on a full-time basis when he was invalided out of the War in 1942. His work of the 1950s is distinguished by its meticulous linear detail – for example, his portrait of Francis Bacon of 1952 delineates each eyelash, in a manner reminiscent of the German 'New Objectivity' painters between the Wars. By the later 1950s Freud, under Bacon's influence, broadened his style, using hog bristle brushes rather than sable and his technique became more painterly, with a broader 'sweep,' and less intricate in detail.

Unlike Bacon, Freud works directly from the model over a long period and normally paints people he knows well. 'If you don't know them it can only be like a travel book.' *Portrait of the Artist's Mother* painted in 1984, is part of a series of portraits of his mother, Lucie Freud, begun in 1972. In it Freud embodies his idea of portraiture, which he has explained in the following manner: 'I know my idea of portraiture came from dissatisfaction with portraits that resembled people. I would wish my portraits to be *of* the people, not *like* them. Not having a look of the sitter, *being* them. I didn't want to get just a likeness like a mimic, but to *portray* them, like an actor . . . As far as I am concerned the paint *is* the person. I want it to work for me just as flesh does.' *Portrait of the Artist's Mother* is one of the most powerful and striking of Freud's most recent works.

In the late 1960s there was an observable trend among younger painters in both America and Europe towards photo-realism. Photographs had been used as a means to an end by painters since the introduction of photography in 1839. The Romantic painter Eugène Delacroix was one of the first to advocate their use and was a charter-member of the first photographic society in France in 1851.

The range of of artists included under the general heading of American photo-realism is a very wide one, particularly as realism was the dominant style in American art until the Armory Show of 1913. Chuck Close, one of the leading exponents of the style who has used photographs for his work since 1967, explains his aims in the following manner: 'I am trying to make it very clear that I am making paintings from photographs and that this is not the way the human eye sees it. If I stare at this it's sharp, and if I stare at that it's sharp too. The eye is very flexible, but the camera is a one-eye view of the world . . .' The use of photographs in the painting process gives Close's work a striking detachment and coolness in relation to its subject matter. The very objective rendering of the faces of friends who are the main subject matter of Close's work can be seen as the diametric opposite of such a subjective style as Abstract Expressionism.

Chuck Close's *Nat* (1972) for example is a colossal five foot six inches close-up, and in the original at least it is very clear that 'this is not the way the human eye sees,' a startling effect of unexpected scale difficult to appreciate in reproduction. Close, who was born in Monroe, Washington, and had his first one-person show in 1967, asserts that his main objective is to 'translate photographic information into paint information' and explains the monumental size of his work as a means of forcing 'the viewer to focus on one area at a time. In that way he is made aware of the blurred areas that are seen with peripheral vision.' The startling realism of the image is heightened by its neutral rendering and the limited amount of paint used.

Richard Estes also works from photographs but in a radically different manner from Close. His subject matter is the urban landscape and he selects the material for his painting from many contact-sheet photographs taken, as he explains, 'to make up for the fact that one photograph really doesn't give me all the information I need.' Estes studied at the Chicago Art Institute and began painting fulltime at the age of thirty, limiting his subject matter to the urban landscape, trying to paint, in his own terms, 'not something different, but something more like the place I've photographed. Somehow the paint and the intensity of color emphasize the light and do things to build up form that a photograph does not do.' *Food Shop* (1967), for instance, demonstrates this in its meticulous rendering of detail, an ordering of the elements of the composition that is reminiscent of the seventeenth-century Dutch townscapes of such an artist as Pieter de Hooch, whose work has a parallel geometric structure. In *Food Shop*, Estes seems to emphasize the squares and rectangles of his subject, along with the reflections in the window (which enable us to see the other side of the street) and the curious effects of light, both the internal neon lighting of the shop, and the reflected area of clouds and sky.

A parallel to Estes' work may be seen in the paintings of Don Eddy. Eddy worked as a photographer for some years before becoming a painter and uses photographs as a basis for his work, often a single photograph, as in *New Shoes for H* (1973). The painting poses an intriguing puzzle for the viewer, offering as it does a series of conflicting images, with only the narrow strip on the extreme left of the painting giving a clear and direct view of the street. The rest is reflected and distorted by the glass in a fashion that is familiar yet ambiguous in its displacement of reality. Eddy uses bright colors and paints everything — the shoes of the title, buildings, traffic, whether reflected or seen directly — in uniform focus and with typically bright, unshadowed color. The brilliance of the color is related to the 'H' of the title — Eddy here pays tribute to both Henri Matisse and Hans Hofmann.

In Germany, however, figurative painting after 1960 took a very different form. Georg Baselitz, for example, is one of several painters born during the period of World War II who were deeply conscious of their nationality, and yet wished to reach back a generation before the experience of War. The non-objectivity of Baselitz (who trained in both East and West Germany, studying at the Berlin College of Fine Arts from 1957 to 1964 and teaching there from 1983) and others of his generation has led to such painters being termed Neo-Expressionist and parallels drawn between their work and that of the German Expressionists working before World War I, particularly Kirchner. Baselitz' work utilizes a kind of primitivism familiar from the work of earlier Expressionist painters, particularly, in recent years, that of Emil Nolde and something also to the example of the Norwegian symbolist painter Edvard Munch. The violent colors of Baselitz's work and the distorted forms create what the artist has termed an 'aggressive disharmony' of the kind displayed in *Supper in Dresden* (1983). Here Baselitz explores an image familiar in Western Christian painting, that of the Last Supper of Christ, which gives the work its formal structure; but here the artist reverses the image so that it appears as a reflection, and violently distorts the figures so as to subvert further the viewer's expectations: the images appear both familiar and puzzling. Baselitz in fact paints his canvasses as they appear to the viewer, often employing deliberate trails of paint to demonstrate that they are indeed worked on in this way and not simply reversed in the hanging.

The American artist Julian Schnabel is, like Baselitz, often classified as part of the international direction in the art of the 1980s, sometimes described as 'Bad Painting,' by reason of the deliberate crudity of its style. Schnabel, virtually self-taught as an artist, paints in a neo-Expressionist manner that owes a debt to such artists as Kokoschka. Schnabel uses universal imagery in his search for what he terms the 'collective subjective.' His techniques are unconventional: he often works in oils on large-scale unstretched canvasses and with the addition of fragments of domestic pottery to create an effect somewhere between a shimmering oil painting in extraordinarily thick impasto (heavy layers of paint) and a relief sculpture.

Another German painter, Albrecht Penck, whose friendship with Baselitz began around 1955, was consistently turned down for formal art training over a considerable period in both Dresden and East Berlin, although he had begun to paint at the age of ten and had trained as a commercial draftsman. Penck visited Baselitz in West Berlin the day before the Berlin Wall was built, returning to the East that evening. He was not able to live in the West until 1980. In such a painting as *Metaphysical Passage through a Zebra* of 1975, Penck explores a complex series of images drawn from primitive art (cave paintings in particular) and urban graffiti, in a fashion that is somewhat reminiscent both of Miro's Surrealist forms and the work of Dubuffet. Penck's individual signs appear comprehensible in themselves but mysterious in their relationships with each other.

However the most celebrated of contemporary German painters, Anselm Kiefer, is more accessible in his imagery, although his work has often been the subject of controversy, both in Germany and abroad. Kiefer, born in the last year of World War II, was a pupil of the leading German postwar sculptor and influential artistic and political theorist, Joseph Beuys. Kiefer explores his country's past in a series of paintings devoted to its culture, mythology, and landscape.

Kiefer's powerful images often contain the pictorial metaphor of an attic as a space apart from the life and activity of a house or, by extension, a nation, a place that also represents perhaps the idea of individual and national self-discovery. In *Father, Son, and Holy Ghost* of 1973, the forest (a potent image in German art and literature, used in the postwar period by Max Ernst, among others) both supports and provides the wood for the attic. In the attic are three ritual fires that burn without consuming. Kiefer makes complex use of his country's myths and legends as well as the history of Germany's immediate past: 'You cannot just paint a landscape after tanks have passed through it, you have to do something with it.'

The war and its effects are also an important theme in the work of the

American-born painter R B Kitaj, who has lived in London since 1960. Kitaj was born in Ohio and in a cosmopolitan career has studied at the Cooper Union, the Akademie, Vienna, the Ruskin School of Art, Oxford, and, at the age of 25, at the Royal College of Art, London, where he had a considerable influence on the work of his younger 'Pop' contemporaries, especially David Hockney. Kitaj's work is a rich and complex interweaving of personal, philosophical and historical allusion.

Cecil Court, London WC2 (The Refugees), painted in the winter of 1983/84, for example, contains Kitaj's self-portrait at the very front of the picture, reclining on a chrome and leather couch, a twentieth-century design classic by the architect Le Corbusier. Kitaj is dressed in the clothes he had worn for his recent marriage, and the whole dream-like painting reflects the artist's desire for his work to be 'enshrouded' by a 'confessional aura' an element of Kitaj's work which sometimes obscures its meaning. Cecil Court, an alleyway of specialist bookshops running from Charing Cross Road to St Martin's Lane in the very heart of London, has changed very little in the past 25 years, and it has rich personal significance for Kitaj, who first went there on his arrival in his adopted city. The place 'fed so much into my dubious pictures from its shops and their refugee booksellers, especially the late Mr Seligmann (holding flowers at left) who sold me many art books and prints.' The complex composition takes the form of a stage setting, or, as Kitaj has described it, of a shop sign. Kitaj explores the experience of European refugees like the artist's own family. Some of the figures 'were largely cast from the beautiful craziness of Yiddish Theater.'

The English artist Howard Hodgkin was born within a year of Kitaj and is also regarded internationally as one of the leading artists working in Britain today; but here the resemblance ends. Hodgkin studied at the Camberwell School of Art, London, and Bath Academy of Art, where he later taught. He has traveled extensively, placing particular importance on the influence of both India and Venice on the development of his work. His work is characterized by its jewel-like color and small size. Hodgkin acknowledges the influence of the Mughal miniatures he collects on his work as both painter and printmaker. The titles of Hodgkin's work convey their domestic settings and private nature, as in *Dinner at Smith Square* of 1975-79, a work that evokes dinner with old friends who are art collectors. The apparent spontaneity of the image is deceptive as the paintings are worked on for long periods in the attempt to encapsulate an occasion which has private and particular meaning for the artist. As Hodgkin has stated: 'My pictures are finished when the subject comes back and the painting actually becomes a "physical object" that stands for feeling.' The intimacy of the scene recalls the interiors of such earlier painters as Bonnard, and Hodgkin's device of painting an integral wood surround both draws the spectator into the enclosed world of his painted panel and emphasizes the private nature of the image.

In conclusion, several of the major threads of twentieth-century painting may be seen in the work of the British artist John Walker, who trained at Birmingham College of Art and at the Académie de la Grande Chaumière, Paris. Walker moved to New York in 1970, and has been Professor of Painting and Drawing at Cooper Union, New York, Visiting Professor at Yale and Dean of the Victoria College of Arts, Melbourne. Walker aims, as he puts it, 'to stay just this side of abstraction' in his work, and his recent work, particularly after his experience of Australia and Oceania, has tended to become more figurative. *Conversation*, like Walker's other mature work, was produced in a fashion that recalls early Abstract Expressionism, without conscious thought, and as a work 'that's a piece of me, whatever I'm into at that time.' Indeed the evocative shapes of *Conversation*, together with Walker's manner of working and stated aims recall André Breton's definition of Surrealism as 'purely psychic automatism through which we undertake to express . . . the actual functioning of thought.'

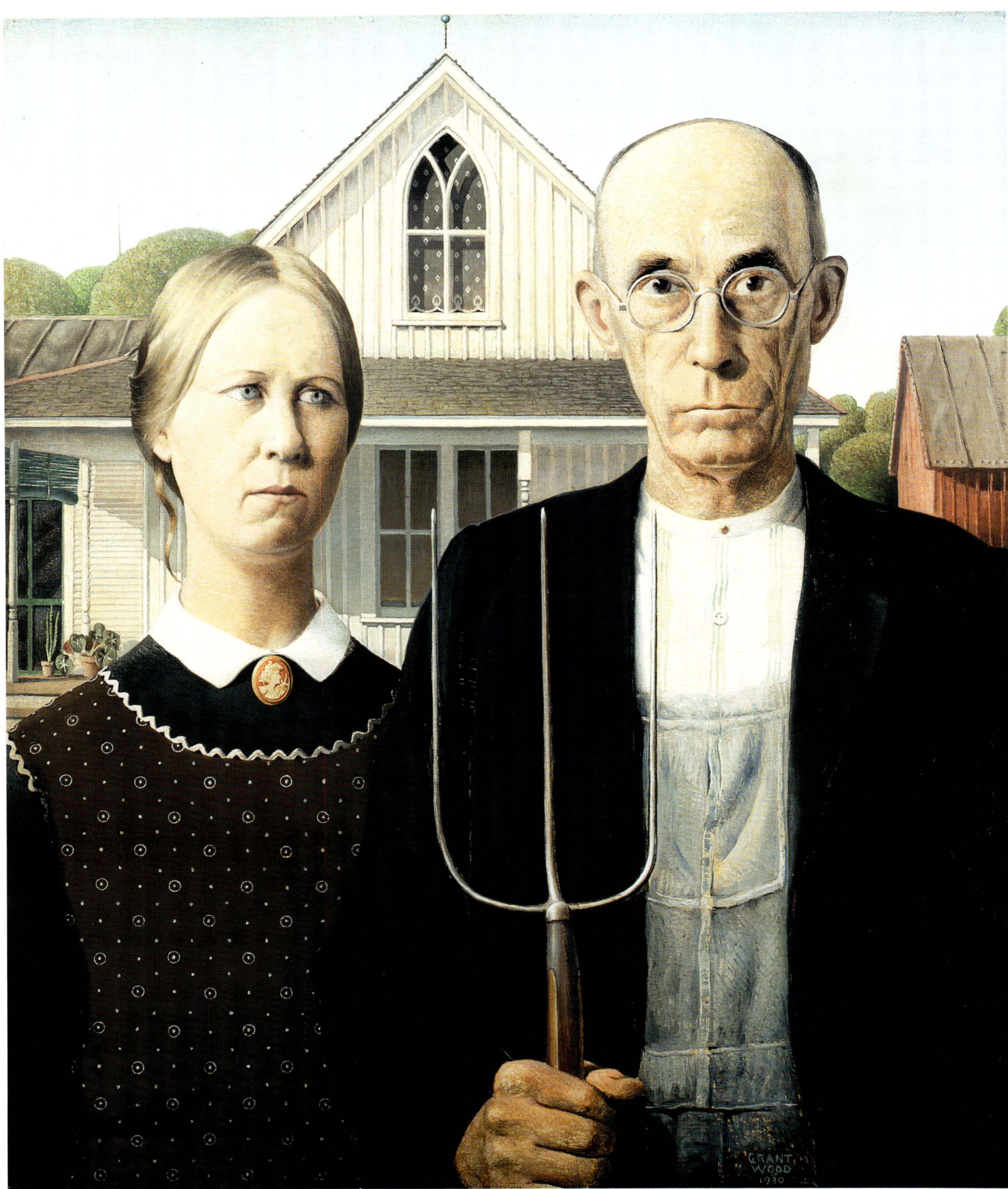

Grant Wood
American Gothic 1930
Oil on beaver board, 30×25in (76×63.3cm)
The Art Institute of Chicago
Friends of American Art Collection
© *DACS, 1989*

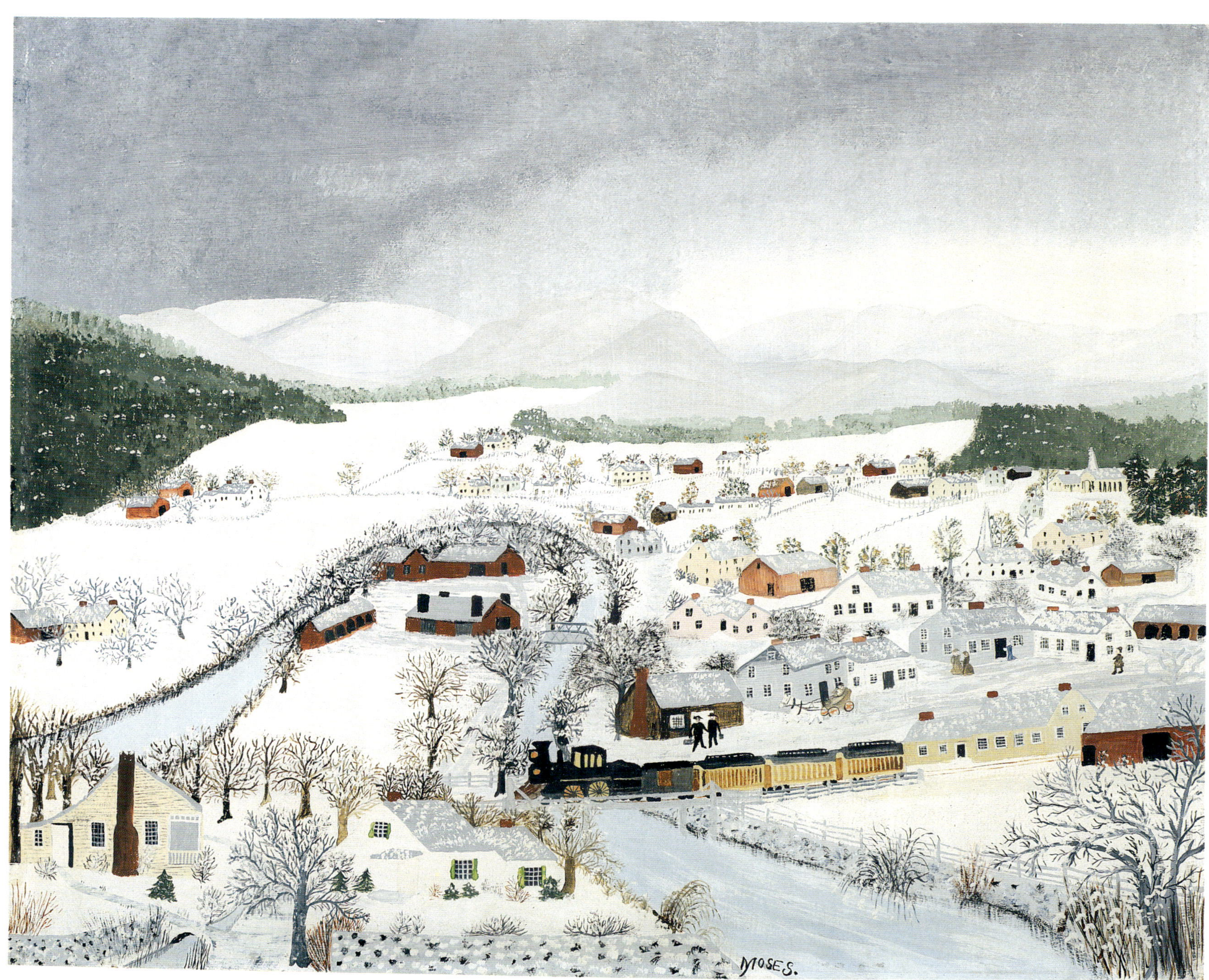

Grandma Moses
Hoosick Falls in Winter 1944
Oil on masonite, 19¾×23¾in (50.1×60.3cm)
The Phillips Collection
© *Grandma Moses Properties*

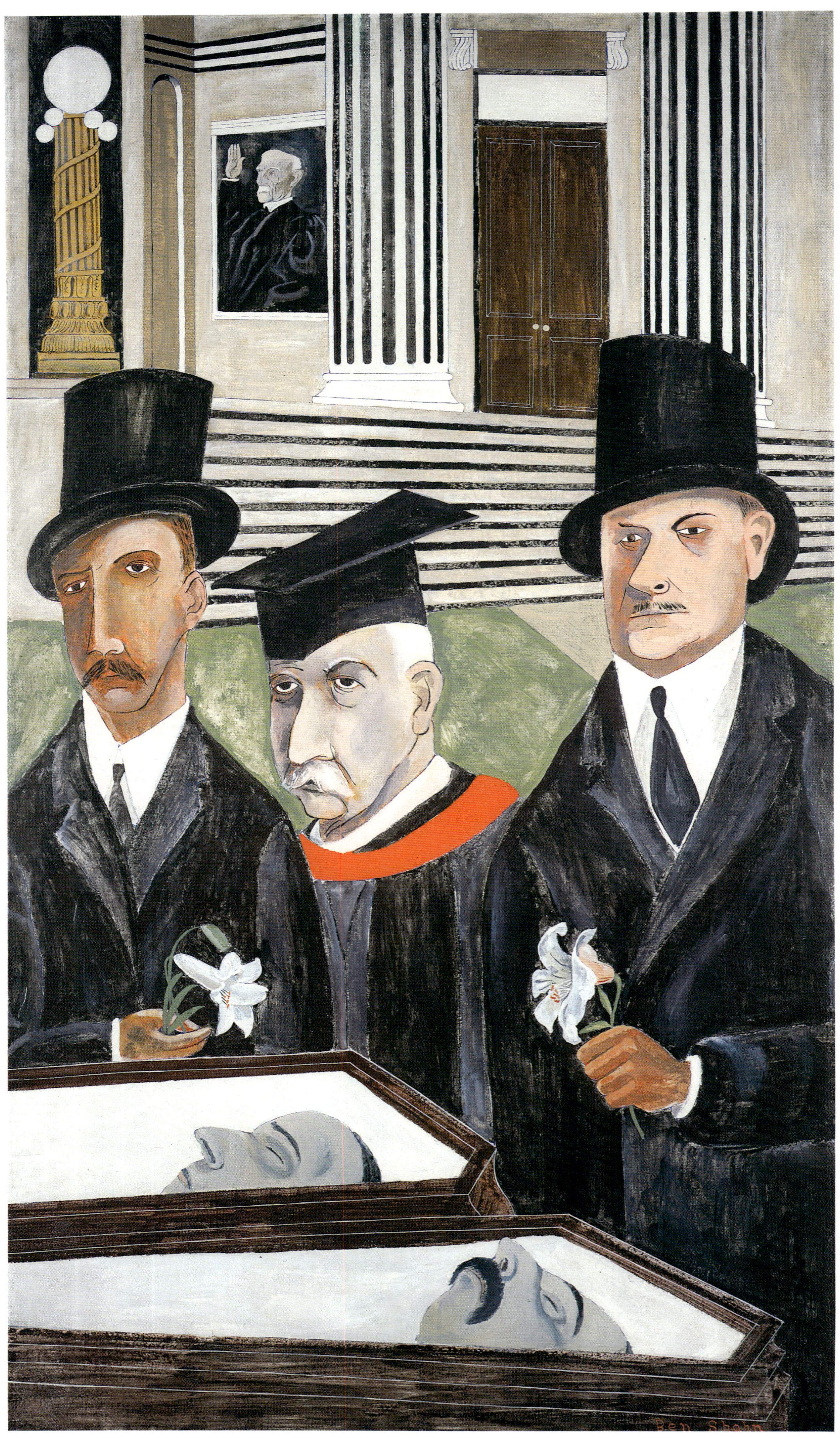

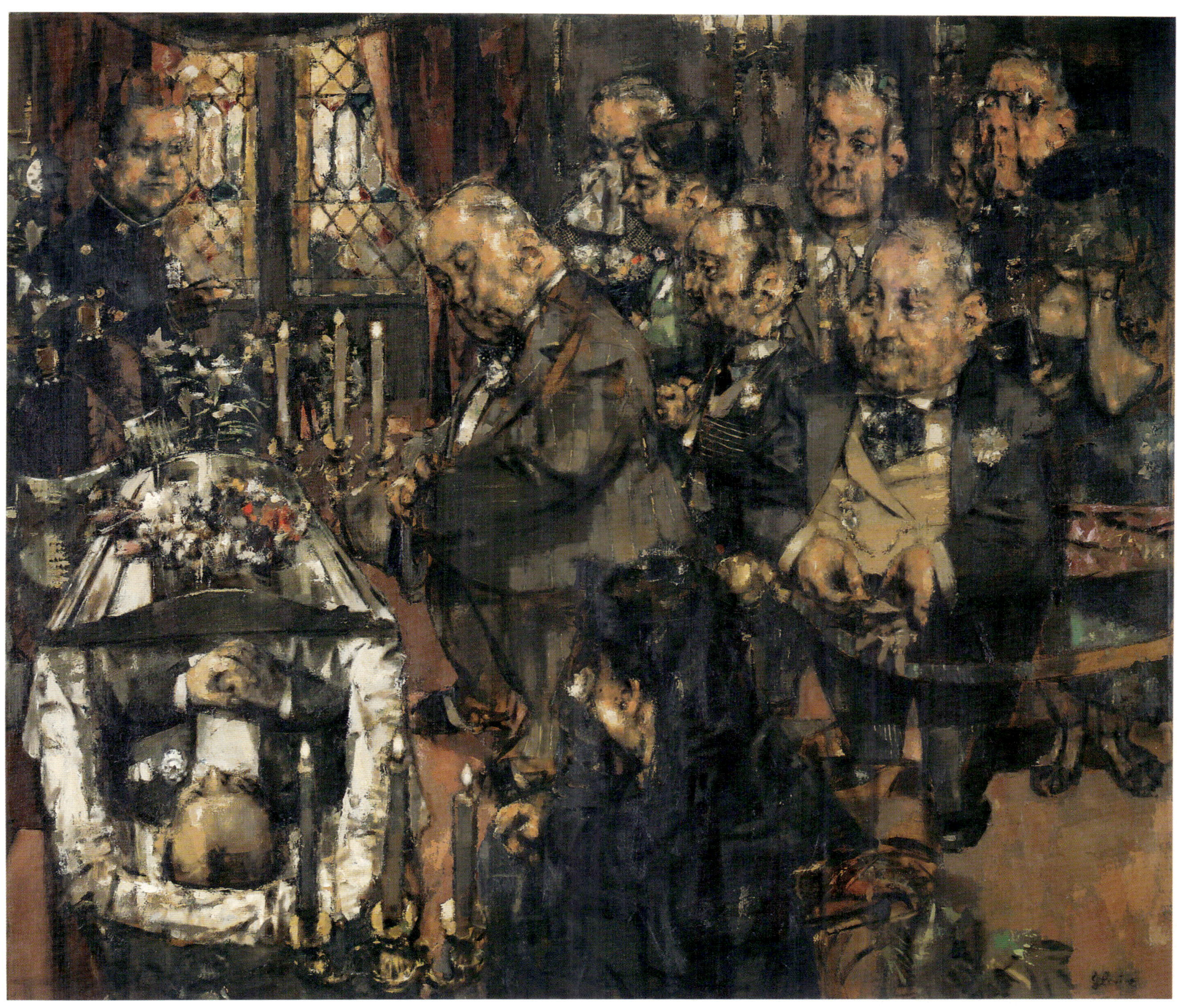

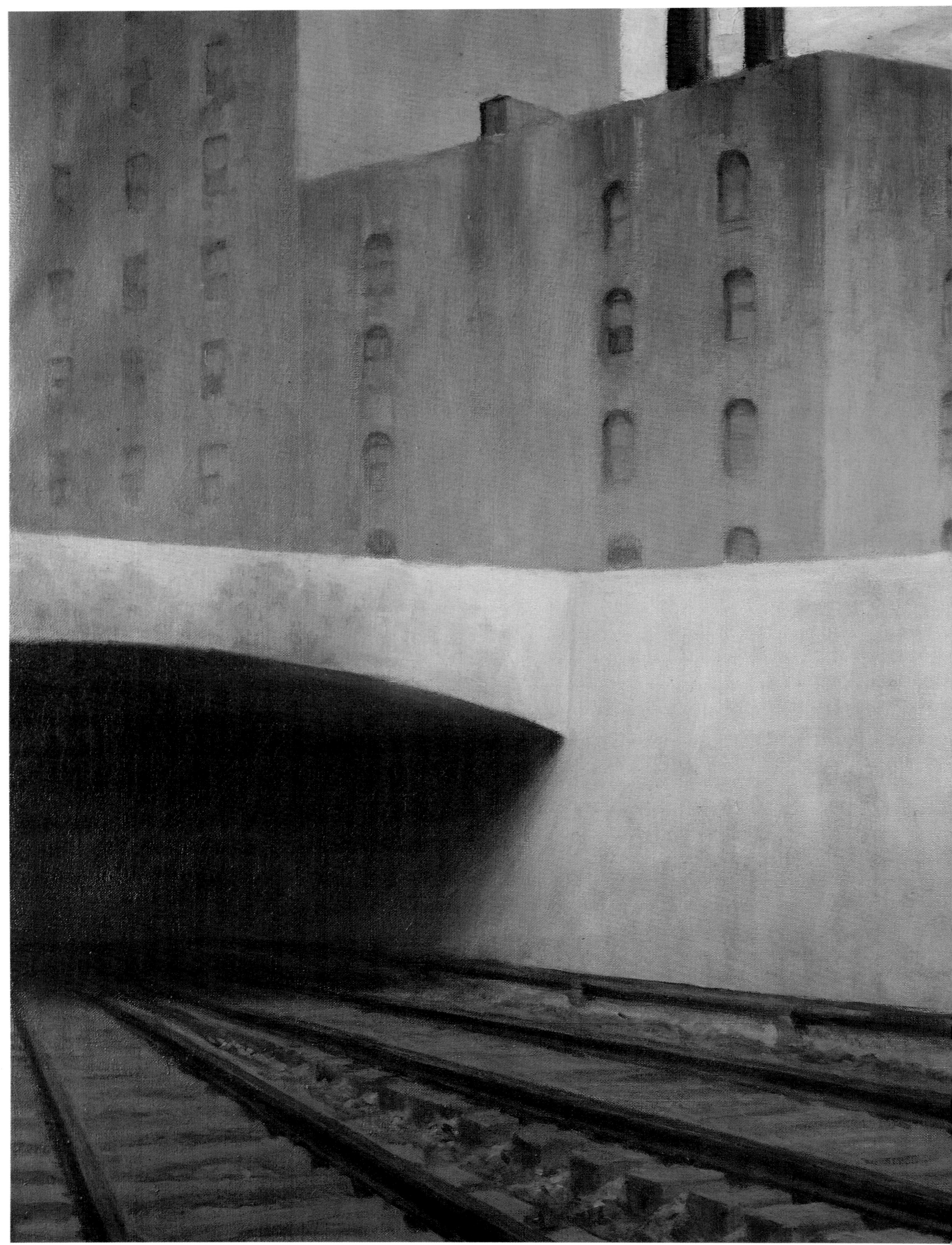

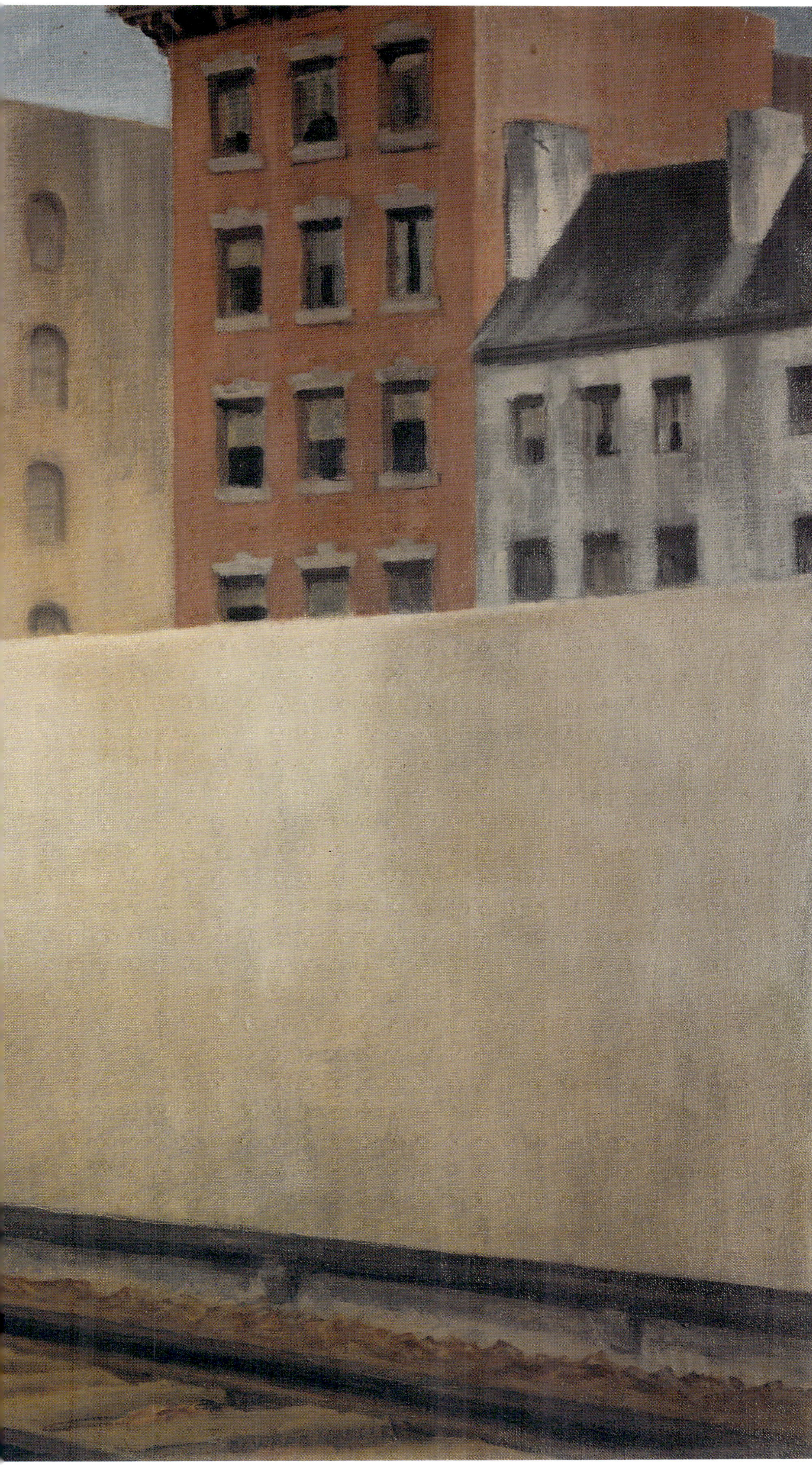

Edward Hopper
Approaching a City
1946, Oil on canvas, 28⅛×36in
(68.9×91.4cm)
The Phillips Collection

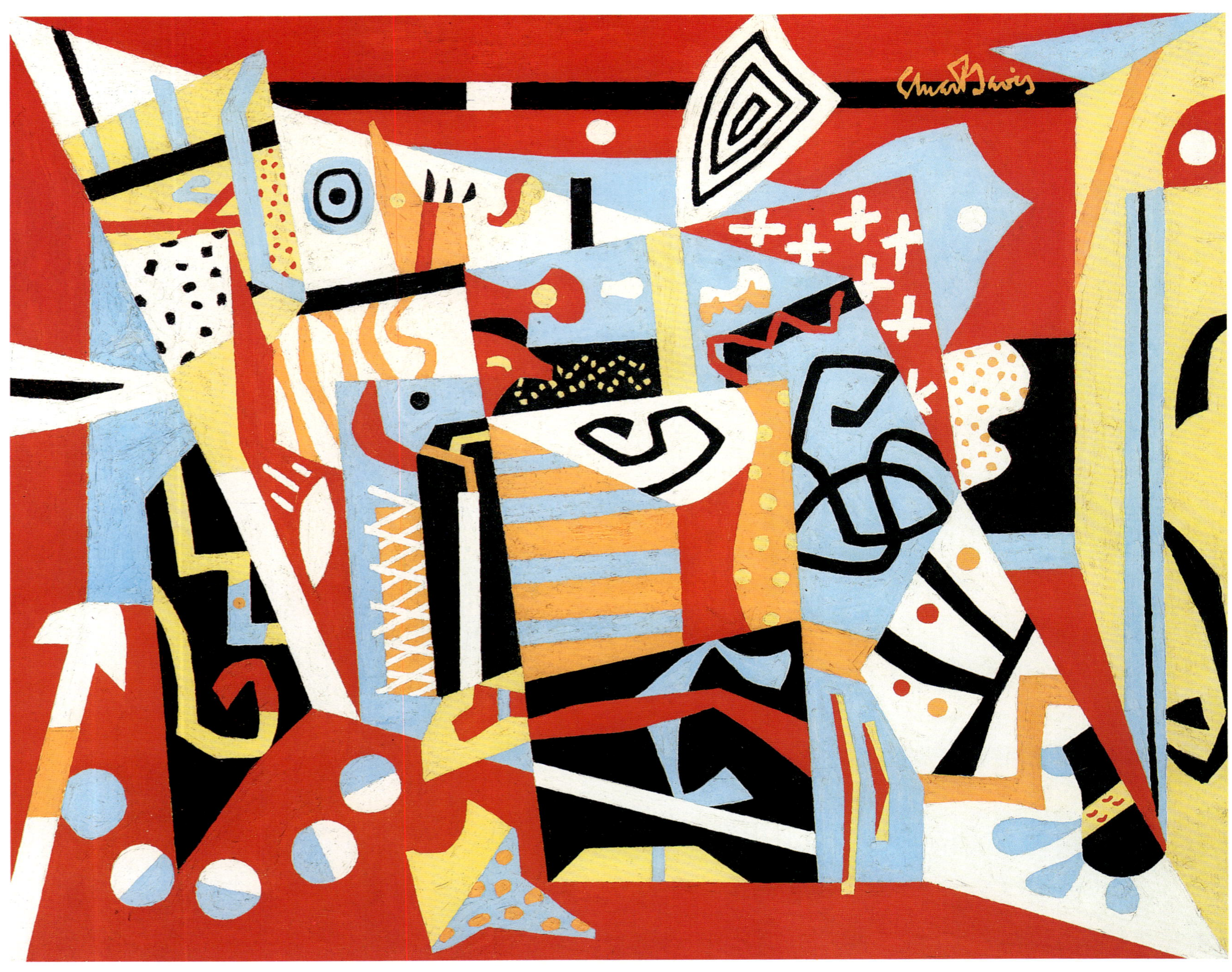

Stuart Davis
Hot Stillscape for Six Colors – 7th Avenue Style 1940
Oil on canvas, 36×45in (91.4×114.3cm)
Museum of Fine Arts, Boston
Gift of the W H Lane Collection and M Karolik Collection
by Exchange

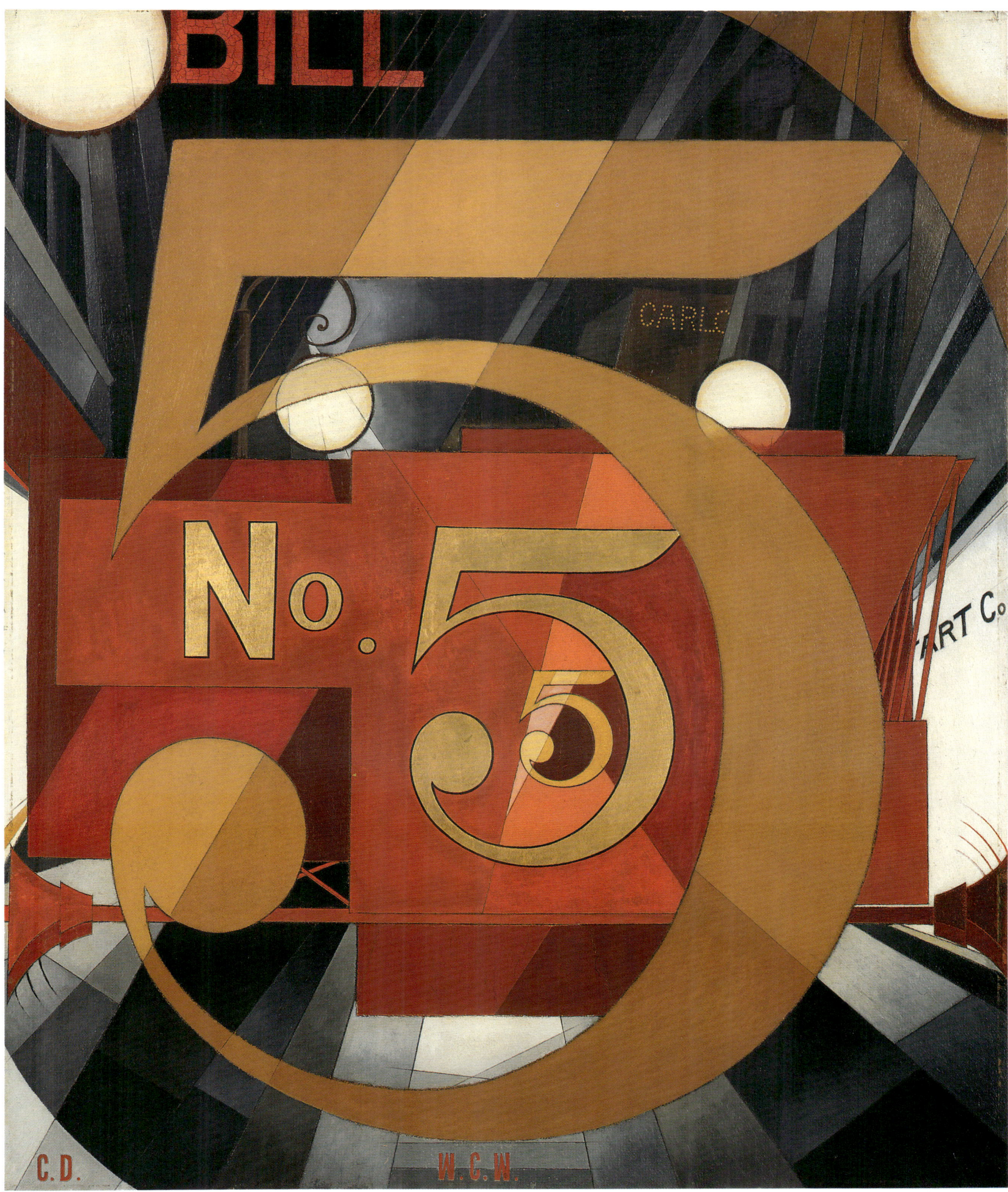

Charles Demuth
The Figure 5 in Gold 1928
Oil on composition board, 38×29¾in (91.4×75.6cm)
The Metropolitan Museum of Art, New York
The Alfred Stieglitz Collection

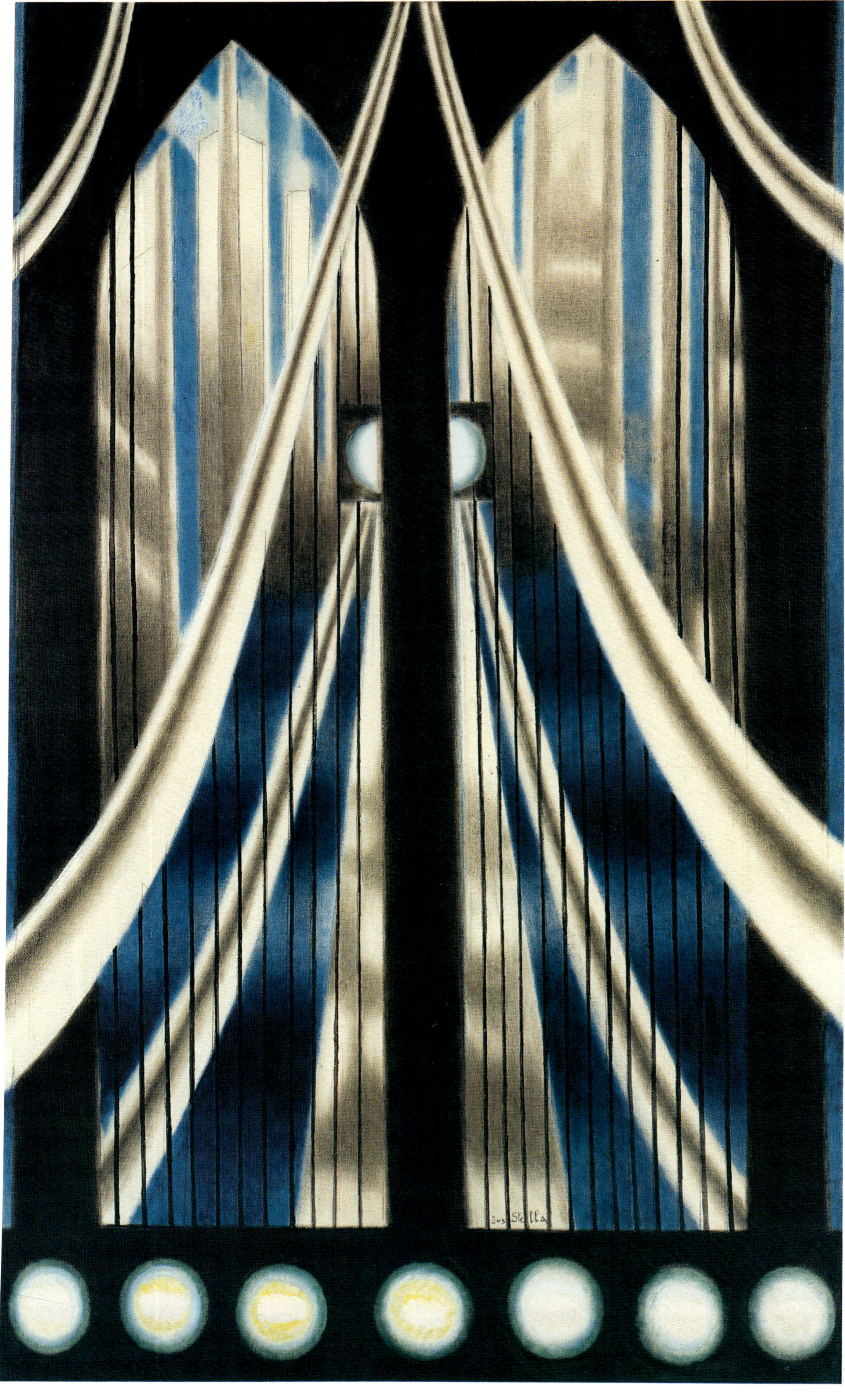

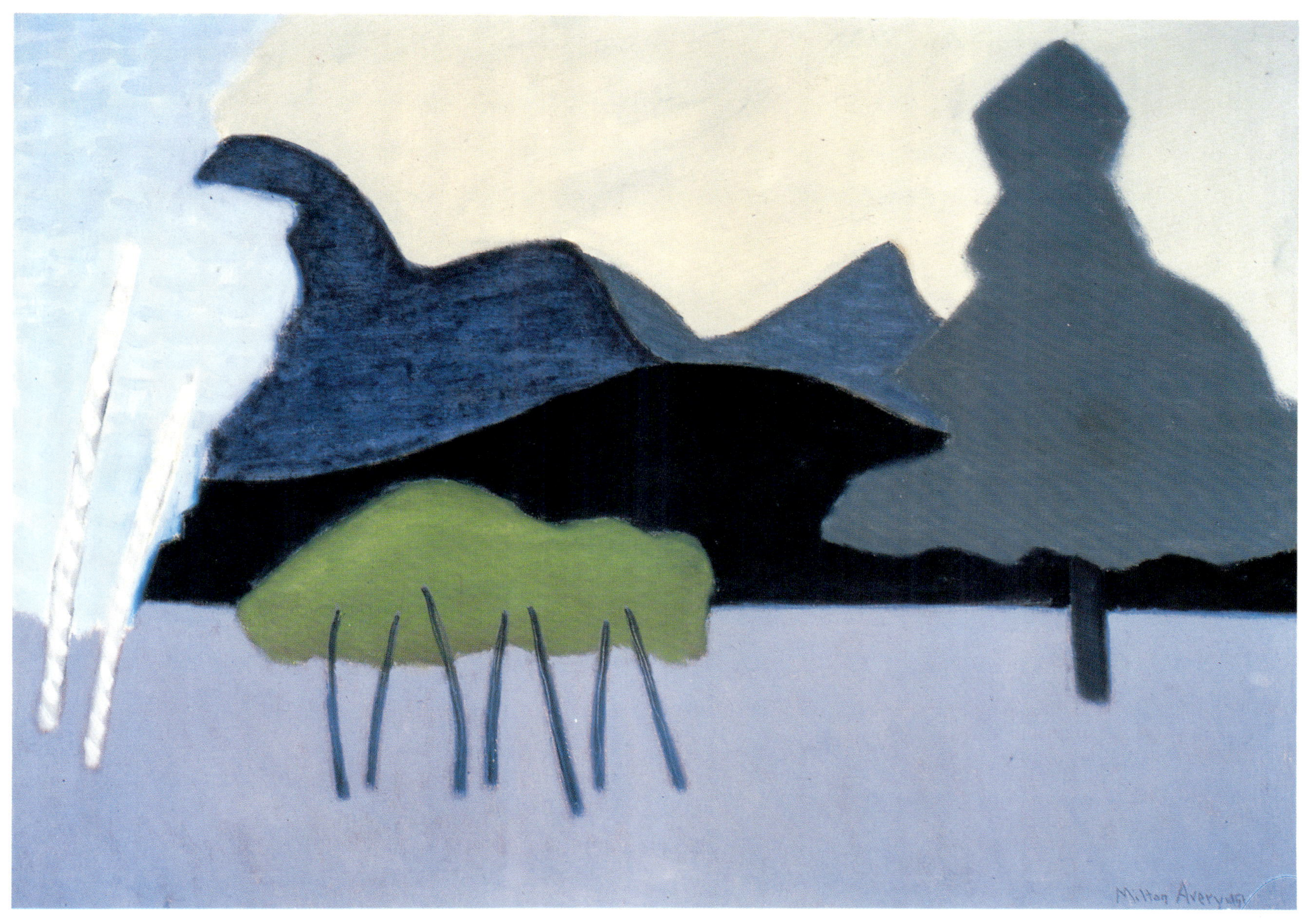

LEFT:
Joseph Stella
Bridge 1936
Oil on canvas, 50⅛×30⅛ (127.3×76.5cm)
San Francisco Museum of Modern Art
WPA Federal Arts Project Allocation to the San Francisco
Museum of Modern Art

ABOVE:
Milton Avery
Clear Cut Landscape 1951
Oil on canvas, 32⅛×44in (81.6×111.8cm)
San Francisco Museum of Modern Art
Gift to the Women's Board
© *ARS NY/Milton Avery Trust, 1989*

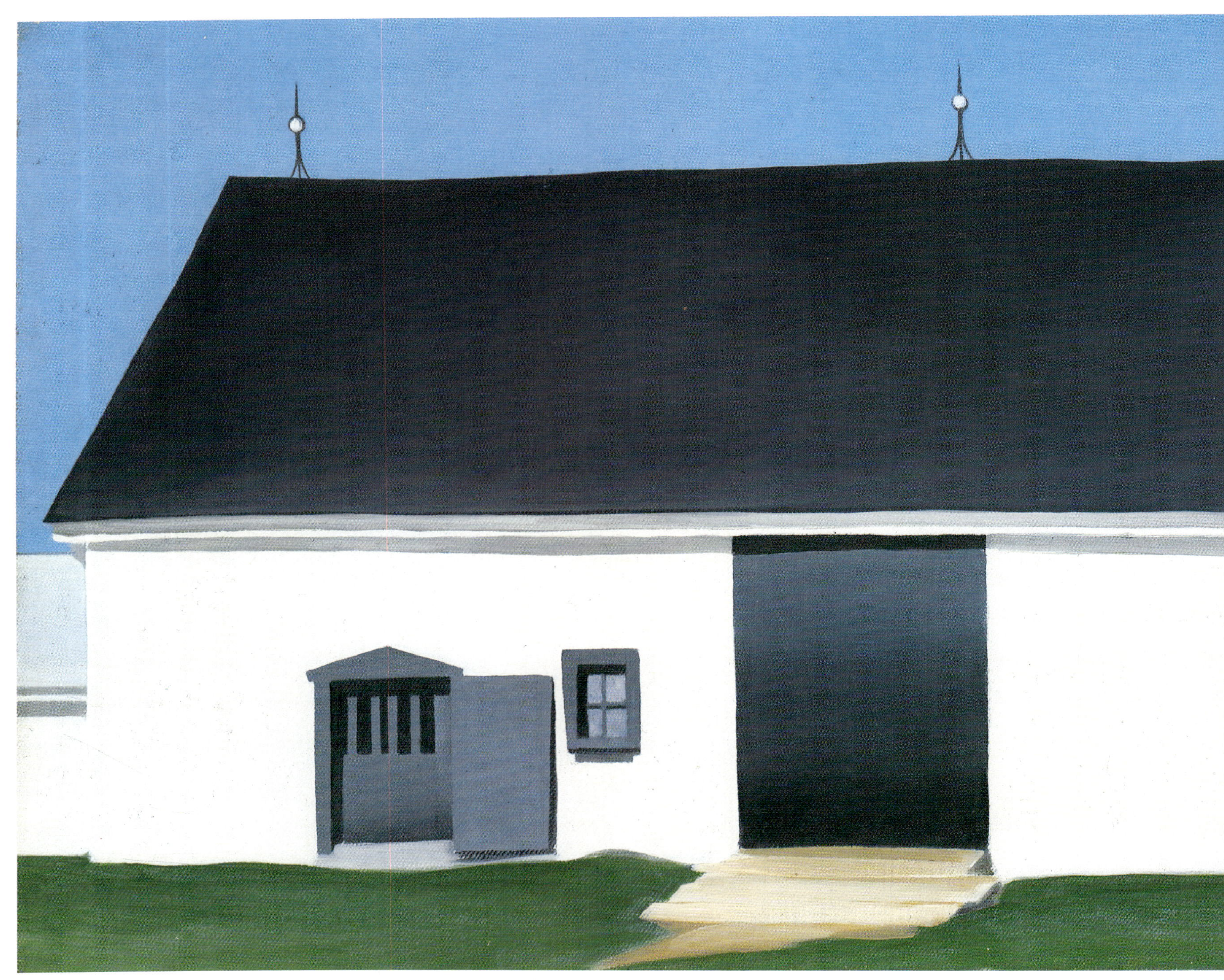

Georgia O'Keeffe
White Canadian Barn No 2 1932
Oil on canvas, 12×30in (30.5×76.2cm)
The Metropolitan Museum of Art, New York
The Alfred Steiglitz Collection

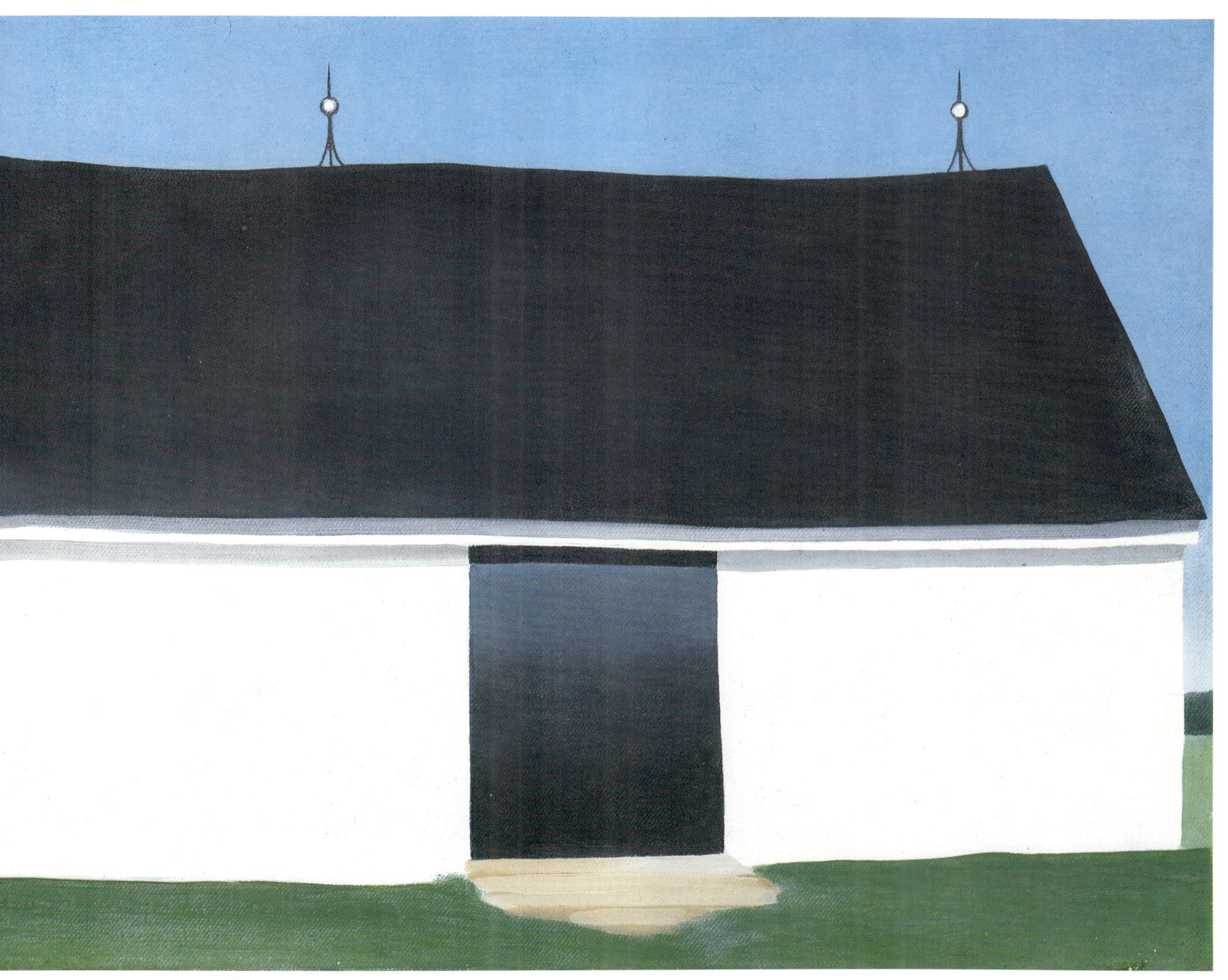

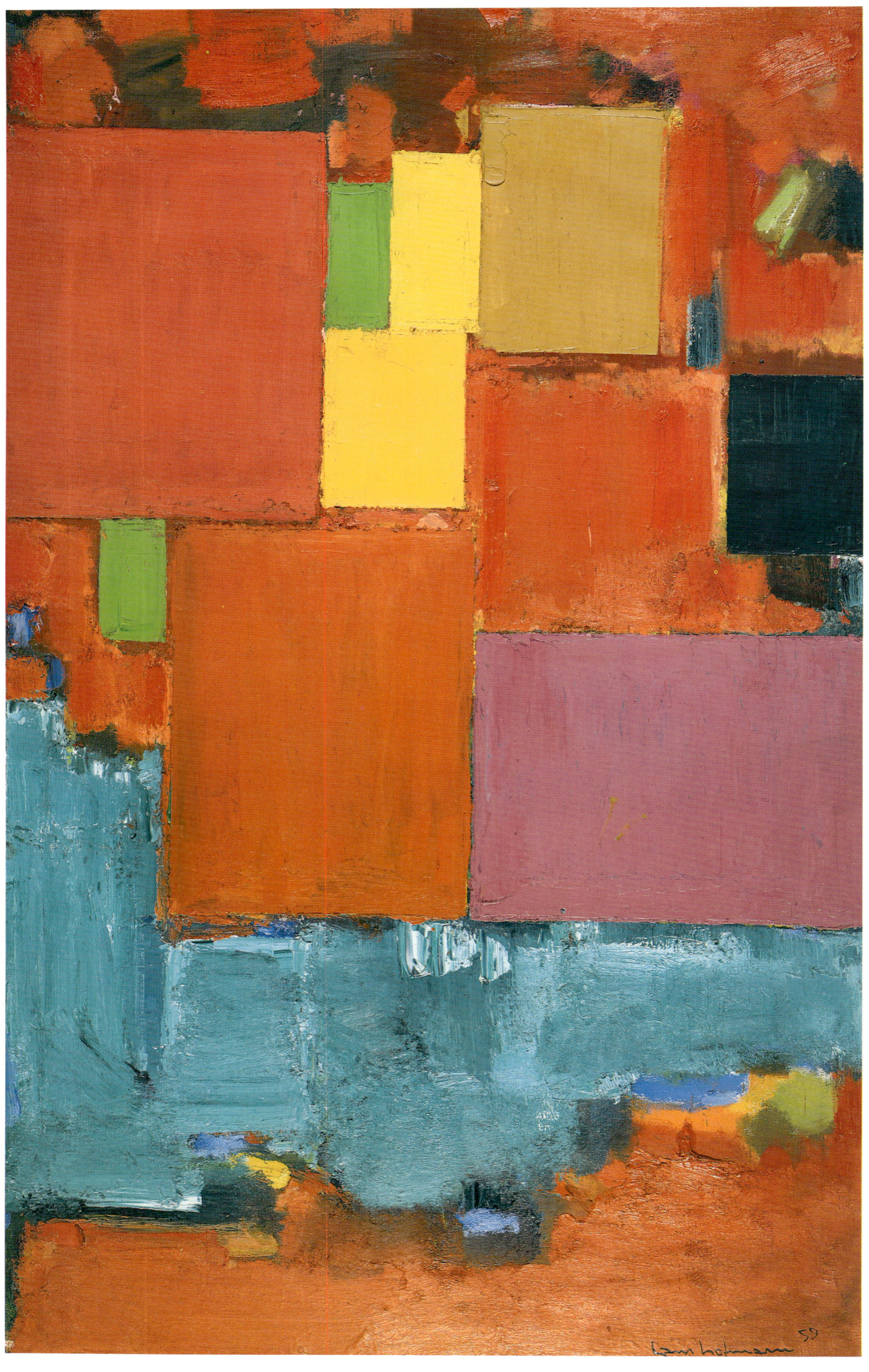

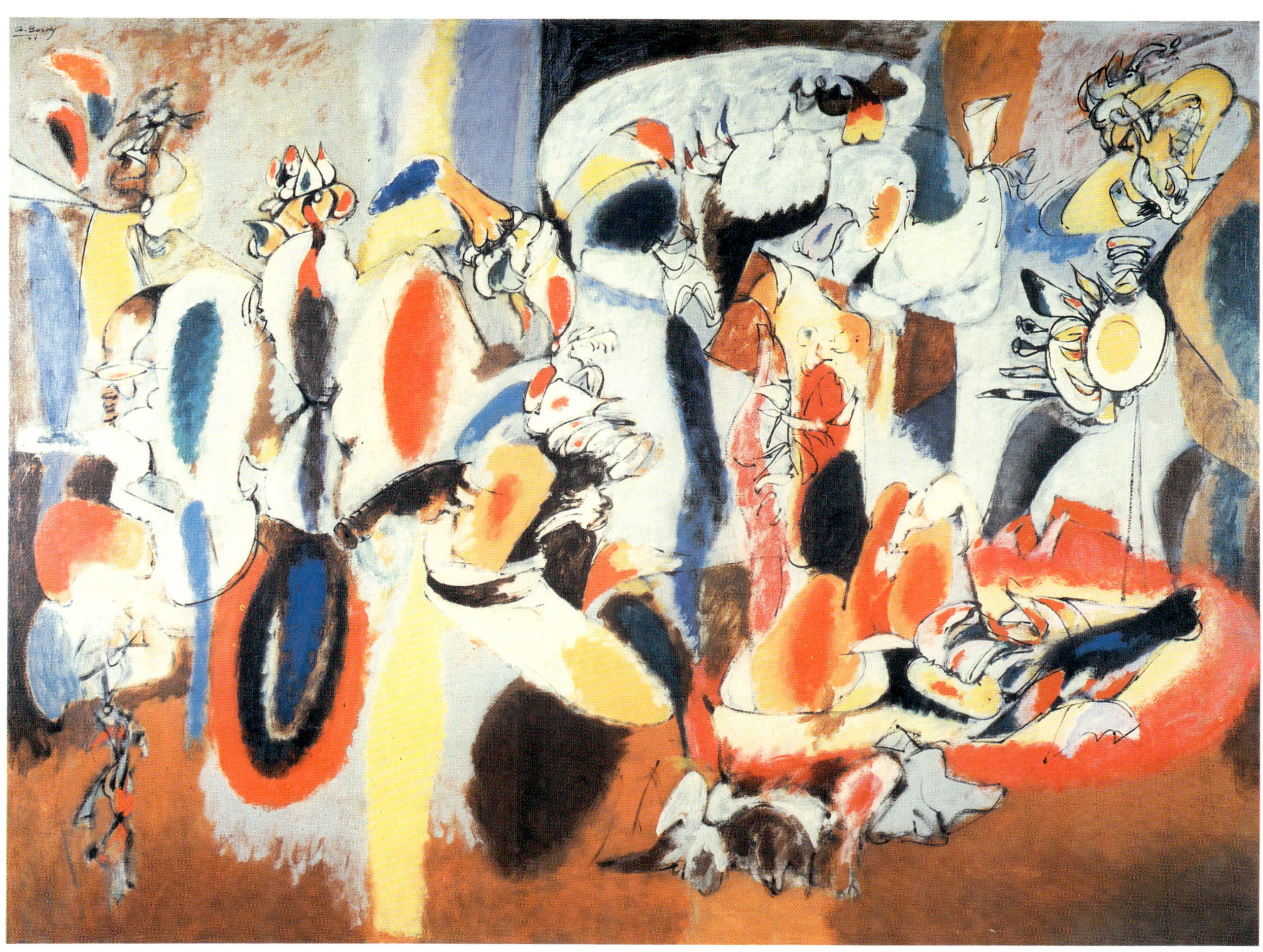

Hans Hofmann
Pompeii 1959
Oil on canvas, 84½×58⅛in (214.6×147.6cm)
Tate Gallery, London

ABOVE:
Arshile Gorky
The Liver is the Cock's Comb 1944
Oil on canvas, 73¼×98in (186×248.9cm)
Albright-Knox Art Gallery, Buffalo, New York
Gift of Seymour H Knox

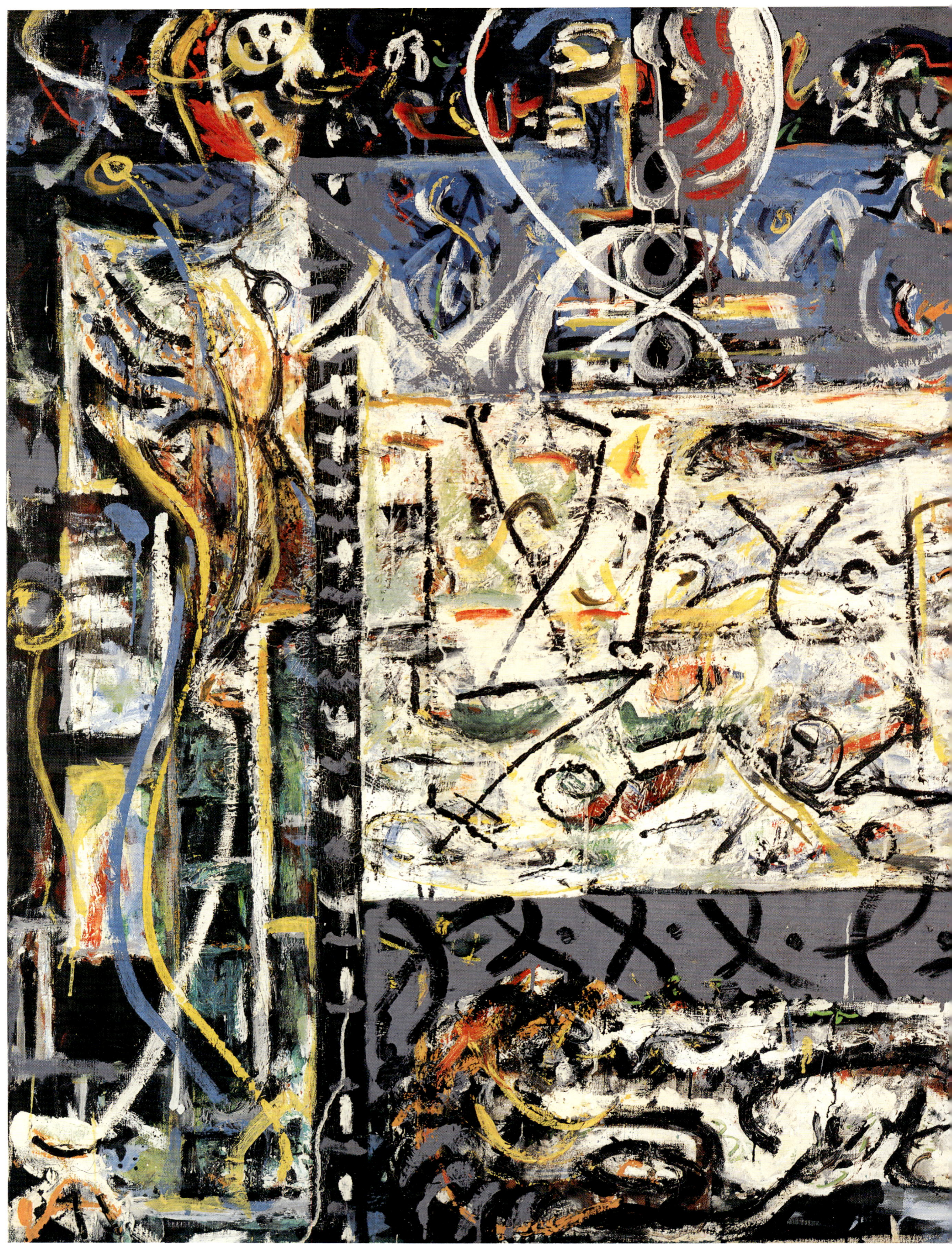

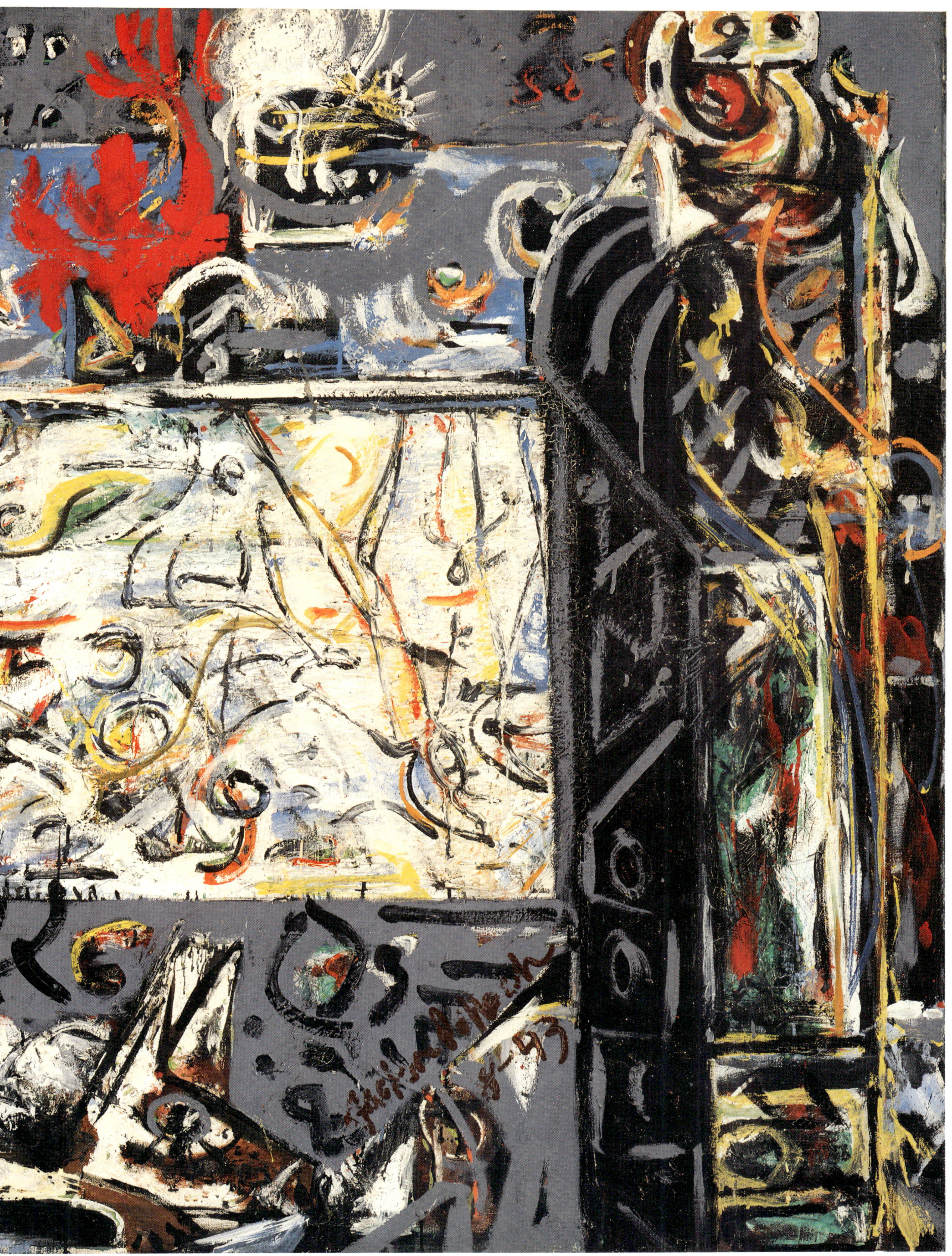

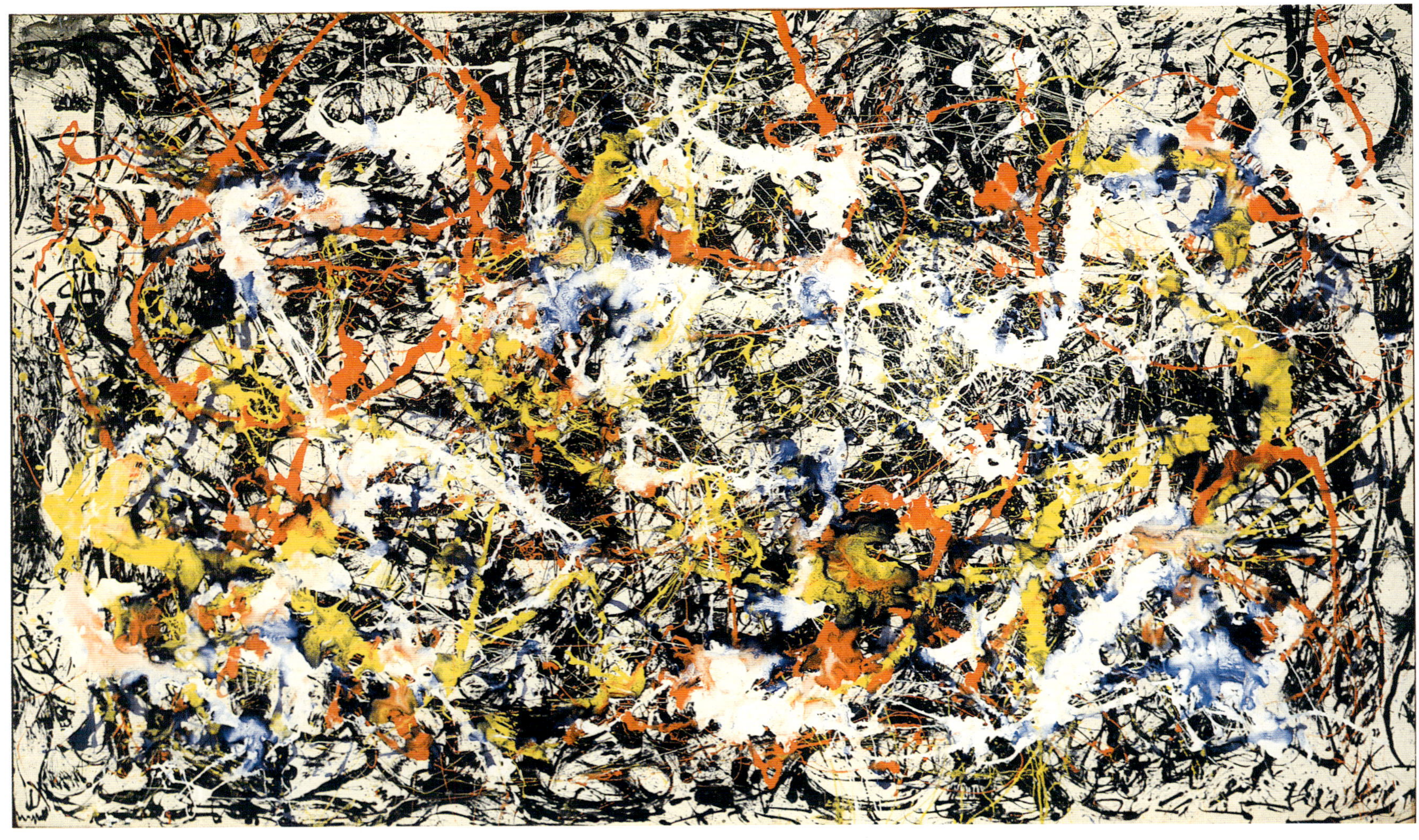

128

ABOVE:
Jackson Pollock
Convergence 1952
Oil on canvas, 93½×155in (237.5×393.7cm)
Albright-Knox Art Gallery, Buffalo, NY
Gift of Seymour H Knox, 1956
© *ARS NY/Pollock-Krasner Foundation, 1989*

PREVIOUS PAGES:
Jackson Pollock
Guardians of the Secret 1943
Oil on canvas, 48⅜×75⅝in (122.9×191.5cm)
San Francisco Museum of Modern Art
Albert M Bender Collection
Albert M Bender Bequest Fund Purchase
© *ARS NY/Pollock-Krasner Foundation, 1989*

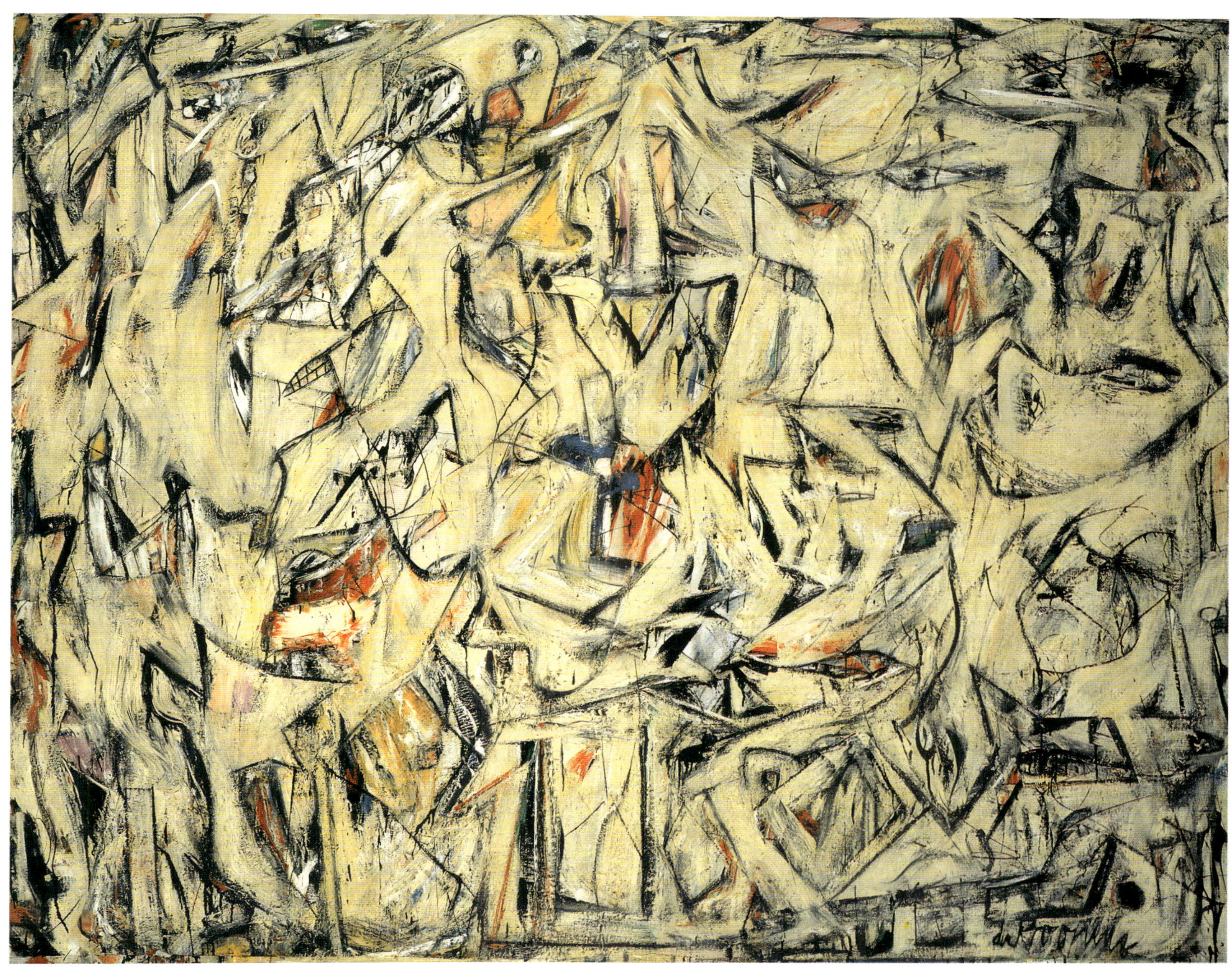

Willem De Kooning
Excavation 1950
Oil and enamel on canvas, 80×100in (203.2×254.3cm)
The Art Institute of Chicago
Gift of Mr and Mrs Noah Goldowsky and Edgar Kaufmann Jr

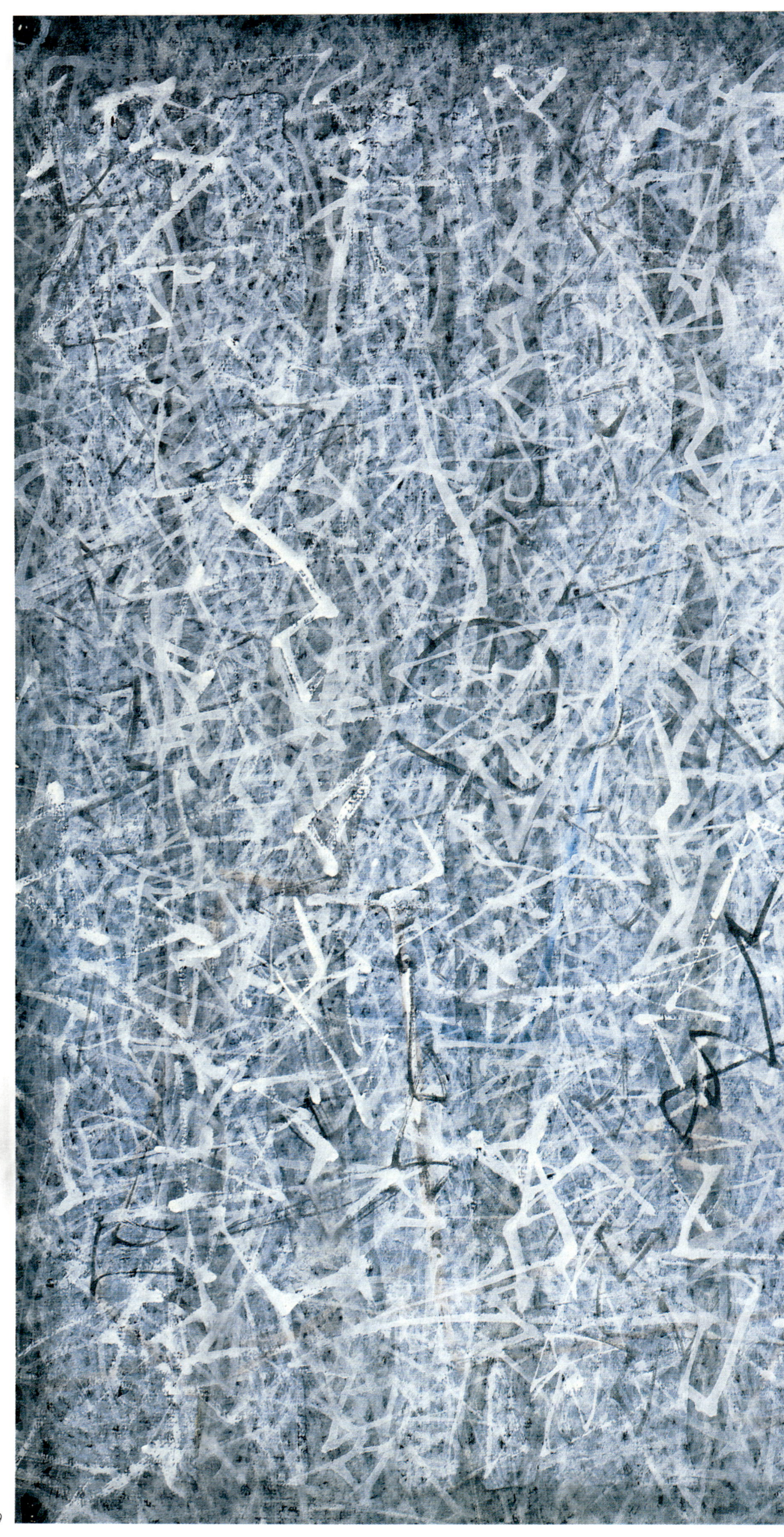

Mark Tobey
Shadow Spirits of the Forest 1961
Tempera on paper, 19×24¾in (48.4×63.2cm)
Kunstsammlung, Nordrhein-Westfalen, Düsseldorf
© *COSMOPRESS, Geneva, DACS, London, 1989*

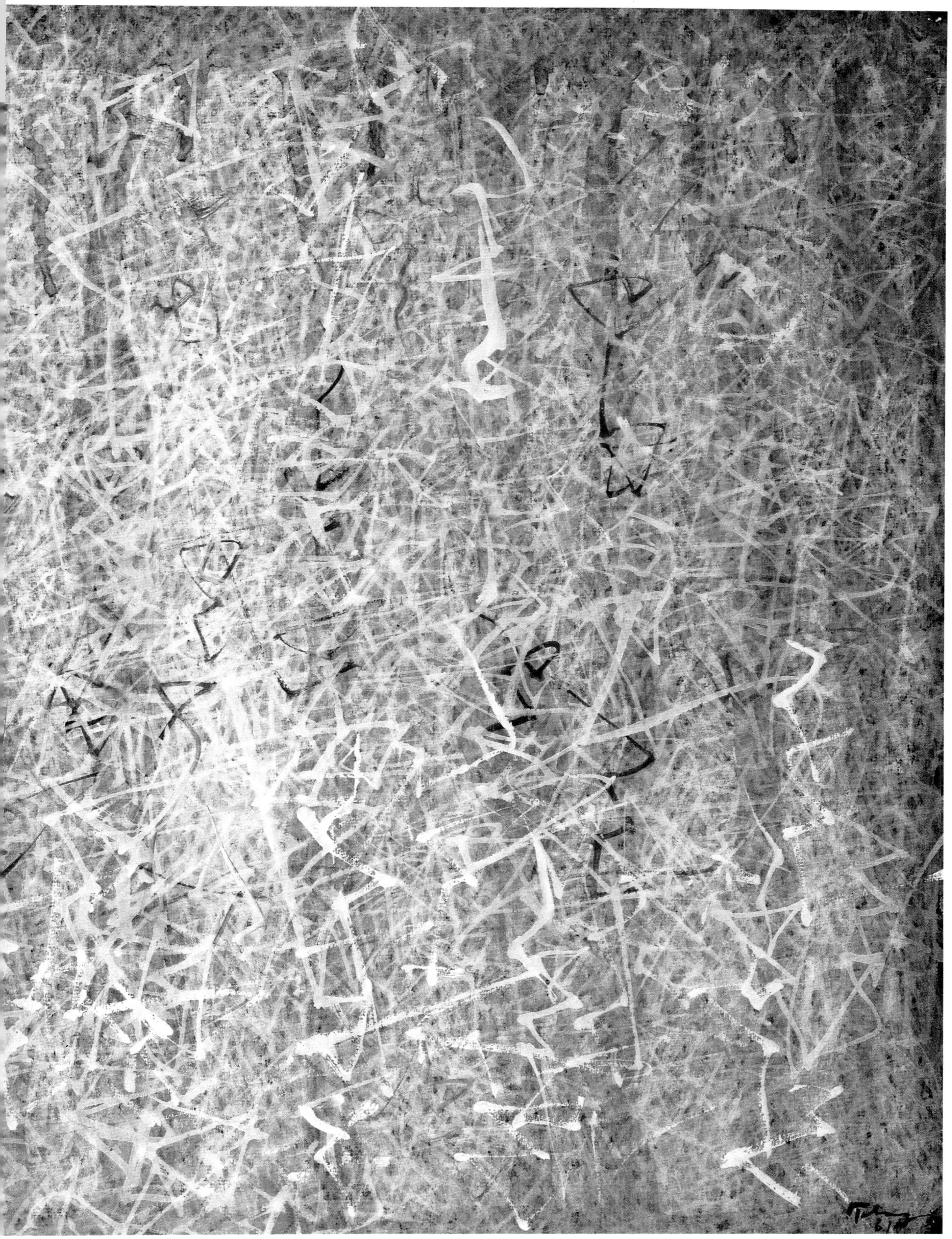

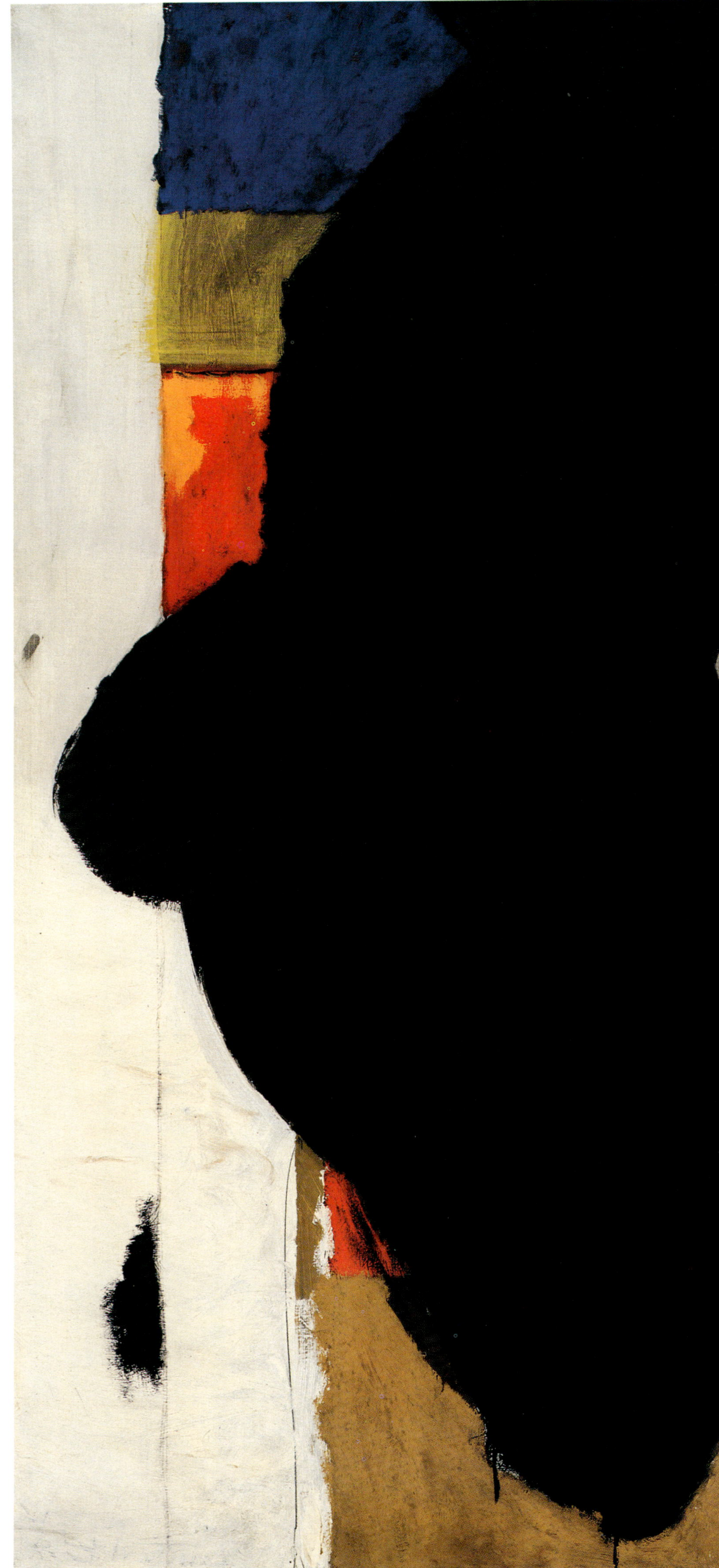

Robert Motherwell
Elegy to the Spanish Republic No 34 1953-54
Oil on canvas, 80×100in (203.2×254cm)
Albright-Knox Art Gallery, Buffalo, NY
Gift of Seymour H Knox, 1959
© *DACS, 1989*

OVERLEAF:
Clyfford Still
1957 – D No 1 1957
Oil on canvas, 113×159in (287.2×403.86cm)
Albright-Knox Art Gallery, Buffalo, NY
Gift of Seymour H Knox

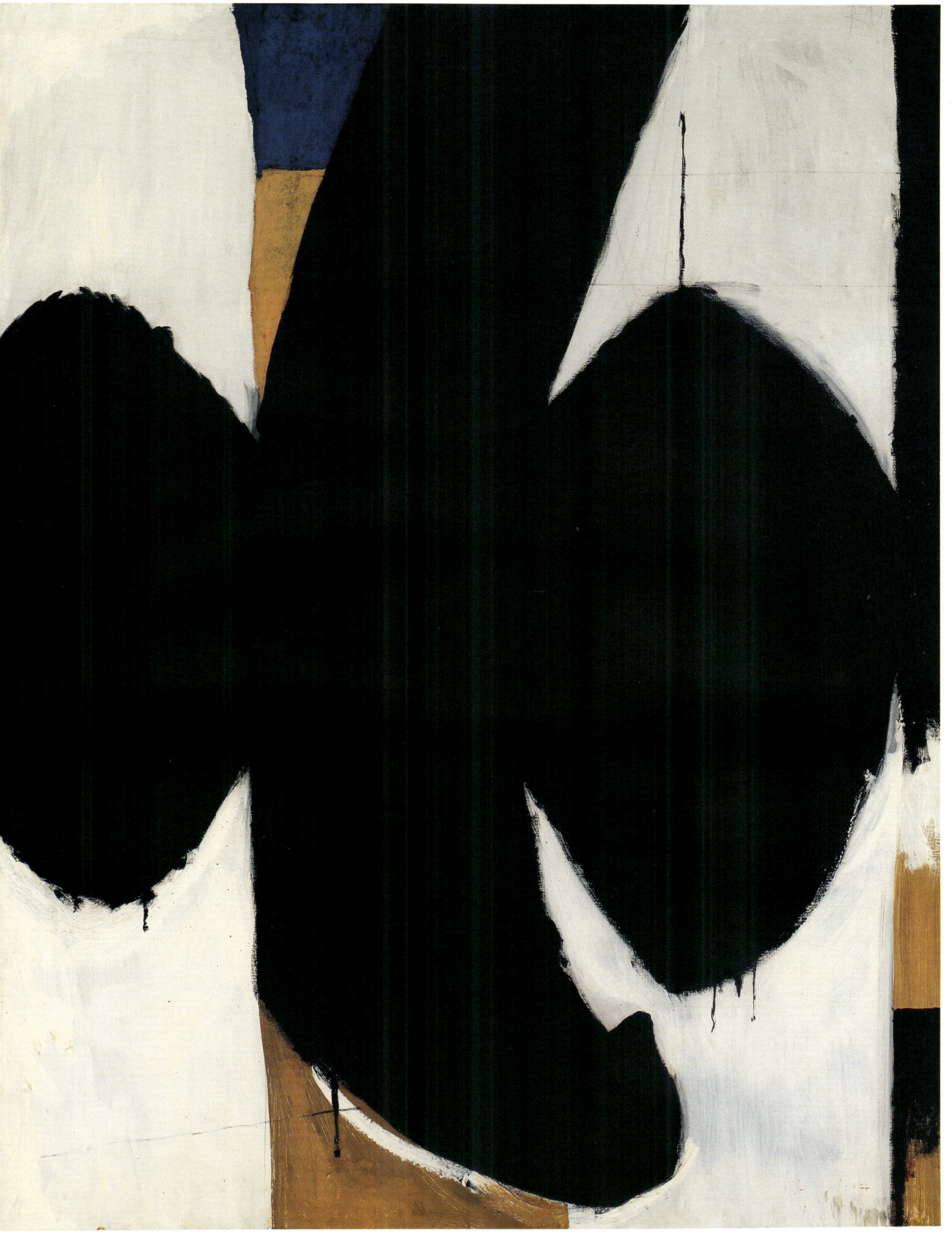

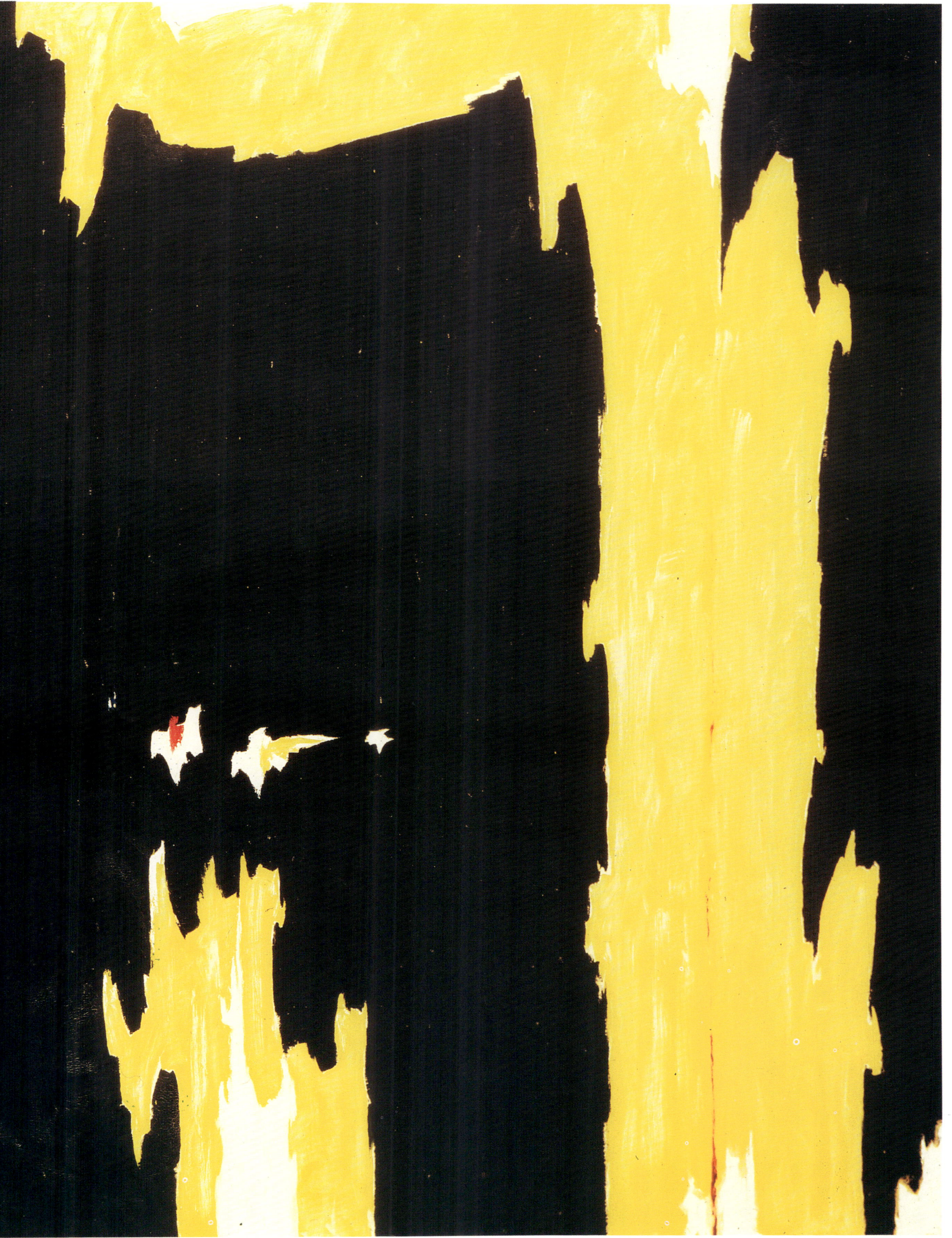

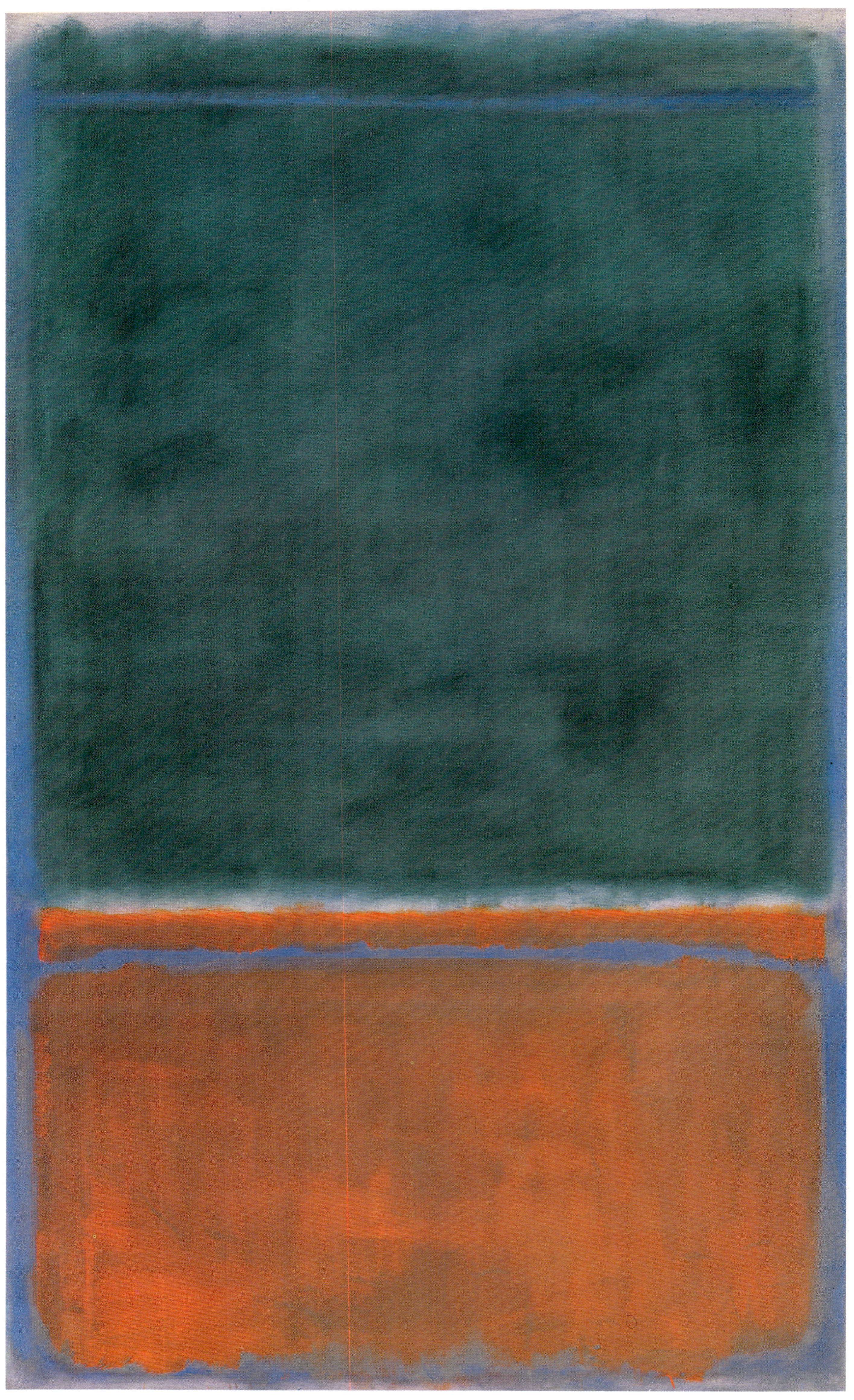

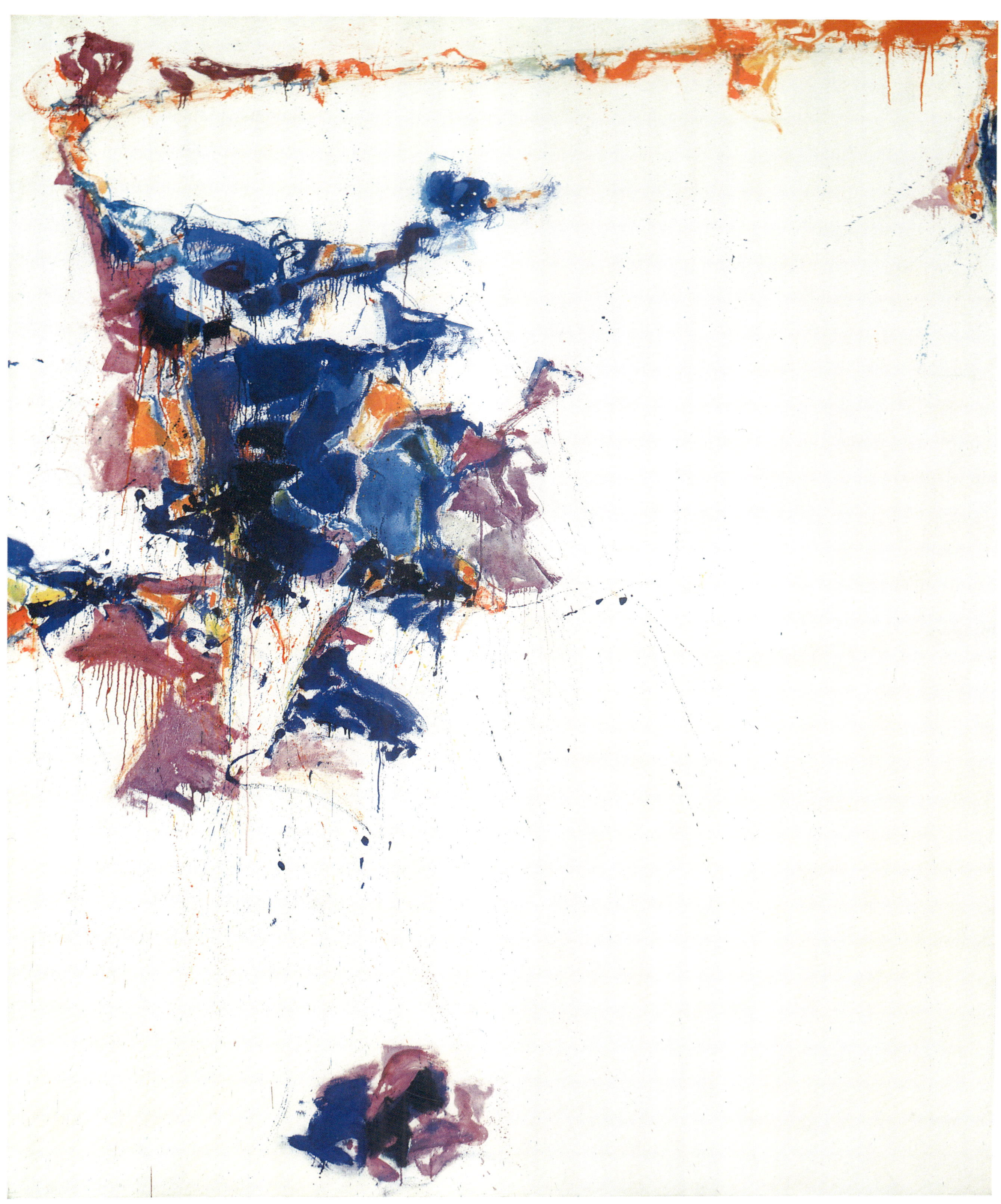

LEFT:
Mark Rothko
Green and Maroon 1953
Oil on canvas, 91¼×54¾in (231.8×139.1cm))
The Phillips Collection, Washington, DC

ABOVE:
Sam Francis
The Whiteness of the Whale 1957
Oil on canvas, 104½×85½ (265.4×213.8cm)
Albright-Knox Art Gallery, Buffalo, New York
Gift of Seymour H Knox, 1959

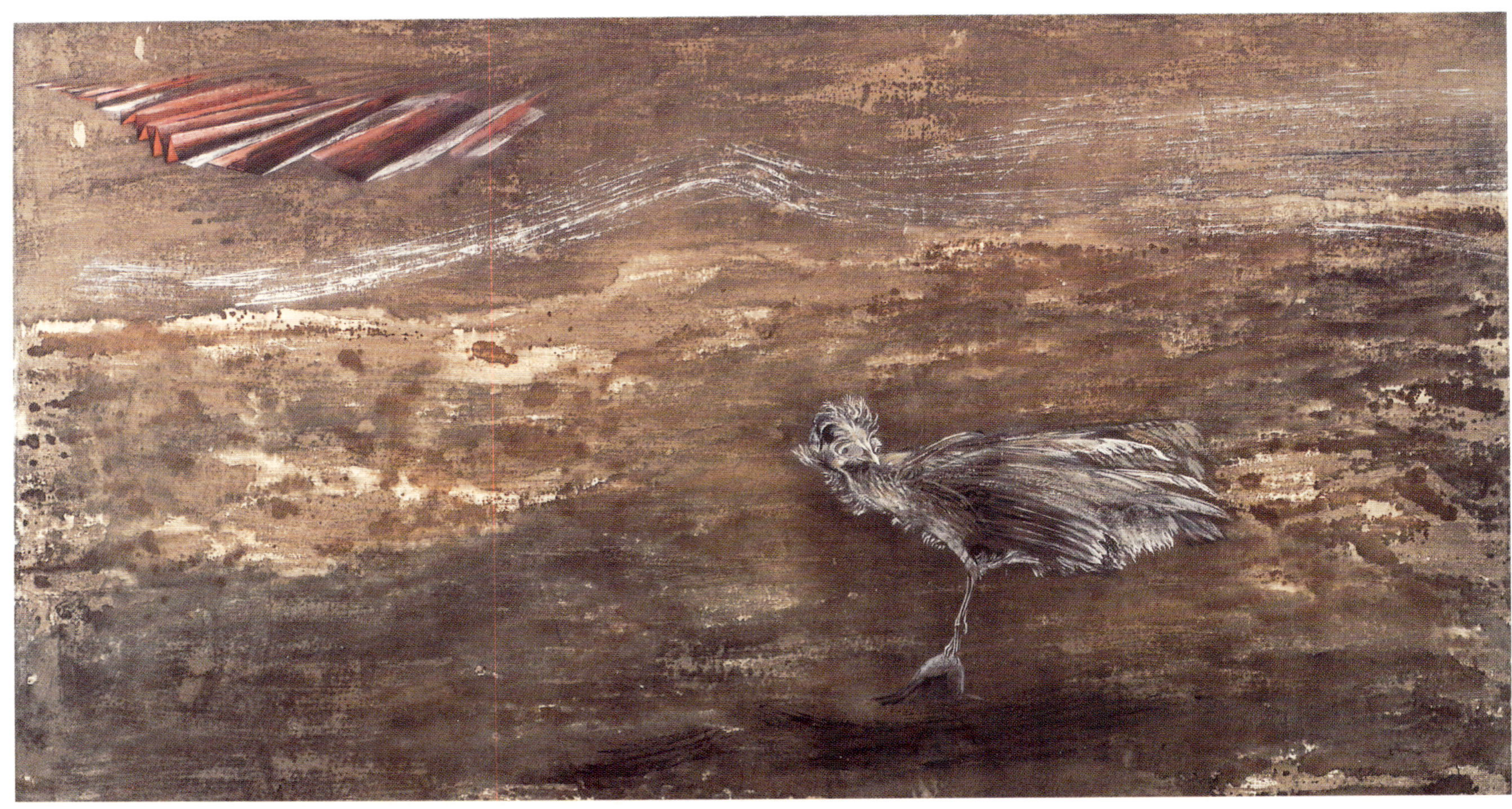

Morris Graves
Bird Maddened by the Sound of Machinery in the Air 1944
Watercolor on rice paper, 32⅝×59⅜in (82.9×150.8cm)
San Francisco Museum of Modern Art
Anonymous Gift

Barnett Newman
Covenant 1949
Oil on canvas, 47¾×59⅝in (121.3×151.4cm)
Hirshhorn Museum and Sculpture Garden
Smithsonian Institution
Gift of Joseph H Hirshhorn, 1972

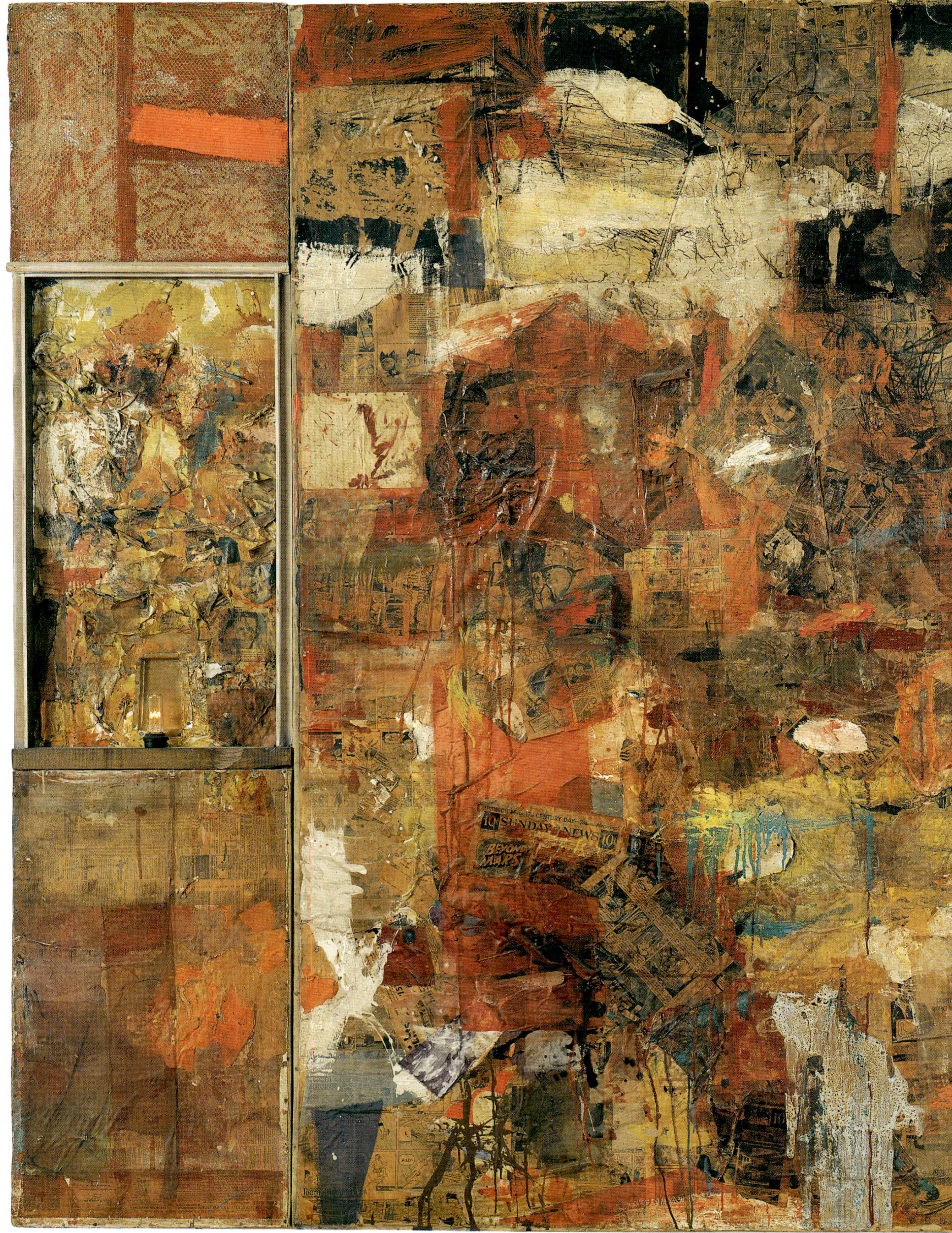

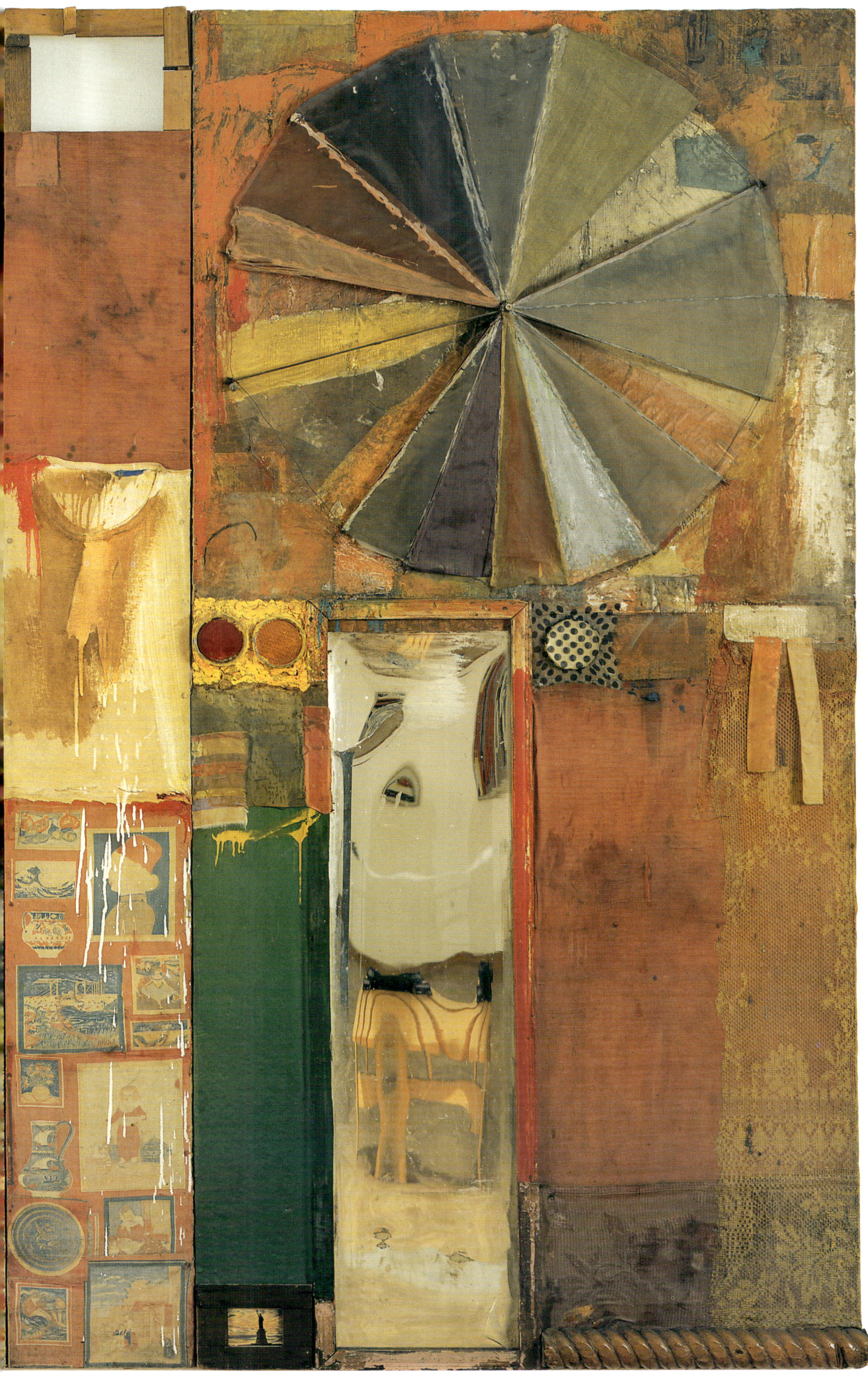

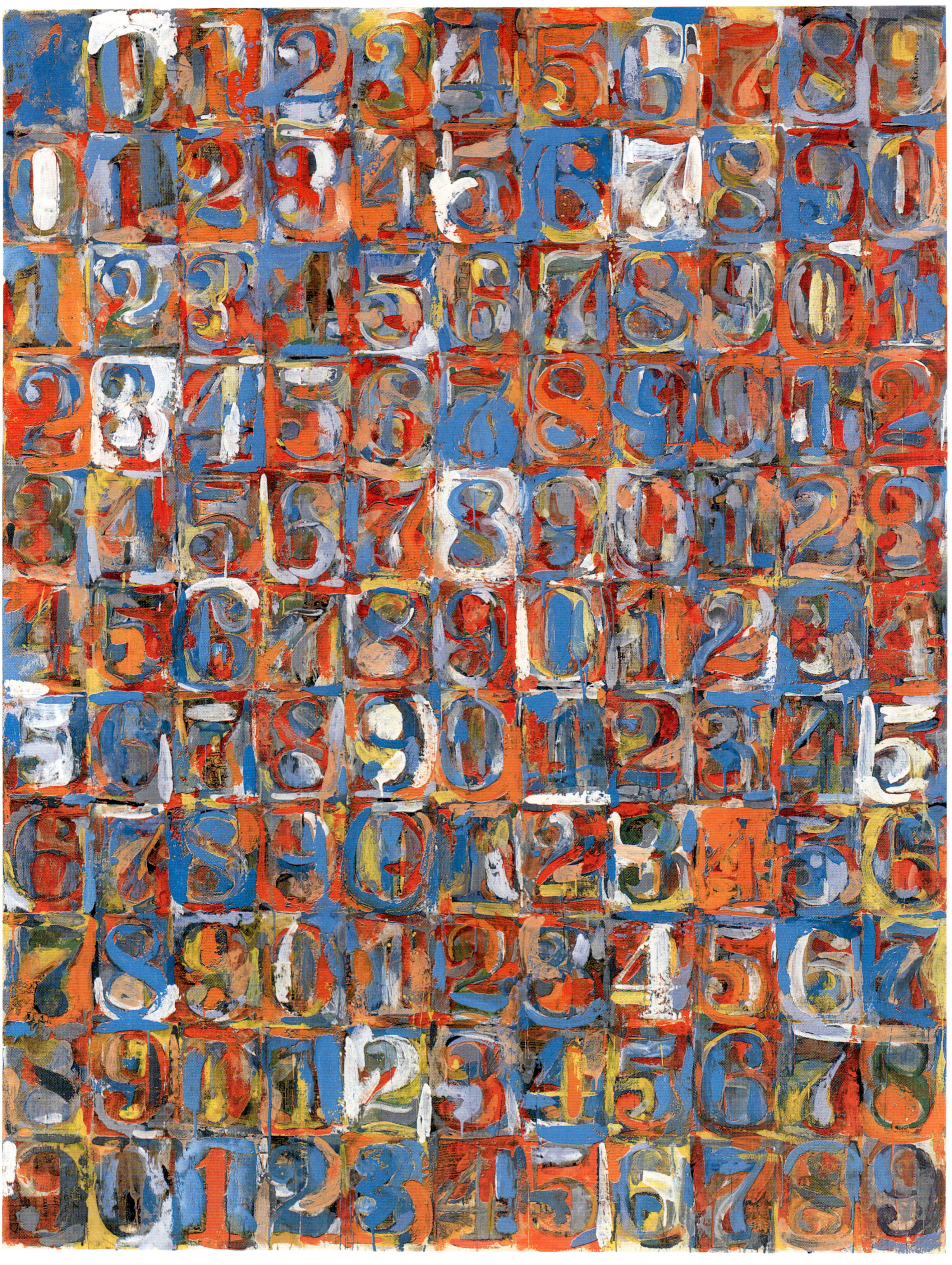

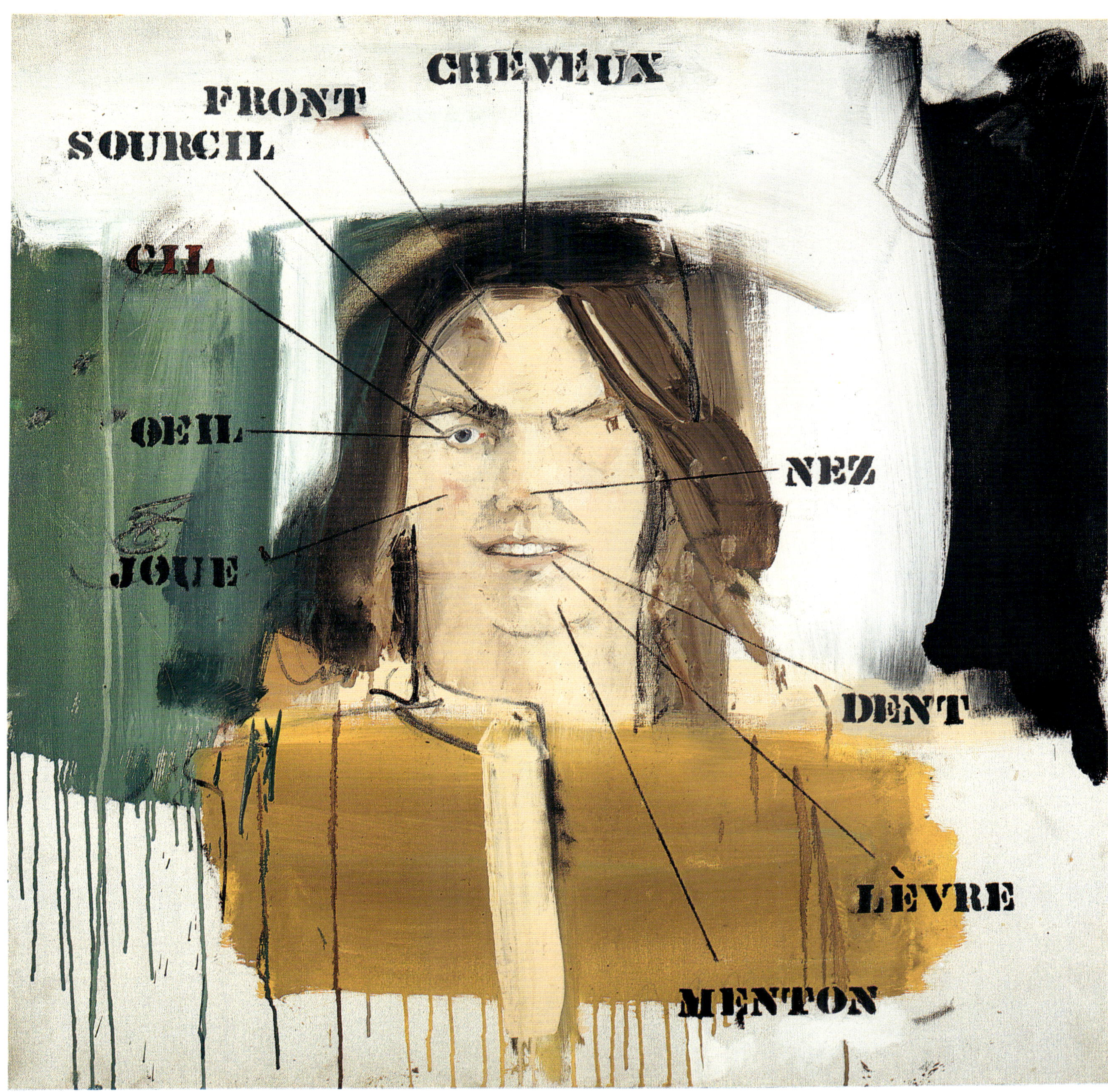
CHEVEUX
FRONT
SOURCIL
CIL
OEIL
JOUE
NEZ
DENT
LÈVRE
MENTON

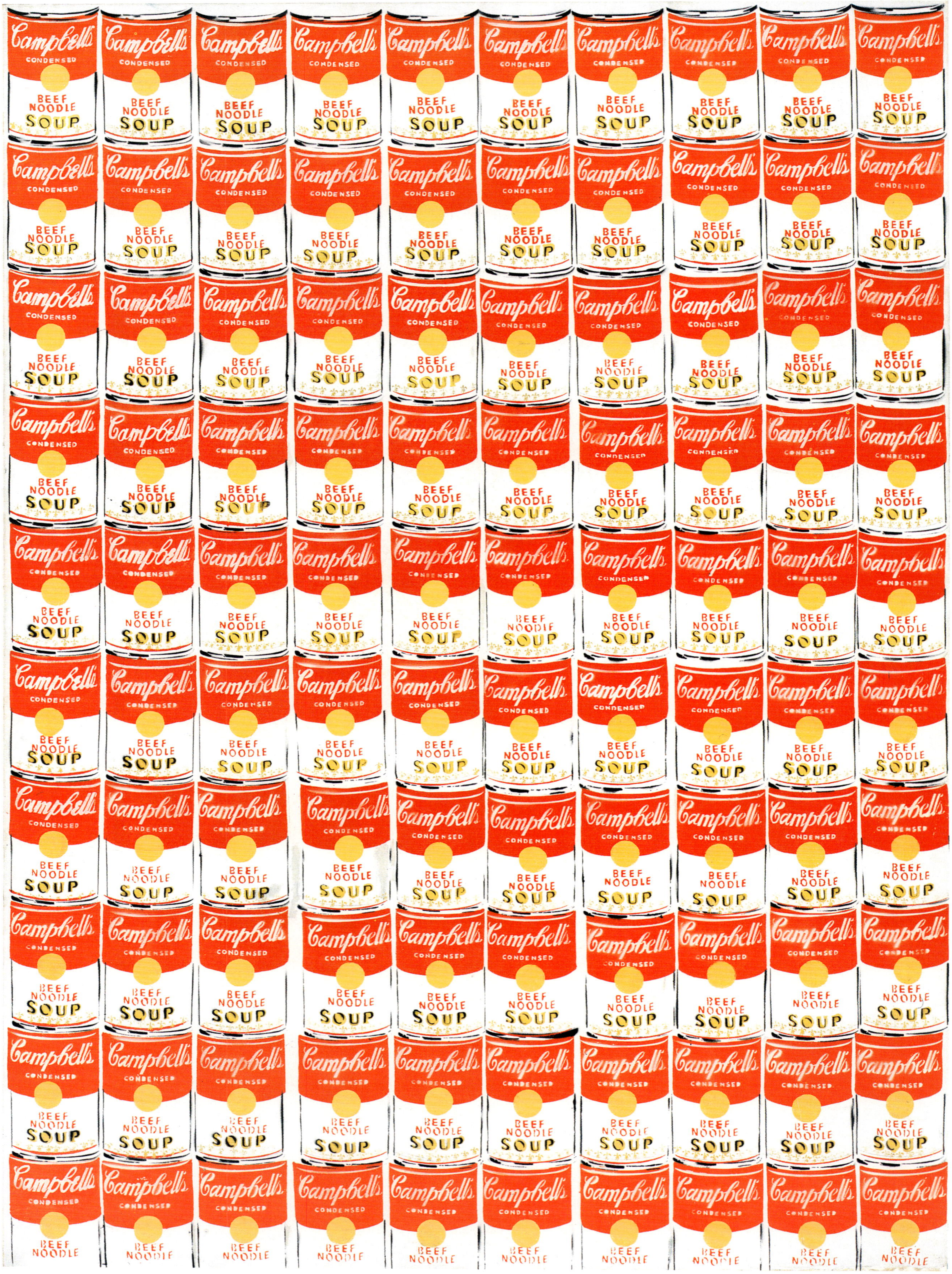
Campbell's
CONDENSED
BEEF
NOODLE
SOUP

Andy Warhol
100 Cans 1962
Oil on canvas, 72×52in (182.9×132cm)
Albright-Knox Art Gallery, Buffalo, New York
Gift of Seymour H Knox, 1963
© *The Estate and Foundation of Andy Warhol, 1989/ARS NY*

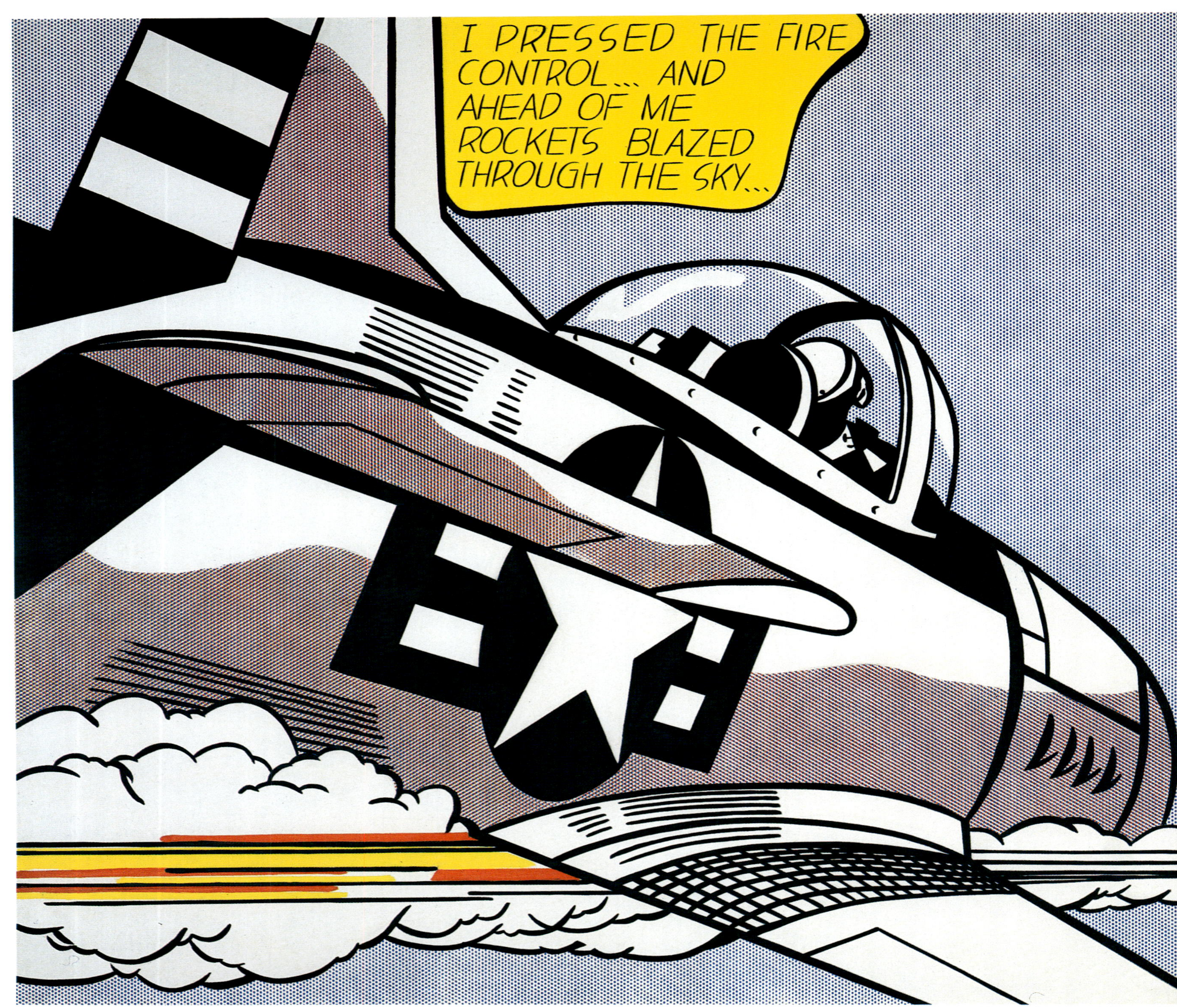

Roy Lichtenstein
Whaam! 1963
Acrylic on canvas, 68×160in (172.7×406.4cm)
Tate Gallery, London
© *DACS, 1989*

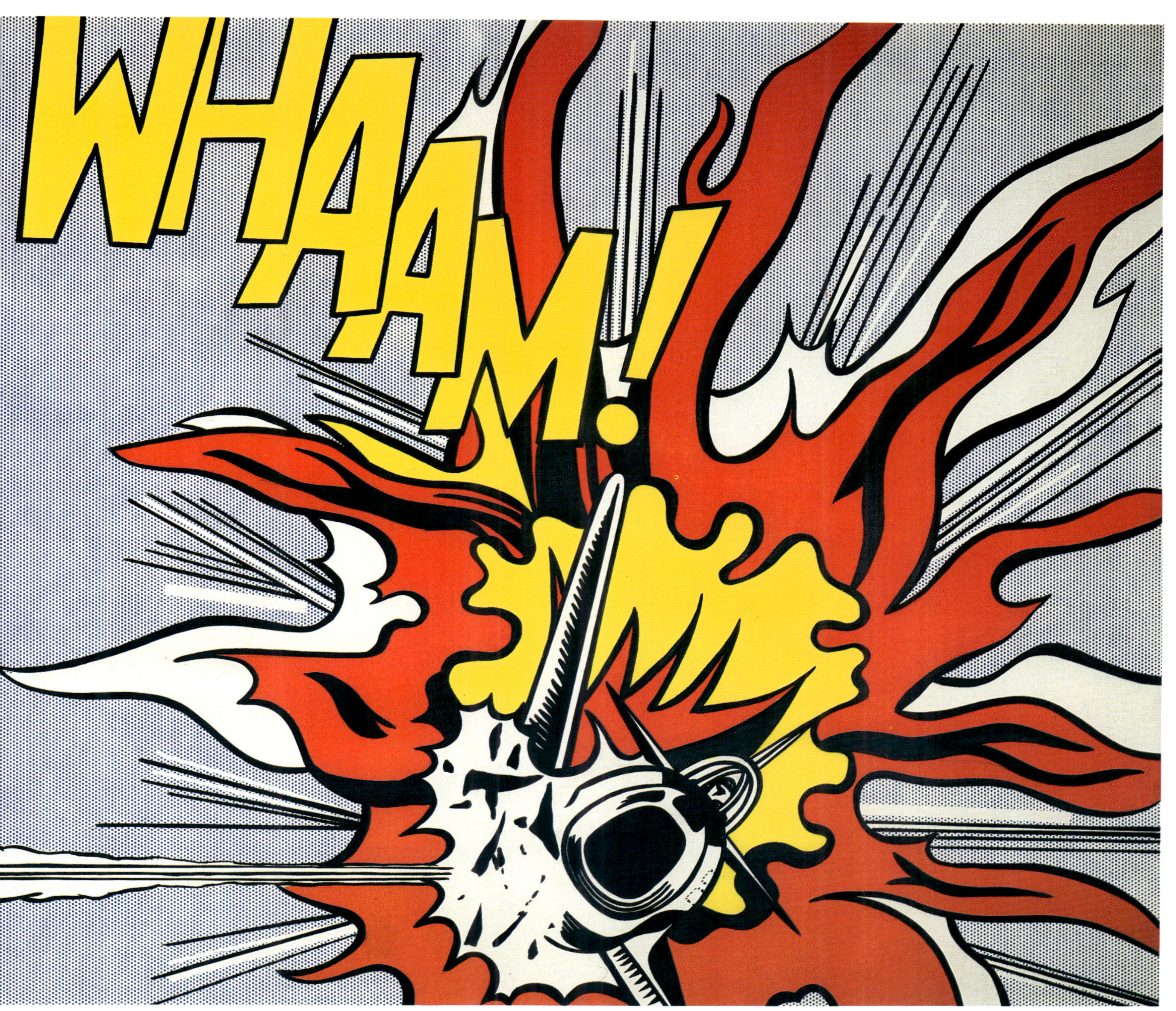
WHAAM!

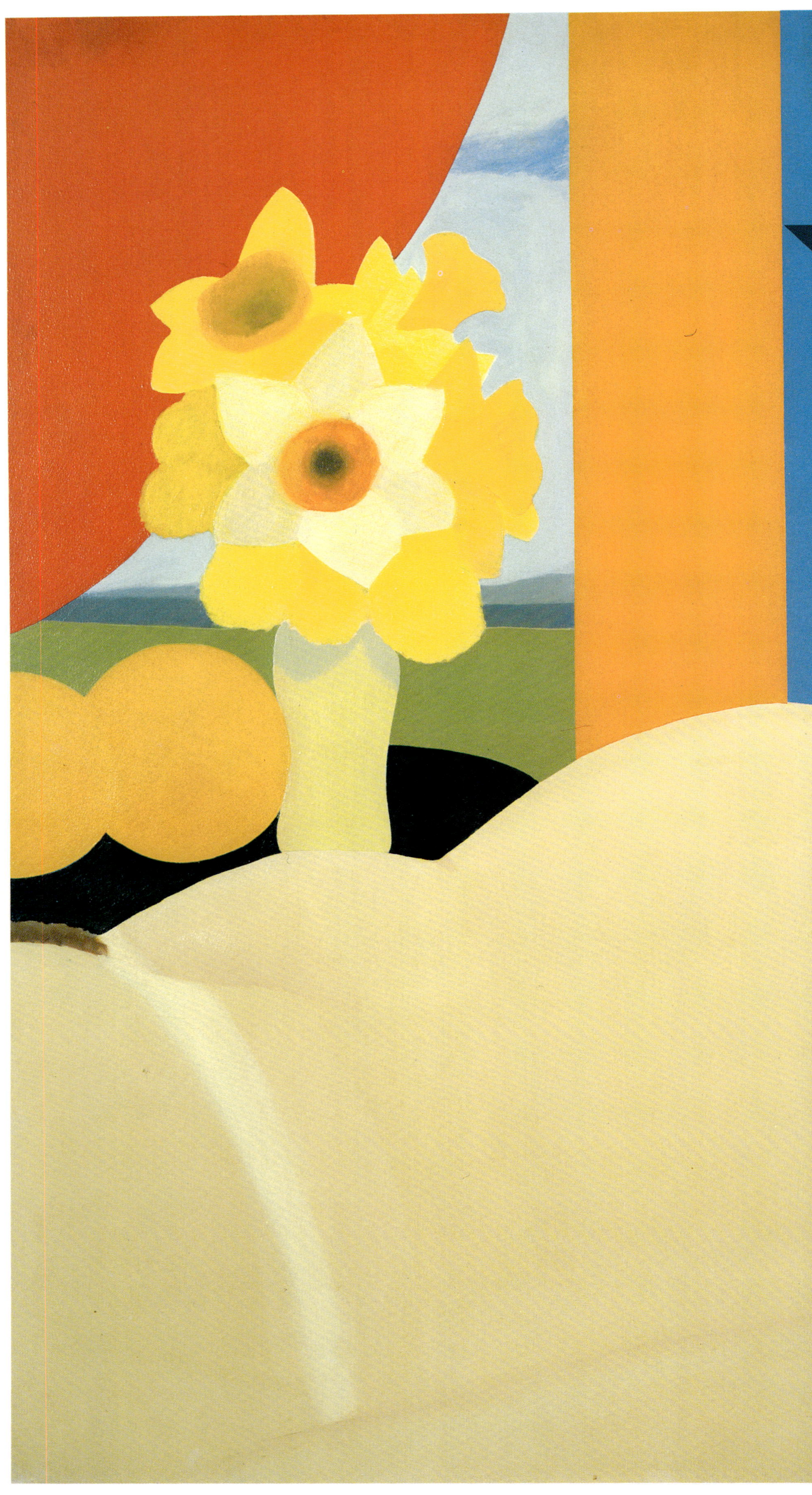

Tom Wesselmann
Great American Nude, No 57 1964
Synthetic polymer on composition
board, 48×65in (121.9×165.1cm)
*Collection of Whitney Museum of
American Art, New York
Purchased with funds from the
friends of the Whitney Museum*
© *DACS, 1989*

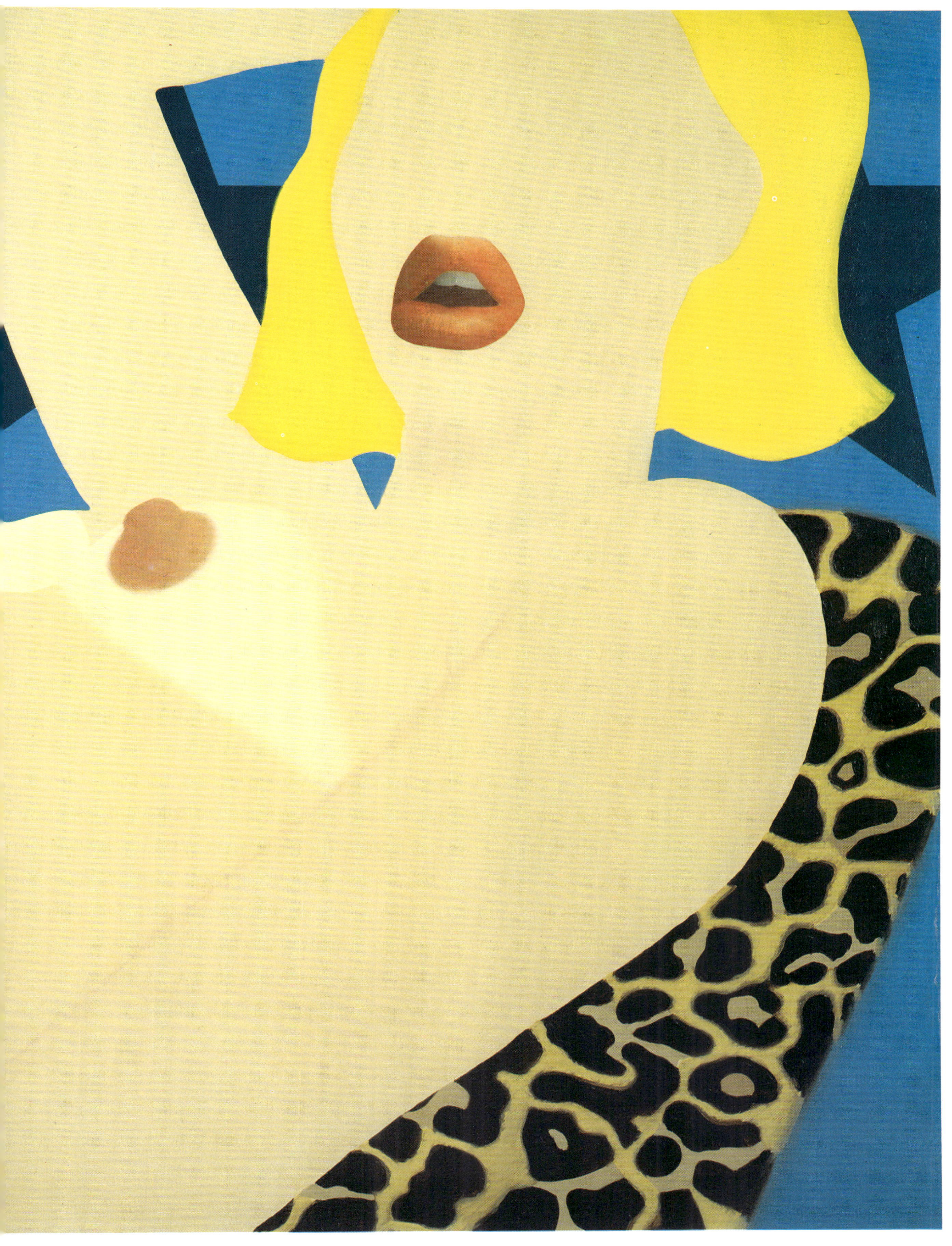

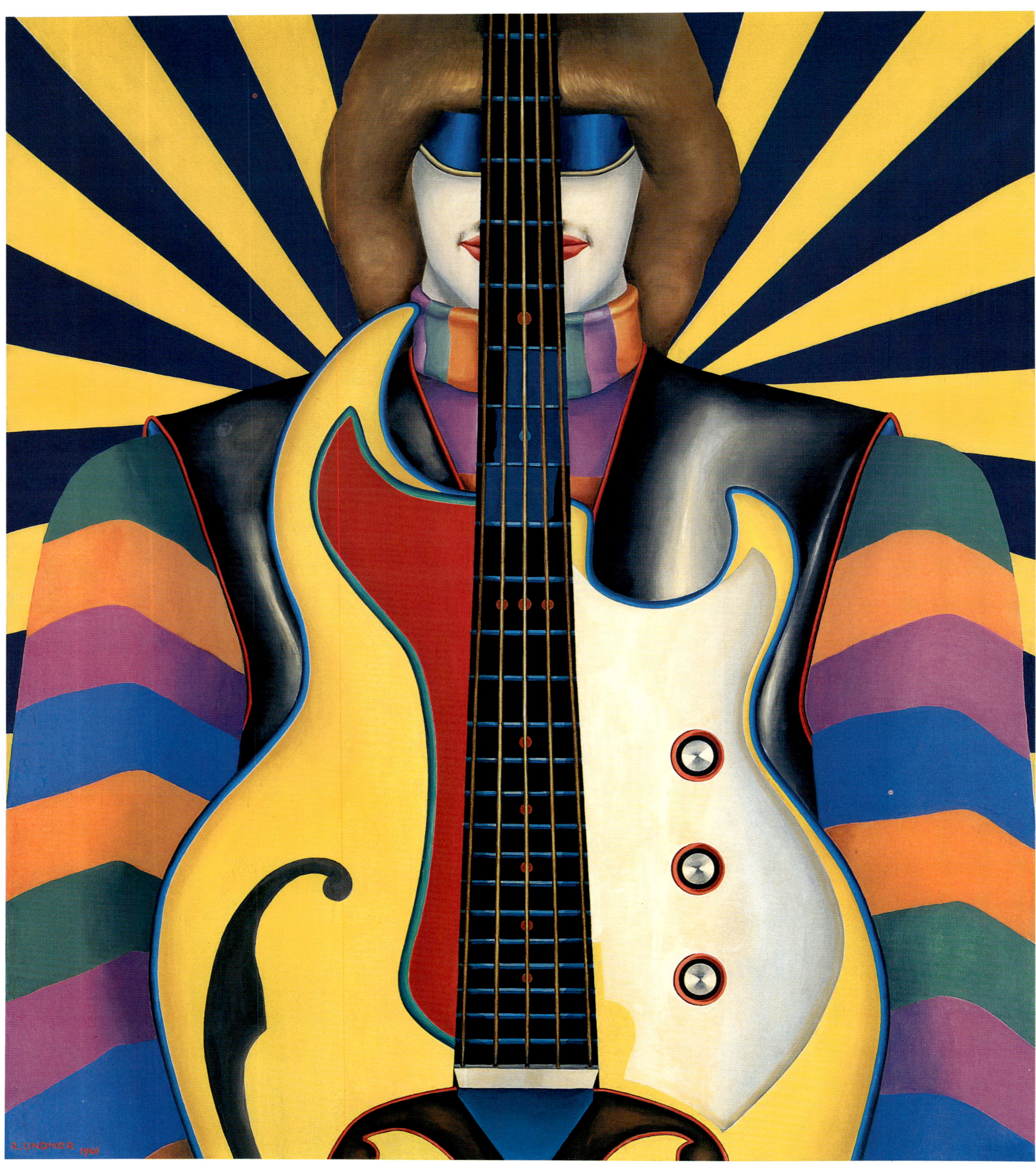

Richard Lindner
Rock-Rock 1966
Oil on canvas, 70×60in (177.8×152.4cm)
Dallas Museum of Art
Gift of Mr and Mrs James H Clark

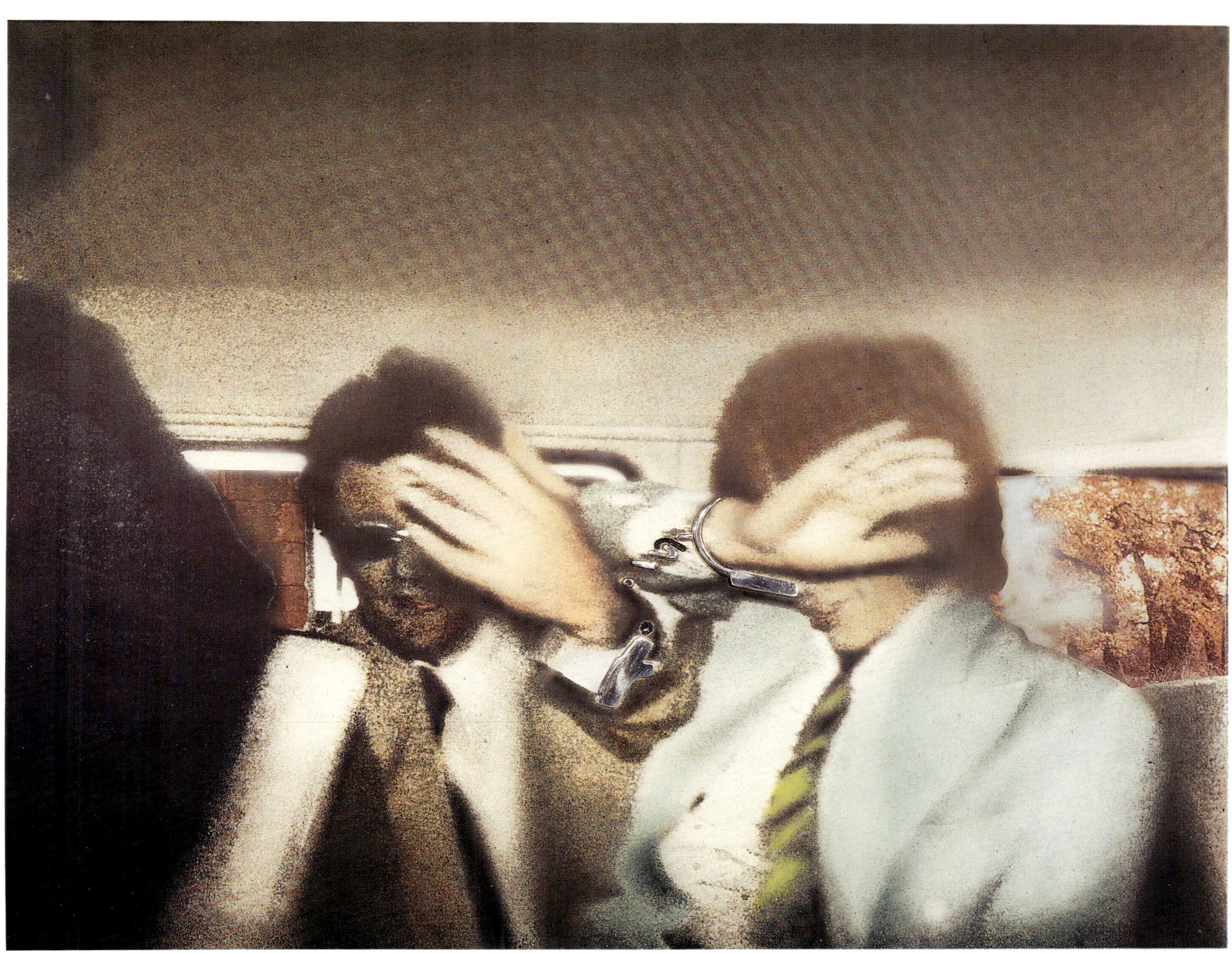

Richard Hamilton
Swingeing London 1968-69
Acrylic with metal on canvas, 26½×33½in (67.3×85.1cm)
Tate Gallery, London
© *Richard Hamilton 1989, all rights reserved DACS*

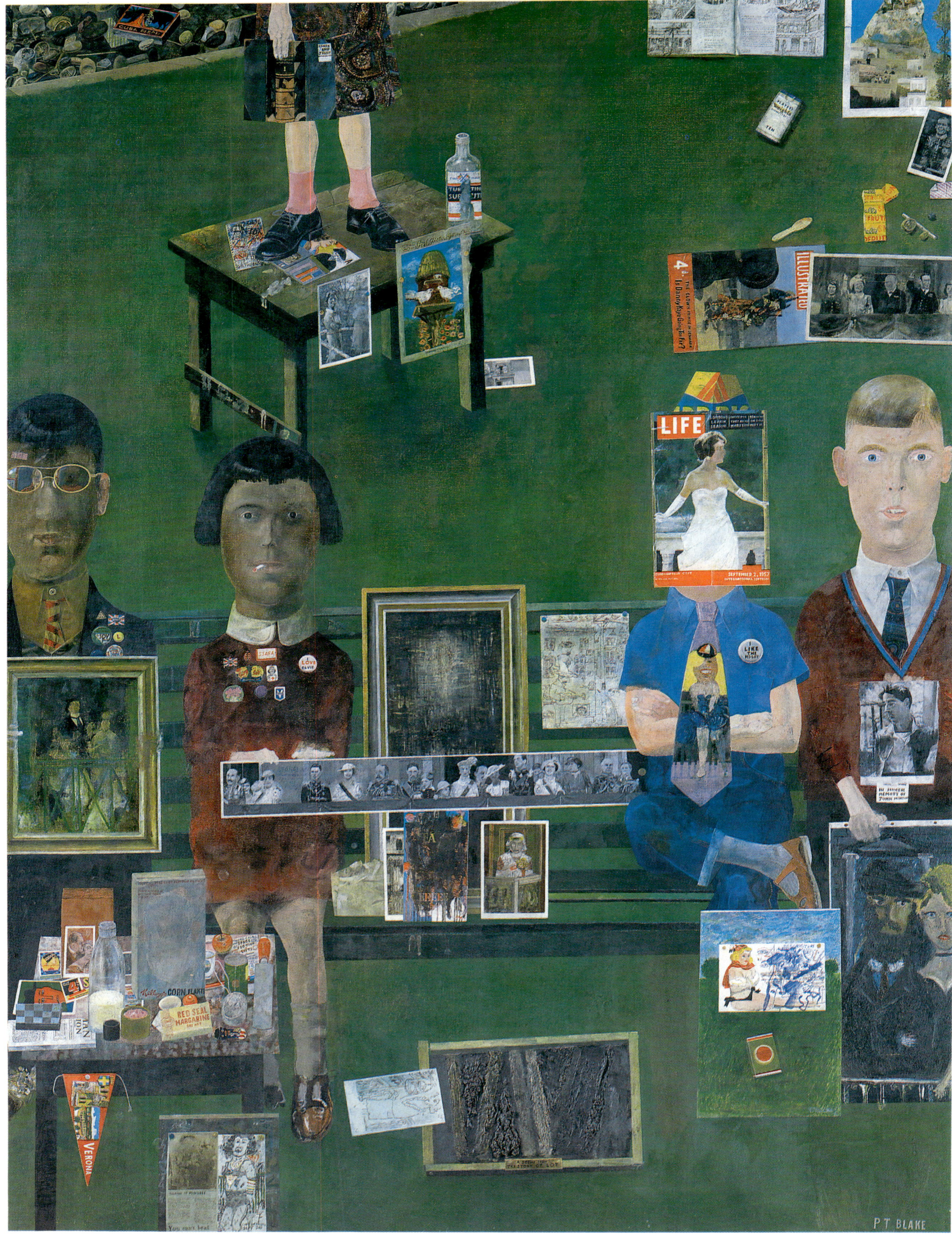

CUBA LIBRE
LIFE
SEPTEMBER 2, 1957
ILLUSTRATED
CORN FLAKES
RED SEAL
MARGARINE
VERONA
P T BLAKE

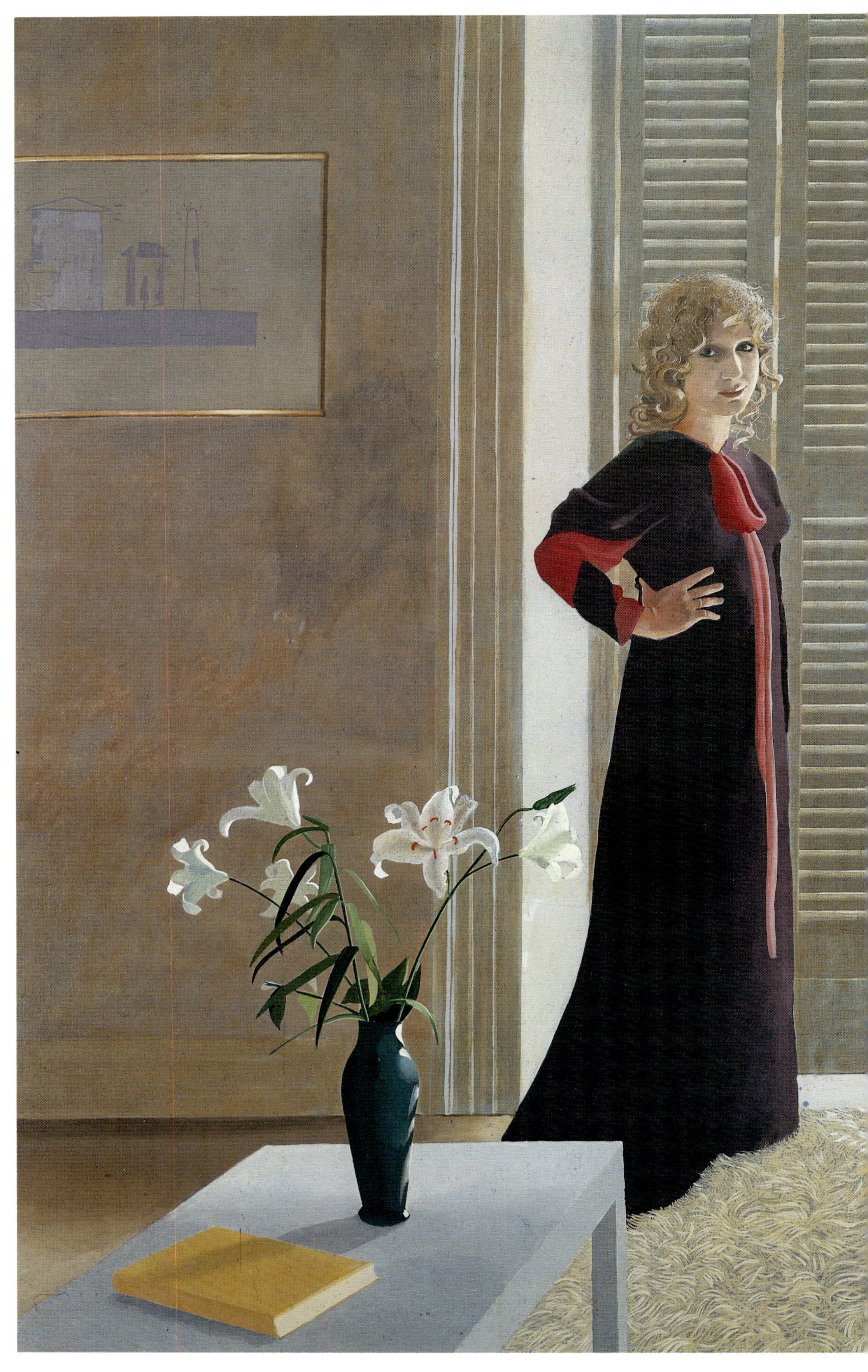

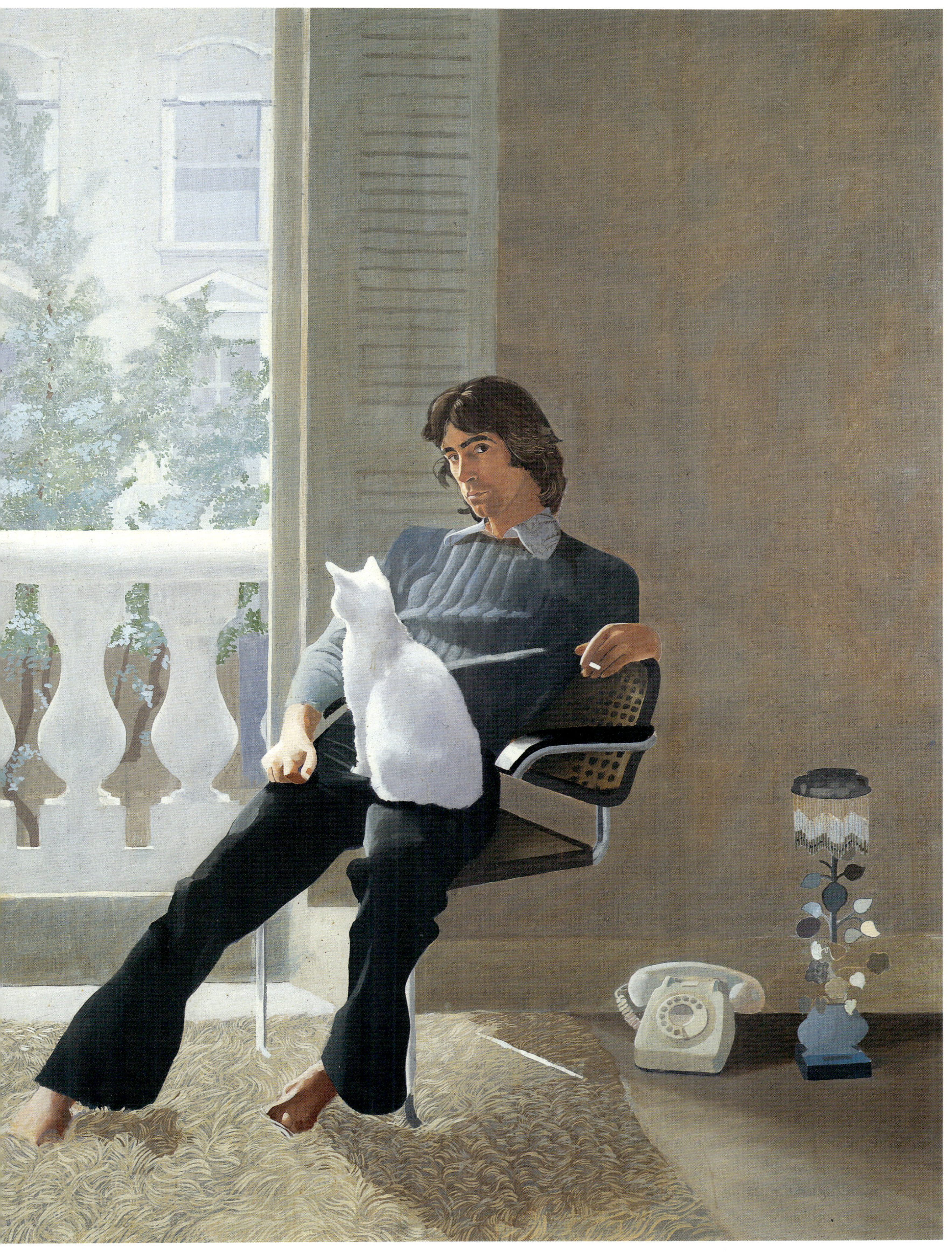

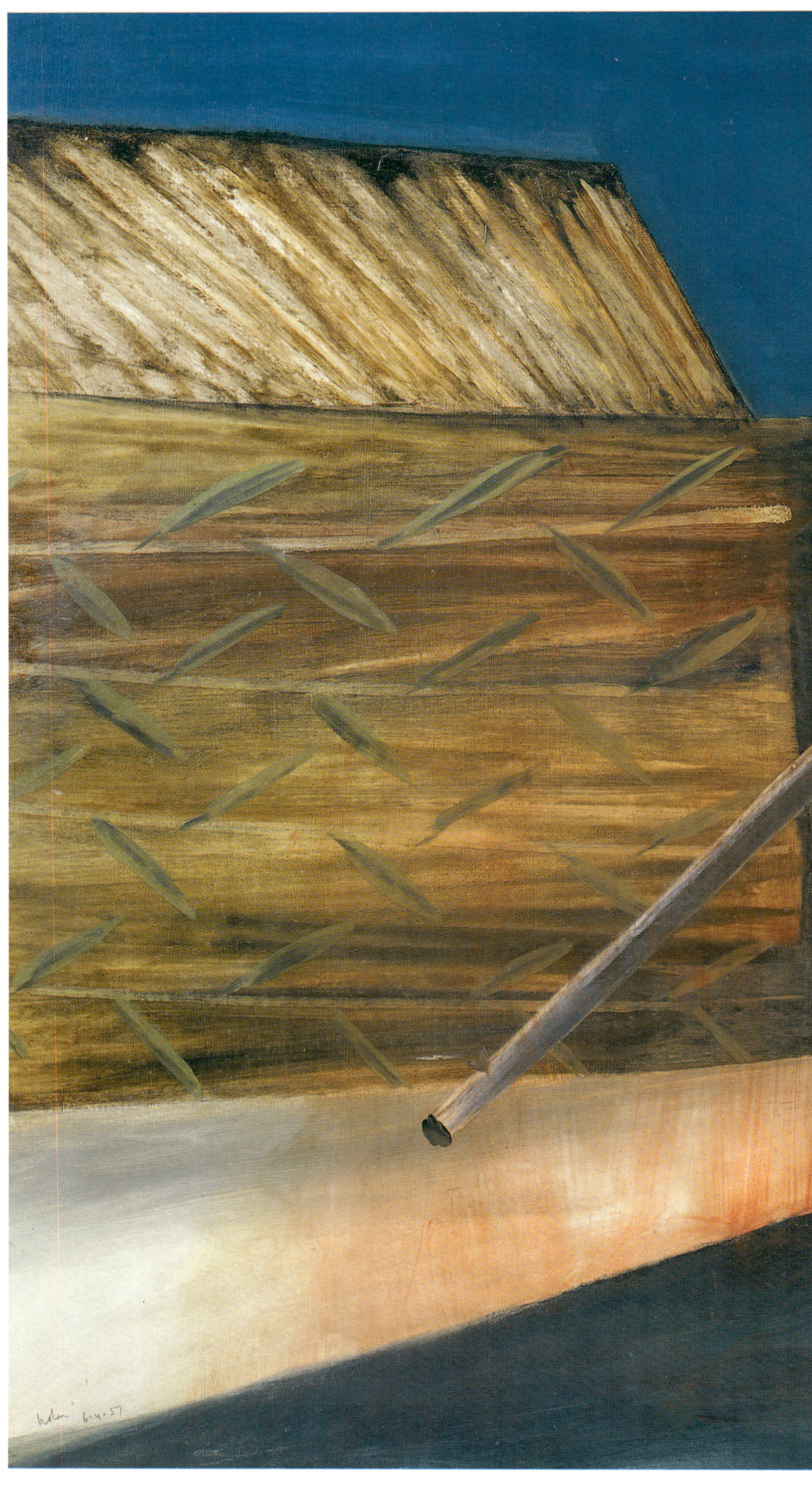

Sidney Nolan
Glenrowan 1956-57
Acrylic on canvas, 36×48in
(91.4×121.9cm)
Tate Gallery, London

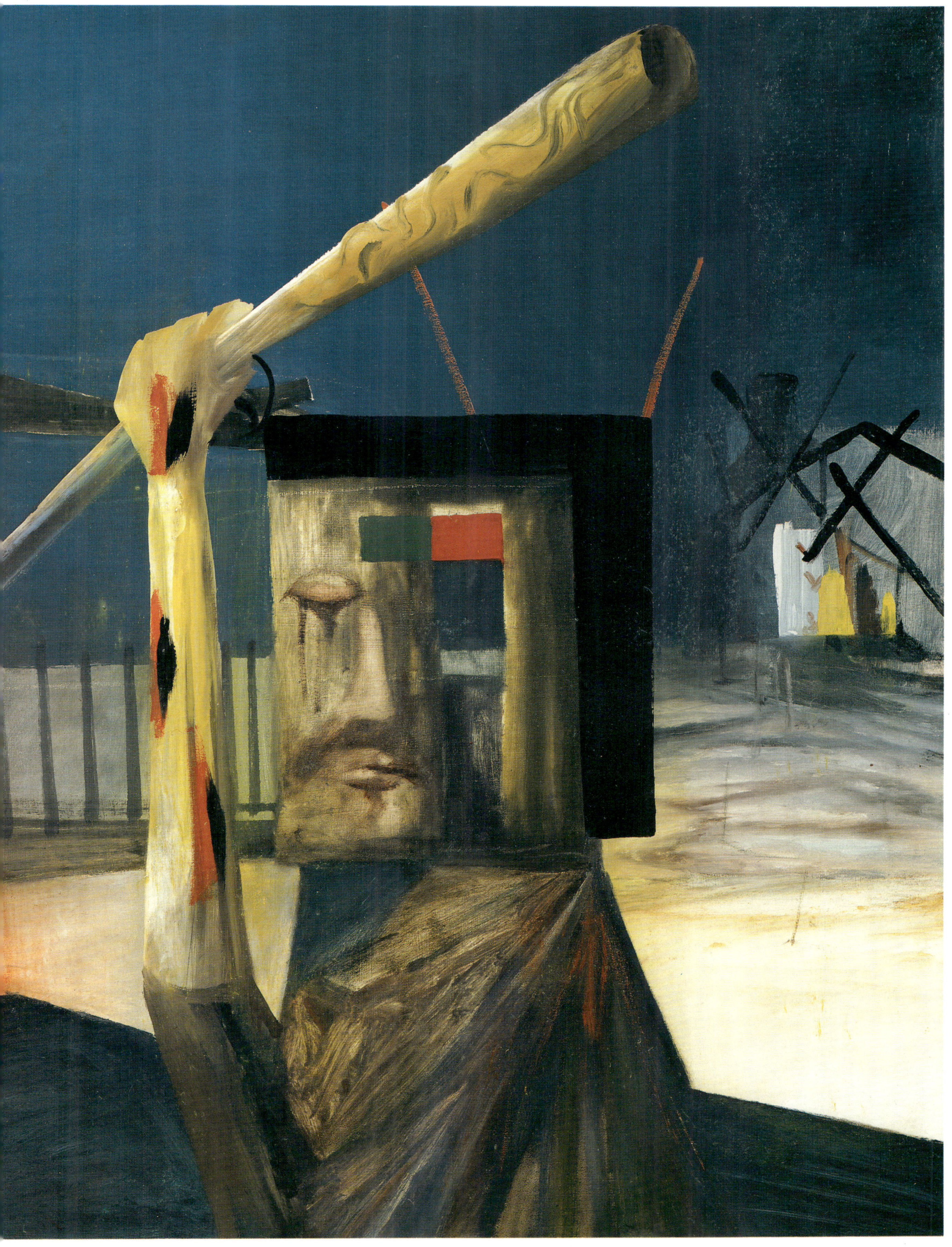

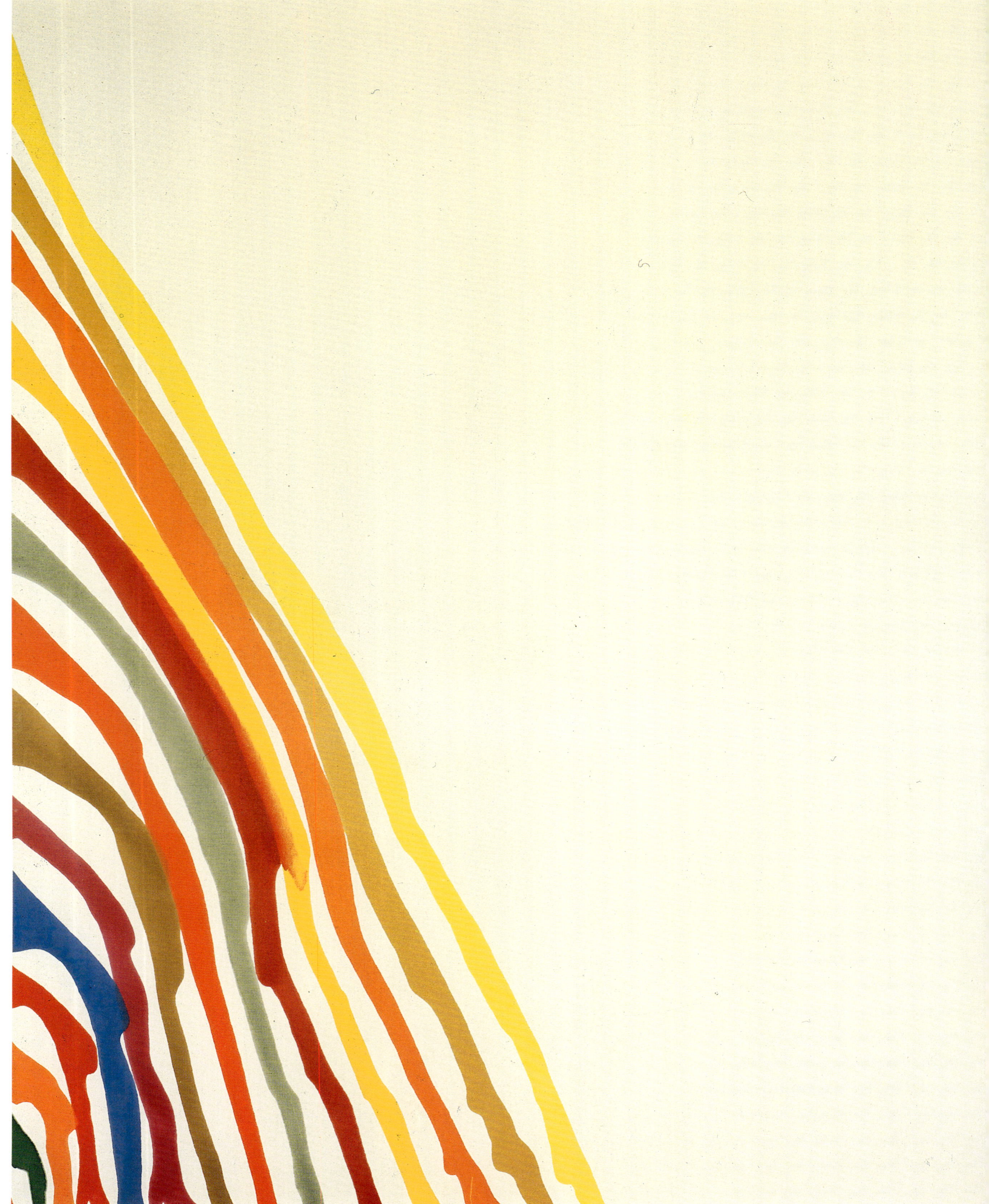

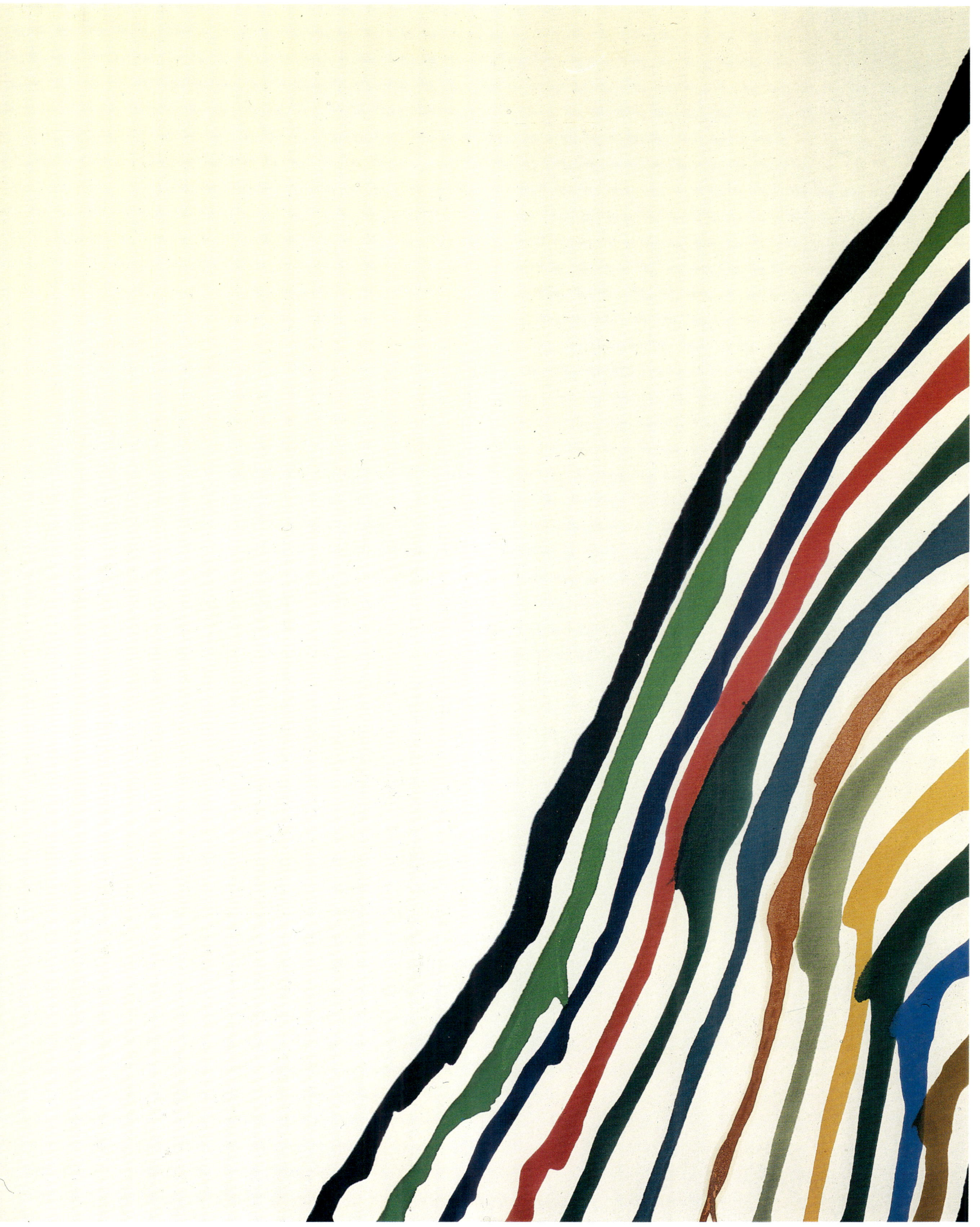

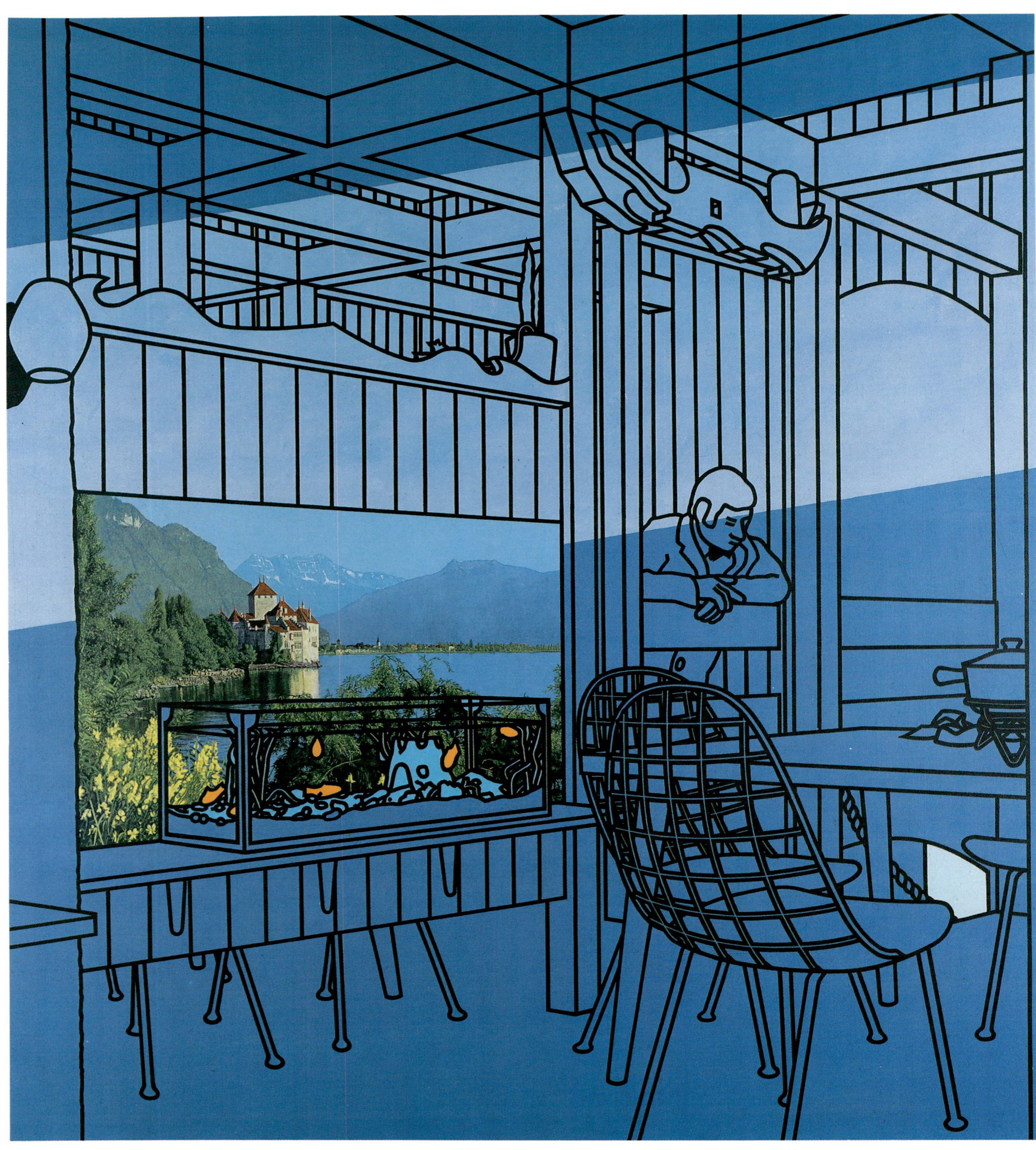

Patrick Caulfield
After Lunch 1975
Acrylic on canvas, 98×84in (248.9×213.4cm)
Tate Gallery, London
© *Patrick Caulfield, all rights reserved, DACS, 1989*

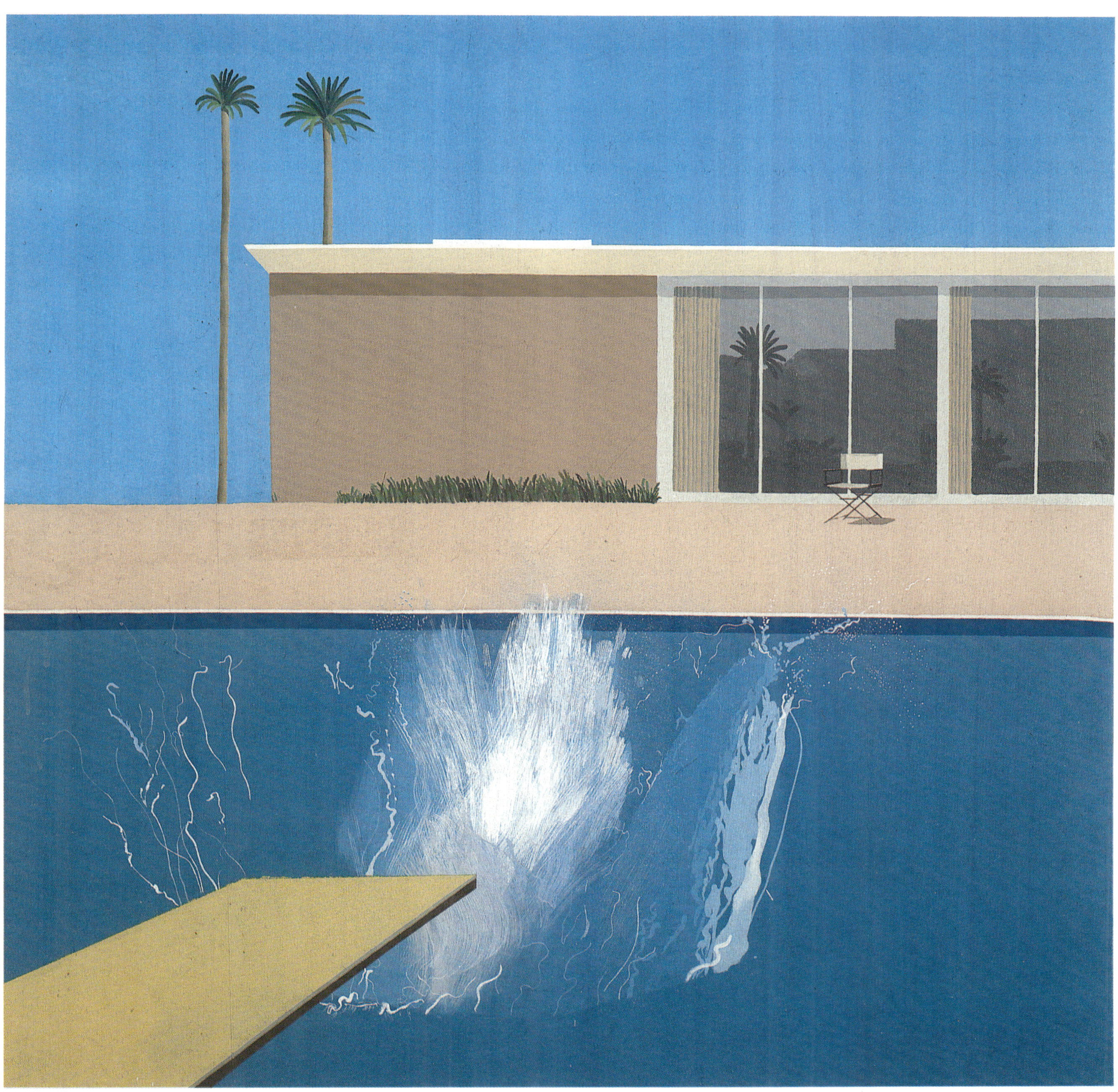

David Hockney
A Bigger Splash 1967
Acrylic on canvas, 95½×96in (242.6×243.8cm)
Tate Gallery, London

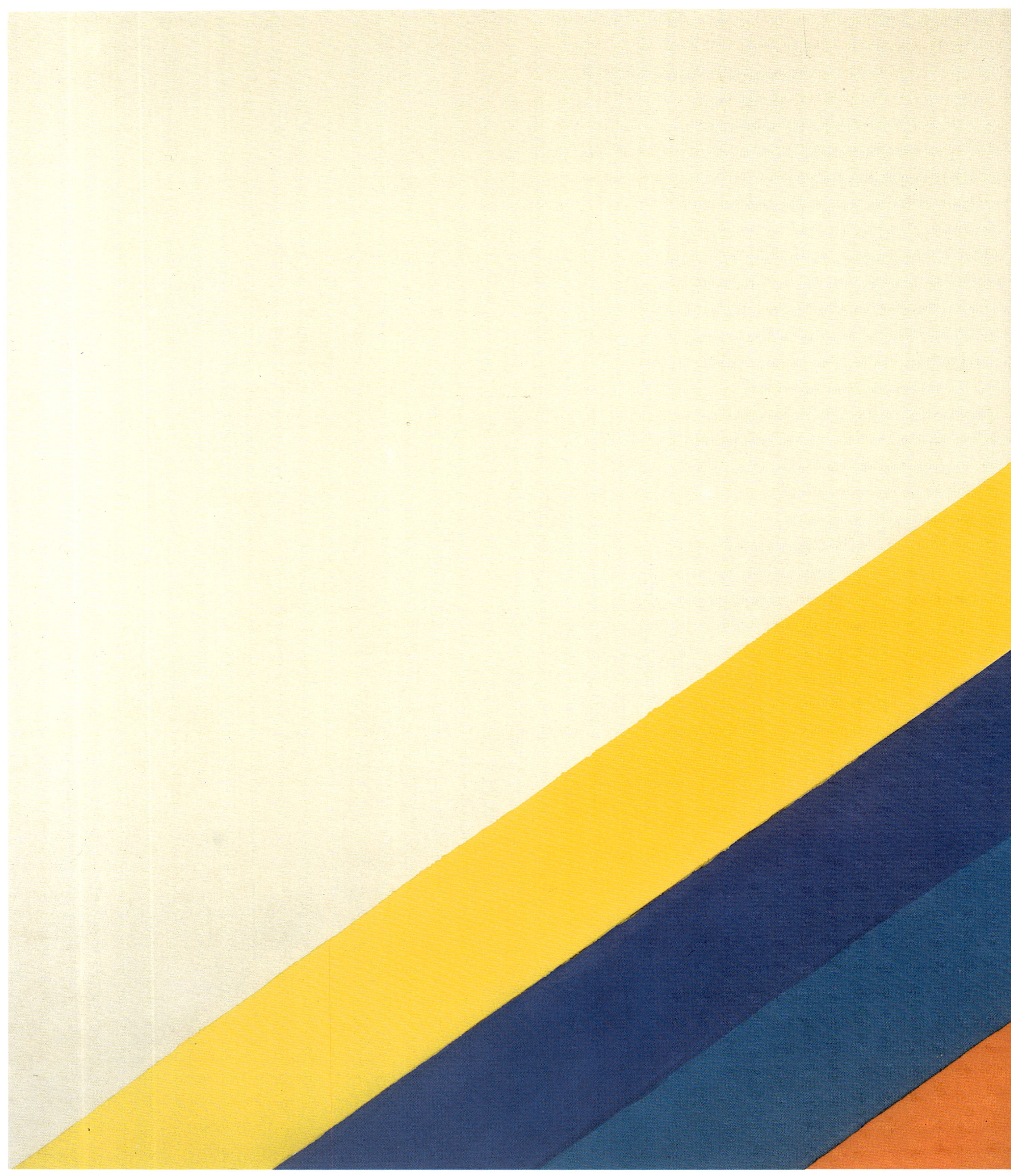

Kenneth Noland
Bend Sinister 1964
Synthetic polymer on canvas, 92½×162½in (235×411.5cm)
Hirshhorn Museum and Sculpture Garden
Smithsonian Institution
Gift of Joseph H Hirshhorn
Photo: John Tennant © DACS, 1989

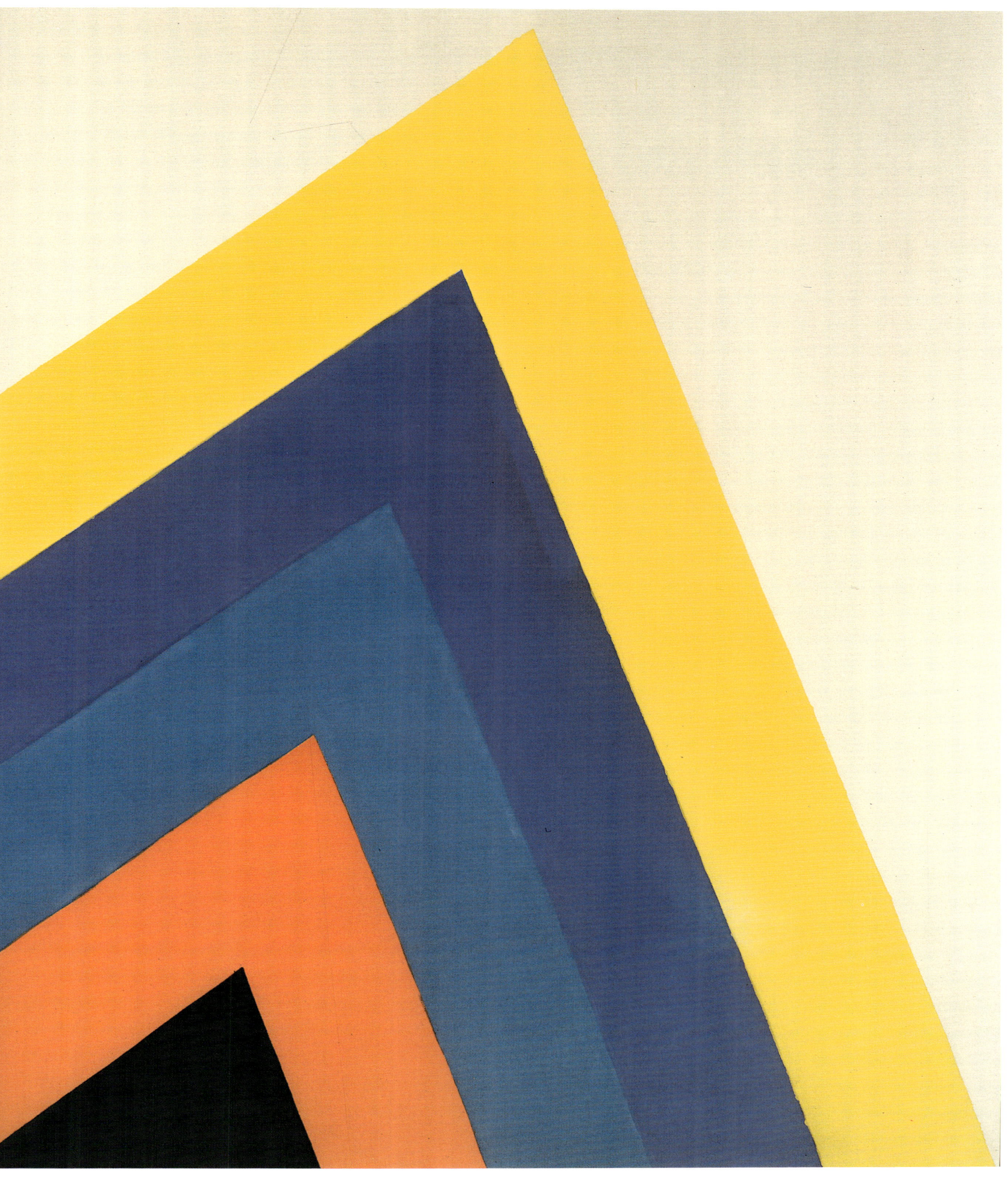

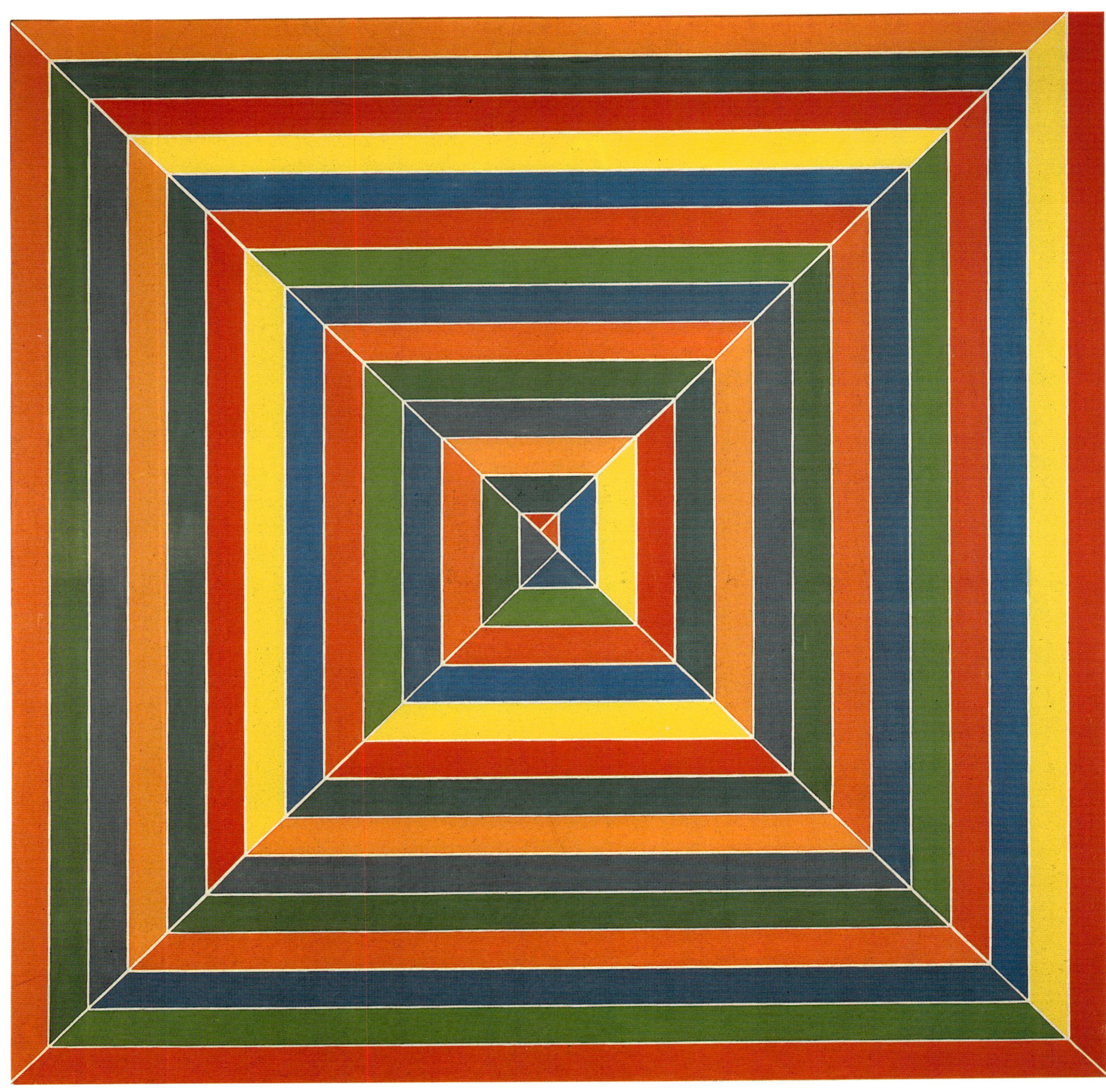

Frank Stella
Hyena Stomp 1962
Alkyd on canvas, 77×77in (195.6×195.6cm)
Tate Gallery, London
© *ARS NY, 1989*

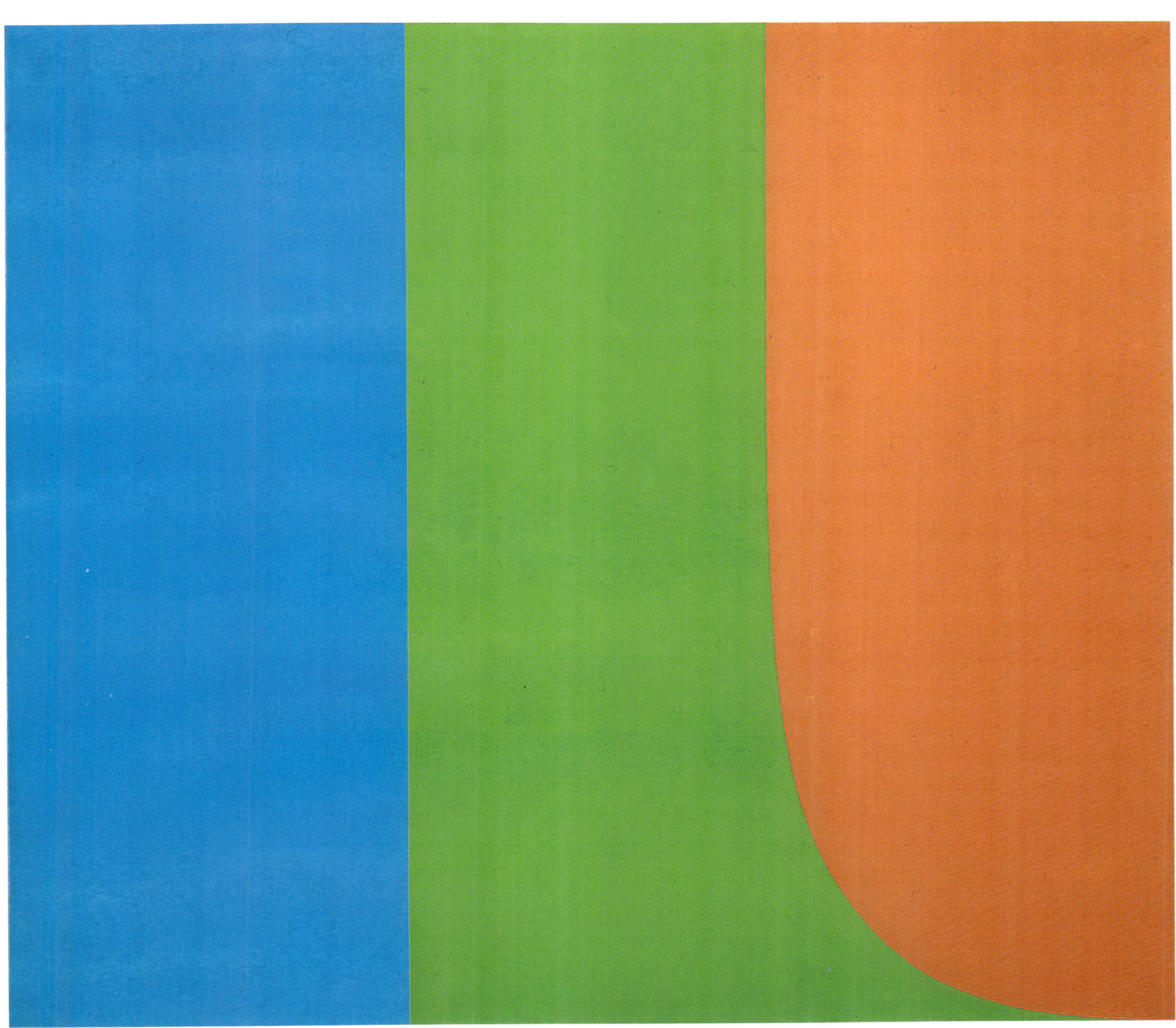

Ellsworth Kelly
Red, Green, Blue 1965
Oil on canvas, 91×91in (231.1×231.1cm)
Stedelijk Museum, Amsterdam
© *DACS, 1989*

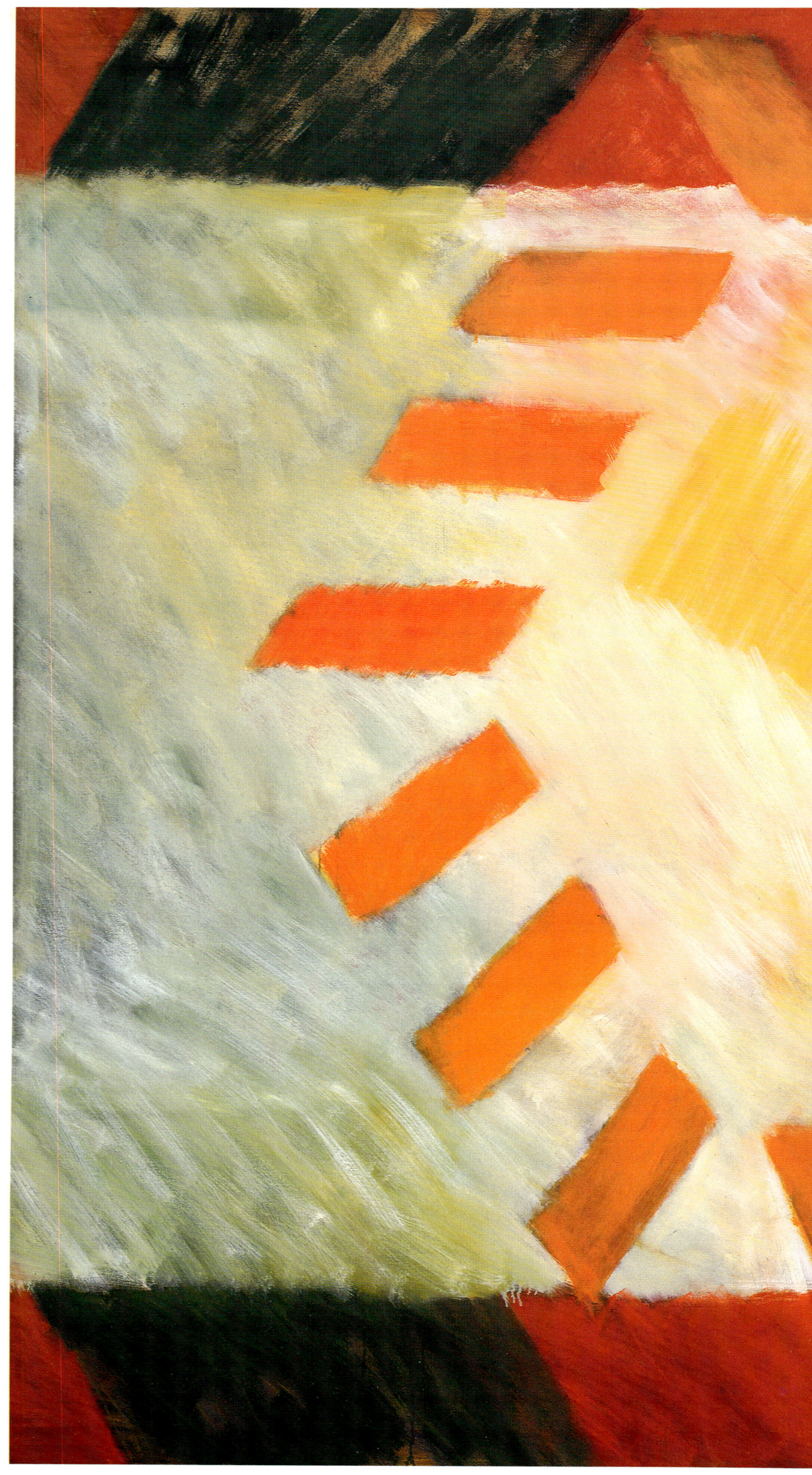

Richard Smith
Panatella 1961
Oil on canvas, 90×120in
(228.6×304.8cm)
Tate Gallery, London
© *DACS, 1989*

OVERLEAF:
Bridget Riley
Late Morning 1967-68
Acrylic on canvas,
89×141½in (226.1×359.4cm)
Tate Gallery, London

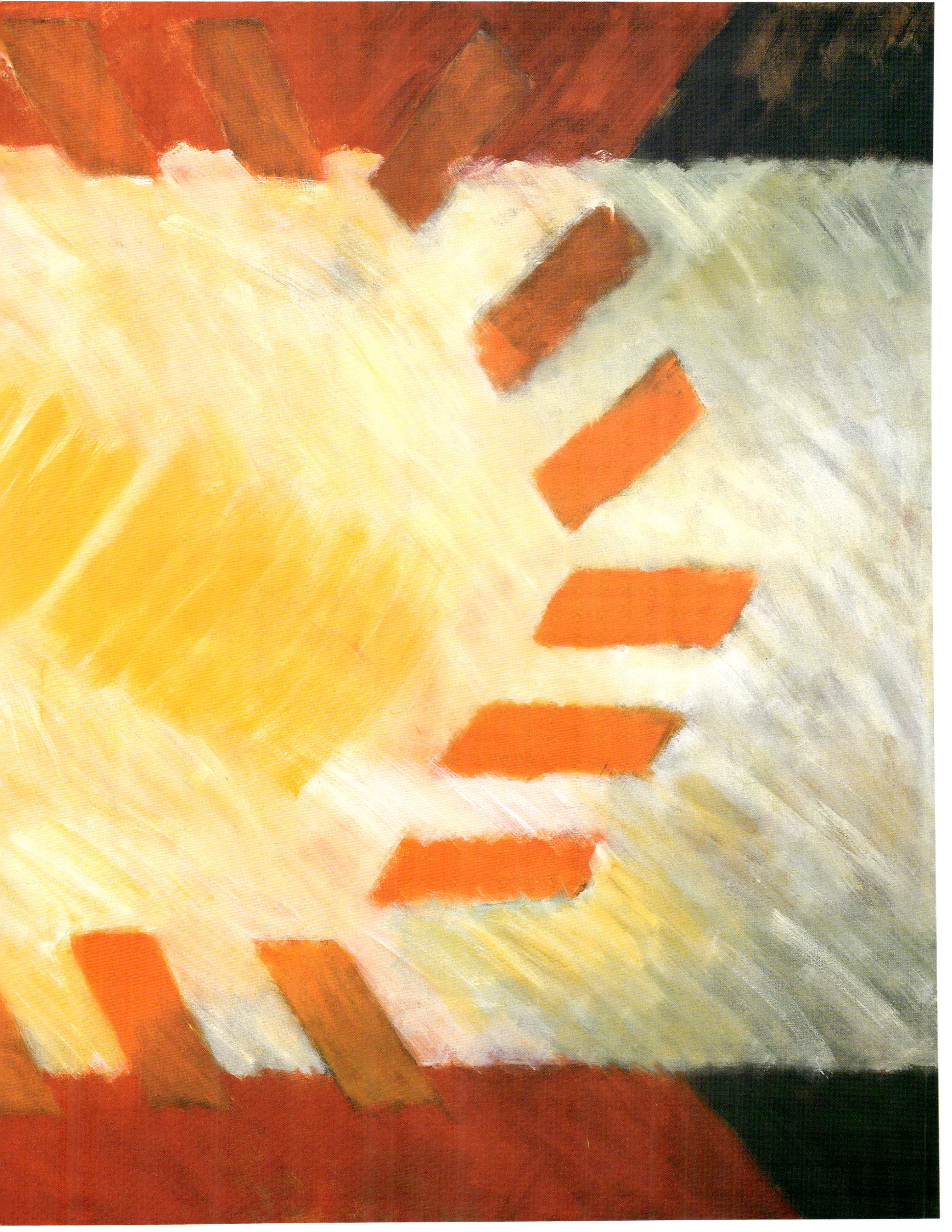

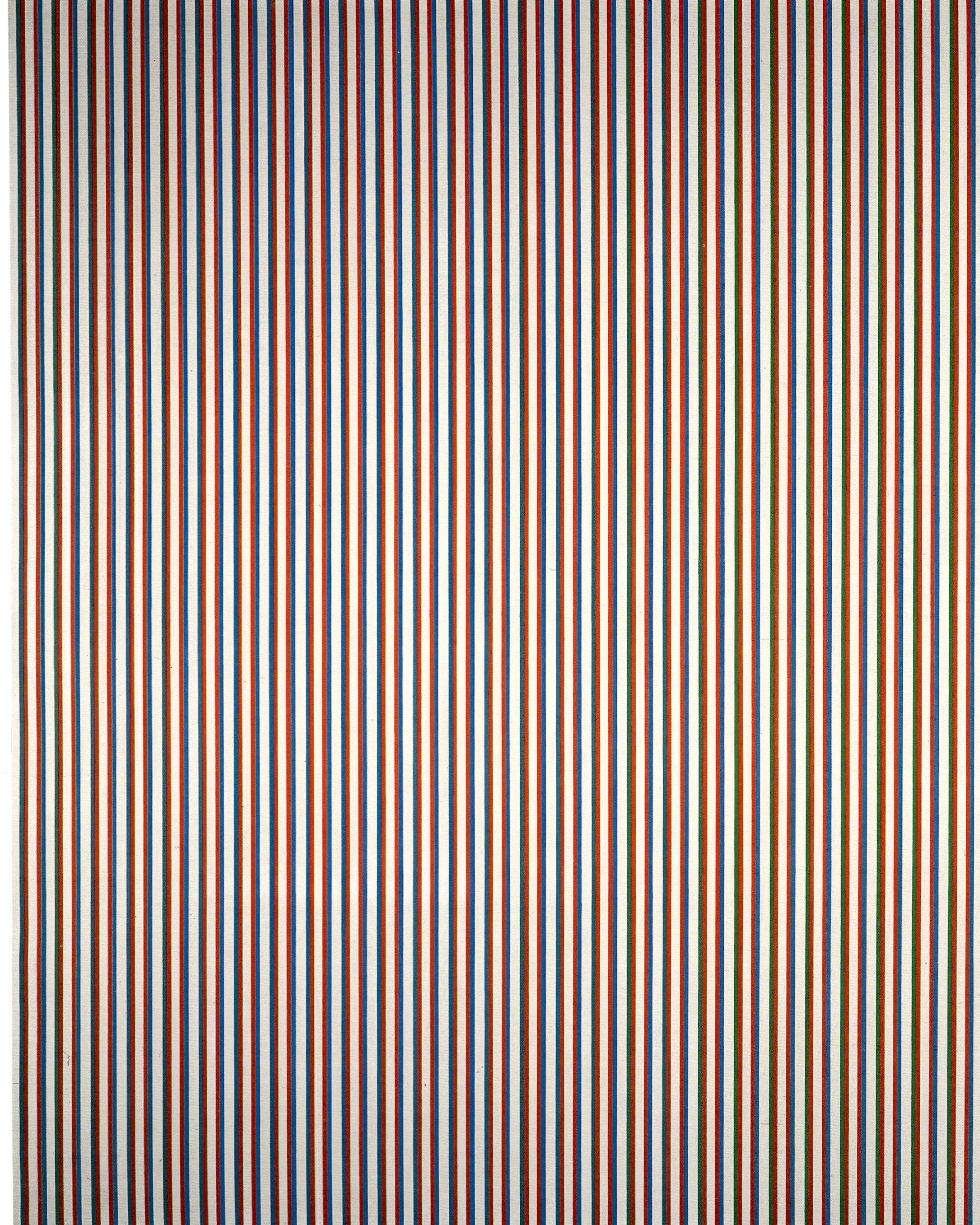

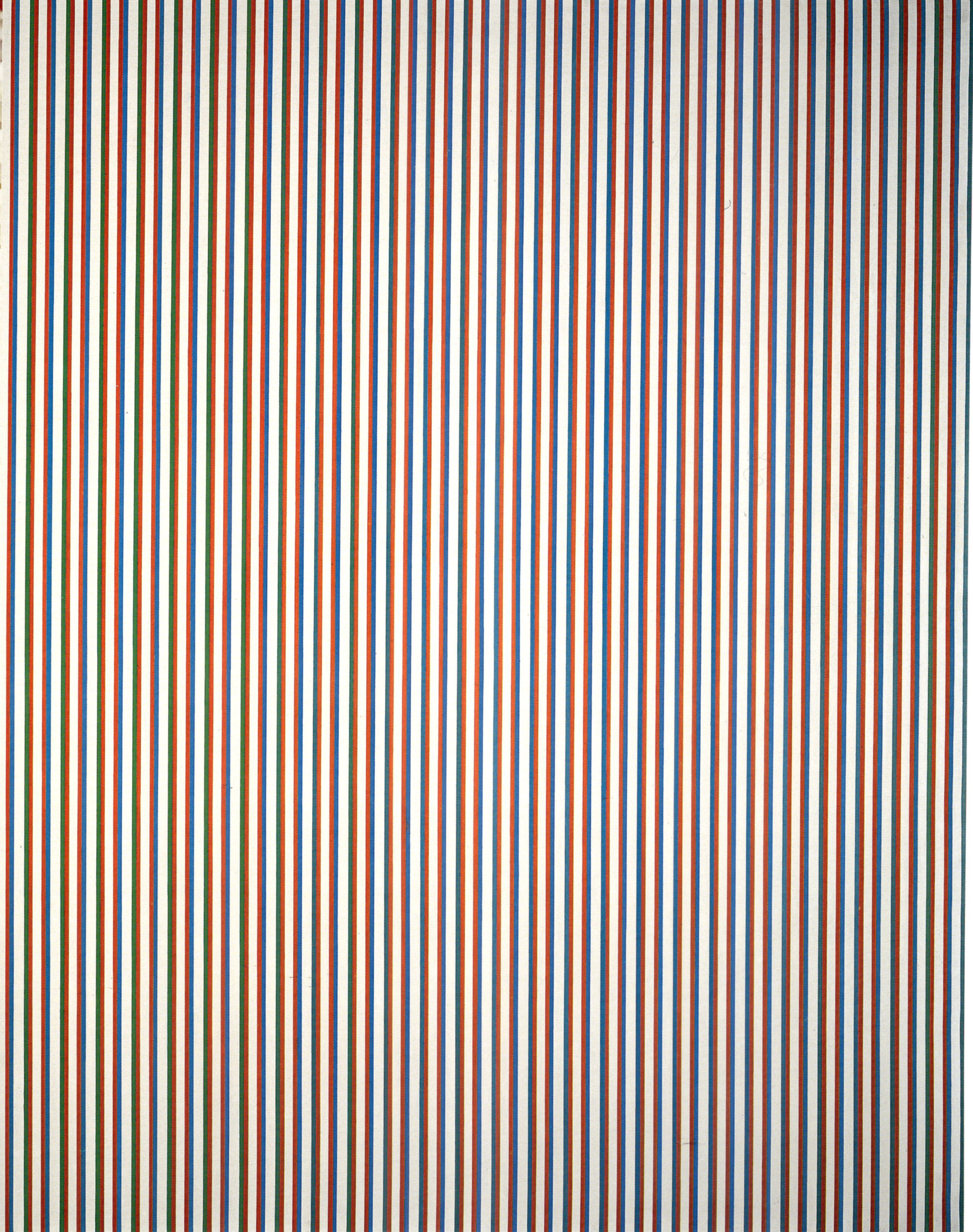

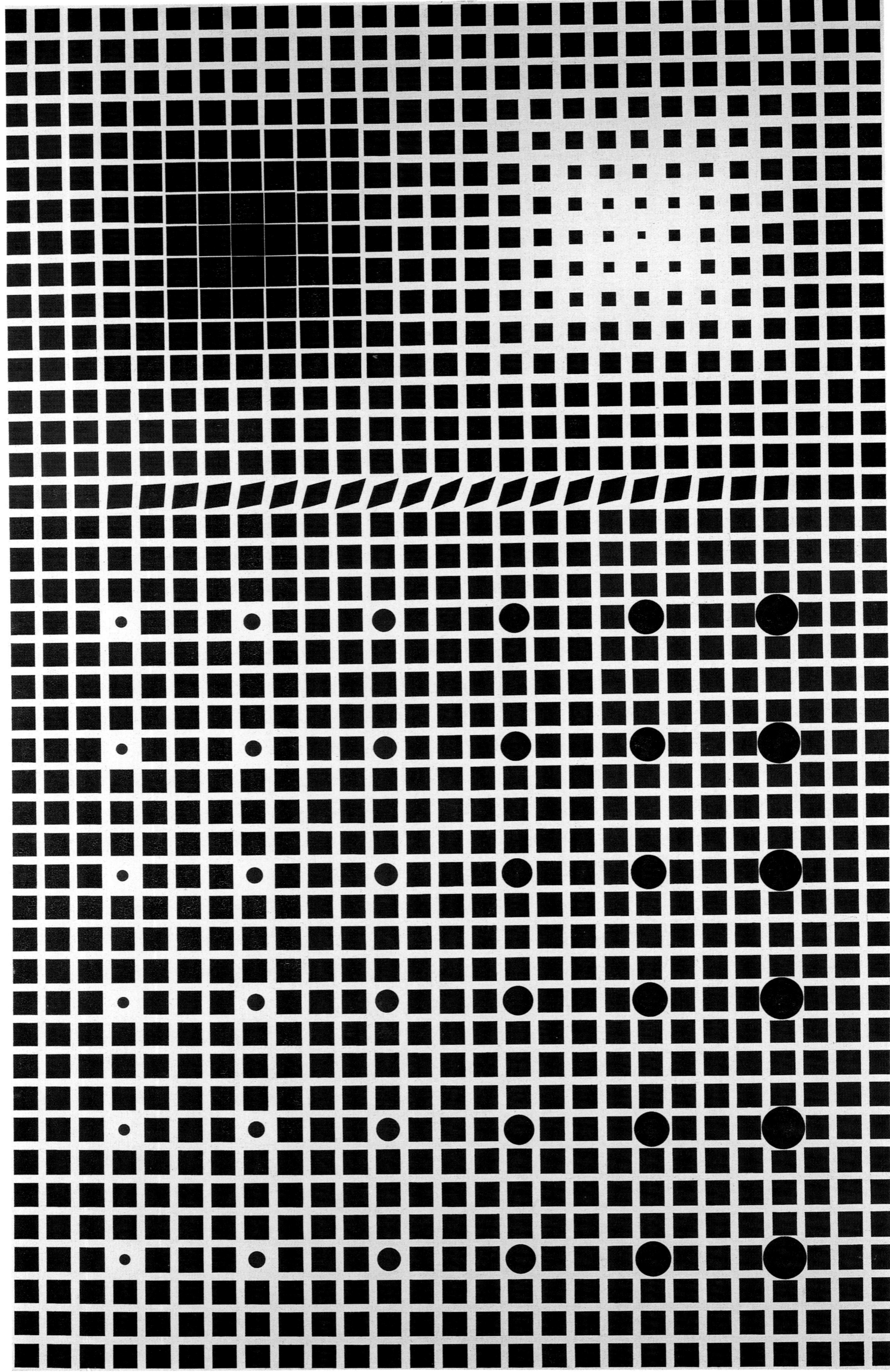

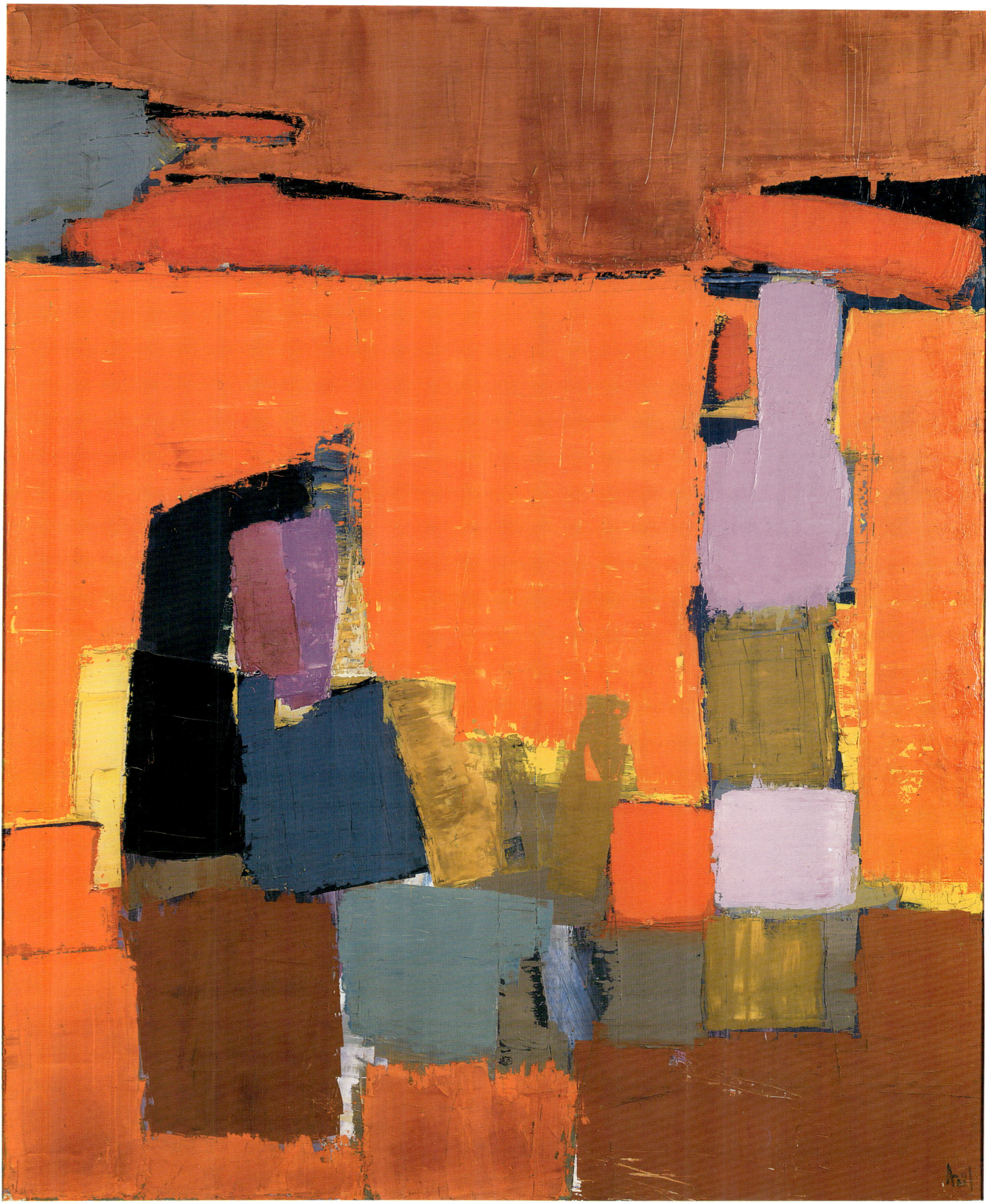

LEFT:
Victor Vasarely
Supernovae 1959-61
Oil on canvas, 95¼×60in (241.9×152.4cm)
Tate Gallery, London
© *DACS, 1988*

ABOVE:
Nicolas De Staël
Figure by the Sea 1952
Oil on canvas, 63⅝×51in (161.6×129.5cm)
Kunstsammlung Nordrhein-Westfalen, Düsseldorf
© ADAGP, Paris, DACS, London, 1989

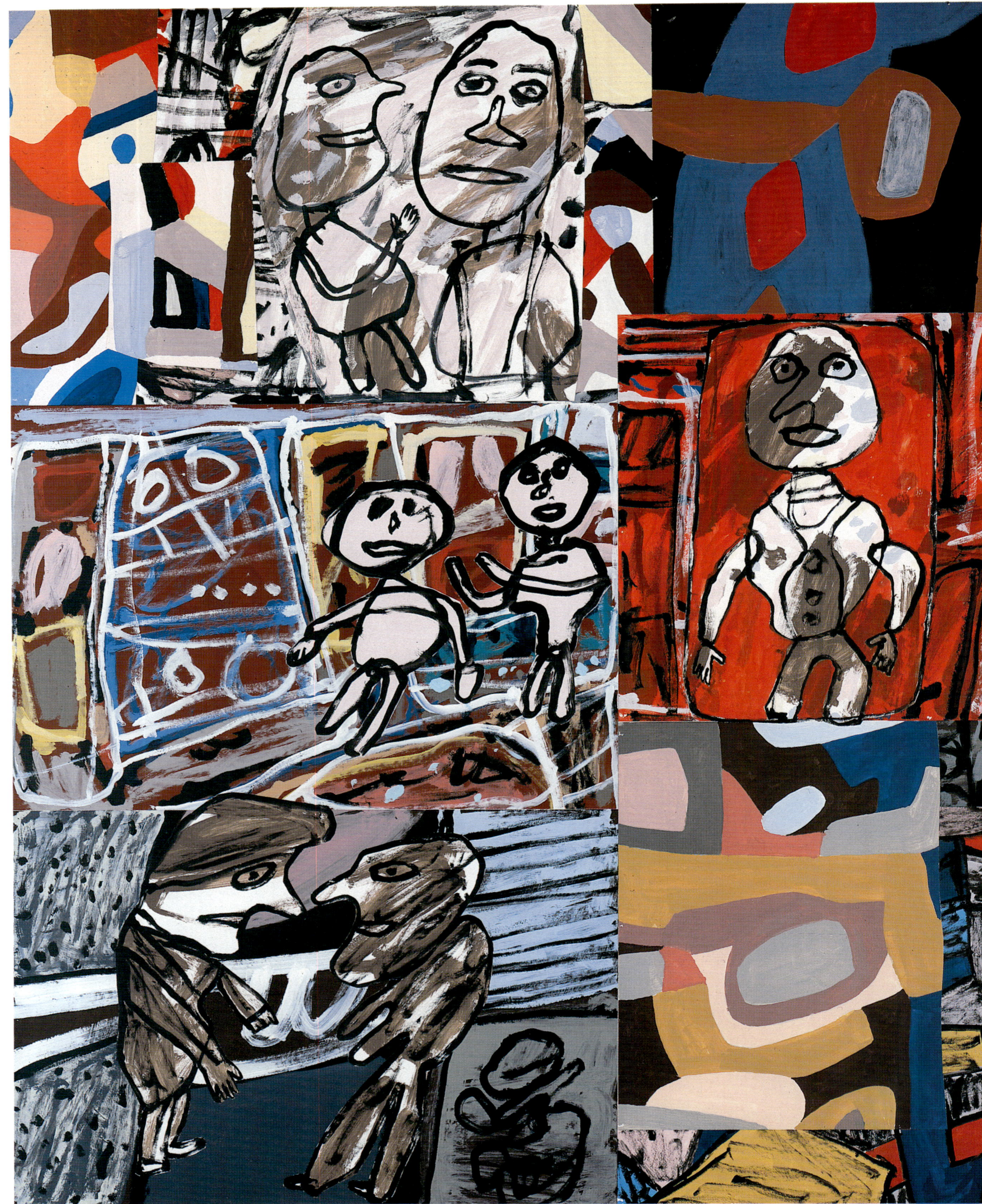

Jean Dubuffet
The Ups and Downs 1977
Acrylic and paper on canvas, 84×134½in (213.4×341.6cm)
Tate Gallery, London © ADAGP, Paris, DACS, London, 1989

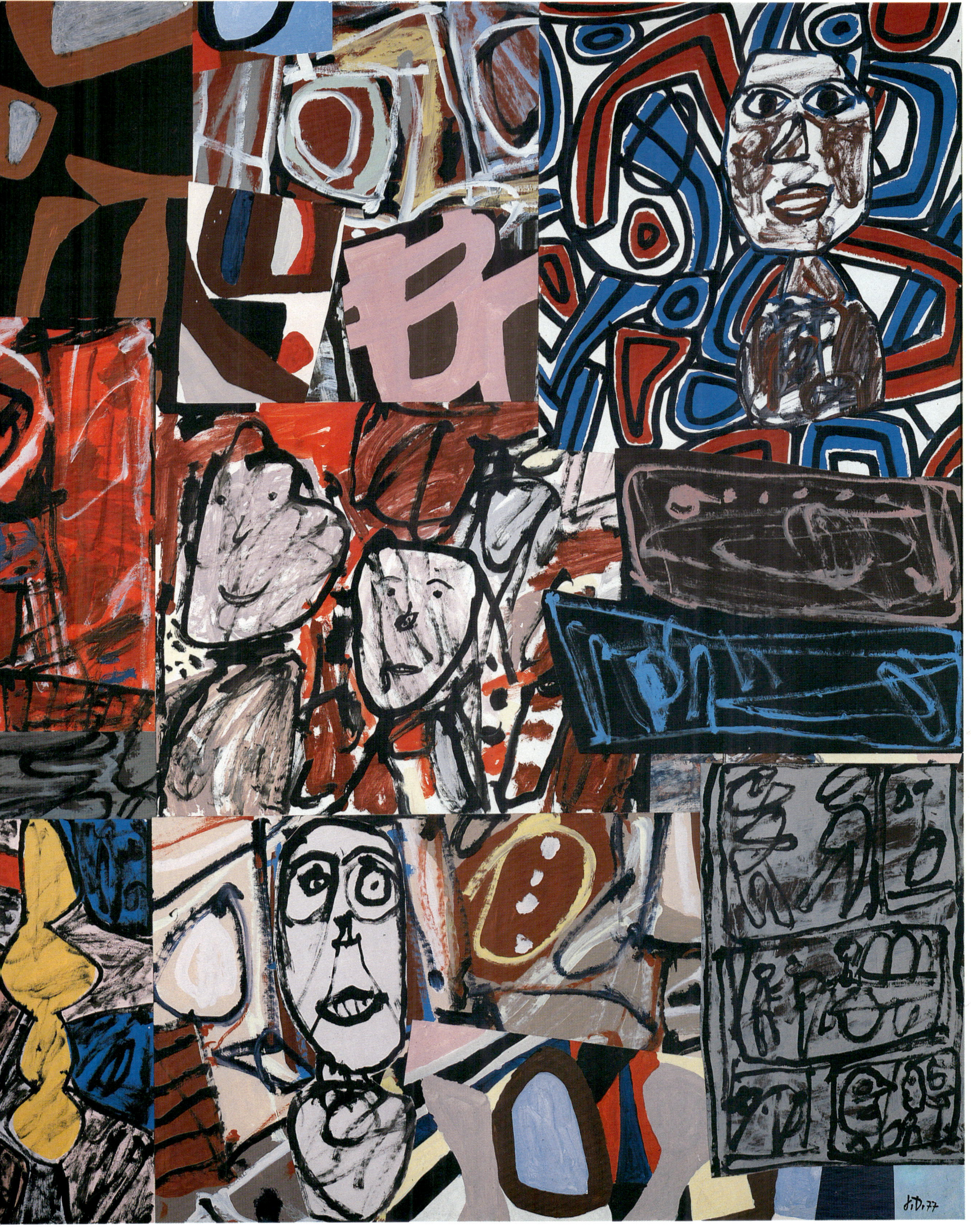

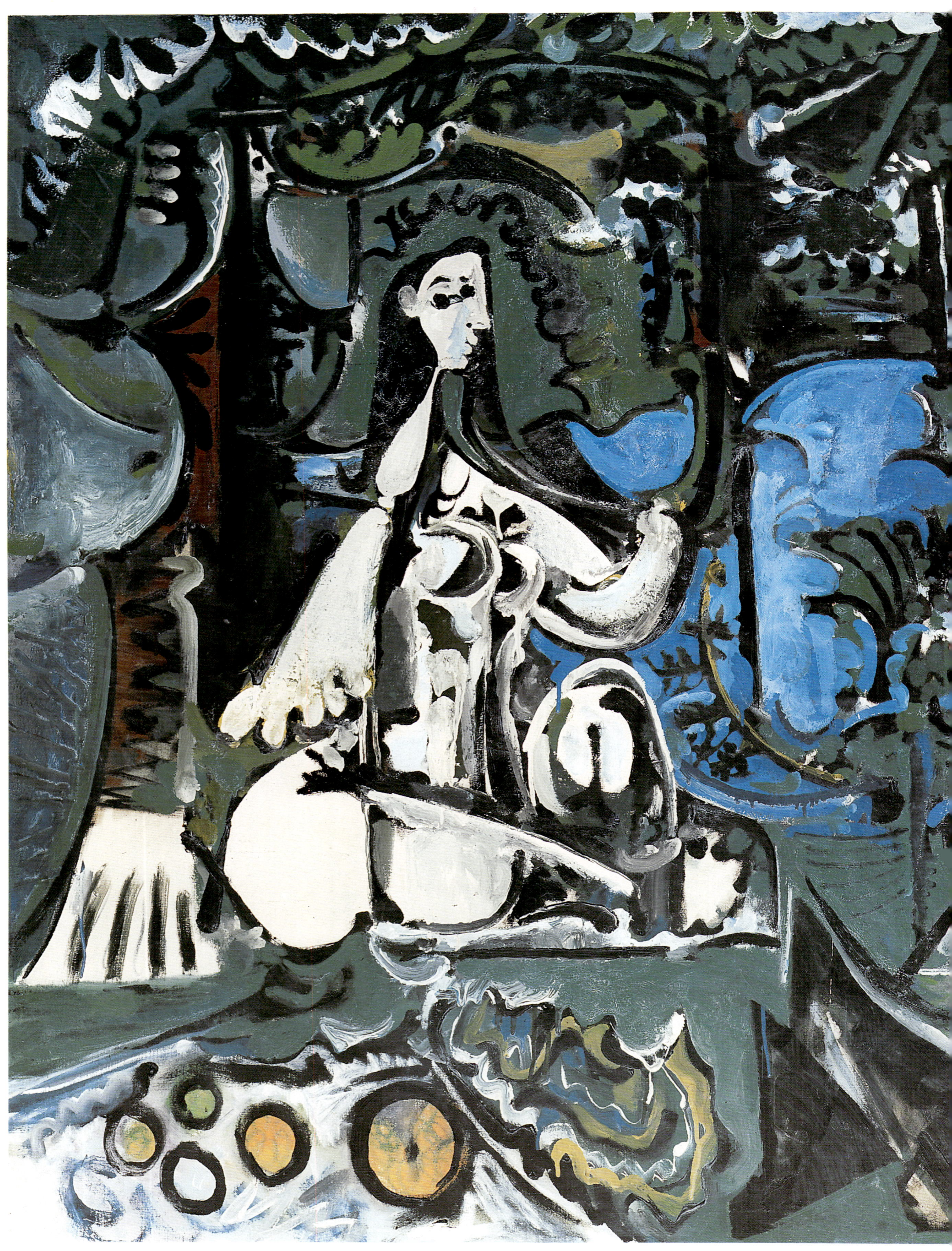

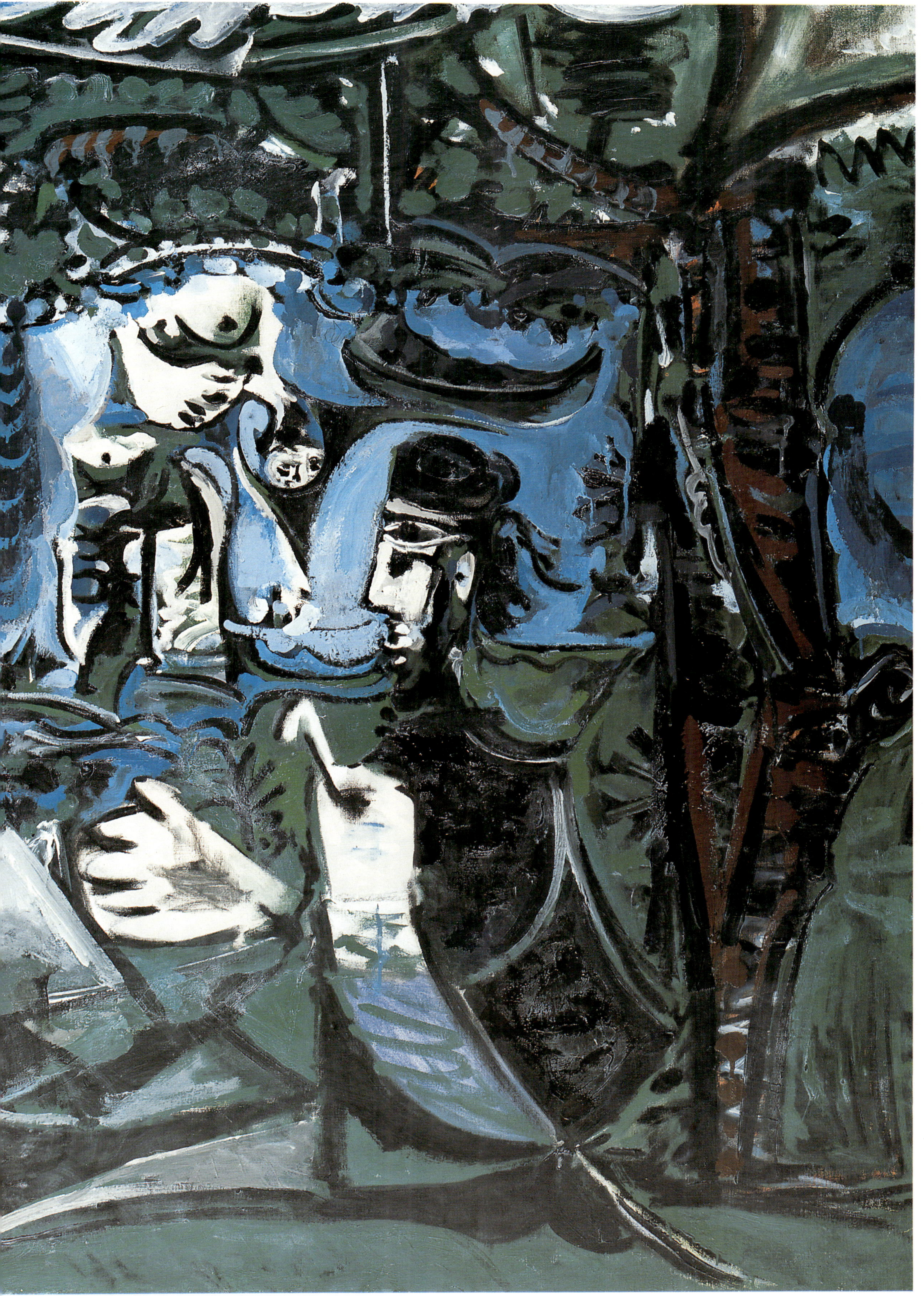

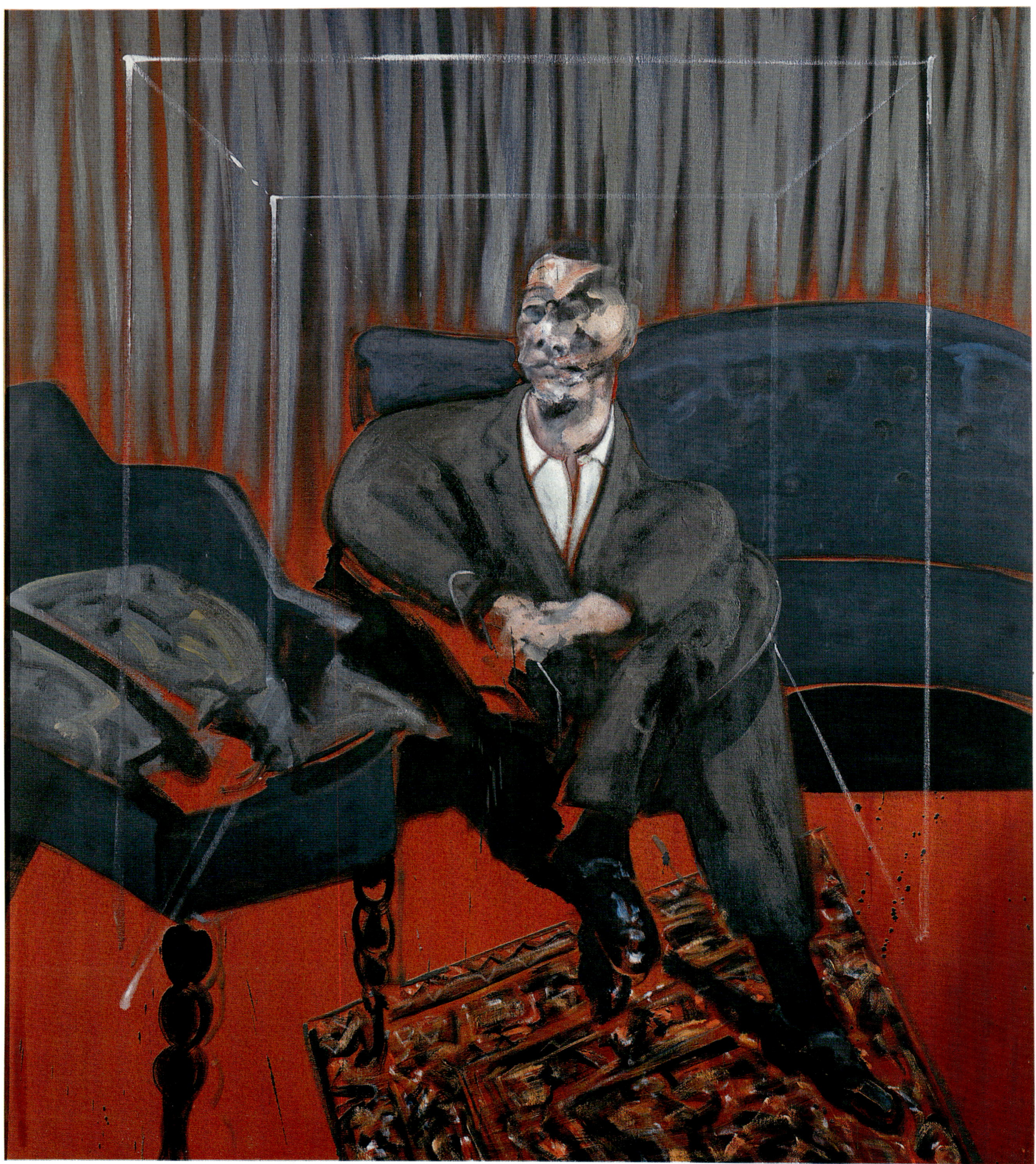

ABOVE:
Francis Bacon
Seated Figures 1961
Oil on canvas, 65×56in (165.1×142.2cm)
Tate Gallery, London

PREVIOUS PAGES:
Pablo Picasso
Le Déjeuner sur l'Herbe 1960
Oil on canvas, 51¼×76⅞ (130×195cm)
Picasso Museum, Paris © DACS, 1988

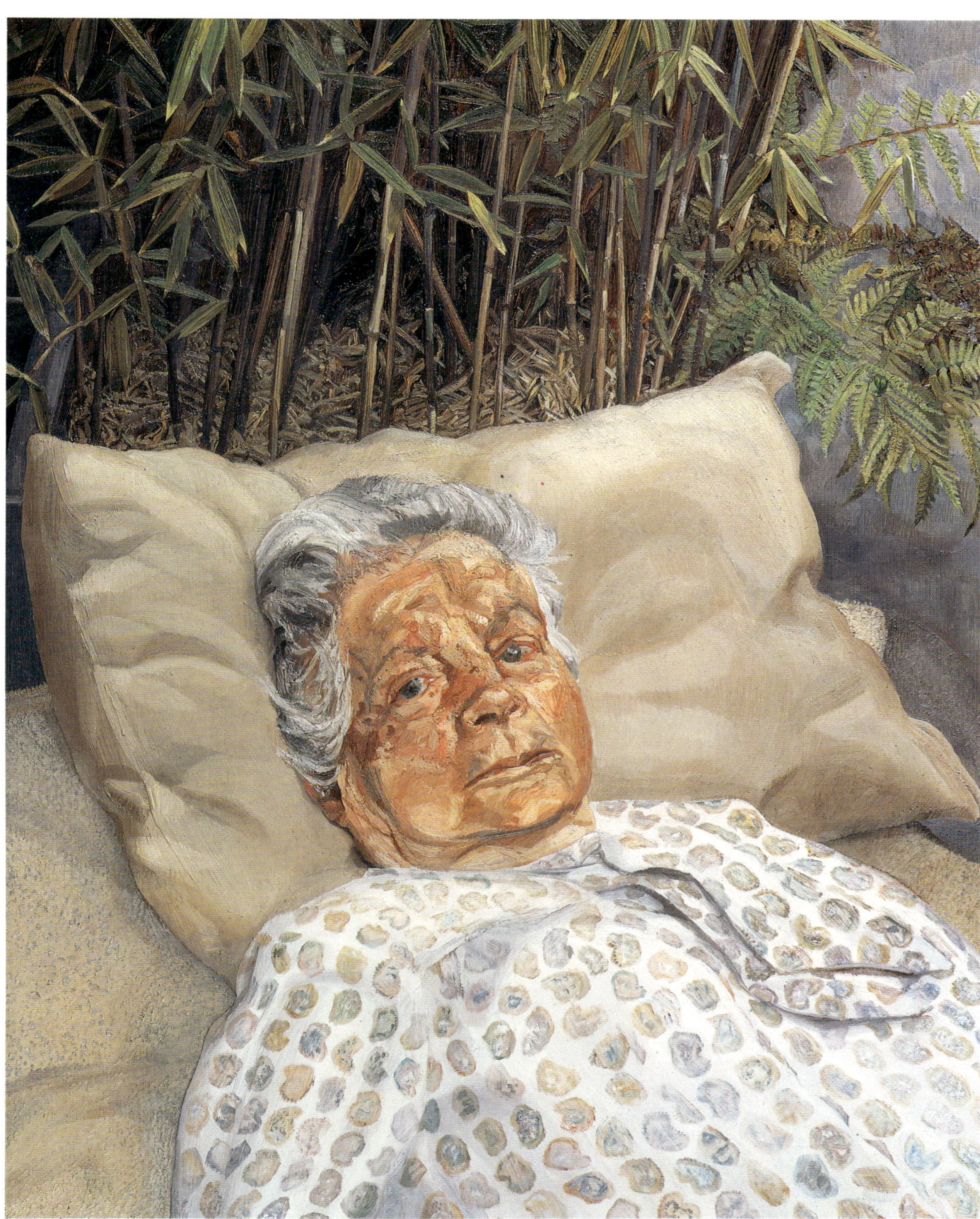

Lucian Freud
The Painter's Mother 1984
Oil on canvas, 34½×27⅝in (87.6×70cm)
Private collection
Photo courtesy of James Kirkman

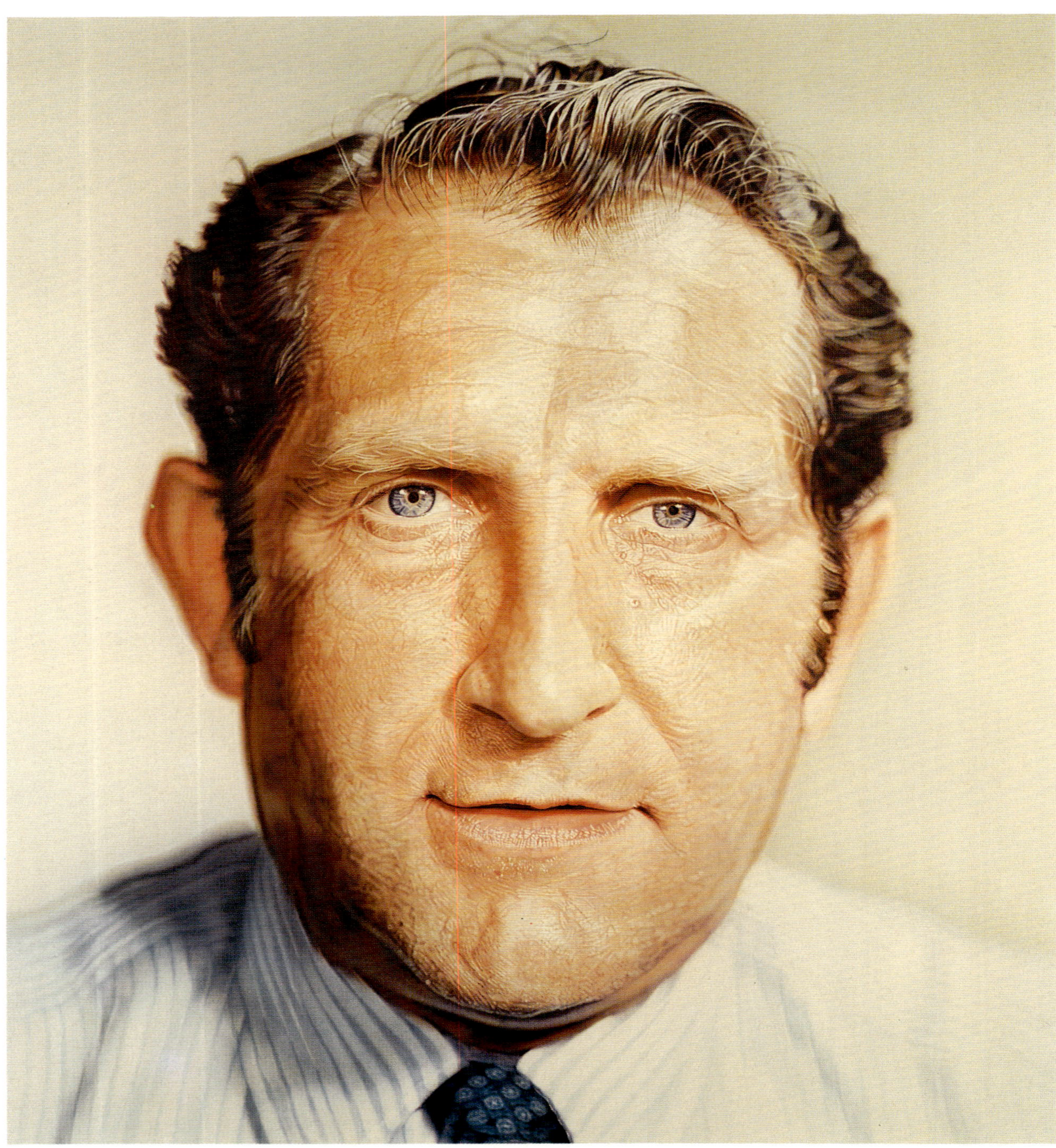

Chuck Close
Nat 1972-73
Gouache on paper, 63×57in (160×145cm)
Budapest Nationalgalerie
Sammlung Ludwig, Aachen

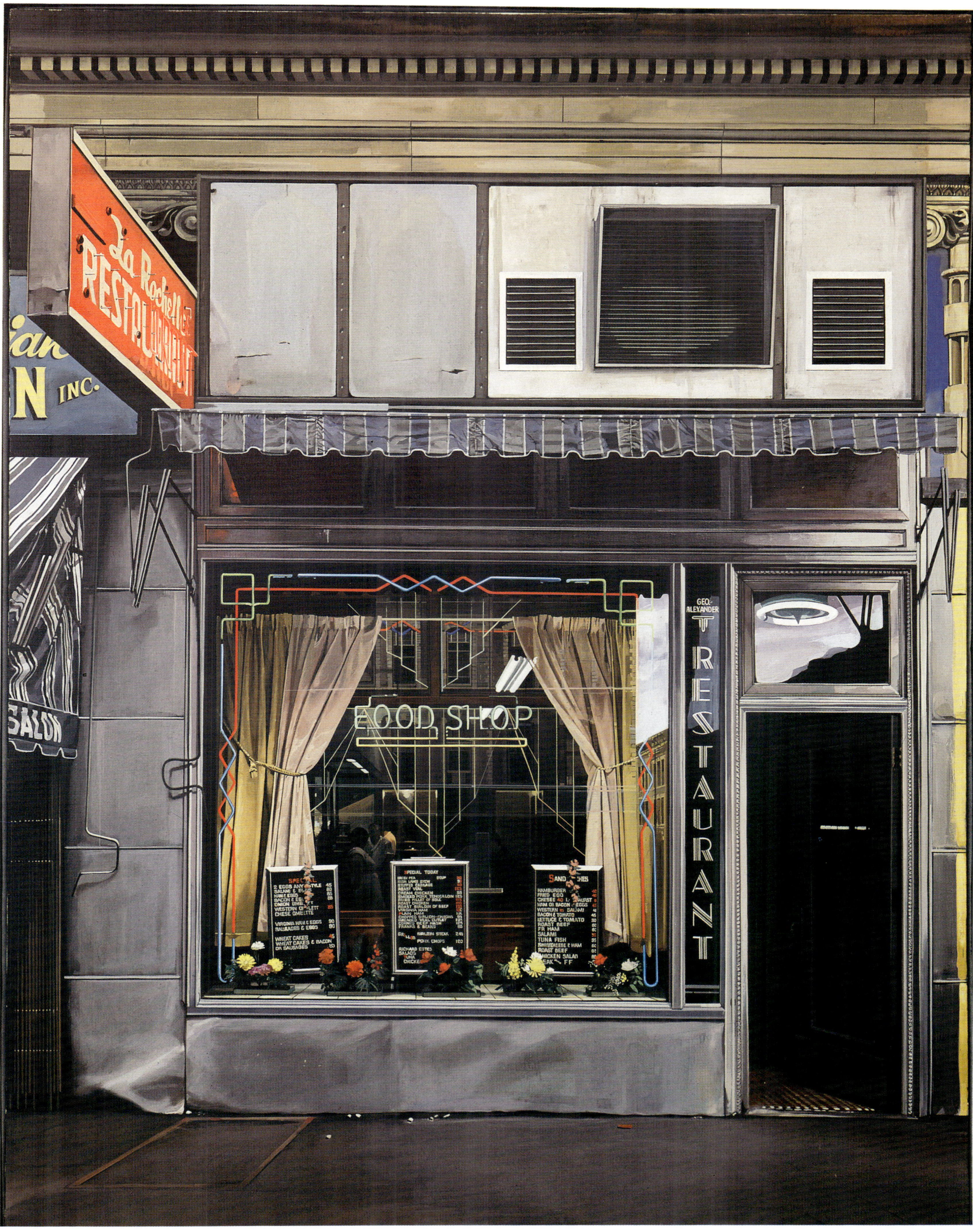

Richard Estes
Foodshop 1967
Acylic on canvas, 65⅜×48⅝in (166×123.5cm)
Museum Ludwig, Cologne

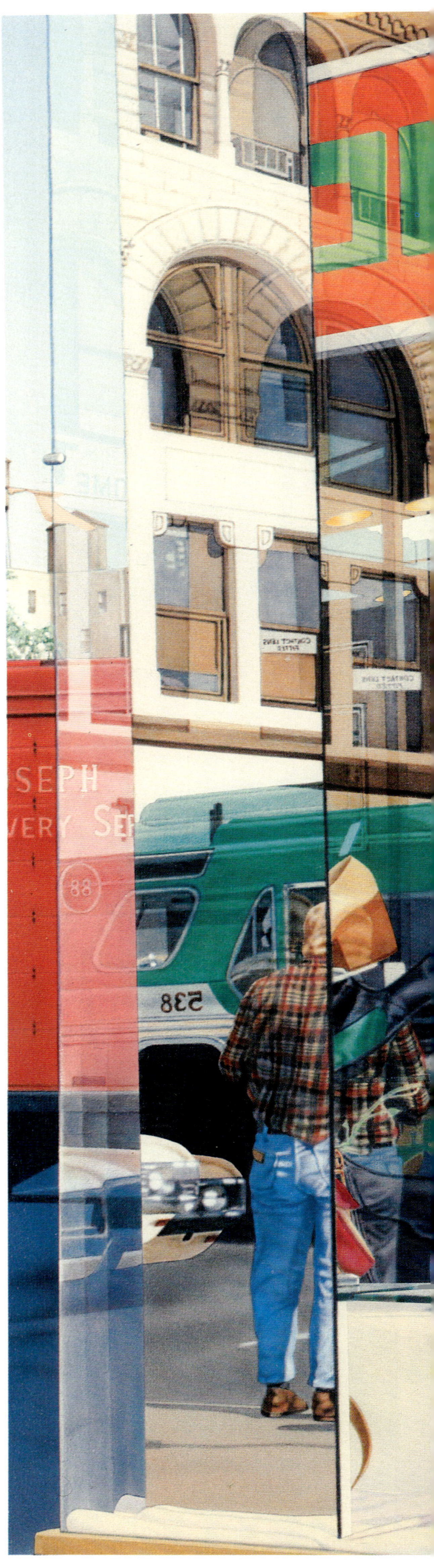

Don Eddy
New Shoes for H 1973-74
Acrylic on canvas, 44×48in (111.8×121.9cm)
The Cleveland Museum of Art, Ohio
Purchased with a grant from the National Endowment for the Arts and matched
by gifts from members of the Cleveland Society for Contemporary Arts

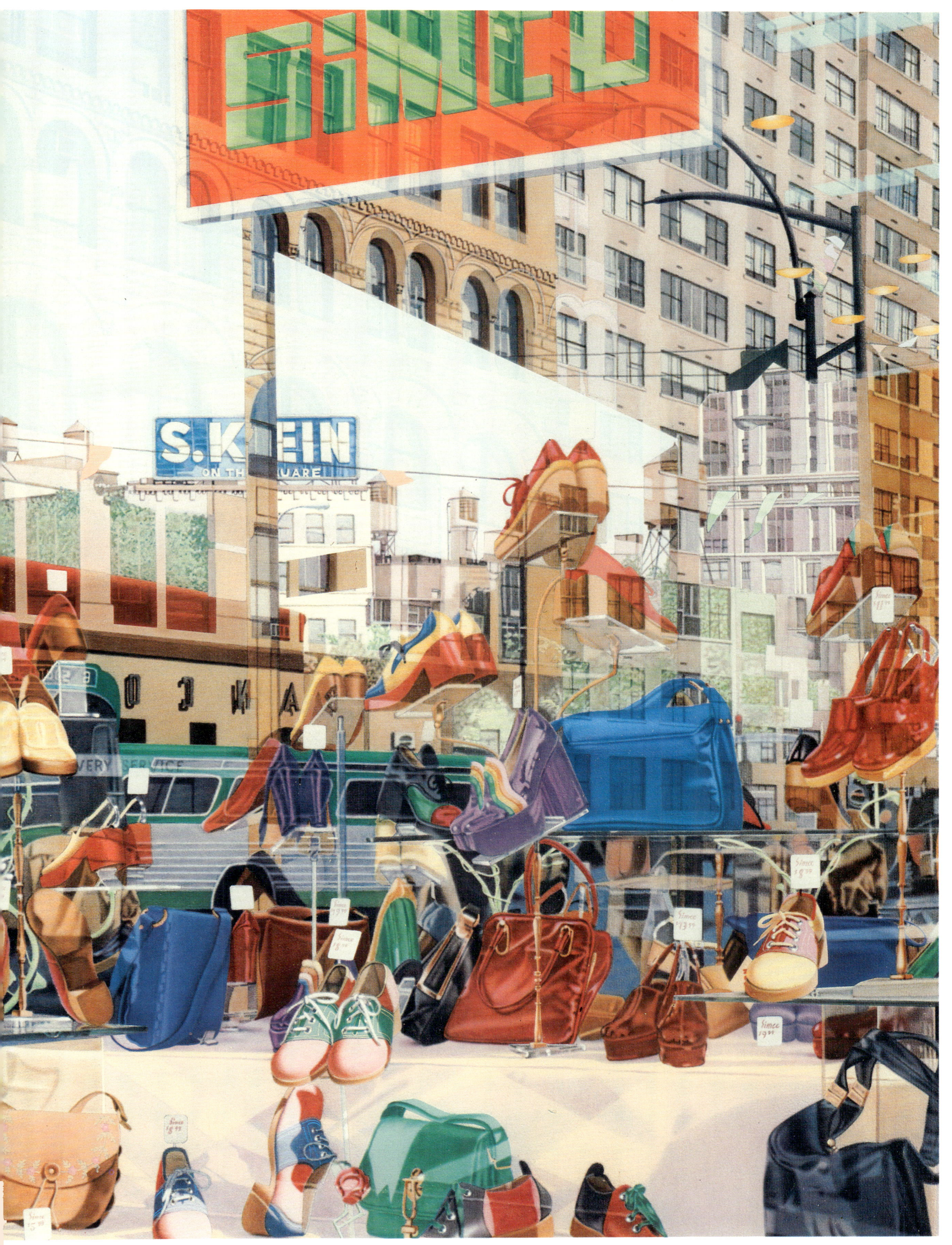
SIMCO
S.KLEIN
ON THE SQUARE

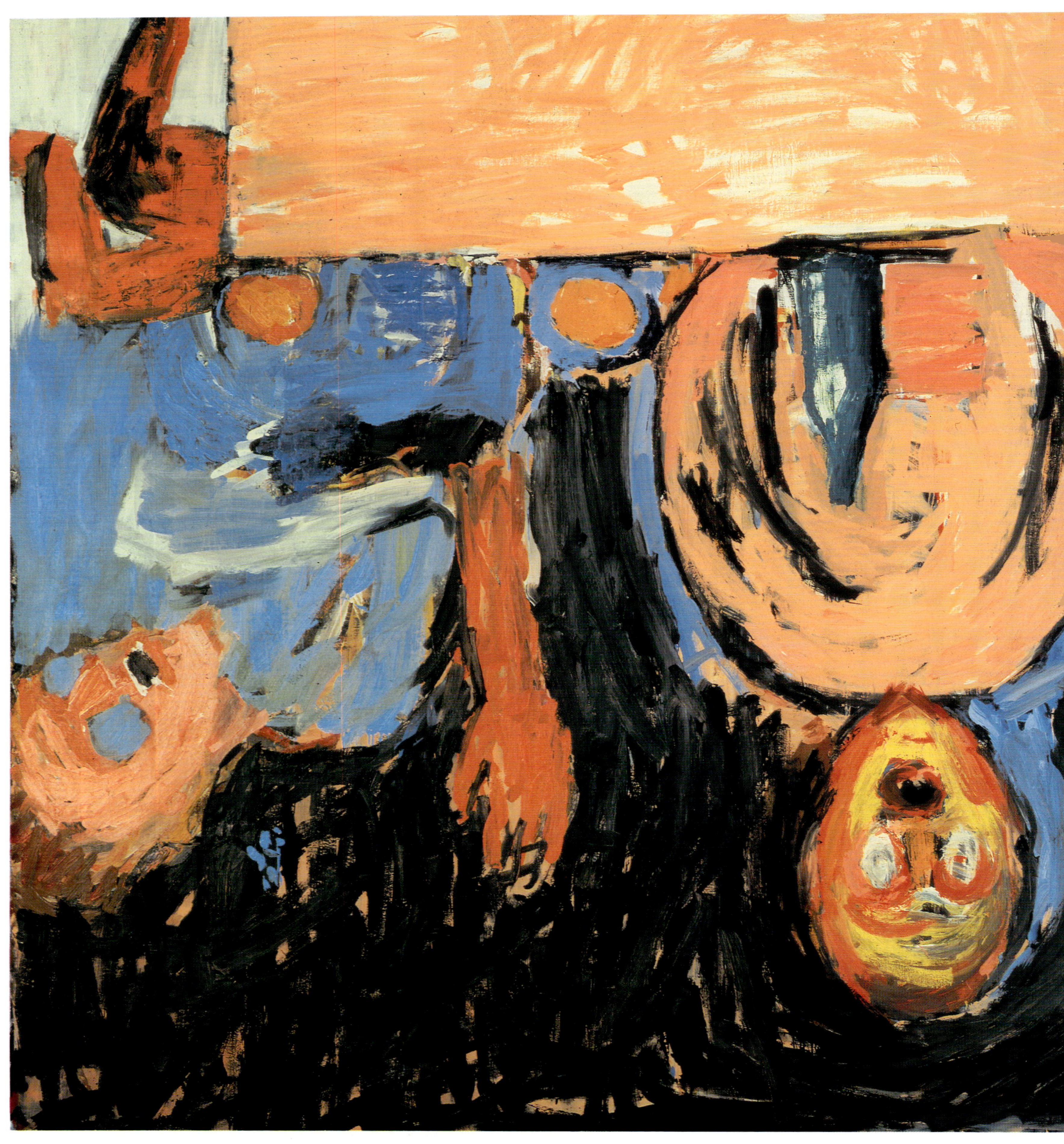

Georg Baselitz
Supper in Dresden 1983
Oil on canvas, 110×177in (279.4×449.6cm)
Saatchi Collection, London

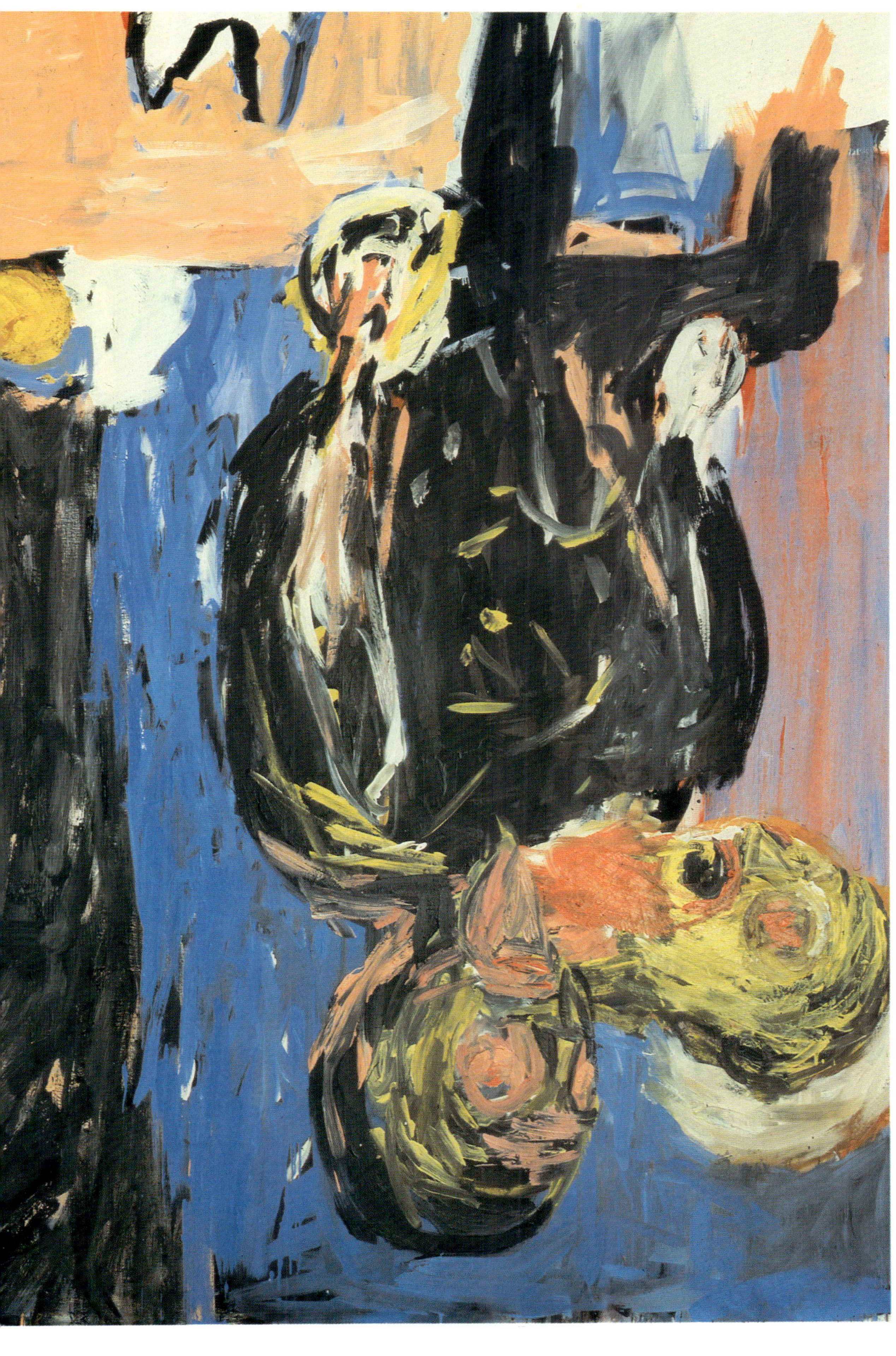

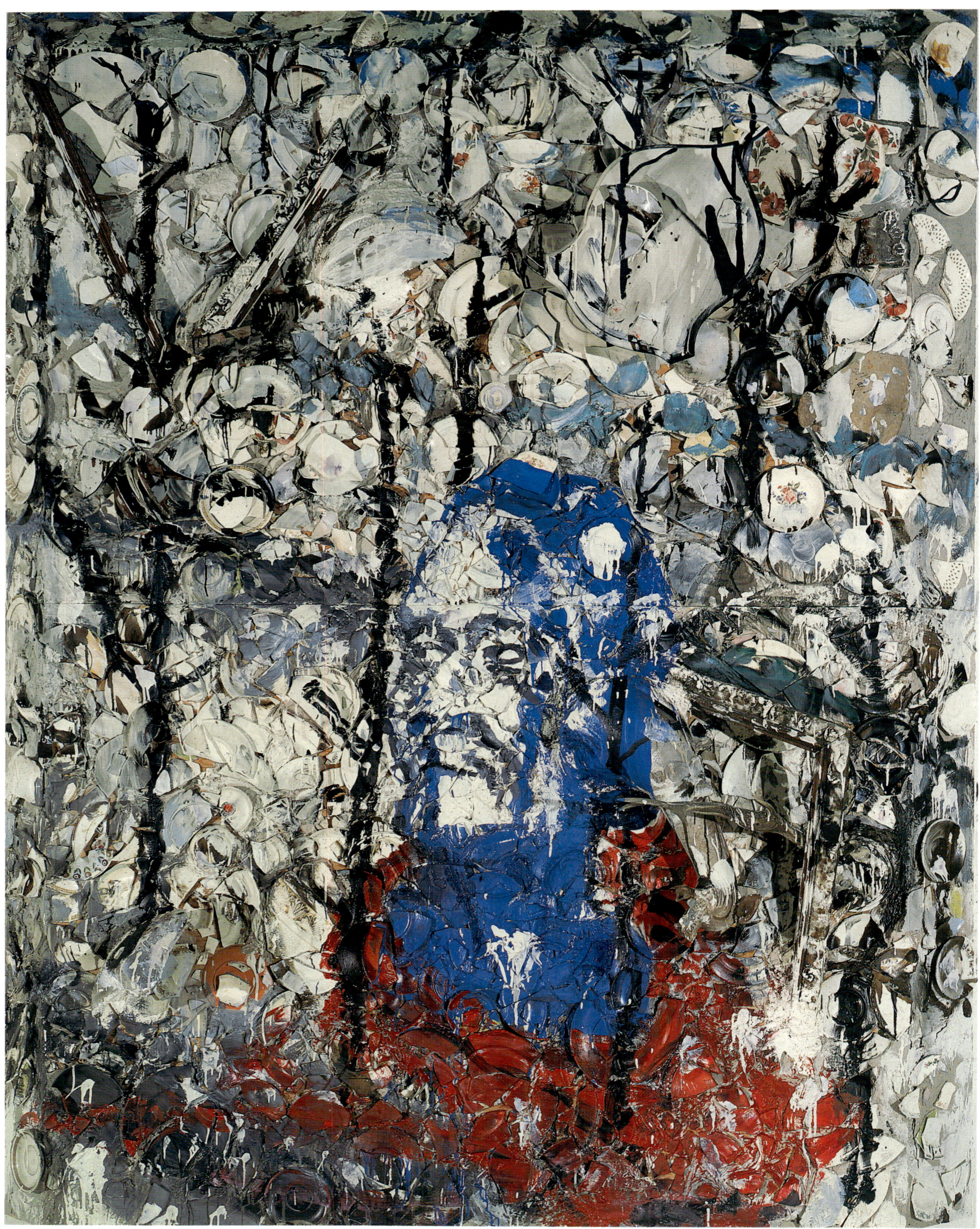

Julian Schnabel
Winter (Rose Garden that Jacqueline Built as a Girl) 1982
Oil, crockery, antler, wood, and bondo on wood,
108×84in (274.3×213.3cm)
Saatchi Collection, London

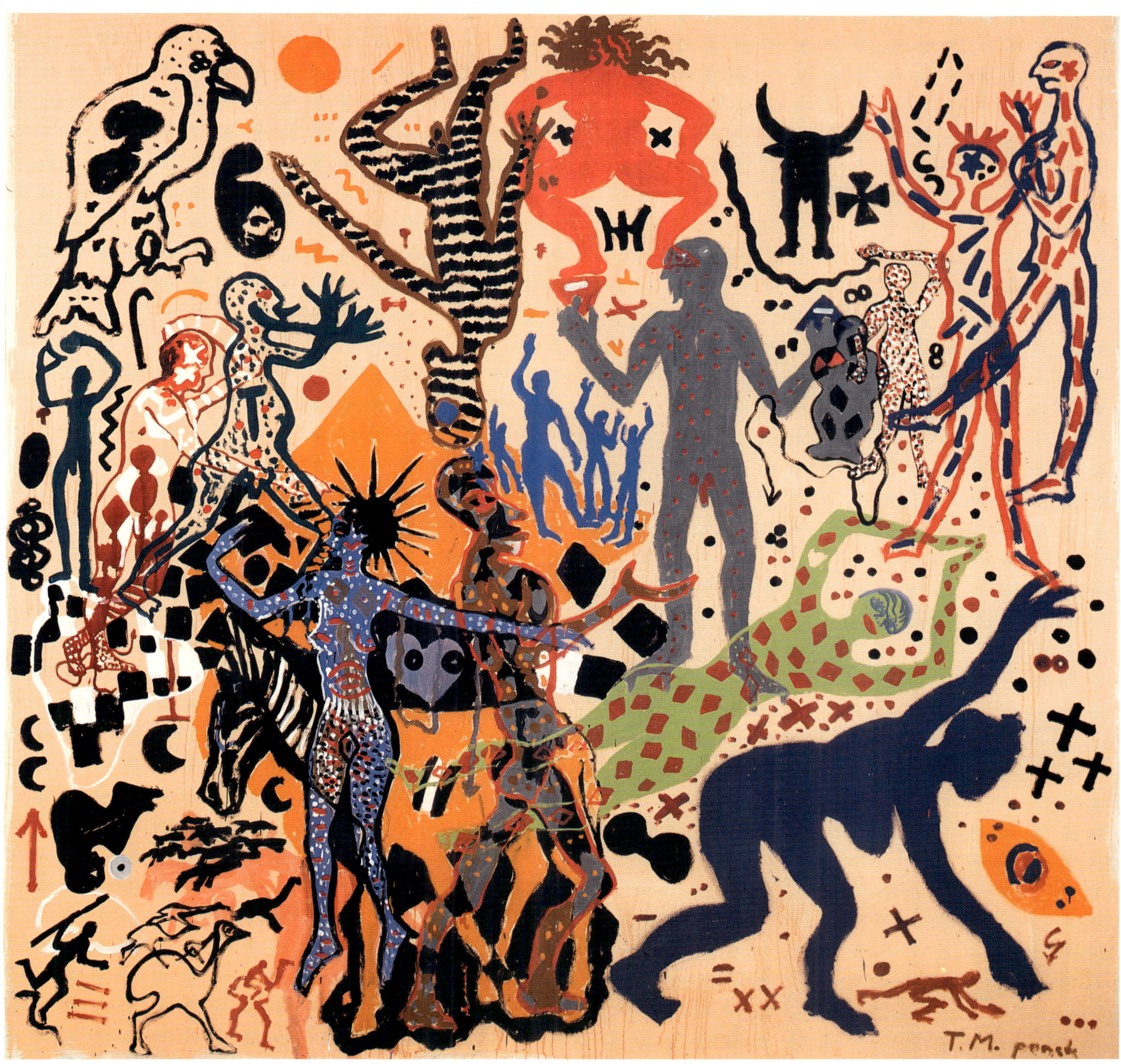

Albrecht Penck
Metaphysical Passage Through a Zebra 1975
Oil on canvas, 112¼×112¼in (285×285cm)
Budapest-Nationalgalerie, Sammlung Ludwig, Aachen

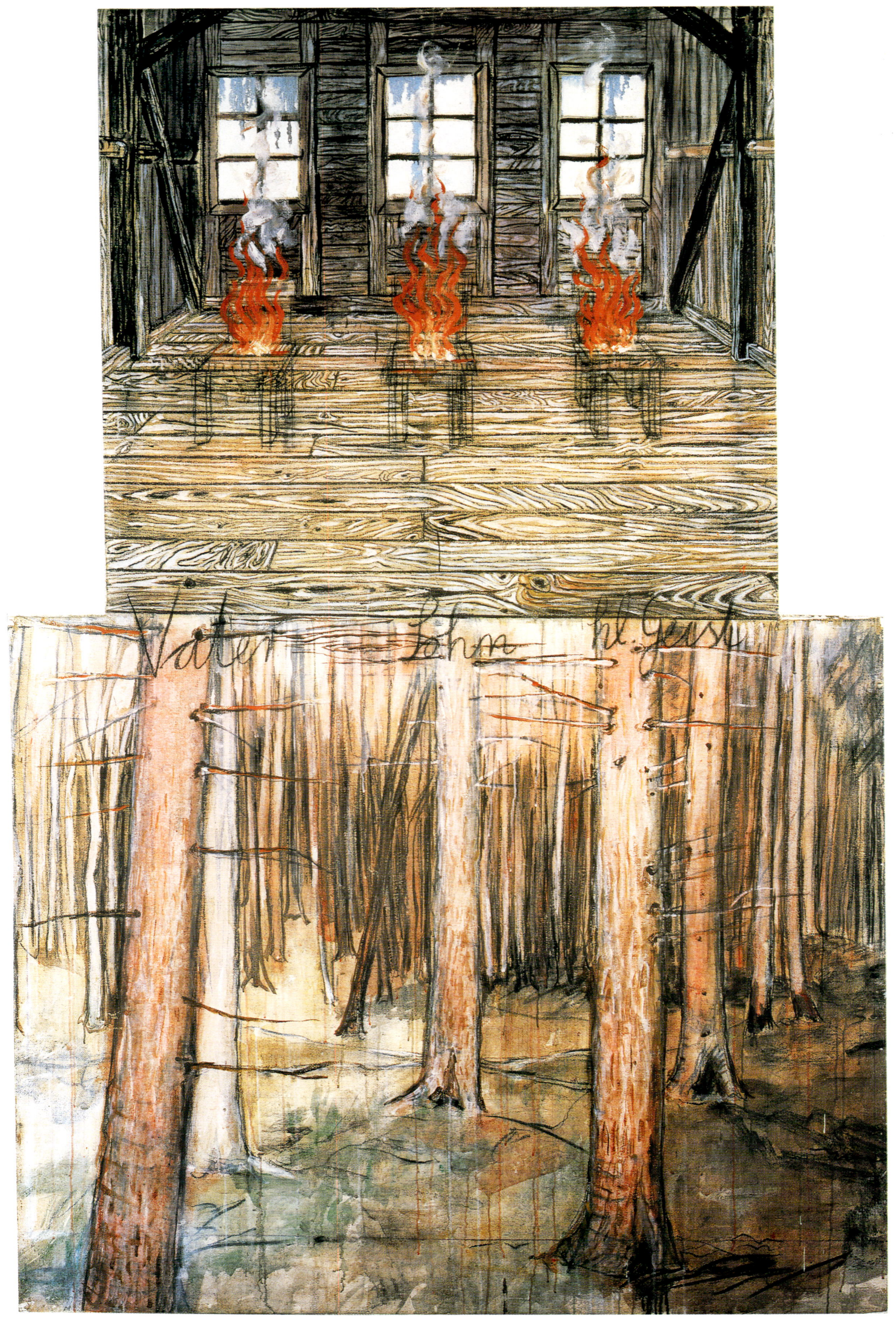
Vater
Sohn
hl. Geist

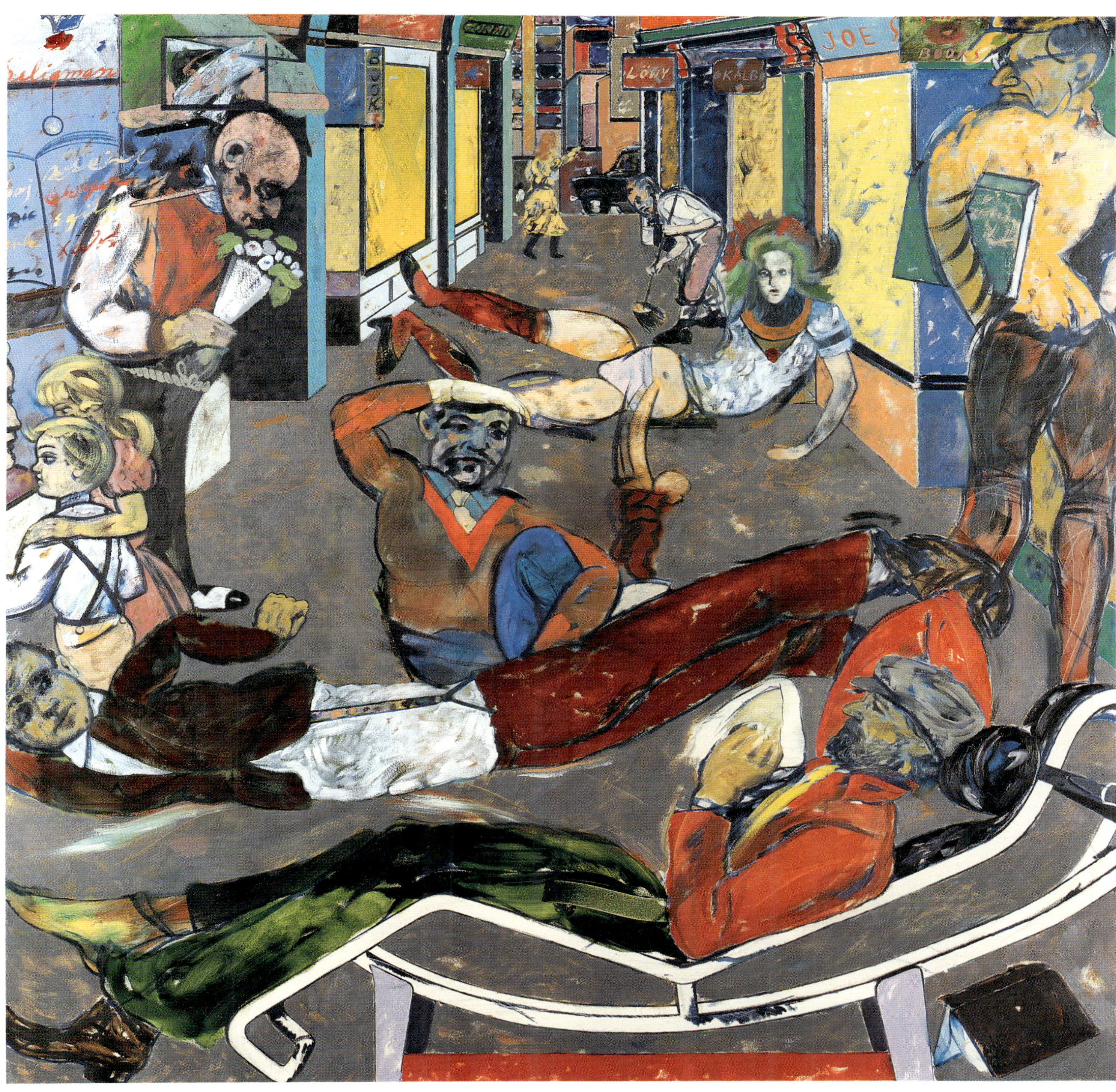

LEFT:
Anselm Kiefer
Father, Son, and Holy Ghost 1973
Oil on canvas, 113⅜×74⅜in (288×189cm)
Van Abbe Museum, Eindhoven
Mr M Sanders & Mrs J Sanders

ABOVE:
R B Kitaj
Cecil Court, WC2 (The Refugees) 1983-84
Oil on canvas, 72×72in (183×183cm)
Tate Gallery, London

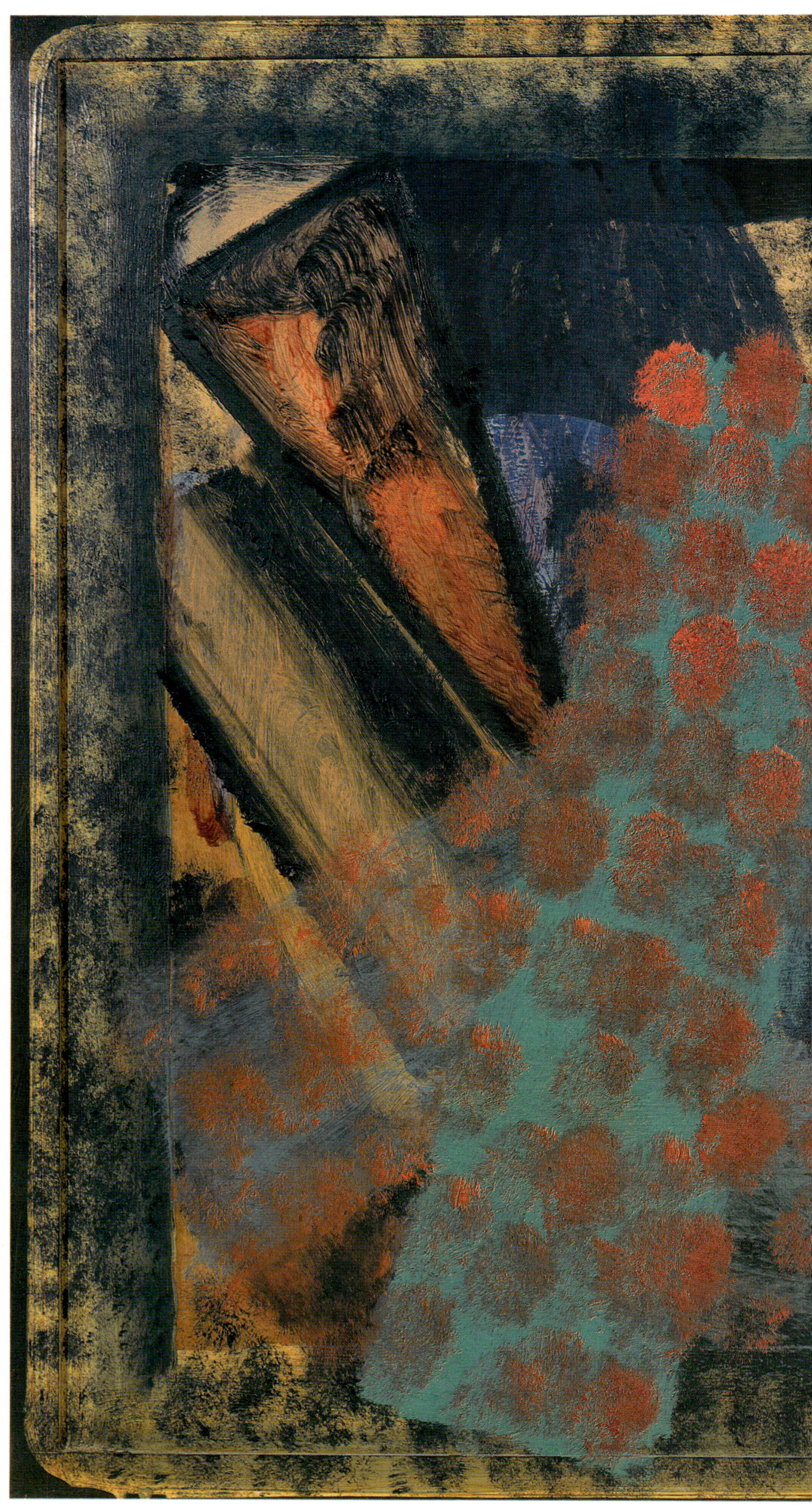

Howard Hodgkin
Dinner at Smith Square 1975-79
Oil on wood, 37¼×49¼in
(94.6×125.1cm)
Tate Gallery, London

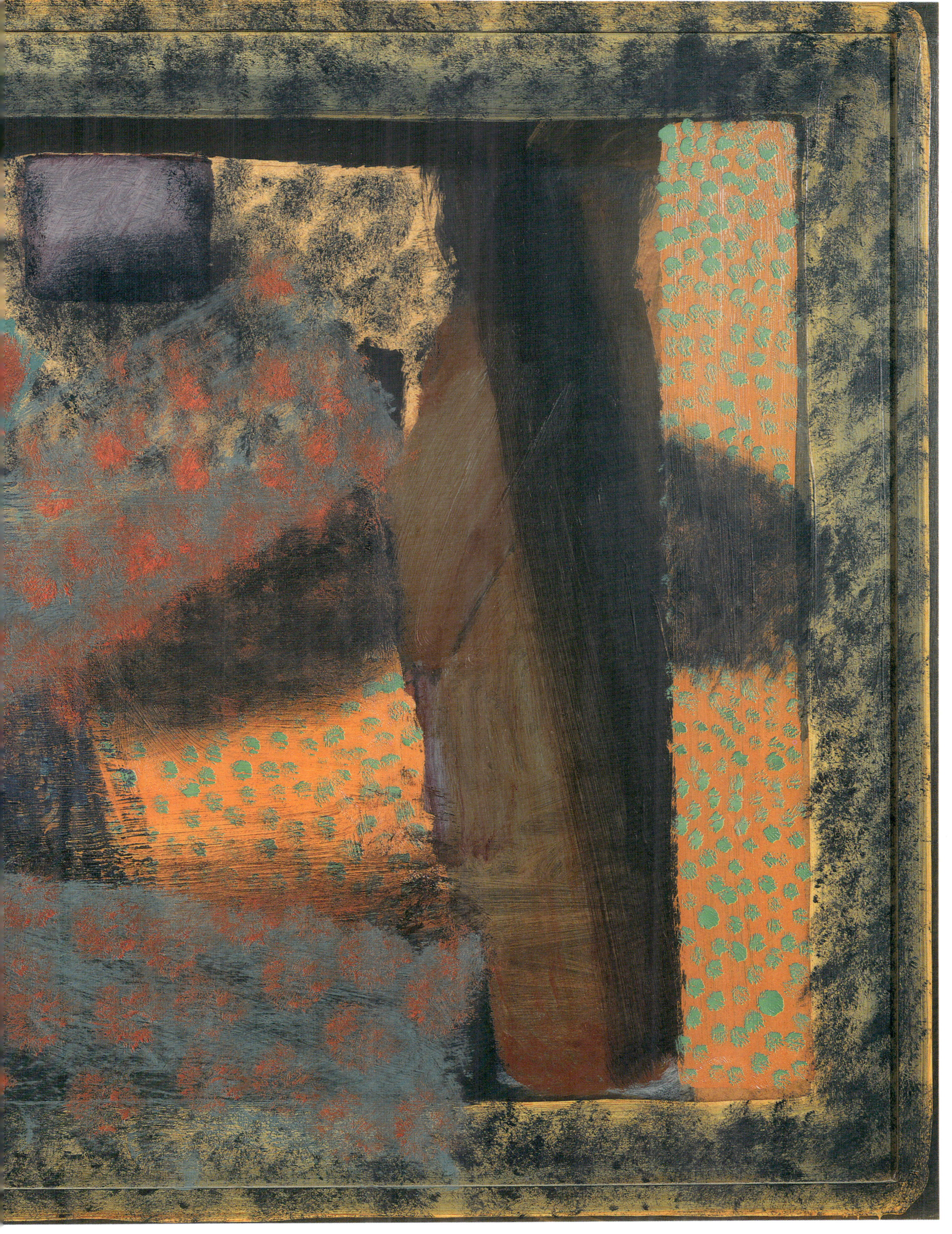

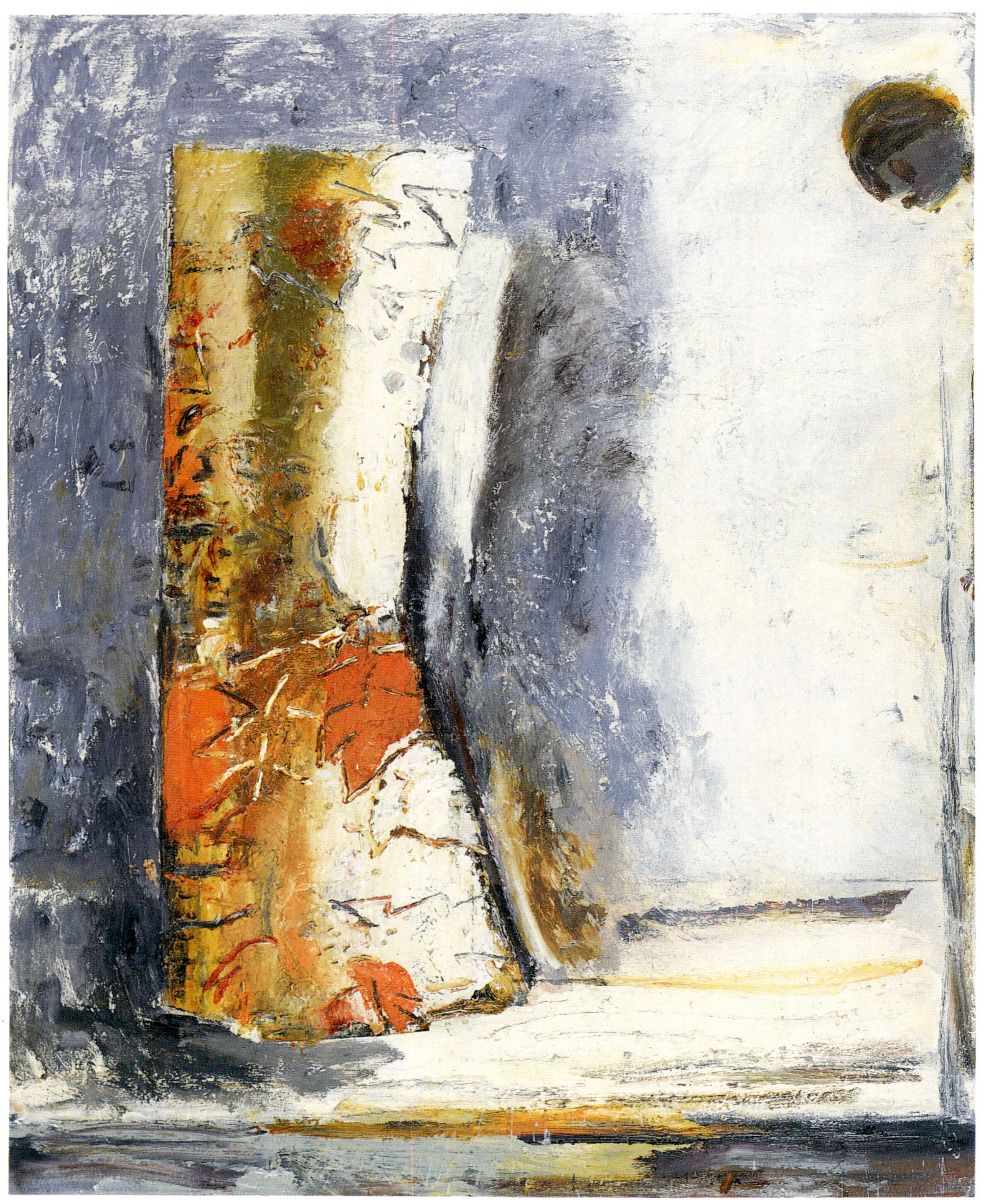

John Walker
Conversation 1984
Oil on canvas, 84¼×66¾in (214×169.4 cm)
The Arts Council of Great Britain Collection

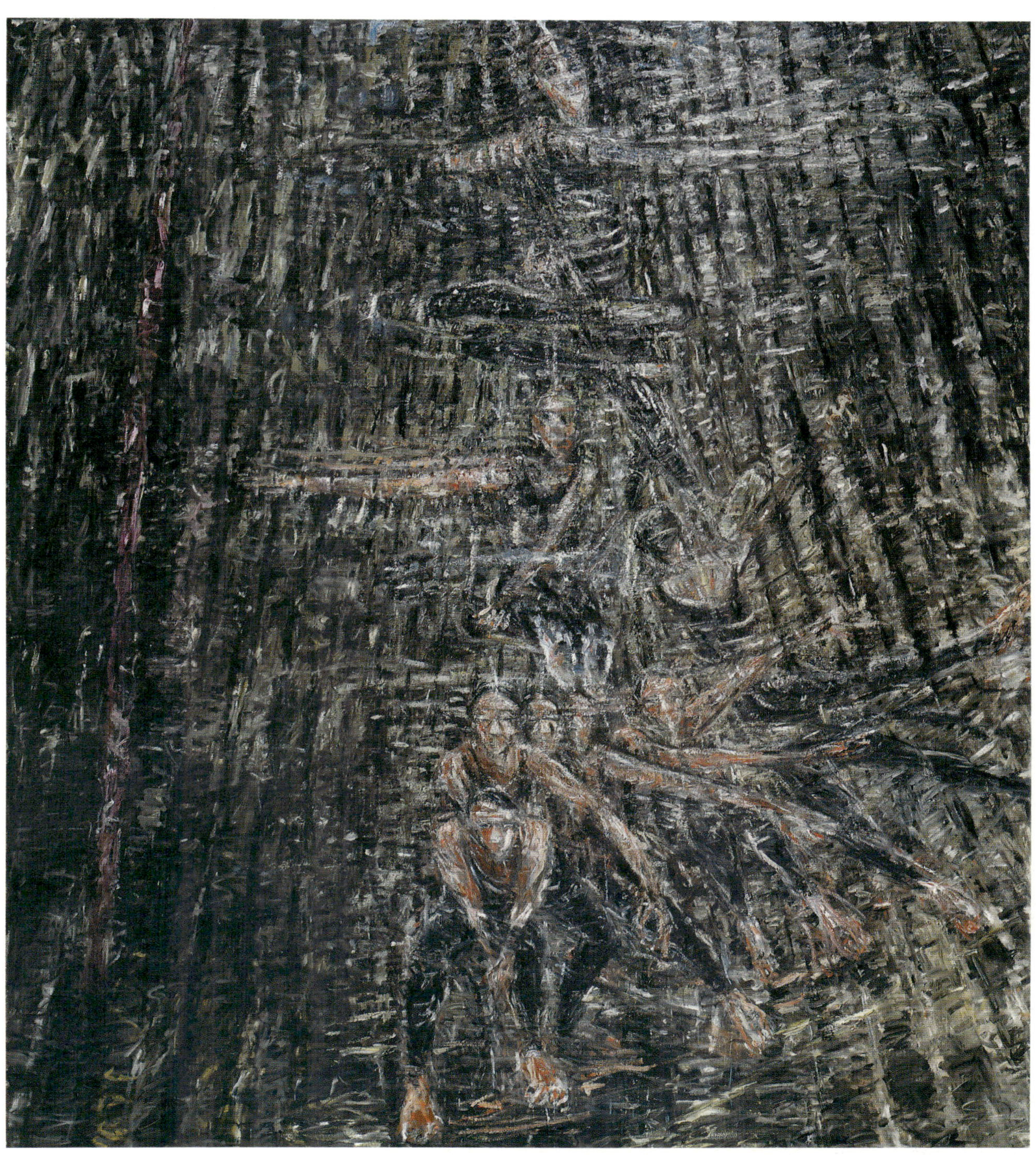

Susan Rothenberg
Vertical Spin 1986-87
Oil on canvas, 142×112½in (360.7×285.7cm)
Tate Gallery, London